Volume 13

DIRECTORY OF WORLD CINEMA FINLAND

Edited by Pietari Kääpä

intellect Bristol, UK / Chicago, USA

First Published in the UK in 2012 by Intellect, The Mill, Parnall Road, Fishponds,
Bristol, BS16 3JG, UK

First published in the USA in 2012 by Intellect, The University of Chicago Press,
1427 E. 60th Street, Chicago, IL 60637, USA

A catalogue record for this book is available from the British Library.

Publisher: May Yao
Publishing Manager: Melanie Marshall

Cover photo: *Laitakaupungin Valot*, 2006, Sputnik/The Kobal Collection

Cover Design: Holly Rose
Copy Editor: Michael Eckhardt
Typesetting: Mac Style, Beverley, E. Yorkshire

Directory of World Cinema ISSN 2040-7971
Directory of World Cinema eISSN 2040-798X

Directory of World Cinema: Finland ISBN 978-1-84150-617-3
Directory of World Cinema: Finland eISBN 978-1-84150-666-1

Printed and bound by Cambrian Printers, Aberystwyth, Wales.

DIRECTORY OF WORLD CINEMA
FINLAND

Acknowledgements 5

Introduction by the Editor 6

Film of the Year 9
Rare Exports

Directors 12
Aki Kaurismäki
Erkki Karu
Matti Kassila
Mikko Niskanen
Pirjo Honkasalo
Rauni Mollberg
Risto Jarva
T.J. Särkkä
Teuvo Tulio
Valentin Vaala

Stars 46
The Emergence of the Star System
Kati Outinen
Matti Pellonpää
Tauno Palo
Vesa-Matti Loiri

Industrial Spotlight 61
The Economics of Finnish
Cinema Part 1: 1910–1935

Scoring Cinema 65

Silent Cinema 72
Essay
Reviews

War 84
Essay
Reviews

**Contemporary Film and
Literature** 100
Essay
Reviews

Social Realism 126
Essay
Reviews

Genre 170
Essay
Reviews

Comedy 200
Essay
Reviews

Children's Film 220
Essay
Reviews

Documentary 228
Essay
Reviews

Cinema and the Environment 236
Essay
Reviews

Global Finland 250
Essay
Reviews

**The Futures of Finnish
Cinema** 262

Recommended Reading 266

Finnish Cinema Online 268

Test Your Knowledge 270

Notes on Contributors 273

Filmography 275

Intellect's *The Directory of World Cinema* series has been conceptualized as an archive of knowledge catering for a wide readership and a substantial contribution to global film culture. To meet these requirements, this collection provides an overview of Finnish cinema and its historical and cultural developments. Simultaneously, it provides fresh critical takes on these developments and the specific films that most dynamically embody them.

While film historians and organizations such as the National Audiovisual Archive (Kansallinen Audiovisuaalinen Arkisto) have conducted excellent extensive studies of Finnish film culture, critical inspection of Finnish cinema remains limited, at least in English. Not long ago, leading film critic and historian Peter von Bagh introduced the challenges facing anyone working in the field in his English language 'guide' to Finnish cinema:

> The effort of introducing the cinema of a small, distant country is half-doomed in advance. Almost nothing is known of Finnish cinema outside its borders. I can only guess that a foreign spectator approaches it as if it was a science fiction experience. As with most small countries, Finnish cinema is mostly provincial, relegated to immediate oblivion even in its own surroundings. (Olov Qvist and Von Bagh 2000: 211)

This collection seeks to discourage such pessimism. Finnish cinema has followed global trends and patterns of development throughout its history (with substantial and necessary variations, of course). To take a preemptive stance and explain its themes and peculiarities as something akin to the work of an alien being does not fully capture the complex efforts of film producers nor the reading capacities of domestic and foreign spectators.

The level of commitment by both Intellect and the contributors indicates the advances made in both the production and study of Finnish cinema. The contributors to this volume construct a long-form argument about speaking to a global audience in a critical vernacular that can be understood beyond the cultural borders of domestic readership. Simultaneously, all contributors acknowledge the many culturally-specific aspects indigenous to Finland and provide explanations to fill in any contextual gaps in knowledge. To these ends, this collection does not belittle the reading competence of non-Finnish audiences nor does it presume that they are fluent in the machinations of the Finnish film industry. All contributors also retain a sufficiently critical perspective on the films and the cultural-historical developments that underlie them so as not to make this only a work of celebration. Instead, while we do highlight more positive aspects of the history of Finnish cinema, we are also conscious of maintaining an appropriate critical distance. Thus, the outcome reflects the intellectual rigour and hard work of all the contributors and the editorial team at Intellect, especially Melanie Marshall. I wish to thank the Ella and Georg Ehrnrooth Foundation for their support on this project. As ever, this collection is dedicated to Yan.

Pietari Kääpä

References

Olov Qvist, Per and Von Bagh, Peter (2000), *A Guide to the Cinemas of Finland and Sweden*, Westport, CN: Greenwood Press.

INTRODUCTION
BY THE EDITOR

The Finnish film industry is enjoying one of its most successful times in decades. In 2010, audience attendance at the domestic box office reached over 7 million spectators, out of which 2 million were tickets sold to Finnish films. This comprises the biggest share (27%) of the domestic box office for Finnish releases since the early 1970s. Furthermore, two of the most successful films of the year were domestic productions, the children's musical *Risto Räppääjä ja polkupyörävaras/Risto Räppääjä and the Bicycle Thief* (Rantasila, 2009) and the road comedy *Napapiirin sankarit /Lapland Odyssey* (Karukoski, 2010). Meanwhile, successful international co-productions were anomalies only a few decades ago. In 2010, several films were produced in collaboration with international production companies or funding organizations, including both *Lapland Odyssey* and Jalmari Helander's *Rare Exports* (2010). These films have not only received screenings in international festivals, winning several prestigious prizes, but also commercial releases in the US and markets Europe-wide.

While Finnish films have met with extensive criticism from domestic audiences throughout cinema history (often for very good reasons), this rhetoric has changed, at least in comparison to the prophecies of doom that penetrated much of the critical discussion from the beginning of the 1960s to the late '90s. Wider developments in film culture have played an important role in these changes, including increasing variety in film genres, marketing initiatives, exhibition practices, the re-emergence of a star system, and the consolidation of both commercial and art house auteurs. It would seem that Finnish cinema has overcome many of its past challenges.

While the above paints a rosy picture of the industry's fortunes, we must still remember that these are accomplishments of what Mette Hjort has called a 'small nation cinema'

(2007). This is an industry catering for a small population of a linguistically marginal country, and any success here may be considered minor on a global scale. Yet, this does not invalidate the artistic and commercial successes of the Finnish producers. Finland may be a prosperous Northern European nation still inhabited by a largely ethnically homogeneous population, but this does not diminish the value of interrogating its developments nor its fallacies. While Finland may not be as 'sexy' as other more politically-contentious cinemas, it has much to teach us about the relationship between globalization and film culture. Indeed, the advances made here are substantial indicators of a globalized field of cultural production and the increasing interconnectivity of its creative industries.

This collection will reveal a complex industry mobilizing a range of artistic and production-related techniques to maintain its competitive vitality. Debates on not only cultural identity and nationhood, but also multiculturalism and transnationalism are increasingly played out in cinema, allowing films to participate in wider social and cultural developments in Finnish society. To these ends, this *Directory* is aimed at both domestic and international readers, and it will cover some familiar ground for those initiated in Finnish cinema. But this is not intended as another dogmatic exploration of Finnish cinema designed to fill in all the boxes on matters of national importance. Neither do we seek to reinforce dominant international perspectives on Finnish cinema – i.e. small scale industry dominated by sociorealist art house films. Because of the types of Finnish films which have traditionally succeeded abroad, the international preconception of Finnish cinema is one of morose Nordic depression, populated by lonely, isolated individuals who seek to dilute their misery with alcohol consumption and violence, brought on by an uncaring society and geographical isolation. This is certainly the stereotype evoked in the international reception for films such as those produced by the Kaurismäki brothers, especially Aki. Additionally, animated films such as *Niko – Lentäjän poika/The Flight Before Christmas* (Hegner and Juusonen, 2008) and fantasy tales such as *Joulutarina/Christmas Story* (Wuolijoki, 2007) have shown a different side of the nation to international audiences. But to what extent are these exoticized depictions any more progressive than the frequent bleakness of the art house films? To these ends, this collection demonstrates that there is more to Finland than Santa Clauses and alcoholic depression.

The contributions to this volume cover the whole range of Finnish cinema, not only in terms of genre, art and commercial films, independent productions and blockbuster cinema, but also its industrial-historical context. The industrial situation of Finland has followed a largely similar pattern with many other European film industries as it developed from a disparaged form of entertainment with clear international connections into a specifically and emphatically national film industry in the 1930s. The following era was one of prosperity, 'the golden age', attributed to increasing acceptance of cinema as an art form, buoyed by a population hungry for entertainment during and after WWII, all complemented by a studio system with a large-scale production output. As television and other forms of leisure consumption increased, the industry found itself in financial difficulties and many of the large studios faced bankruptcy proceedings or had to, in any case, downscale their production output substantially. The 1970s and '80s were a period of constant downturns and attempts at innovation, and it is only in the twenty-first century that the film industry has gained a steady form of growth. Yet, the industry is still largely structured around the domestic market and producers face overwhelming competition from Hollywood. These are only some of the wider developments and considerations that the articles in this collection address.

A crucial part of this collection's aim is to expand not only global interest in Finnish cinema, but also the parameters in which it is discussed. All contributors to this volume are informed by historical understanding of the interconnections of the domestic cultural industries with international geopolitical, economic, artistic and industrial developments. Appropriately for a film industry increasingly building global connections, we are able to include articles on the Japanese perceptions on contemporary Finnish cinema as well as co-production initiatives with Chinese film producers. Other contributors provide historical perspectives on Finland's transnational connectivity with the Nordic countries and the US. To debate the multifaceted nature of Finnish cinema, the contributions construct an image of an ever-transforming and dynamic national industry, facing challenges and meeting opportunities with occasional success stories and also frequent failures.

This book is not a mere celebration of Finnish cinema or a condemnation of past mistakes. Rather, it is a critical evaluation and a historical study of its diversity and ongoing development. This collection does not intend to chronicle the 'best' Finnish films of the past 100 years as such an endeavour is always a subjective enterprise. Instead, films have been selected on the basis of representability and divided by their nominal genre. But as is clearly evident, these sorts of divisions are only arbitrary and perfunctional rather than clear guidelines for discussing the importance of these films. Most of the films can, and have to, be categorized in multiple ways as they frequently combine genres and appeal to both art house and multiplex patrons. Thus, this is not an exhaustive guide of Finnish film culture or its great directors, but instead, it expands our understanding of this film culture as part of the global cinematic landscape. The aim of this book, then, is to make sure that marginalized and 'non-exotic' cinemas like that of Finland are recognized as part of global film culture.

Pietari Kääpä

References

Hjort, Mette and Petrie, Duncan (2007), *The Cinema of Small Nations*, Edinburgh: University of Edinburgh Press.

Rare Exports: A Christmas Tale, Filmcamp.

FILM OF THE YEAR
RARE EXPORTS

Jalmari Helander's *Rare Exports* is a real anomaly in the history of Finnish cinema. The tale of a monstrous Santa Claus who punishes children by beating them to death takes its genre inspiration from 1980s Steven Spielberg and John Carpenter films, and combines this with an exploration of broken family dynamics set in a reindeer herding community in northern Finland. At times, it plays like a blockbuster horror film, at others it resembles typical *juntti* comedies (a form of Finnish humour focusing on immature men and their misadventures). The film was a huge success on its domestic release, garnering over 200,000 spectators and generally favourable reviews. This success was partly buoyed by a large-scale hype campaign and advance word of its success at international festivals. While it lost out to Dome Karukoski's road comedy *Lapland Odyssey* (2010) at the annual Jussi Awards, it garnered all the accolades in the technical categories. This critical success for what is explicitly a genre-based production is symptomatic of the politics of contemporary Finnish film culture. No longer the site of art cinema, it is clear that popular Finnish films hold a crucial place in the nation's film culture.

Rare Exports is based on two short films Helander produced for internet distribution, *Rare Exports Inc.* (2003) and *Rare Exports: Safety Instructions* (2005). These films focus on three hunters of the indigenous species of Santa Claus, who roam free in the plains of northern Lapland and who can be dangerous if provoked. However, they can be domesticated through extensive training, after which they are dressed up in red Coca-Cola overcoats and shipped to exotic destinations. The feature film is a prequel to the short films, and expands on their established mythology. Legend tells us that a monstrous Santa was unleashed on the local Sami population, but was finally defeated and buried in the fell of Korvatunturi. In the present day, a group of scientists are performing mysterious excavations at the fell and causing plenty of consternation with the locals. One day, the dig goes quiet and the reindeer of the region are slaughtered. Soon, Pietari (Onni Tommila), the 8-year-old son of a single father, is receiving nightly visitations by a naked, thin man outside his window. His father soon captures the prowler and sets out to investigate the mystery behind this feral creature. The film is comprised of two distinct halves: the first one setting the foreboding tone with suggestive sightings of the creepy elves (the naked, old men) and slaughtered reindeer; the second half culminates in a large-scale confrontation involving rampaging elves and helicopter battles.

Produced with the comparatively low budget of €1.5 million, the film is very impressive in its sustained atmosphere and its visual effects – in fact, it works considerably better than many of its Hollywood competitors. This is underlined by its 89 per cent positive rating at the film website *Rotten Tomatoes*, where horror films rarely receive such accolades. The film received a limited release in the American markets and favourable comments from critics like Roger Ebert. It also generated substantial buzz at the Toronto and Locarno Film Festivals, winning awards and generating all the makings of a cult hit.

A large part of this international success has to be attributed to the ways *Rare Exports* combines culturally sensitive material with its blockbuster conventions. The humour between the three hunters is largely reliant on stereotypes of Finnish masculinity, and uses local vernacular and customary idioms to a great extent. Furthermore, the final confrontation between the protagonists and the hordes of elves takes place in a reindeer ranch, and provides a culturally-specific field of action for events that may otherwise be familiar to viewers from Hollywood. Yet, the film is clearly intended for international markets as the title and use of English in its credits imply. Its local flavour is thus to be understood as a form of exoticism that appeals to international audiences and helps to distinguish the film from similar monster tales. Indeed, the reception it received in the US underlines this exotic conceptualization. But the conclusion of *Rare Exports* can be understood in self-reflexive ways as we follow the complex process of packaging the elves and shipping them abroad. The suggestion here is that the film producers are entirely aware of the international demand for national exotica and are shipping their

Rare Exports: A Christmas Tale, Filmcamp.

own set of 'rare exports' for consumption by the foreign audiences. This is the rarest of exports in Finnish cinema: a film that is both culturally specific and populist enough to appeal to wide audiences.

Yet, in its domestic context, *Rare Exports* is not considered an exotic film. Rather, it was a genuine blockbuster with good audience figures and critical reception. Whereas most of the foreign reviews understandably drew attention to the unusual qualities of the film, Finnish reviews discussed its entertainment and technical qualities. If exoticism was perceived by the Finnish critics, this was to do with the successful implementation of Hollywood conventions into a Finnish setting. *Rare Exports* is a clear embodiment of the globalization of the Finnish film industry, and comes at a time when concrete efforts are being made to expand the confines of the national cinema. Simultaneously, it empha-sizes the need to remain nationally-specific as it would have been unlikely to receive the type of commercial success, at least in the international markets, without its exotic qualities. While genre films (as in commercial genre narratives utilizing conventions of mainstream popular cinema) have certainly been produced in Finland before, this is the first example of a truly successful attempt to capitalize on the market. It remains to be seen if the film remains an anomaly or if producers will be able to create other examples of genre-based national cinema. For now, the film sets the tone for this volume in its combination of acknowledging national cinematic history and attempting to reinvent these ideas for the global markets and their wide audiences.

Pietari Kääpä

Aki Kaurismäki.

DIRECTORS
AKI KAURISMÄKI

Aki Kaurismäki began his film-making career as an actor and writer on his older brother Mika's graduation film *Valehtelija/The Liar* (1981). Following *The Liar* the brothers worked together on *Saimaa-ilmiö/The Saimaa Gesture* (1981), *Jackpot 2* (1981) and *Arvottomat/The Worthless* (1982). Pietari Kääpä calls these first four films the brothers' 'template films' as they 'establish the representational and argumentative basis of much of the Kaurismäkis' subsequent work' (2010: 9). Where Mika Kaurismäki has gone on to making a range of different kinds of films – from road films to music documentaries and dark relationship comedies – Aki Kaurismäki has become more clearly profiled as an 'auteur' film-maker with a recognizable cinematic world and a thematically and aesthetically con- sistent output. Kaurismäki's 2002 film *Mies vailla menneisyyttä/The Man Without a Past* won the Grand Prix at the Cannes Film Festival, and was the first ever Finnish film to be shortlisted for a foreign language Oscar.

The protagonists in Kaurismäki's films generally occupy positions of low social status: when not in prison or unemployed they are industrial butchers, garbage collectors, dish washers, etc. Some are utterly friendless. They operate within the norms of soci- ety to the best of their abilities, often thwarted in their efforts by unfortunate personal circumstances that lead them into violence and, consequently, further into the margins of society. In the cases of Nikander and Taisto, the respective protagonists of *Varjoja paratiisissa/Shadows in Paradise* (1986) and *Ariel* (1988), the violence is sudden and impulsive. For Rahikainen of *Rikos ja rangaistus/Crime and Punishment* (1983) and Iris of *Tulitikkutehtaan tyttö/The Match Factory Girl* (1990) the step into crime is premeditated, an exercise in control over their environment. Death, suicide, shame and loneliness are recurring themes, and protagonists' efforts at improving their social standing usually fail or are aborted: the proposed new garbage collection business in *Shadows in Paradise* never eventuates; a building contractor takes to desperate measures following his bankruptcy in *The Man Without a Past*; Koistinen's imprisonment thwarts any – already hopelessly optimistic – plans he had of running his own security company in *Laitakaupun- gin valot/Lights in the Dusk* (2006). The comparative 'winners' of society provide telling juxtaposition, more commonly in supporting roles such as Ilona's unctuous employers in *Shadows in Paradise* or Iris' callous lover in *The Match Factory Girl*. *Hamlet liikemaa- ilmassa/Hamlet Goes Business* (1987) is a rare example of a film where main characters have high social standing and are surrounded by material wealth, and Mrs Sjöholm in *Kauas pilvet karkaavat/Drifting Clouds* (1996) is an equally rare example of a sympathetic wealthy character. Despite the gloomy elements in the films, they also have a heightened sense of the ridiculous: from the temperamental canopy of Taisto's white Cadillac to the epic journey across Helsinki in *Calamari Union* (1985) that sees a gaggle of Franks and one Pekka succumb to either death or marriage, bursts of anarchy punctuate the oeuvre, and a muted sense of humour marks the work.

The dialogue in Kaurismäki's films is highly stylized and archaic, and often also lends a subtle humour to the narrative. The marriage of short and functional phrases with old fashioned, even romantic imagery, draws deliberate attention to the way characters com- municate with each other and creates a sense of whimsy: in *The Man Without a Past*, the protagonist, M (Markku Peltola), casually mentions having been to the moon; in *Ariel* Taisto (Turo Pajala) is pleased to hear Irmeli (Susanna Haavisto) already has a child – after all, it will save them time in forming a family. Silence is also important in Kaurismäkian film, and the acting style is distinctive in its minimalism: it accommodates long pauses and resists expressions of emotion. Kaurismäki has explained that his approach to acting is consciously similar to Brecht's: he too believes 'that "acting" should be avoided in films [and] the actor should regard himself as a narrator who only *quotes* the character he is playing' (Cardullo 2006: 7).

The socially marginal status of the characters is emphasized by the films' spatial and temporal defamiliarization: for example, while Kaurismäkian films are predominately

Aki Kaurismäki.

urban their cityscape has few obvious landmarks that would indicate where the action takes place. Henry Bacon (2003: 92) argues that while in some ways the city is identifi-able as Helsinki – at least to its residents – at the same time the way Helsinki is depicted creates a sense of 'strangeness'. According to Bacon, Helsinki itself is out of place, contributing to and reflecting the protagonists' estrangement from society. Drawing on Bacon's analysis, Pietari Kääpä (2006) similarly refers to Kaurismäki's Helsinki as an 'impressionistic snapshot' of the city, while Sirpa Tani (2007) argues that the films' aes-thetic transforms the city: for Tani, the diegetic city does not refer to a physical reality, but to an imagined past. Indeed, a sense of nostalgia complicates the sense of past and present in the films: while the problems faced by the protagonists reflect the time in which the films were made, the settings and visual style of the films recall a range of past time periods. The concurrent representation of several time periods foregrounds the continual changes in Finnish society, and many commentators see Kaurismäkian melancholy and nostalgia as reactions to the changes in Finnish society since the 1960s. Tytti Soila, for example, describes Kaurismäkian cinema as reflecting a Finnish national identity in 'limbo between the demolished world-view of the former Soviet Union and an onrushing Euro-Americanism' (2002: 197).

The aesthetic consistency of Kaurismäki's films results not only from the control of the director, who often also writes and produces his films, but also from the consistency over time of other collaborators, such as the cinematographer Timo Salminen. Responsible for sound, editing and set design respectively, Jouko Lumme, Timo Linnasalo and Markku Pätilä also play an important part in creating the Kaurismäkian aesthetic. Peter von Bagh (2006: 156–57) describes with some amazement how Kaurismäki and Salminen can work together on set for several hours in near-silence, and how quickly Pätilä's design crew creates the 'Kaurismäkian' world for the camera. Jim Jarmusch has also recounted an exchange with Kaurismäki, illustrative of the director's and his crew's pace and efficiency:

> He called me a month ago saying, 'I have to finish my script'. It was a Thursday. And I said, 'When are you shooting?' He said, 'I'm shooting on Monday'. Then he left me a message three days ago: 'I wrote the script, I filmed the script, I'm done with the editing'. And I haven't even finished starting to write my script. He's just really annoying. (in Béar 2008: 143)

From the beginning of his directorial career, Kaurismäki's films were well received by film critics. The critical success of Kaurismäki's films has also met with some vocal resistance. Among the popular criticisms of Kaurismäki's achievements were references to the unwavering support of Helena Ylänen, the film critic of the country's largest daily newspaper, *Helsingin Sanomat*, and her potential influence over funding decisions, speculation whether older brother Mika's connections from the Munich Film School had helped Kaurismäki's film career along, and dismay at Kaurismäki's success in receiving Finnish Film Foundation funding and other government bursaries (see for example Savo 1985: 3; Pouta 2003: 41). Indeed, Kaurismäki has been among the more successful of the Foundation's funding applicants, and in 1999 the head of the Foundation, Erkki Astala, admitted that both Mika and Aki Kaurismäki's critical successes abroad led to more lenient criteria being applied to their funding applications (Arolainen 1999). More recently, the Finnish national broadcaster YLE granted funding towards Kaurismäki's new film *Le Havre* (2011) and Olli Saarela's *Harjunpää ja pahan pappi/Priest of Evil* (2010), despite the broadcaster's funding operations being otherwise suspended due to budget uncertainties (Anon 2010).

The Kaurismäkis' privileged position in the Finnish film industry has been at odds with the taste of broader Finnish cinema-going public. As Pietari Kääpä (2010: 34–40) notes, both of the Kaurismäki brothers' films have generally been released only to a very limited number of screens, with at most eleven but more typically around half a dozen prints in circulation. In practice the small number of prints limited even the potential audience of the films to patrons of small cinemas in the capital city and a couple of other larger towns: the films certainly did not aim for a *national* audience. However, Kaurismäki's films reach a much larger domestic audience through television than they do during their initial theatrical releases (Nestingen 2005: 283). Ari Honka-Hallila, Kimmo Laine and Mervi Pantti (1995: 221–22) even refer to the televised reincarnations of films as their opportunities to enter the 'national shared memory', citing *The Match Factory Girl* as an example.

Tytti Soila points out that the director 'has painstakingly worked on creating a public persona in line with his cinematic universe' (2002: 195), and James Caryn notes the similarity between Kaurismäki's persona and the characters of his films, describing the director as 'the prototypical Kaurismaki character: a droll personality, stingy with words yet offering vast irony through his impassive presence' (1990). Crucial to Kaurismäki's persona is the image of a reluctant interviewee, a would-be hermit. Esa Mäkinen (2008) notes the paradox inherent in Kaurismäki's public profile: despite the hundreds of interviews the director has given over the years, the popular perception is of him as a man who avoids publicity at all cost. The image of a reluctant celebrity combines with that of a hard-drinking, hard-smoking, bad-tempered *enfant terrible*. Kaurismäki is also well-known for his cinephilia, and his films include references to the work of many other film-makers (see for example Timonen 2006; Von Bagh 2006). Kaurismäki was also instrumental in founding the formality-free Midnight Sun Film Festival in a small town north of the Arctic Circle in 1986, and has worked as a producer and distributor for other people's films.

In recent years, Kaurismäki's public profile has increased and he has become further identified as a national figure. In addition to receiving numerous awards for his films, in 2008 he was named Academician of Cinema, a lifetime honorary title conferred by the president. Kaurismäki has also gained some notoriety with high profile political protests: for example, he declined to attend the New York Film Festival in 2002 as a protest following Iranian director Abbas Kiarostami being denied a visa by the United States. Kaurismäki also boycotted the 2003 Oscar gala, even though *The Man Without a Past* had been nominated as Best Foreign Language Film, because of the United States' foreign policy. For the same reason, Kaurismäki refused to submit *Lights in the Dusk* for consideration for the Academy Awards after it had been selected as the Finnish candidate.

Sanna Peden

References

Anon (2002), 'Kaurismäki boycotts NY festival after Kiarostami snub', http://www.guardian.co.uk/film/2002/oct/01/news. Accessed 9 January 2011.

Anon (2010), 'Yle rahoittaa Kaurismäen ja Saarelan Elokuvia', *Helsingin Sanomat*, 5 March.

Arolainen, T. (1999), 'Elokuvan tukiraha kasautuu', *Helsingin Sanomat*, 24 April.

Bacon, Henry (2003), 'Aki Kaurismäen Sijoiltaan Olon Poetiikka', in Kimmo Ahonen, et al. (eds), *Taju kankaalle. Uutta Suomalaista Elokuvaa Paikantamassa*, Turku: Kirja-Aurora, pp. 88–97.

Béar, L. (2008), *The Making of Alternative Cinema*, vol. 2, London: Praeger.

Cardullo, Bert (2006), 'Finnish Character', *Film Quarterly*, 59: 4, pp. 4–10.

Honka-Hallila, Ari, Laine, Kimmo and Pantti, Mervi (1995), *Markan Tähden. Yli Sata Vuotta Suomalaista Elokuvahistoriaa*, Turku: Turun yliopiston täydennyskoulutuskeskus.

Kääpä, Pietari (2010), 'The National and Beyond: the Globalisation of Finnish Cinema in the Films of Aki and Mika Kaurismäki', Oxford: Peter Lang.

Kyösola, Satu (2004), 'The Archivist's Nostalgia', in A. Nestingen (ed.), *In Search of Aki Kaurismäki: Aesthetics and Contexts*, Ontario: Aspasia Books, pp. 46–62.

Mäkinen, Esa (2008), 'Aki Kaurismäki and His Carefully Crafted Public Image', *Helsingin Sanomat – International Edition*, 22 May.

Nestingen, Andrew (2005), 'Aki Kaurismäki's Crossroads: National Cinema and the Road Movie', in A. Nestingen and T. G. Elkington (eds), *Transnational Cinema in a Global North*, Detroit: Wayne State University Press, pp. 279–306.

Pouta, H. (2003), 'Aki Kaurismäen Tie Oscar-ehdokkaaksi', *Apu*, 13, pp. 38–40.

Savo, M. (1985), 'Kaurismäki-syndrooma', *Kinolehti*, 2, pp. 2–3.

Soila, Tytti (2002), 'The Face of a Sad Rat: The Cinematic Universe of the Kaurismäki Brothers', in Yvonne Tasker (ed.), *Fifty Contemporary Filmmakers*, London: Routledge, pp. 195–204.

Timonen, Lauri (2006), *Aki Kaurismäen Elokuvat*, Helsinki: Otava.

Toiviainen, Sakari (2002), *Levottomat Sukupolvet: Uusin Suomalainen Elokuva*, Helsinki: SKS.

Von Bagh, Peter (2006), *Aki Kaurismäki*, Helsinki: WSOY.

DIRECTORS
ERKKI KARU

Erkki Karu was 48-years-old when he died in 1935. In his sixteen-year film career he directed eighteen fiction films, most of them features, produced 40, and established two of the biggest film production companies ever to operate in Finland. Karu was undeniably one of the most significant figures in the history of Finnish cinema. All the same, by the time his life was cut short by meningitis, he had mainly worked in the field of silent cinema. Popular as his films were in the 1920s and 1930s, they are now largely forgotten, whereas directors like Valentin Vaala and Hannu Leminen, who made their careers in the studio era, are still cherished by Finnish audiences.

Before his film career, Karu worked as a carpenter, baker and goldsmith, but these occupations didn't satisfy his creative mind. As he had been interested in theatre and acting since his childhood days, Karu joined a small itinerary theatre group in 1907, at the age of 20, with which he travelled around the country as an actor for four years. Then, in 1911, he established his own travelling theatre company. During summers, Karu made a living by painting coulisses for other companies, and in 1915 he set up a workshop that specialised in coulisse construction. Next year he was made the manager of a small theatre in Forssa. The theatre flourished under Karu's management until 1918 when the Civil War broke out. In the 1910s, Karu had not only got himself acquainted with Finnish theatre, but he had also gained considerable knowledge of his home country and its people (Uusitalo 1988: 11–35).

The Finnish film industry emerged from the Civil War with new vitality. A number of new production companies were established after the war months, but most of these were short-lived. In 1919, Karu got a chance to try film-making together with established cinematographer Frans Ekebom. They made two slapstick comedies, both directed by

Karu: *Ylioppilas Pöllövaaran kihlaus/Student Pöllövaara's Betrothal* (1920) and *Sotagu-lashi Kaiun häiritty kesäloma/War Profiteer Kaiku's Disrupted Summer Vacation* (1920). Aesthetically, these films bear traces of popular foreign slapstick comedies of the day, but the setting is clearly Finnish. In late 1919, Karu, together with Karl Fager and Teuvo Puro, established Suomen Filmikuvaamo (Suomi-Filmi from 1921), which was to be the most important and long-lived of the new film companies.

Karu worked as the chief manager and director of Suomi-Filmi, though both Puro and Konrad Tallroth directed films for the company as they had more experience: Puro had already worked on the first Finnish fiction film *Salaviinanpolttajat/The Moonshiners* (with Louis Sparre, 1907) and Tallroth had directed a number of films in the 1910s both in Fin-land and Sweden. Suomi-Filmi's first feature film production was *Ollin oppivuodet/Olli's Years of Apprenticeship* (dir. Teuvo Puro, 1920), in which Karu has a small role. Soon, Karu gave up acting altogether as it seems that he did not feel entirely comfortable with the art form. He worked as a film producer and wrote the script of one minor film before his cinematic breakthrough came with *Koskenlaskijan morsian/The Logroller's Bride* in 1923.

The Logroller's Bride was a critical and commercial success. The film is based on a popular novel of the same name written by Väinö Kataja in 1914. The story of a family feud on the brink of a wild rapid is set in the not-so-distant past. *The Logroller's Bride* was highly regarded for its phenomenologically realistic representation of ethnographic detail and the natural landscape. Nature is not merely something in the background of the events, but closely tied to the ongoing drama as an indicator of emotions of the characters. Joyous events often take place outdoors in beautiful landscapes, while con-frontations tend to take place in front of bushes or rocks – or even indoors. The precari-ous shootings of the rapids became a great attraction for contemporary audiences and, according to contemporary film reviewers, people stood in lines just to see lobby cards representing these scenes (Seppälä 2007). *The Logroller's Bride* can be considered the first Finnish lumberjack film. Indeed, the lumberjack became something equivalent to the cowboy in American cinema. The influence of Mauritz Stiller's *Sången om den eldröda blomman/Song of the Scarlett Flower* (1919), which had done well at the box office in Finland, can be seen especially in the scenes revolving around rapids. It is no wonder that journalists soon talked about Karu as Finland's Stiller.

The Logroller's Bride was the first Suomi-Filmi production to make a profit (Uusitalo 1988: 73). Already in 1922, the company had gained considerable critical praise with two productions based on Finnish national literature, *Kihlaus/The Betrothal* (dir. Teuvo Puro) and *Anna-Liisa* (dir. Teuvo Puro and Jussi Snellman), both produced by Karu. According to Ari Honka-Hallila, Suomi-Filmi's earlier products were too cosmopolitan in nature to be distinct from imported foreign films (1995a: 45). When Karu directed an adaptation of *Nummisuutarit/The Village Shoemakers*, probably the best-known Finnish play, in 1923, he had his formula – films were to faithfully focus on national literature and representa-tions of the country and its people. This soon became known as Karu's line of film pro-duction. As Suomi-Filmi did not have noteworthy competitors in the 1920s, this line was largely that of Finnish cinema of the time.

When it comes to film style, Karu's works are closer to the tableau style of European cinemas of the 1910s than the classical Hollywood narration. Takes are long and deep, images are large, and characters stand in front of the camera with their chests and faces clearly seen. Analytical editing with its patterns of shot/reverse shots and close-ups are sparsely used. As a film-maker, Karu didn't shy away from theatre, but rather embraced many of its stylistic features, which is no wonder considering his past stage career and Suomi-Filmi's involvement in the business of coulisse construction. Actually, many of Karu's films are inherently intermedial. They feature well-known theatre actors, rely heav-ily on source texts and even include some of the source text dialogue in the intertitles.

Numerous settings and compositions are reminiscent of canonised Finnish paintings. These were all viable means of making Finnish films distinct from imported foreign films.

Popular and praised as they had been, Karu's films became criticised in the late 1920s. Young critics and film-makers began to argue that the Finnish national cinema did not meet the standards set by the best foreign cinemas and that it relied too heavily on the national tradition and arts of the past. One argument against Karu was the low number of exported Finnish films. Foreign audiences, many agreed, were not interested in representations of Finnish national culture. Even though copies of *The Logroller's Bride* were sold as far as Japan, Karu's dream of making Finnish films popular abroad had failed. Those who stood against Karu argued for the importance of modern subject matters represented with, as they saw the matter, a more cinematic use of montage and rhythm. Karu's answer was *Meidän poikamme/Our Boys* (1929), a film set in the military world, which did well at the box office. However, it was not an international success.

Karu's films should not be seen as a homogeneous group. Kari Uusitalo has divided Karu's films into six distinct categories (1988: 191–92). First of all, slapstick comedies and farces, which allowed Karu to practice and experiment. They are the most international of all his films, as they are modelled after foreign slapstick comedies. These films are based on original scripts and the emphasis is on physical comedy and witty intertitles rather than on ethnography and landscape. The second category is that of rural films with which Suomi-Filmi began to flourish. These were the best known and most appreciated of Karu's films and they were seen as making Finland known at home and abroad. The third category consists of films set by the sea, such as *Myrskyluodon kalastaja/The Price They Pay* (1924) and *Nuori luotsi/The Young Pilot* (1928), appropriate considering his fascination with yachting and the archipelagos. The influence of Swedish films cannot only be seen in the rural films, but also in comedies that parody upper-classes and urban life. One particularly influential film was Mauritz Stiller's *Erotikon* (1920), a sophisticated and subversive film that paved the way for the social comedy. The first film of this category, *Suvinen satu/Summery Fairytale* (1925), a parody of the lives of the idle rich, fell modestly short of expectations at the box office and got lukewarm reviews. However, *Syntipukki/The Scapegoat* (1935) turned out to be a commercial success. The fifth category is that of ideological and patriotic films that depict the Finnish army, the best known of these being *Our Boys* and its two sequels made in the early 1930s. The last category consists of commissioned documentary-like films *Finlandia* (with Eero Leväluoma, 1922) and *Ne 45.000/Those 45.000* (with Risto Orko, 1933).

At the turn of the 1930s, global recession hit Finland. Cinema admissions began to drop at a time when the industry should have invested in synchronised sound technology. Moreover, public radio broadcasts began to gain increasing prominence among domestic audiences. Karu failed to realise the changed economical realities. Instead of tightening Suomi-Filmi's budget, he began to work on a new project: the company was to build a skyscraper in Helsinki. The building was to house Suomi-Filmi's head office and a large film theatre alongside many venues of the film industry (Uusitalo 1988: 128). If Karu's works had been criticised for their lack of internationalism, this clearly was an American dream modelled after Paramount's New York skyscraper headquarters. It was also a dream that could not be fulfilled in Finland at the time for economical, political and practical reasons. Instead of giving up on the project and tightening expenses, Karu remained adamant, which led to severe interpersonal problems within the company. In 1933, thinking he was irreplaceable, Karu sent the corporate executive board a letter in which he asked for resignation. Contrary to his thinking that he would be asked to continue in his post, the board resigned him.

Karu began to make plans for establishing a new company that would inherit Suomi-Filmi's popularity. The old company, Karu was sure, would soon be bankrupt and therefore the new one was to carry a name that would resemble Suomi-Filmi as much as possible. Karu's partner Risto Nylund (who soon changed his name to Risto Orkko) came up with the name Suomen Filmiteollisuus (literally The Film Industry of Finland). The name was modelled after Svensk Filmindustri as was the abbreviation SF. Contrary to Karu's thinking Suomi-Filmi did not go bankrupt without him. Moreover, the company hired Nylund to its service. In late 1933, Karu managed to find himself new associates with whom he finally set up Suomen Filmiteollisuus. As the new company strengthened and Suomi-Filmi got over its financial difficulties, the situation changed in Finnish film production: there were now two equally strong companies competing for the same audience. When Karu died in 1935, the studio era had began in Finland, largely as a result of the work he had done.

Jaakko Seppälä

References

Honka-Hallila, Ari. (1995a), 'Elokuvakulttuuria Luomassa', in A. Honka-Hallila, K. Laine and M. Pantti (eds), *Markan Tähden: Yli Sata Vuotta Suomalaista Elokuvahistoriaa*, Turku: Turun yliopiston täydennyskoulutuskeskus.

Honka-Hallila, Ari (1995b), *Kolme Eskoa: Nummisuutarien ja sen kolmen filmatisoinnin kerronta*, Helsinki: Suomalaisen Kirjallisuuden Seura.

Seppälä, Jaakko (2007), 'Suomalaisen Mentaliteetin Kasvualusta – Kotimaisen Mykkäelokuvan Luontorepresentaatiot', http://www.widerscreen.fi/2007-1/suomalaisen-mentaliteetin-kasvualusta-kotimaisen-mykkaelokuvan-luontorepresentaatiot/. Accessed 20 December 2010.

Uusitalo, Kari (1988), *Meidän poikamme: Erkki Karu ja Hänen Aikakautensa*, Helsinki: Valtion painatuskeskus & Suomen elokuva-arkisto.

Matti Kassila.

DIRECTORS
MATTI KASSILA

Matti Kassila (b. 1924) is among the very few Finnish film directors who grew into film-making during the studio era and managed to remain active during the following decades, surviving the changing modes of film production in the 1960s and 1970s. Kassila began his film career as a props assistant and a continuity supervisor at Suomi-Filmi, while simultaneously serving as an apprentice in theatre. After directing several short films, he ended up as a feature film assistant director at the rivalling company Suomen Filmiteollisuus (SF), and having been in charge of much of the production of Edvin Laine's comedy *Aaltoska orkaniseeraa/Aaltonen's Missus Takes Charge* (1949), he was given a chance to direct his first feature film. *Isäntä soittaa hanuria/The Head of the House Plays the Accordion* (1949) was a fairly standard rural comedy from a script assigned to Kassila by the producer T. J. Särkkä, but as Kassila proved to be a reliable and efficient director, he soon became one of the few trusted young employees at SF.

Between 1950 and 1962, Kassila directed twenty feature films. While most of the other major directors of the 1950s remained loyal to one producer, Kassila regularly negotiated his terms with the major production companies, being able to realize one of his own ideas every now and then in exchange for customized projects set by the producers. Among the latter were, for example, *Professori Masa/Professor Masa* (1950), a political comedy-drama about a professor of sociology who, disguised as a working man, becomes involved in harbour workers' strike, and *Kuriton sukupolvi/Wild Generation* (1957), a remake of Mika Waltari's play about the unruly if fundamentally benevolent youth.

The film projects initiated by Kassila himself varied in kind. *Radio tekee murron/The Radio Commits Burglary* (1951), co-written by the future director Aarne Tarkas, was a film noir story of a reporter who breaks into an art museum in order to broadcast the whole course of events but gets involved with real criminals. The film was acknowledged for the swift pace of its narration and dialogue, its credibility – it was based on an actual broadcast by a well-known reporter – as well as its on-location and night-for-night shooting, which was something rarely seen in Finnish cinema. *Elokuu/The Harvest Month* (1956) was an adaptation of a novel by F. E. Sillanpää. Using Kassila's own voice-over narration, characteristic for many of his films, *The Harvest Month* is a lyrical account of the last day of the life of a channel guard, an alcoholic wannabe writer, who reminisces about his life and unfulfilled love. An unforeseen critical success in Finland – it won six Jussi Awards, the Finnish equivalent to the Oscar – *The Harvest Month* was also the second Finnish film ever to make the official selection at the Cannes Film Festival.

In between major production companies, Kassila also pioneered in independent production. *Radio tulee hulluksi/The Radio Goes Mad* (1952), a farcical sequel to *The Radio Commits Burglary*, was funded by the independent film-maker Teuvo Tulio. *Lasisydän/Heart of Glass* (1959), produced by Kassila and his cinematographer Osmo Harkimo, was a notable attempt to break out of the conventions of studio film-making. It is a road movie influenced by art cinema – or a 'walking film' as Kassila calls it – about a successful but frustrated glass designer who wanders aimlessly in the countryside. Shot with light equipment mainly outdoors, using only post-produced sound and introducing a jazzy score, this was one of the first serious aspirations of Finnish cinema towards modernist narration.

Some of Kassila's most remarkable projects from the studio era were first suggested by the company, but then turned into something more personal. *Sininen viikko/Blue Week* (1954), adapted from a short story by Jarl Hemmer, was an eternal triangle involving a young working-class man, a young woman and her elderly husband. Taking a morally ambiguous stance and heavily influenced by Ingmar Bergman's films of the early 1950s, this film used the sea and the archipelago as an impressive borderline milieu – empty and full of meanings at once.

Adapting Mika Waltari's detective novel *Komisario Palmun erehdys/Inspector Palmu's Error* (1960) was also suggested by T. J. Särkkä. Reluctant at first, Kassila found an angle to the story when promised a big enough budget for a 1930s period piece. The epoch was achieved not only by costumes and set design, but also by the use of heavy old arc lamps that were found in the studio warehouse. The success of the film led to three sequels. *Kaasua, komisario Palmu!/Gas, Inspector Palmu!* (1961) and *Tähdet kertovat, komisario Palmu/It Is Written in The Stars, Inspector Palmu* (1962) were set in contemporary Helsinki, but what was common for all the films was a peculiar combination of suspense, horror, comedy and modernist narrative devices: frequent use of, for example, freeze frames, quick zoom-ins and self-conscious narrators coloured the narration, and the musical score by Osmo Lindeman blended popular music with dissonant modernist music and electric sound effects. Yet another sequel, *Vodkaa, komisario Palmu/Vodka, Inspector Palmu* was made in 1969, in colour. No longer scripted by Waltari, the last film is a political thriller, albeit with a comic touch, dealing with Finnish-Soviet relations. Due to the stylistic idiosyncrasy of the films, the distinctive central characters and the strong atmosphere of Helsinki, the Palmu-series has probably the most devoted cult following of all films from the studio era; as an emblem of this, Helsinki City Transport suggests a tram tour around Helsinki with stops near the most memorable shooting locales of the films.

During the subsequent decades, Kassila continued to make films, although on a less regular basis than during the studio years. Among the highlights are *Päämaja/Headquarters* (1970), an account of the last stages of the Finnish-Soviet Continuation War from the perspective of the commander-in-chief and his headquarters; *Niskavuori* (1984), a heritage style remake of a classic family saga; and *Ihmiselon ihanuus ja kurjuus/The Glory and Misery of Human Life* (1988), Kassila's final return to F. E. Sillanpää and the themes of alcoholism, aging and waning artistic creativity.

Besides directing feature films, Kassila has been active in other branches of film culture. He has, for example, scripted and directed television films and documentaries – notably the Soviet-Finnish co-production *25 vuotta ystävyyttä/25 Years of Friendship* (1973) – and been involved in film politics, acting as production manager of the Finnish Film Foundation from 1977 to 1979 and as a member of its board on several occasions. Also, he has published novels and two valuable volumes of memoirs.

Kimmo Laine

DIRECTORS
MIKKO NISKANEN

Mikko Niskanen is often described as one of the most skilful Finnish directors of young and amateur actors. Part of this skill can be attributed to his background, having been raised in poor conditions in the Finnish wartime and post-war countryside, a topic to which he returned in several of his films. Niskanen was born in 1929, and spent his childhood in Konginkangas, in rural central Finland. Despite having been trained as a mechanic, Niskanen travelled to the entrance exams of The Finnish Theatre Academy on the recommendation of his recital instructor, and was accepted in 1947. After three years of actor training, Niskanen toured different regional theatre companies and did small roles in films. The latter led to a firm interest in film art and, in 1958, to a scholarship to study film directing in Moscow at the All-Union State Institute of Cinematography (VGIK), where Eisenstein and other Soviet masters had taught. The school based its teachings on understanding montage, influences of which can be seen in Niskanen's film work.

After returning to Finland, Niskanen produced his directorial debut *Pojat/The Boys* (1962), which followed a group of teenage boys during the Continuation War, in the midst of a community of home front Finns and German soldiers stationed in Finland. It is a masterful debut film about the damage wartime circumstances cause to children, and amongst the film's young, skilfully handled amateurs, the central performance by Vesa-Matti Loiri stands out. *Sissit/Commando Assault* (1963), based again on a story by Paavo Rintala, was logistically a huge task for a young director: this sarcastic wartime tale demanded command of a huge crowd of extras, and extensive creation of battle scenes and pyrotechnics. As with *The Boys*, Niskanen's eye for details and editing carves out the central theme about the cost of war on the human psyche. The third part of his war trilogy, *Hopeaa rajan takaa/Silver from Across the Border* (1963), is a lighter film, an adventure-type tale of a group of men returning to the former Finnish, now Soviet-controlled, home town to take the silver left behind during the Winter War evacuation. The film's lighter tone was also underlined by the selection of the main actor, TV comic Pertti 'Spede' Pasanen.

After a stint in directing regional theatre, Niskanen was hired by the National Broadcasting Corporation YLE to educate TV staff in camerawork and direction. During this time he produced documentaries and short films and also a television film, *Elokuva jalostavasta rakkaudesta/A Film about Affinating Love* (1967), a metafilm about the making of a film in Hrustsev-time Soviet Union, but done in Finnish with Finnish actors. The film can be seen as a shift to a period, during which Niskanen started making films about the relationship between the personal and the political, pictured against the hectic student movement period of the 1960s. At the same time, these films became some of the central works in the Finnish New Wave cinema.

Käpy selän alla/Skin skin (1966) depicts one summer in the life of four university students, two males and two females. The film's impressionistic scenes of the four tenting in the woods are true New Wave imagery, and the young actress, Kristiina Halkola, singing the film's theme song '*Laulu rakastamisen vaikeudesta*'/'A Song About the Difficulty of Loving', are memorable in their free young rebellion, and helped the film to become a central text for a younger generation. Niskanen continued with youth depictions in his next two films *Lapualaismorsian/Girl of Finland* (1967) and *Asfalttilampaat/Asphalt Love* (1968). The former used the premiere of Lapualaismorsian in March 1967 at the Helsinki Student Theatre as a background story in the film: its main characters, featuring many of the same young actors (Kirsti Wallasvaara, Eero Melasniemi, Pekka Autiovuori) in all three of his youth films, also participate in the theatre play, which became the launching platform for left-wing political student theatre in Finland. *Asphalt Love* was a more problematic production as Niskanen had to change the script on the demand of producer Jörn Donner, and the film's depiction of young love against repressive social surroundings never quite achieved his aims.

Niskanen again shifted focus in his film-making in the 1970s as he returned to his native countryside. In March 1969, Niskanen heard the news about a farmer shooting four policemen in his home region, and he knew immediately that he had found the topic of his next film. The result is Niskanen's masterpiece *Kahdeksan surmanluotia/ Eight Deadly Shots* (1972), released both as a theatrical version and a four-part television drama. Niskanen used this real-live event to analyze the social situation of the countryside. The result is a sharp-eyed, but also darkly poetic vision about the small farmers' struggle in the countryside during the late 1960s, early 1970s. Simultaneously, the film highlights Niskanen's immersion in his film-making: for him, the films and their main characters are often a continuation of his inner struggle, and he threw himself into film-making deeply enough to sometimes alarm his co-workers.

Meanwhile, Niskanen also produced a remake of the classic tale, *Laulu tulipunaisesta kukasta/Song of the Bloodred Flower* (1971), based on a Johannes Linnankoski novel. A tale of a lumberjack Don Juan of the early twentieth century, the topic seemed outdated for parts of the audience, but reflects the director's turn towards rural topics. This was followed by another literary topic, Ilmari Kianto's *Omat koirat purivat/Bitten By My Own Dogs* (1974), one of Niskanen's numerous television productions, in which he connects strongly with Kianto's autobiographical story about the writer's wartime court case struggle.

In 1974, Niskanen resigned from YLE, established his own production company, Käpy-Filmi, and started spending more time in central Finland, where he was building his own mansion to house the company. In *Pulakapina/The Horse Rebellion* (1977), the first feature by Käpy-Filmi, Niskanen again turned towards historical topics, this time a 1930s local rebellion, which turned into an analysis on the post-1929 economic hardship of a western Finland farming community. As was often the case, Niskanen performed one of the main roles. The film got mixed reviews, and contrary to Niskanen's former box office hits, gained meagre results at the box office. A better, though overtly pathetic and thematically uneven accomplishment, was the contemporary story *Syksyllä kaikki on toisin/Autumn Is To Change It All* (1978), in which a small town bank manager (again the director himself) gets caught in the midst of local politics, with dire effects on his family.

Niskanen's contemporary countryside studies, however, produced one post-*Eight Deadly Shots* jewel: *Ajolähtö/Gotta Run!* (1982). The film centres on three young men in the midst of social and economic metamorphosis of the Finnish countryside, which forced part of its countryside population to leave their home, many of them immigrating to Sweden and Norway. One of them ends up working on a Norwegian oil rig, another in the harbours of southern Finland before drifting to Sweden, and the third one stays home, working local jobs. Again, Niskanen had an eye for spotting promising young amateurs (Tero Niva, Timo Torikka and Heikki Paavilainen) and his way of allowing them to improvise their dialogues in lengthy pre-shoot discussions worked wonders. The film was favourably received by the critics, received several Jussi awards, and re-established Niskanen for audiences. Niskanen returned to young people and their struggle towards adulthood with *Mona ja palavan rakkauden aika/Mona and the Time of Burning Love* (1983), in which he now depicts the inner struggles of a young woman with a religious calling. The main role went to the 17-year-old Anna-Leena Härkönen, who, besides being active in local youth theatre, also had literary ambitions, and later became a popular novelist.

Niskanen's countryside background attracted him to the novels of Kalle Päätalo, one of Finland's bestselling authors, whose self-biographical novel series about a boy's struggle through his teen years and early adulthood in hard lumberjack work in north-east Finland touched Niskanen, who shared similar experiences. *Elämän vonkamies/ Life's Hardy Men* (1986) and *Nuoruuteni savotat/The Timbercamp Tales* (1988) are in style and tone more mainstream film-making than Niskanen's early, Soviet-montage-influenced films or his '60s New Wave trilogy, and less clear in their sociopolitical analysis than *Eight Deadly Shots*. But they again reveal Niskanen's skill with young actors, and his camera's loving eye for everyday details and realism in depicting manual work.

Mikko Niskanen passed away in 1990 with some of the central works of postwar Finnish cinema under his belt, after a colourful life of creating theatre, teaching and directing different types of films. He also underwent personal mental battles with self-doubts and alcoholism and several failed marriages, which contrasted with his charming, almost Russian-style colourful enthusiasm for art and life.

References

Toiviainen, Sakari (1999), *Tuska ja hurmio. Mikko Niskanen ja hänen elokuvansa*, SES/SKS.

DIRECTORS
PIRJO HONKASALO

Pirjo Honkasalo is perhaps the most prolific internationally-recognized Finnish documentary director working today, though she also directs fiction films, and the lines between documentary and fiction are often fluid in her work. Honkasalo's work is characterized by a strong psychological strand – her work always studies the inner worlds of the characters of the films. Widely travelled, her subject matters range geographically from Finland to Japan, Russia, Chechnya and India. Honkasalo is also interested in the ethics of film-making, which she sees as the major difference between fiction and documentary film-making: with documentaries, the film-makers bear responsibility for the individual fates they depict.

Born in 1947, Honkasalo entered film school at the age of 17, according to her own words to avoid becoming an engineer, a profession most of her family had chosen. Upon graduation, she continued her film studies at Temple University in Philadelphia. She also took courses in the anthropology department, and was influenced by the school's anthropological film events. Honkasalo worked as an assistant director for Rauni Mollberg and as a still photographer for Mikko Niskanen. She has worked as a cinematographer for numerous film projects, especially for Jörn Donner, whose company produced most of Honkasalo and Pekka Lehto's co-productions. She also did a stint as a regional art coordinator in central Finland.

The first half of Honkasalo's career consists of co-productions with other directors. Pekka Lehto has especially proven to be a fruitful collaborator: *Ikäluokka/Age Class* (with Pekka Lehto, 1976) is a short documentary capturing Finland from the perspective of working people of different ages, and *Vaaran merkki/The Sign of Danger* (with Lehto, 1978) paints a portrait of a Finnish neo-Nazi leader. *Kainuu 39/ Two Forces* (with Lehto,

1979) combines fiction and documentary forms in covering a historical event from 1939, when one Finnish village on the Soviet border started cooperating with the occupying Soviets. Similar techniques are also used in *Tulipää/Flame Top* (with Lehto, 1980), a historical drama about the novelist Algot Untola alias Maiju Lassila, which was selected for the Cannes Official Selection series in 1980. The film's different temporal levels would show up again in such works as *Da Capo* (with Lehto, 1985). *Yhdeksän tapaa lähestyä Helsinkiä/Nine Ways to Approach Helsinki* (dir. Jörn Donner, 1982) gives a refined view of Helsinki and its inhabitants during different seasons and times.

A shift towards intimate portrayals of contemporary people happened with *250 grammaa – radioaktiivinen testamentti/250 Grammes: A Radioactive Testament* (with Lehto, 1983), for which Honkasalo and Lehto managed to hire the Russian star actor Nikita Mihalkov. The portrait of a Russian girl dying with cancer ominously echoes the Chernobyl incident, which happened three years after the shooting. Similar intimacy can also be found in *Da Capo*, notable also for being the director's first cooperation with screenwriter and future partner, Pirkko Saisio. The film, again, took a real character, now a 1930s child genius violinist Heimo Haitto, as a starting point to study the abusive relationship between the manager and the child star.

Honkasalo's brand of documentary-making came into full bloom with the 'Trilogy of the Sacred and Satanic': the first, *Mysterion* (1991), about an Estonian-Greek Orthodox monastery, was Honkasalo's last co-direction, this time with Eira Mollberg; *Tanjuska ja 7 perkelettä/Tanjuska and the 7 Devils* (1993), portrays the exorcism of devils from a mentally ill girl by a charismatic, but possibly evil priest; and *Atman* (1996) is about an Indian mystic's 6000 kilometre pilgrimage, for which Honkasalo won the Joris Ivens prize in Amsterdam in 1996. The combination of the poetic and the fantasy-like was also present in her fiction film *Tulennielijä/Fire-Eater* (1998), which covers wartime and postwar Finnish and European history through the story of twin girls who end up working in a circus.

In the twenty-first century, Honkasalo has re-engaged with the documentary form with resounding success. One of most awarded Finnish films ever is *Melancholian 3 huonetta/ The 3 Rooms of Melancholia* (2004), which is a three-part documentary on the effect of the Chechen war on both Russian and Chechen children. The film has been shown in over 100 countries and won significant awards at notable festivals such as Venice and Sundance. Honkasalo's successes and career are thus increasingly international as can be seen from her latest production, *Seitti – kilvoittelijan päiväkirja /Ito: A Diary of an Urban Priest* (2009), which was produced with the support of Japan's NHK, and draws a personal portrait of Yoshinobu Fujioka, a former boxer, now a Buddhist priest and bar owner in Tokyo.

Honkasalo is stimulated not only by the sacred and Satanic, but also by the poetic and political. In her capable hands, the topics acquire a poetic, hypnotic pictorial quality – Honkasalo does most of the filming herself. As Variety's John Anderson (2010) writes (about *Ito*), Honkasalo has the gist of elevating non-fiction to the level of pure art.

Eija Niskanen

References

Anderson, John (2010), '*Ito: A Diary of an Urban Priest* - Review Print', *Variety.com*, 5 October.

Hytönen, Jukka (1999), '"Totuus ei löydy kameraa heiluttamalla" – Pirjo Honkasalon haastattelu', *Filmihullu*, 1.

Saglier, Viviane (2010), 'Pirjo Honkasalo: "The more in the margin the better"', 24 November, www.nisimazine.eu/pirjo-honkasalo.html.

Sedergren, Jari (n.d.), 'Pirjo Honkasalo', www.kava.fi/pirjo-honkasalo.

Rauni Mollberg.

DIRECTORS
RAUNI MOLLBERG

Rauni Mollberg is one of the most notable Finnish directors, although he has not been that prolific in feature-length films: his filmography contains many short films and important made-for-television productions, and he also acted as the theatre department director for YLE (Finland's national broadcasting company) between 1968 and 1986. Mollberg's films work with universal human themes, including sexual awakening, forbidden love, religion and the destructive power of violence. He had a great appreciation for nature and the ordinary everyday life, which resulted in critics labelling his films as alternatively naturalistic and spectacular. His films are all based on literary works, and he consistently treated his sources with great respect. Mollberg was well-known for finding the best unknown amateur actors and actresses for his films and he knew how to form a great and fruitful relationship with his colleagues.

Rauni Antero 'Molle' Mollberg was born on 15 April 1929 in Hämeenlinna, Finland. Between 1948–50, he studied at the Finnish Theatre School in the same class as Mikko Niskanen (another great Finnish director) – in the 1950s he worked both as director and actor in hundreds of plays in the theatre. This is where he got the chance to know Finland's provincial theatres and their actors, faces that had not been used on television or in the cinema. It was not until later that he got the chance to use his knowledge of these actors and actresses thoroughly when he made his first feature film in 1973 (at the age of 44): *Maa on syntinen laulu/The Earth Is a Sinful Song* (1973) is based on the novel of the same title by Finnish author Timo K. Mukka. When Mollberg read the novel, he found it visually so enchanting that he wanted to adapt it right away. He bought the rights and began the preparatory work with Mukka. Since not a single company showed interest in making the film, Mollberg decided to produce it on his own. This labour of love paid off as it was screened at the 24th Berlin International Film Festival, which was a huge step for Mollberg and Finnish cinema as a whole. This earthy tale turned out to be a great success in many countries, and has been one of the biggest box-office successes in the history of Finnish cinema, selling 709,000 tickets.

The film depicts the life of the rural people in northern Finland before the Second World War. Its main themes are nature, family, love and death – all notions embedded with taboos. The story focuses on Martta, an 18-year-old Lapp girl, who lives in a peasant community with her parents and grandfather. She meets Oula, a Sami reindeer herder with whom she falls in love. Her father forbids her relationship with Oula and threatens to kill the herder. The whole film is dominated by naturalism: the actors are mostly amateurs or local people with no acting experience, they do not wear any make-up that could make them look more glamorous – they appear just the way they are and still manage to be very convincing in their cinematic roles. There is a lot of nudity and many sex scenes; a calf is cut in pieces while still inside the cow's womb; reindeers are slaughtered; everything is harsh and realistic; pleasure is a simple thing in these people's lives. The spectacular pictures of the Finnish landscapes are in direct opposition to the lives of these people, and sometimes this contradiction makes it seem as if we are gazing at a documentary film. Mollberg was nevertheless criticized for not being faithful enough to Mukka's novel, but veracity to the literary source is not the intention. Rather, the film is all about the experience, of immersion into the lifestyles depicted.

Aika hyvä ihmiseksi/Pretty Good for a Human Being (1977), a period film based on the novels by Simo Puupponen (better known by the pen name Aapeli), followed Mollberg's debut production. He won the Best Director award for it at the Naples Film Festival and at the Finnish Jussis. Mollberg had been very interested in Aapeli's novels in his youth, and he even wrote his first theatre adaptation of the novel *Pikku Pietarin piha/The Courtyard of Little Peter* in 1959, which was the starting point for all his future adaptations. *Pretty Good for a Human Being* is an ensemble film with multiple characters of equal importance, and it takes place in the 1920s, where memories of the Civil War were recent. The adapted material is complex and sprawling, but Mollberg managed to knead it into an organic whole, an 'adult' version of the books. The film emphasizes situations where there is no more place for logic, where people need to find new meanings for their lives so they can forget about the war and live a normal everyday life in the community. In this community every individual character is interdependent of the others, as everyone fulfils vital social roles (health inspector, blacksmith, policeman, coachman, bailiff, musician, janitor, dancer, etc.). There is only one person in this community who does not fit in: Karoliina. She comes and disappears mysteriously; she keeps the people together and teaches them essential rules for living together, for loving and caring about each other – like a celestial creature. *Pretty Good for a Human Being* continues Mollberg's focus on community and the social roles of individuals, but it also expands his oeuvre with its themes of civil war and the infusion of comedic elements.

Mollberg's third feature film is *Milka - elokuva tabuista/Milka - A Film About Taboos* (1980), a title which tells us a lot about the film, and about the cinema of Rauni Mollberg. It was screened at the 31st Berlin International Film Festival, where it was nominated for the Golden Bear. Just like his first feature, *Milka* is based on Timo K. Mukka's novel (*Tabu*, 1965), which focuses on Milka's story, a 14-year-old girl who lives with her mother and misses her dead father, searching for true love in her life. Instead of true love, she gets impregnated by an older man, Ojanen, who moves into their home and has an affair with her mother, then leaves them with a child. Milka learns that life has some tough laws which cannot be changed, so she prays to God for answers. The story takes place in northern Finland again, where the scenery provides a hopelessly emphatic background to the events – the film was accordingly praised for its poetic cinematography. Mollberg again used amateur actors for the production and his focus on idiosyncratic themes (a young girl's sexual awakening and spiritual growth in a world where love is blood-flavoured and tragedy hides in every corner) is conveyed in several sexually explicit scenes involving the 17-year-old Irma Huntus, who played Milka. These scenes were to cause her severe problems in her home village, an example of real life imitating art. *Milka* is not as harsh as *The Earth is a Sinful Song*, as its contemplative and poetic imagery makes the film seem like a moving painting – there is constantly something to be gazed at, yet this never takes the form of grotesque realism seen in the earlier film. The protagonist is never left alone in her misery – the viewers accompany her through all the hard times, leaving plenty of room for sympathy and in-depth engagement with the most sacred of emotions. *Milka*'s reception was largely positive, contributing to what was already a good year for Mollberg as he was also honoured with the Pro Finlandia medal for his contributions to Finnish culture.

Tuntematon sotilas/The Unknown Soldier (1985) is Mollberg's most widely-known film. This is an updated version of Väinö Linna's novel of the same title, made 30 years after Edvin Laine's classic adaptation, and was received rapturously. Mollberg's version was one of Finland's most expensive films at the time of its release and it was also the fourth highest-grossing product at the domestic box office in the 1980s. Mollberg's project was already in development at the end of the 1970s, but there was huge debate over whether a remake should be produced, and it only received production support from the Finnish Film Foundation in 1982. The debate focused on two perspectives: why make another film about the war; and why remake an already classic narrative, one canonised in Finnish culture? In response, Mollberg argued that the narrative of the war needs to be passed on to the next generations, which was reflected in the casting of many young faces in the leading roles. The film's premiere was held on Finland's Independence Day (6 December) in 1985, and received largely favourable reviews and massive box office success.

Mollberg's narrative follows largely the same patterns as Laine's version, but the new version changes a crucial aspect of the thematic focus: instead of the necessity of national defence and the honour of war, Mollberg's version emphasizes the horrors and inhumanity of war as it tries to immerse the viewers into the events. The film is shot on handheld camera, so the soldiers are constantly running, attacking, crawling and shaking, and all of the battle scenes are edited to gain a rhythmic, ever-increasing tempo. While Laine's version was based on documentary material, Mollberg's version emphasizes the notion that the war may be a part of shared national history, but it is also a time when the worst of human weakness and exploitation come to the forefront. While the film is certainly unique in the annals of Finnish cinema and has its share of cinematic greatness, it could never match the canonical status afforded to Laine's version.

Mollberg's fifth feature *Ystävät, toverit/Friends, Comrades* (1990) was in production for three years and was ultimately screened in the '*Un Certain Regard*' section at the Cannes Film Festival in 1991. Although this is a literary adaptation as well, Mollberg decided to abandon the realism/naturalism of his earlier work for this brutal tale of greed and power. The story was written by Joni Skiftesvik, who strongly criticized Mollberg upon the release of the film, as the final product changed and removed a lot of Skitesvik's themes and added new ones without consulting him. The story focuses on revered nickel tycoon Arno Jurmala, who seemingly has everything: a beautiful wife (Lisa), lots of money, fame and friends. When he celebrates his birthday, the guest list is full of significant business-men and politicians from all over the world. These people have no idea who Jurmala really is (or perhaps they know this too well) as he is a rotten man who would do anything to make more money. He kills his competitors and employees if necessary, and even trades with the Nazis and Soviets, depending on who is winning the war at the time. He also mistreats his wife who cannot have children, forcing her to become a drug addict. Mollberg does a great job of portraying the atmosphere of decadence and political corruption in the 1930s, but it is hard to decide whether he sympathizes with Jurmala or not. The character is very powerful and willing to forsake conventional morality, but Mollberg hesitates to make him pure evil and, instead, focuses on contrasting the drasti-cally opposite qualities of this man. He is simultaneously delicate and brutal, exploitative and exploited. It is clear from the international sweep of this epic that Mollberg intended to produce something more than purely products aimed at the domestic market – the director originally wanted Meryl Streep for the part of Lisa Jurmala, which never came to be. Regardless, the final product is a clearly important and expansive epic.

Four more years passed until Mollberg came up with a new feature, which was to be his swan song: *Paratiisin lapset/Children of the Paradise* (1994) is based on Jouni Lompo-lo's short story. The story focuses on Eva, a strong-willed and ambitious businesswoman whose dream is to build a spa called Paradiso Baltica. Legislation and bureaucracy cause constant obstacles and other people conspire to make her work more difficult. The film's première attracted a great deal of attention, but both the public and the critics rejected it, even generating discussion about the death of Finnish film. The film is a strange mix of human comedy, loud satire and a dramatically-stylized multilayered creation: its characters do not act in the natural way that they usually do in Mollberg's films as their behaviour is best characterised as theatrical and hysterical. Audiences were used to Mollberg's human naturalism, and this time the director 'betrayed' these expectations and made a satirical comedy about the greediness of the Finnish society. A comedy where laughter gets stuck in the viewers' throat is obviously a strange and paradoxical phenomenon, and this is largely why people were so disappointed in Mollberg's film: they recognized themselves in the characters.

After his last feature film, Mollberg was active for ten more years in different parts of the domestic cultural industries. He made six more short films, of which three were made for television. He was often called the 'Academic Mollberg' because he was prolific in different aspects of cultural policy and education, a notion made complete as he received the honorary title of Academician in 1989. He died on 11 October 2007.

Emőke Csoma

DIRECTORS
RISTO JARVA

Risto Jarva is one of the most significant directors in Finnish cinema. He emerged as a vital force in the so-called New Wave movement of the 1960s, providing a distinct and fresh voice to domestic film culture. His films often combine documentation of contemporary social concerns with formative innovation. In fact, he frequently uses documentary effects in his fictional films to complement their probing critical explorations of contemporary society. Key themes of his work are wide-ranging, including such important concerns as social alienation, the impact of technology on individuals, class politics, and the relationship between urbanisation and the environment. Jarva's films may share similarities in theme and form, but all of them are clearly independent pieces of cinematic art. Observing his filmography as a whole gives the impression of a passionate and varied artist, simultaneously politically committed and painfully aware of the economic realities of the film industry.

Jarva's career began as a chemical engineer, but he soon found his calling by joining the film club Montaasi, where he was not only inspired by the films viewed, but also by the opportunity to produce his own. This was the gestation of the production company Filminor, around which important cultural figures such as Peter von Bagh and Jaakko Pakkasvirta clustered. Filminor started its operations by producing short films on contemporary social topics, including the role of women in society, environmental considerations, pollution, urbanisation, and the role of individuals in all these. Many of the topics would become key issues in Jarva's future films as it was increasingly clear that for him the power of cinema was in its potential for social commitment and participation.

Yö vai päivä/Night or Day (1962) was Jarva's first feature production and followed a group of researchers on a UNESCO organized trip to Finland. The film contains a common thematic strand for Jarva in its exploration of national heritage from alternative, seldom-seen perspectives. To capture this collision of traditional imagery and foreign curiosity, the film crew not only visits the capital city, but ventures to the countryside and its lakes. Through this, we receive a cinematic capture of a nation in transition. Similar concerns are evident in *Onnenpeli/A Game of Luck* (1965), which can be considered one of the key documentations of Helsinki and its increasing modernization. Documentary techniques are heavily present in these two films and they even occasionally resemble something close to *cinema vérité*. By capturing the process of change, the film not only effectively mirrors the mindscapes of its young protagonists who feel at odds with normative society, it also captures the changing ways in which national identity works in a society which has transformed from a predominantly rural to an urban one in the space of only a few decades.

Documentary techniques and experimental form are also present in Jarva's follow up *Työmiehen päiväkirja/The Diary of a Worker* (1967), which is considered the first real proletarian film produced in Finland. The narrative is very conventional as it follows the marriage between a middle-class woman and a factory worker. However, the way in which this story is told is anything but ordinary. The monochrome cinematography and largely understated style bring to mind not only the works of Robert Bresson, but the formative innovations of the French *nouvelle vague*. This is especially the case with the film's denouement, where the camera pans into outer space, necessitating that we consider the lives of these individuals not only as reflections of contemporary themes, but also universal ones. These ideas were contextualized in an unexpected setting with *Ruusujen aika/Time of Roses* (1969), one of the first ever science fiction films produced in Finland. The film is an exploration of a utopian totalitarian society where information and the media are controlled by governmental forces and supported by the benevolent apathy of the population.

He continued to explore the impact of technology on individuals in *Bensaa suonissa/ Gas in the Veins* (1970). This exploration of rally culture expands beyond its immediate confines to wider concerns of technological over-determinism on individual social identity, or how technology increasingly shapes humanity's self-conceptualisation. *Kun taivas putoaa…/When the Heavens Fall* (1972) zoomed in on the role media plays in interpersonal and societal relationships. Its critical exploration of the lengths to which sensationalist reporting neglects any moral journalistic concerns touches on contemporary fears over the power of the media. Suggestively arguing that the propagators of tabloid reporting have spiralled out of control, the film provides a representation of the dehumanizing effects media technology can have on individuals. This critical focus on contemporary society found its culmination in 1973's *Yhden miehen sota/One Man's War*, a critical examination of the Great Migration (the rapid structural changes of Finnish society from a rural to an urban society). Migration of individuals from the countryside to the cities and their often despairing living conditions are portrayed in the most dystopian of ways in this film which intersperses fictional talking head interviews with raw documentary-like footage. Alongside Mikko Niskanen's *Kahdeksan surmanluotia/Eight Deadly Shots* (1972), the film is one of the most harrowing of depictions of the state of the nation in these challenging times.

Jarva's career illuminates the tension between the idealism of political commitment and the realistic demands of the market throughout the period of substantial restructuring of domestic cinema. Government support was only a part of a film's budget, and the majority of the production had to be financed through independent investment, production deals, pre-selling and international co-production. While this situation provided film-makers with authorial freedom, it also often created a need for personal financial investment. Considering the less than stellar financial returns of most of his self-consciously politicised films, it is not surprising Jarva decided to re-orientate his style of film-making in the mid-1970s. In the funding application for the comedy *Mies joka ei osannut sanoa ei/The Man Who Couldn't Say No* (1975), Jarva stated:

> My directorial career will be in dire straits if a connection with the audience cannot be found. First of all, the film in question does not deal with contemporary reality or directly engage with socially-relevant questions. Rather, the hopes for the future are more to do with a romanticized past.

The result of this reorientation were 'gentle' comedies such as *Loma/Olympian Holiday* (1976) and *Jäniksen Vuosi/The Year of the Hare* (1977), resulting in suggestions that 'Finland's first great auteur' was wasting his talent on populist comedies (Cowie 1990). Others, however, suggest that this change of tactic resulted in films that still maintain the critical perspective of Jarva's earlier films. These films turned away from austere reflections on current social issues in favour of more fantastic, even farcical scenarios involving protagonists attempting to escape their constricted social circumstances. *The Year of the Hare* is a good example of Jarva's methodology as it provides a timely commentary on the state of the nation, touching on important ecological themes while managing to maintain a levity that allows it to appeal to popular audiences.

The Year of the Hare's method of bridging the gap between art and entertainment raises a significant and curiously prophetic point about the importance of heritage and tradition in regaining the interest of the domestic audience, The Finnish Film Foundation's annual reports and projections, especially from the late 1970s onwards, are abundant with references to 'reclaiming national audiences' by producing 'national films' that appeal to a mass audience. Caught in the space between aspirations towards high culture and populist realities, film-makers had to balance precariously between the guaranteed funding of high culture and appeasing a public that had different ideas about what they wanted to see at the cinema. Jarva's films were able to find a balance between these different demands as they were largely popular with national audiences, qualified for the status of official culture through critical reception and funding from the Finnish Film Foundation, and dealt with traditional national history and reworked Finnish cultural traditions. In essence, Jarva's thematic re-orientation can be seen as one of the first concrete symptoms of the change of tactics within the domestic national cinema that was to occur during the next decades, where the drive to produce and preserve national culture would meet with the demands of the audiences.

Jarva was one of the most significant auteurs in Finnish cinema and his influence is still felt. He died in a tragic car accident on his way home from the premiere of *The Year of the Hare* in 1977.

Pietari Kääpä

References

Cowie, Peter (1990), *Finnish Cinema*, Helsinki: VAPK-publishing.
Documents available at http://www.ristojarvaseura.fi/

DIRECTORS
T.J. SÄRKKÄ

Of all the Finnish film producers, T. J. Särkkä (1890–1975) comes closest to the arche-typal image of a film mogul. Särkkä held an autocratic position in Suomen Filmiteollisuus (SF), the biggest production company in Finland from the late 1930s to the early 1960s and, like his Hollywood colleagues, he was a most controversial public figure, loved and feared, respected and despised alike. Unlike Hollywood producers, however, due to the relatively small scale of production, he was able to personally operate on many levels of film practice, not only as the president of the company and the central producer, but also as a prolific director and screenwriter. Emphasizing his all-round job description, he preferred to designate himself as 'the first errand boy of the company'.

Särkkä was well in his forties when he entered film business in the mid-1930s. Having majored in Russian philology, he had made a career as a bank manager and as a manag-ing director of the Association for Finnish Work, an organization established for promot-ing domestic industry, before getting acquainted with Erkki Karu. Former president of Suomi-Filmi, the leading film production company of the 1920s, Karu had established SF in 1933. Särkkä became a shareholder and a member of the board, and when Karu died unexpectedly in 1935, Särkkä took his position as the president of the company. With very little experience in actual film-making, he also inherited Karu's dual role as not only the head, but also as the main creative force of the company.

Under Särkkä's management, SF soon began to make profit, which was facilitated by the fact that by the mid-1930s Finland had more or less recovered from the Great Depression. SF started with one shooting crew and one or two films a year, but in 1939 they already had four shooting crews and eight premières. Despite certain difficulties during the Winter War period (1939–40) and the post WWII period, caused by material shortage and political tensions, film-making continued with minor interruptions during the war years. In fact, domestic films were more popular than ever, and *Kulkurin valssi/ The Vagabond's Waltz*, a historical romance film directed by Särkkä in 1941, broke all previous records with its over 1.2 million spectators.

In the 1950s SF's production volume increased, reaching its high point in 1954 and 1955 with fourteen new feature films a year. The unforeseen success of the epic war film *Tuntematon sotilas/The Unknown Soldier* (dir. Edvin Laine, 1955) was, paradoxically, a turning point. The huge returns of the film were invested into new productions. This led to considerable overproduction, while constantly rising production costs and declining attendance simultaneously pushed the film industry into deepening problems. Unlike its main rivals, Suomi-Filmi and Fennada-Filmi, SF had always concentrated mainly on feature film production, which made it more vulnerable when the public's interest in traditional domestic films began to fall in the face of television and other competing audio-visual media, swift suburbanization, and other major social and cultural transformations. Särkkä produced his last films in 1963, and two years later SF petitioned for bankruptcy. Both Suomi-Filmi and Fennada-Filmi carried on producing feature films, but on an irregular basis, and after the launching of a state subsidy system – first channelled through state film awards from 1961 and then through the Finnish Film Foundation from 1969 – the studio production system was more or less replaced by new modes of production, run by small, independent and often short-lived companies and package-unit productions.

Throughout three decades Särkkä was the unchallenged leader figure of SF. While important decisions had to be passed by the board in Suomi-Filmi and Fennada-Filmi, the role of the board in SF was nominal. In practice it was Särkkä who made decisions for production, and the one who hired and fired people. The decisions were often quick and impulsive, especially in the 1950s, when SF's B-budget productions would spring up at an unforeseen pace. Särkkä would, for example, get an idea of turning a popular hit song into a film; then, lyricist and scriptwriter Reino Helismaa would outline a script, sometimes overnight, and within a few weeks the film would première.

As a scriptwriter and director Särkkä remained active until the end of his career, whereas his main rival Risto Orko who followed Karu as the production manager of Suomi-Filmi, ceased directing in the early 1940s when he became the president of the company. Särkkä scripted more than 40 films and directed 49, ranging from light comedies (*Lapatossu/The Old Railroad Worker* [with Yrjö Norta, 1937]; *Rakas lurjus/Beloved Rascal* [1955]) to biopics (*Runon kuningas ja muuttolintu/The King of Poets and the Bird of Passage* [1940]; *Ballaadi/Ballad* [1944]) and from melodramas (*Naiskohtaloita/Destinies of Women* [1947]; *Kuu on vaarallinen/Preludes to Ecstasy* [1962]) to historical spectacles (*Helmikuun manifesti/February Manifesto* [with Norta, 1939]; *Tanssi yli hautojen/Dancing on Graves* [1950]). His scripts were, with few exceptions, adaptations of novels or plays.

Särkkä's first eleven films were co-directed with Yrjö Norta, a technical expert who had built his own sound recording system in the late 1920s, in use in SF until 1941. In contrast to Orko, neither Särkkä nor some of the directors he hired from the stage like Wilho Ilmari or Edvin Laine showed much interest in film technology. Thus, the obvious role for Särkkä was to concentrate on supervising the actors, while Norta would make the decisions concerning camera angles, lenses, etc. In consequence, the house style of SF was primarily actor- and character-centred: from the grandiose acting ideals adopted by Särkkä and the reliance on established theatre actors to the insensitivity of the early recording equipment and the favouring of high-key lighting and reframing camera movements, everything contributed to focusing on the character. Among the more innovative cinematic experiments was the use of a 'transfocator', a home-developed early version of a zoom lens; this, however, was also often used in order to emphasize the character's reactions with a quick zoom-in.

Despite these technical innovations, Särkkä's style is often considered somewhat ponderous and pathetic. According to cinematographer Felix Forsman, the actors performed like they would perform for 'the third row in a theatre' since Särkkä did not observe the action through the camera lens. On the other hand, Särkkä's disinterest in technology allowed the cinematographers at SF to have more artistic freedom and responsibility than they would have had working with directors with a background in cinema. Indeed, the reliance on technical personnel gives certain credit for the 'genius of the system': numerous stories recount that Särkkä or Edvin Laine would sometimes be away from the shooting location for hours or even for days, and let the personnel be in charge.

Besides being a producer and a film-maker, Särkkä was, arguably, the most influential rhetorician of national cinema in Finland. He started writing about film culture in the early 1930s as the editor of a magazine published by the Association for Finnish Work, emphasizing the potential of the film industry for national economy, but also paying attention to important issues concerning the national film style. By the beginning of WWII, Särkkä had polished his writing into a high style prose, introducing every issue of the company magazine *SF-Uutiset* with an editorial that anchored SF's newest films to the endeavours of national film culture with clever turns. While SF imported only a handful of films over the years, and had little success in exporting their own films, for Särkkä, national cinema very much equalled domestic film production for domestic markets – 'by and for the people', as he liked to emphasize.

Up to the end of WWII the fundamental premise of Särkkä's national rhetoric was that of national integration. In accordance with the governmental politics of the late 1930s, this integration was based on relative inclusion: with the exception of both the extreme left and right, all Finns were welcomed to constitute a nation – and a national film audience. Särkkä wrote in 1939:

> The film audience is made of practically all population groups [...] in no other way can the success of cinema be explained. The working man and the schoolteacher, the farmer and the bank manager, the housemaid and the professional woman all sit side by side at the cinema, as a grand democracy of the auditorium.

During the postwar era Särkkä's national rhetoric – both in his writings and in SF's films – adopted a more exclusive attitude, sometimes converging with the rising populist movement and culminating in the series of *rillumarei* films that glorified the common sense wisdom of the everyman against the urban cultural elite. At the same time, Särkkä, as well as his rivals, still adhered to the idea of an undivided national audience and denied the possibility of making films for fragmented audiences. By the early 1960s this proved to be deadlock situation, ending up in virtual downfall of the traditional modes of film production.

Kimmo Laine

DIRECTORS
TEUVO TULIO

Teuvo Tulio is undoubtedly one of the most important pioneers of Finnish cinema. Tulio began his career in the 1920s as an actor, before establishing himself as an independent producer and director in the 1930s – with only one exception, all of his 16 films are heart-breaking melodramas. Despite the fact that neither the film industry, nor the critics were too fond of his films (especially those produced later in his career), they were extremely popular, especially among female viewers – this is not a coincidence, since Tulio attacked narrow-mindedness and immorality through his female protagonists. Almost all the protagonists of his films are women who are unable to have a normal sexual or spiritual relationship in a hypocritical world dominated by men. These critical views of the patriarchal nature of Finnish society are conducted through the narratives of innocent, poor and naïve girls, who become rich and famous due to their kindness and beauty. But in Tulio's films, as in much of the patriarchally-minded cultural production, social welfare and beauty are always accompanied by various punishments such as misery, loneliness, imprisonment, and sometimes even death.

Tulio (whose real name is Theodor Derochinsky Tugai) was born in 1912, in Rēzekne, Latvia on a train en route to St. Petersburg. He was born to a Turkish-Polish father and a Persian-Latvian mother. At the age of 10, he moved to Helsinki with his mother, and in his teens he got acquainted with the Russian-born Valentin Ivanoff, who later became known as Valentin Vaala in the Finnish film industry. Tulio and Vaala enthusiastically visited cinemas, where they were introduced to all sorts of film styles and genres, and they produced their first, never finished or screened, film in the summer of 1927, which was followed by four feature films in the next years. At that time, their roles were divided to Vaala directing and Tulio acting in the main roles (*Mustat silmät/Black Eyes* [1929]; *Mustalaishurmaaja/The*

Gypsy Charmer [1929]; *Laveata tietä/The Wide Road* [1931]; *Sininen varjo/Blue Shadow* [1933]). In their first collaboration, Tulio played a dark charmer for whose affections women constantly competed, and as their second film expanded on the theme, Vaala became a nationally recognized director. Their third collaboration, *The Wide Road*, was an early example of a Finnish film of which a sound version was produced alongside the silent version. Tulio once again plays a charmer violinist, who conquers not only the hearts of Finnish women, but also those of Parisians. Their last film together was based on Mika Waltari's story *Blue Shadow*, and this time Tulio played the challenging dual role of a thief and a clerk. His exotic appearance, and eroticized roles in particular, were instrumental in making Tulio Finland's own Rudolph Valentino.

Tulio and Vaala parted ways when the production company Fennica folded due to the recession. By now, Tulio was convinced he was ready to prove his talent on the other side of the camera as well as in front of it. He met Yrjö Kivimies and they wrote two screenplays together (*Taistelu Heikkilän talosta/Struggle for the House of Heikkilä* [1936]; *Silja - Nuorena nukkunut/ Silja* [1937]). The results of the collaboration were surprisingly successful, despite (or perhaps because of) Tulio following a strict melodramatic path, while Kivimies preferred a different kind of humour. Tulio started working in Abel Adams' studio (at Adams Film), where he also made his first feature film, the above mentioned *Struggle for the House of Heikkilä*. The film is based on Johannes Linnankoski's short story and takes place in the countryside, where a young couple's future is forbidden due to a prenuptial agreement. Anni detests Toivo Erkkilä, the husband who was designated for her, and her frigidity drives him into the throes of insanity and alcoholism: he not only drinks like a fish, but also tries to earn some respect around the house with a whip. When Anni finally tires of her husband's behaviour, she takes the whip in her own hands and starts to dictate her new rules: she prohibits him from drinking and forces him to stay home, but in true melodramatic fashion, Toivo takes vengeance and poisons Anni.

Tulio's second feature *Silja* was based on the future Nobel Laureate Frans Emil Sillanpää's novel and focuses on Silja, who comes from a wealthy family, but is made a servant, and not only loses her true love, but also gets tuberculosis. This canonical piece of cinematic melodrama defines a cornerstone Finnish film genre, the 'haystack drama'. The characteristics of the genre include abundant use of eye-catching landscapes, classic coming-of-age stories and excessive uses of orchestral music.

Tulio's roots can be traced back to rural life in Latvia, to his beloved farm, where he spent his childhood – many of his recreations of Finnish rurality draw on these subjective memories. Tulio's other main obsession was with his portrayals of female protagonists: suffering women are shown in extreme close-ups, their tearful faces, concentrated mimicry and sudden gestures evoke the deepest of pains in many memorable, if excessive, ways. Initially, the films provide the protagonists with respect, admiration and beauty, but ultimately this is all taken away from them. Prostitution, alcoholism and madness make even the most alluring faces and enchanting glimpses look ugly, evoking pity in the male protagonists and the viewers. This sort of oscillation between sympathy and patriarchal impulses characterizes much of his output.

Regina Linnanheimo was in many ways Tulio's personal muse, with whom he had a great professional and personal relationship (though they never got married) – she always read the screenplays and helped to improve the dialogue. She was also up to date with Tulio's business affairs and, in the 1950s, she single-handedly wrote Tulio's screenplays. In Tulio's third film, *Kiusaus/Temptation* (1938) Linnanheimo's provocative smile and enchanting eyes are highlighted by the usual light and shadow play. *Temptation* takes place on an isolated island, where a young clergyman falls in love with another man's wife. Unfortunately, Tulio's first three movies were lost in a fire that broke out at Adams Film, and only stills of the films survive (with the exception of the first film, of which parts were discovered in 2006 by researchers at the Finnish Film Archive).

The collaboration between Tulio and Adams Film ended with Abel Adams' death in 1938. Consequently, Tulio decided to become an independent producer and his first independent work, *Laulu tulipunaisesta kukasta/The Song of the Scarlet Flower* (1938) was an unexpected breakthrough for the director. The film is based on Johannes Linnankoski's novel and focuses on the rites of passage of a young man, who needs to take more responsibility for his social and sexual acts. In the spring of 1939, Tulio agreed to join the project of a Swedish producer, which was eventually cancelled. To cover his costs, Tulio collaborated with the actor Eino Jurkka, which resulted in Tulio's first and only comedy *Vihtori ja Klaara/Victor and Clara* (1939), based on the comic strip 'Bringing up Father'.

His next feature *Unelma karjamajalla/In the Fields of Dreams* (1940) was based on Henning Ohlson's piece. Its male protagonist was the sharp-faced Kille Oksanen, while the female lead was played by 1939's Miss Europa, Sirkka Salonen. Tulio's career froze for a few years as he was ordered to the frontlines to capture the war on film, and his current project was cancelled due to Oksanen's death in battle in October 1941. Towards the end of the war, he cherished experimentation and asked Nisse Hirn to write a screenplay for him. *Sellaisena kuin sinä minut halusit/The Way You Wanted Me* (1944) was the start of a new era in Tulio's career as the rural locations were replaced with the sinful darkness of the city. Tulio also shot a Swedish version (*Sådan du ville ha mig*) of the film and the lead actress Marie-Louise Fock played the main role in both versions of the film, but the versions differ in some of the side characters as Tulio wanted to use some Swedish actors to break into the Swedish and Danish markets – the ploy was successful and the work also garnered recognition in Bulgaria.

After an extensive break, Tulio reunited with his favourite actress, Regina Linnanheimo for *Rakkauden risti/Cross of Love* (1946). Linnanheimo plays the daughter of a lighthouse keeper who longs for a life in the big city and leaves her father for a treacherous man. The innocent, naïve country girl appears again, driven to the sinful city by her good-natured curiosity. The film's honest sexuality and naturalism gives it an expressionist tinge as it combines the absurd with the sublime, sin with atonement. Like many other Finnish films made in the 1940s, *Cross of Love* is a 'problem film', but its exaggerated fable style makes it more than just another melodrama. The traces of war are everywhere in Tulio's films, as his former, relatively positive, spirit was replaced with a much more desperate, darker tone. Also absent was the lyricism of his previous films, which is partially attributable to cinematographer Erik Blomberg's absence.

Levoton veri/Restless Blood (1946) was completed two months after *Cross of Love*, and its heroine's role was consciously written for Regina Linnanheimo – the role of the hysterical wife gave her a chance to show the audience new sides of her talent. These collaborations with Linnanheimo comprise the golden era of Tulio's career, but this did not last for long as he increasingly began to recycle previous works instead of emphasising experimentation. *Intohimon vallassa/In The Grip of Passion* (1947) is a remake of *Struggle for the House of Heikkila* from 1936, to which he inserted whole scenes from his previous work. Almost all of his subsequent films used well-worn topics, and he not only recycled images but also musical cues.

In the late 1940s, Tulio met the Paramount Studio boss Adolph Zukor in Stockholm and had a conversation with him in Yiddish. Tulio showed Zukor some of his work, leading to a contract for a production for Paramount, which was to be shot in Sweden and directed by Tulio. Tulio's screenplay about a 'logger' hero and his lover (to be played by Regina Linnanheimo, of course) was accepted by the studio, and was to star both Clark Gable and Gary Cooper at various points, but due to the death of Paramount's producer Carl P. York the project was ultimately cancelled.

Tulio's fortunes in Finland were not much better. The screenplay for *Rikollinen nainen/A Woman of Crime* (1952) was entirely written by Regina Linnanheimo. The theme of the film was novel, focusing on a female prisoner suffering from amnesia. Despite Linnan-heimo's committed performance, the audience reacted against what they saw as her overdramatic acting. *Mustasukkaisuus/Jealousy* (1953), a remake of *Restless Blood*, was a serious failure for Tulio. It is one of the few Finnish films which has never been shown in theatres in Helsinki, only to be broadcast on television in 1962. Tulio and Linnanheimo's last collaboration turned out to be *Olet mennyt minun vereeni/You Have Got Me Into My Blood* (1956). The narrative was autobiographical for Linnanheimo, who courageously plays an alcoholic woman unable to cope with getting old and burning out.

By the late 1950s, Tulio was considered old-fashioned, and he lived a quiet life until the production of his last film *Sensuela* (1973). This is also a remake, as it is a colour version of *Cross of Love*. The story begins in Lapland, where Hans, a Nazi soldier, crashes in his plane. He is rescued by a Sami family who takes good care of him, while he falls in love with the beautiful Laila. Laila's father is very strict, so he sends the soldier home and forbids his daughter to have any contact with him. After the war, Hans returns to Lapland as a photographer and meets Laila again, who this time runs away with him to the capital. Things do not go as well as Laila imagined, as she soon finds herself in Hamburg as a prostitute in the red light district. It is clear that the shooting of the film was complicated as most of the film is ridiculously jumbled: wild parties, lots of nudity, a mixture of violence and stuffed animals. The production used equipment from the 1940s, resulting in a 'dreamy' atmosphere – in fact, the images are blurred due to the poor quality of the equipment. *Sensuela* was filmed in English to cater for the international markets, yet the film was an almost catastrophic, ugly failure, and received the K-18 certificate in Finland, a first for a Finnish production. Instead of a national première, it was only screened in Kemi, Kuopio and Pieksamäki and received 650 spectators. Tulio advertised his movie as a ballad, though it was later to gain notoriety as the first Finnish soft porn film.

After this final blow, Tulio sequestered himself from the world. New generations began to discover him only in the final stages of his life as his creations garnered cult reputation in the late 1980s. Despite this new-found appreciation of his talent, Tulio never returned to directing. Yet, his reputation, especially nowadays, is that of a great Finnish auteur, a notion underlined by Aki Kaurismäki's declaration of Tulio as one of his idols; according to him, Tulio is the greatest master of Finnish melodrama.

Emőke Csoma

DIRECTORS
VALENTIN VAALA

With 44 feature films and dozens of documentaries, Valentin Vaala (1909–76) was one of the most prolific Finnish film-makers of all time. His work, ranging from urban comedies and lumberjack films to adaptations of classic literature, in many ways embodies the most professional qualities in Finnish studio production.

Born Valentin Ivanov, Vaala was of Russian origin, and he spoke fluent Russian, Swedish and Finnish. As proof of the prevalently rising enthusiasm for cinema in the 1920s, Vaala and his friend Theodor Tugai (who later became a director of melodramas under the name Teuvo Tulio) started making films in the late 1920s. Their first experiments remained unfinished, but by 1929 Vaala and Tugai had gained enough experience and financial backing to be able to finish two feature films, *Mustat silmät/Black Eyes* (1929) and *Mustalaishurmaaja/The Gypsy Charmer* (1929). Relying on 'gypsy romantic' tradition, these films presented Tugai as the Finnish Valentino, openly emphasizing both ethnic and sexual ambiguity. The critical reception was relatively positive, especially among the young modernists, who welcomed the exoticism of the films as a longed-for counterpoint to the assumedly ethnographic mainstream of contemporary Finnish films.

Vaala and Tugai continued their collaboration for two more films, the former as director and the latter as lead actor. Vaala directed two more independent films – playing also the romantic lead himself in *Kun isä tahtoo…/When Father Wants To* (1935), a comedy loosely based on George McManus' comic strip 'Bringing Up Father' – before being recruited by Suomi-Filmi, the biggest production company in Finland at the time. Recovering from the recession, Suomi-Filmi needed another director to back up Risto Orko, the new production manager and head director. Despite his youth, Vaala was, by the mid-1930s, a relatively experienced director who had, unlike most other potential candidates, picked up his skills in the practice of film-making, not theatre. His professional background was perfectly suited to Suomi-Filmi in its wilful tendency to differentiate its new house style from the assumed theatricality and traditionalism of its quickly expanding rival Suomen Filmiteollisuus. Not only had Vaala proved to be an efficient director capable of shooting quickly and with low budgets, but he also had an eye for urban life and international cinematic phenomena.

It was therefore no surprise that Vaala's first task at Suomi-Filmi was to script and direct modern comedies with urban and/or high society settings, determined and independent female protagonists and swift dialogue. Some of these comedies were based on novels by popular female authors like Hilja Valtonen (*Vaimoke/Substitute Wife* [1936], *Varaventtiili/Safety Valve* [1942]), but during the war years, Vaala, the author Kersti Bergroth, and the female lead of his comedies of the era, Lea Joutseno, became a creative scriptwriting trio working on original scripts. An amateur actress, Joutseno was a perfect choice for portraying the nonconformist and quick-witted lead characters, hilariously rendering the lines specially adapted for her in, for example, *Morsian yllättää/The Bride Springs a Surprise* (1941) and *Tositarkoituksella/With Serious Intent* (1943).

In contemporary interviews, Vaala readily named Frank Capra and Ernst Lubitsch as his most important masters. The choices were telling, exemplifying not only screwball and sophisticated comedy, but mastery of the transparent techniques of 'classical' Hollywood narration. Of all Finnish directors of the studio era, Vaala was arguably the one most inclined towards Hollywood. From early on, he studied the practices of classical scene dissection in detail and, to take only one example, he was the first Finnish director to systematically favour shot reverse shot technique in conversation scenes instead of two shots.

Throughout his career, Vaala remained faithful to sophisticated urban comedies, even though the women's films of the 1930s and 1940s later gave way to more male-centred narratives, like that of *Gabriel, tule takaisin/Gabriel, Come Back* (1951), a 'heartless comedy' about a swindler who seduces elderly women and walks out after conning them out of all their money. Along with the comedies there was, however, another constant thread in his work: starting with the early independent productions, many of his films had a touch of melodrama.

Characteristically, if not quite exclusively, Vaala's melodramatic milieu is rural, as opposed to his urban comedies. Often in the form of family melodrama, these films involve such themes as oppressive religious tradition (*Koskenlaskijan morsian/The Lumberjack's Bride* [1937]), female sacrifice on behalf of the family's fortune and tradition (*Loviisa, Niskavuoren nuori emäntä/Louisa* [1946]) or North/South-dichotomy (*Vihreä kulta/Green Gold* [1940]; *Maaret – tunturien tyttö/Maaret, Daughter of the Mountains* [1947]). Compared with the excessive and sensationalist qualities of Tulio, Vaala's melodramatic style was subtle and considerably highbrow. Indeed, some of Vaala's melodramas had an established literary origin: his readings of the works of Hella Wuolijoki (six films, among them *Niskavuoren naiset/Women of Niskavuori* [1938, remade in 1958]) and F. E. Sillanpää (*Ihmiset suviyössä/People in the Summer Night* [1948]) are valued among the finest literary adaptations in Finnish film history.

From the mid-1930s to the 1970s, Vaala stayed at Suomi-Filmi. During his heyday in the 1930s and 1940s, he had relative freedom to choose his subjects and actors, work on his scripts and even have time to rehearse with the actors, which was anything but typical practice – as long as his films kept on making profit, that is. In the 1950s, as attendance declined and production costs rose, Vaala's position in the company became insecure, resulting finally in an attempt to give him notice in 1963. Firing a respected faithful director, however, earned Suomi-Filmi such an amount of bad publicity that they were forced to find him work at the documentary department. Vaala spent the rest of his career directing mainly customized documentaries of various kinds, from industrial to city films.

Vaala was among the few studio directors valued among the post-studio era critics and film-makers. His level of professionalism was undeniable, and there was enough unity in his work and in his working methods to consider him a genuine auteur. While television and video distribution have guaranteed a place for his films in popular memory, a revived critical interest has emerged since the 1980s, focusing on, for example, the modern and gay sensibilities of Vaala's early independent work and the emancipatory potential of the women's films of the 1930s and 1940s.

Kimmo Laine

STARS
THE EMERGENCE OF
THE STAR SYSTEM

While the star system emerged in neighbouring Sweden and Denmark in the 1910s, actors in the Finnish film industry did not receive this attention until later. Only from the mid-1930s onwards were actors able to both make their living through film-making and gain sustainable popularity with the audience. The concept and discourses of stardom, however, were not unknown even in the previous decades.

Already in the 1910s, actors were the most important part of film advertising as the international notions of picture personalities and emerging stardom reached Finland. The queues blocked the streets when favourite performers appeared on the screen, and bookshops sold a great variety of pictures of the favourite actors. The first film journals *Biograafilehti* and *Bio* (published for short periods of time in 1915 and 1916) focused on presenting famous film personas. Occasionally, they used the word 'star', although the term wasn't in widespread use yet.

When compared with the amount of films imported, domestic production struggled in volume, with only little over twenty Finnish fictional films receiving wide theatrical distribution before 1920. This can be considered one of the reasons for the audiences' focus on international celebrities. In the mid-1910s, many of the favourite performers were Danish, led by Asta Nielsen and Valdemar Psilander. Journal *Bio* even reported how the female audience couldn't help themselves, but burst in tears when 'the Young Apollo' Psilander appeared on the screen. Asta Nielsen, regardless, was the most frequent topic of discussion in the journals. As she filmed in Germany, her new features were forbidden during the Great War in the Russian Grand Duchy of Finland, but her career was reported in both *Biograafilehti* and *Bio*, and her older features were frequently replayed at the cinemas. The audience also favoured a variety of actors and actresses from other countries.

In the genre of short comedies, for example, Max Linder and Charlie Chaplin were much adored, and the performers of Russian melodramas such as Vera Kholodnaya and Ivan Mozzhukhin were highly popular.

The turn of the 1920s brought major changes to Finnish film culture. Suomi-Filmi, established in 1919, was the first company to focus primarily on film production. *Filmiaitta*, a film magazine established two years later, brought the latest film news extensively to the Finnish audience. This time, neither film production nor magazine publication ceased after a couple of features or issues, which contributed to sustaining continuity in domestic film culture. The content of *Filmiaitta* was mainly based upon material translated from foreign film journals or publicity material spread by the distribution companies. Thus, Finnish readers became familiar with international film stars, their careers and private lives. In the early 1920s, the import numbers from the United States rose beyond those of other countries, allowing Hollywood pictures to play a significant role in the Finnish film culture.

Domestic film production, however, did not follow the trends established by international examples, but rather the standards of Finnish theatre. In the 1920s, most of the directors, screenwriters and actors had their background on the stage and many of the films were adaptations of distinguished national literature. Throughout the 1920s and early 1930s film acting was a secondary occupation for stage actors. Both the appreciation of film work and the number of productions were still so low that cinema was not able to offer career opportunities. The values and standards of the theatre also influenced film publicity. The most important rule was to respect privacy. Actors did not reveal their opinions nor discuss their backgrounds, but only focused on their profession (except for short notions that an actress was a devoted wife and mother alongside her career). As they were first and foremost theatre actors, their film publicity focused primarily on their stage performances. In most cases, the result was that any interview was basically a summary of the actor's stage career with a brief introduction to the upcoming film.

As actors were recruited among the established stage professionals, they were somewhat older than those playing leading roles in Hollywood films, for example. The problematic contradiction between beauty and youth and professionalism and appreciation, especially among the actresses, was soon noted. Already in 1924, theatre director and film fan Eino Salmelainen wrote about the collision of ideals and the differences between film and theatre. He used William Shakespeare's *Romeo and Juliet* as an example, emphasizing that an actress had to be twice as old as Juliet to be able to perform the role on the stage. The problem was that when she was experienced enough, she no longer looked like Juliet. Salmelainen noted that this did not matter at the theatre as the audience came to listen to the elocution, not to look at the actresses. Difference was vast in comparison to the cinema as the art of the young and the beautiful.

The Finnish film directors sought solution to the problem of youth and beauty by casting amateurs, inexperienced young women, who had no formal training before or during the film-making. Usually, the amateur was also replaced by a new one for the next film. They had no possibilities to improve as an actress as they were expendable for the film production. In the publicity they were often referred to as 'new stars', but their careers were not supported. They were seldom interviewed and they were more often paralleled with mannequins than with stage professionals: their utmost skill was literally to look sweet in the latest fashion. Heidi Blåfield (1900–31) was an exception to the rule, as she was both appreciated for her professional abilities and considered young and beautiful.

The lack of domestic stars was widely discussed in the late 1920s. It was emphasized that there were plenty of skilled actresses for the so-called 'granny roles' (i.e. older stage professionals), but no young actresses who could gain international success like Swedes Anna Nilsson and Greta Garbo. The discussion focused on analyzing the photogenicity (or the lack of it) among the newcomers and debating the characteristics of stardom.

Practically no attention was paid to the fact that the Finnish film industry devoted no effort to star-making and promotion of the newcomers. The star system and publicity functions of Hollywood were well-known, but they were not adopted.

The early 1930s brought major changes in the film production. The financial difficulties rising from the 1920s Depression, the coming of sound and poor business ventures culminated in 1932–33, when the whole industry was about to collapse. After surviving this close call, film production reformed itself and the production numbers grew rapidly during the latter half of the 1930s. Also, for the first time, attention was paid to the promotion of actors. Already in 1934, newly established company Suomen Filmiteollisuus cast Ester Toivonen, who had recently won the Miss Europe beauty pageant. She received masses of publicity and all together sixteen roles in the years 1934–43, despite her limited acting skills. From then onwards, actors played a key part in the rivalries between film companies.

Many of the most loved film stars started their careers in the mid- or late-1930s. The greatest of the actresses, and one of the first whose fame was carefully constructed, was Ansa Ikonen, who had her film debut in 1935. She recollects in her memoirs the director's comments to her after casting: 'Now, Miss Ikonen, we are going to make you a star'. She was dressed in the latest fashion and her hair was bleached platinum blonde. New elaborate film magazines and other glossy papers focused on promoting her as a great star even before her first film premiere. Her first opposite actor was Tauno Palo, who had already appeared in a couple of film roles, and was to become the greatest Finnish film star. Their first mutual film Kaikki rakastavat/Everybody Loves (Vaala, 1935) provided instant success and made them the number one film couple of Finnish cinema. Altogether, they collaborated on twelve films between 1935 and 1956.

Alongside their film careers, Ikonen and Palo were part of the Finnish National Theatre. The film companies kept recruiting leading actors and actresses from the most important stages, but in the late 1930s, cooperation proved to be problematic. The actors had strict contracts with the theatres, which gave only a small amount of time for filming – mostly during the nights. As their prime career was on stage, they were not dependent on the film companies and were easily able to, for example, change the employer if a competing film company offered a higher salary. At the same time, theatres wanted to restrict their film projects even more. The rising film production numbers, instead, increased the demand for actors who would have both photogenicity and the necessary acting skills.

As a response, film companies once again started recruiting amateurs, especially for the roles of leading ladies. No longer were these beautiful young women expendable but investments: they got annual contracts, training, styling and publicity. Between the years 1936 and 1939, Regina Linnanheimo, Helena Kara, Tuulikki Paananen, Sirkka Sari, Sirkka Sipilä and Laila Rihte rose to stardom without a theatre background. As film production was their sole income, they were much more reliable investments than the stage professionals, and they were more seldom able to change employer.

The Finnish press played a significant role in the emergence of stardom in the latter half of the 1930s. The film companies set up their own advertising magazines and other journals were also interested in the upcoming stars. The press still retained its respectful attitude towards the film stars, but new forms of publicity fostered the interest of the audience. Young celebrities shared their opinions about film-making, beauty treatments and fashion, and got their carefully stylized pictures on the magazine covers.

In the upcoming years, new stars were born and some of the old ones left the industry, but by the end of the 1930s the Finnish star system was formed. Its structure was gender-biased as most of the male actors held important positions on most respectable stages of Finnish theatre. In comparison there were more female stars who only acted on-screen and had no connection to the theatre. The film companies offered annual contracts for the most adored performers – both film and stage professionals – and the production numbers were relatively high. The 1940s was the golden era for Finnish film stars especially, and at the height of their fame were, for example, Tauno Palo, Ansa Ikonen, Regina Linnanheimo and Helena Kara, who all had started their film careers and gained stardom in the 1930s.

Outi Hupaniittu

Tulitikkutehtaan tyttö/The Match Factory Girl (1990), Villealfa Productions

STARS
KATI OUTINEN

The Man Without a Past, Sputnik Oy.

Outinen was born in 1961, and entered the prestigious Theatre Academy of Helsinki after completing high school. She trained under the infamous Jouko Turkka, known for his emphasis on the physicality of an actor's work (Johnson 2010: 107–08). While still in high school she appeared as Lissu in *Täältä tullaan, elämä/Right on Man!* (Suominen, 1980), the film that announced the arrival of a 'new Finnish cinema' with its focus on disenfranchised teenagers in Helsinki. The film depicts a class of social misfits with Lissu the only girl among them. Lissu's is a small part, as most of the film focuses on one of the boys, Jussi. However, early on in the film she makes her absences known: she frequently gets up and leaves unexpectedly, any excuses or goodbyes replaced by profanities. She rises to greater prominence in the last few minutes of the film, as she shows a jagged kindness to Jussi and finally watches him fall to his death as he is chased by a security guard. At the time still an amateur actor, Outinen displays in Lissu's character a striking conflict between resilience and fatalism. Lissu has become an iconic character in Finnish cinema, and so when Outinen played the mother of a similarly disenfranchised youth in *Sairaan kaunis maailma/Freakin' Beautiful World* (Lampela, 1997), Sakari Toiviainen (2002: 50) saw in her cameo performance the sign of yet another generational change in Finnish cinema.

In an interview with Pamela Tola (2007: 128), Outinen states that following the release of *Right on Man!* she felt emotionally cut off from friends and exposed to the duplicity of people due to her sudden status as a local celebrity. As a qualified actor she also became increasingly disillusioned by the film and theatre industries' meagre offerings for female actors: roles were limited to small parts as girlfriends of main characters or otherwise restricted to one-dimensional depictions of virgins, mothers or prostitutes.

There was also often pressure to appear naked on the stage or screen, or even requests from directors for actresses to have breast implants inserted; degrading experiences which significantly diminished her commitment to a career in acting (Tola 2007: 129–34). Outinen states that she regained her joy of working when she began collaborating with the director Aki Kaurismäki, who she felt had a fairly gender-neutral approach to filmmaking (ibid.: 129). Outinen is undoubtedly best known abroad for her Kaurismäkian acting – a profile in *Elle* (2002) even refers to her as '*la Kati d'Aki*' – although her Kaurismäkian roles are well-known and, to a degree, defining in Finland as well: for example, a profile on the Theatre Academy of Helsinki website describes her as personifying her generation in her Kaurismäkian roles (Vento 2007).

Outinen first worked with Kaurismäki on *Varjoja paratiisissa/Shadows in Paradise* (1986) as Ilona, a check-out operator. Since *Shadows in Paradise*, Outinen has become a principal player in Kaurismäki's ensemble of actors: she has been Ofelia in *Hamlet liikemaailmassa/Hamlet Goes Business* (1987), Iris in *Tulitikkutehtaan tyttö/The Match Factory Girl* (1990), Tatjana in *Pidä huivista kiinni Tatjana/Take Care of Your Scarf, Tatjana* (1994), Irma in *Mies vailla menneisyyttä/The Man Without a Past* (2002) and Ilona in *Laitakaupungin valot/Lights in the Dusk* (2006), among others. In four of the films, Outinen played opposite Matti Pellonpää, and the pair were due to reprise their roles from *Shadows in Paradise* when Pellonpää suddenly died: instead of cancelling the film or recasting the role, Kaurismäki rewrote the film so that Outinen could play Pellonpää's part. Hanna Laakso (2000: 32) has argued that Outinen's characters in Kaurismäki's films are not properly individualized: the characters are used to depict broader, social trends and situations, revealing little of internal, personal motivations. However, Laakso recognises *Kauas pilvet karkaavat/Drifting Clouds* (1996) as introducing a change to Outinen's performance, as Ilona's expressions and gestures communicate more of her emotions and internal world than in earlier films: the heightened emotion of Outinen's performance no doubt draws from the very real sense of loss caused by Pellonpää's death.

Outinen has won several awards over the years, among them three Best Actress Jussis, or Finnish national film awards (*The Match Factory Girl*, *Drifting Clouds*, *The Man Without a Past*), as well as an honorary mention for *Right on Man!* Outinen also won the Best Actress prize at Cannes for her work in *The Man Without a Past*. In addition to film work, Outinen has had a long career in the theatre. After graduating from the Theatre Academy she worked for ten years for the KOM theatre, and has since appeared with Helsingin Kaupunginteatteri (Helsinki City Theatre), Helsingin Kesäteatteri (Helsinki Summer Theatre) and Ryhmäteatteri (The Group Theatre). Outinen has appeared in several television and radio productions, and she remains an active performer today. In 2002, she was appointed professor of acting at the Theatre Academy of Helsinki, where she currently serves her second five-year term (TEAK 2009).

Sanna Peden

References

Anon (2002), 'Portrait: La Kati d'Aki', *Elle*, 4 November.

Cardullo, Bert (2006), 'Finnish Character', *Film Quarterly*, 59: 4, pp. 4-10.

Johnson, J. (2010), *The New Finnish Theatre*, Jefferson, NC and London: McFarland.

Laakso, Hanna (2000), '"Blank Faces": Kohti Kriittistä Näyttelijäsuoritusta – Kati Outisen Näyttelijäsuoritus Aki Kaurismäen Elokuvissa', Master's dissertation, Turku: University of Turku.

TEAK (2009), 'Kati Outinen. Näyttelijäntyön Professori', http://www.teak.fi/kati_outinen. Accessed 7 January 2011.
Toiviainen, Sakari (2002), *Levottomat Sukupolvet: Uusin Suomalainen Elokuva*, Helsinki: SKS.
Tola, Pamela (2007), *Miksi Näyttelen?*, Helsinki: Ajatus Kirjat.
Vento, M. (2007), 'Tyhmyyttäkin Täytyy Käsitellä Älykkäästi', *TEAK*, http://www2.teak.fi/teak/Teak202/5c.html. Accessed 7 January 2011.

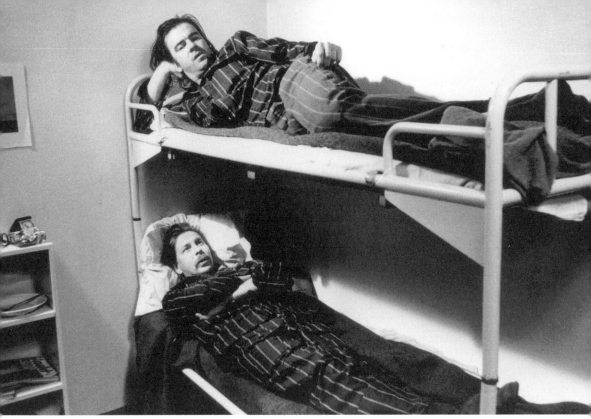

Ariel, Villealfa/Finnish Film Foundation.

STARS
MATTI PELLONPÄÄ

Matti Pellonpää was born in 1951, and appeared regularly on radio as early as 1962 in the children's programme *Lastenradio*. Pellonpää studied at the Theatre School (now Theatre Academy of Helsinki), and had a prolific theatrical career throughout the 1970s. He performed in and wrote many spoken word plays for the radio, among the more popular of which were his *Winnie the Pooh* audio plays with actor Kari Väänänen. He performed in several films, often in small roles, until securing his first lead role in Mika Kaurismäki's *Arvottomat/The Worthless* (1982). Pellonpää had studied camerawork and lighting, and so understood how to adapt his acting practice to the needs of the particular technique or lens being used by the cinematographer (Peltsi 2005).

In addition to being considered a consummate professional of theatre and cinema – albeit ill-suited for lengthy theatrical contracts – Pellonpää is often described as a bohemian spirit, and Lauri Timonen's (2009) affectionate character study makes frequent mention of the actor's alcohol consumption and nomadic lifestyle. An early documentary of the actor, Eero Tuomikoski's *Se minun töistäni – Matti Pellonpää* (1984), also worked on building the bohemian persona: for example, in a memorable scene Pellonpää strips down for a bath, describing the donation history of everything he is wearing. The documentary has been made available on the 'Living Archive' website of the Finnish National Broadcasting company (YLE Elävä Arkisto 2007), and the synopsis on the site describes Pellonpää as a 'vagabond whose possessions fit into a single shoe box, although there is no firm evidence a shoe box ever existed'. Clearly, the narrative of Pellonpää or 'Peltsi' as a bohemian traveller contains an element of satire and self-deprecation.

By all accounts, the stable group of cast and crew members that formed around Aki and Mika Kaurismäki, with Pellonpää perhaps the first among equals, formed a close-knit group of friends, whose idiosyncrasies and inside jokes often made their way into the films themselves. Through his frequent appearances in the director's films, Pellonpää came to be known as Aki Kaurismäki's alter ego, particularly in the character of Nikander. Nikander first appeared in *Rikos ja rangaistus/Crime and Punishment* (1983), Kaurismäki's first solo directorial venture, as a friend of the Raskolnikov-figure Rahikainen, and was the main protagonist in *Varjoja paratiisissa/Shadows in Paradise* (1986). Roger Connah (1991: 298) describes Nikander as '[a] man without qualities'. Satu Kyösola (1993: 50) has also identified Nikander as being free of excessive markers of identity. Discussing *Shadows in Paradise*, Kyösola states that unlike the female protagonist Ilona, whose name lends itself to multiple interpretations, Nikander offers no opportunities for plays on words or symbolic meaning. Instead, the name explicitly links the character to *Crime and Punishment*. Indeed, in *Shadows in Paradise*, Nikander refers to information given about him in the earlier film, such as having worked in an abattoir and having a sister who used to go to university in Stockholm. What is clear is that Nikander is an intertextual figure, moving fluidly within the Kaurismäkian oeuvre. Pellonpää's sudden death in 1995 brought an end to the development of Nikander, as *Kauas pilvet karkaavat/Drifting Clouds* (1996) would have been the third instalment in the character's own trilogy.

After Pellonpää's death, his friends organized a memorial concert in his honour. Performers included some of the best-known Finnish rock and punk bands of the 1980s, such as Juice Leskinen Grand Slam, Popeda and Eppu Normaali. The Leningrad Cowboys were also featured, as was Pellonpää's band from his Theatre School days, Johan Lewis & Korjaa Boys. The profit from the concert was donated to the Finnish Red Cross' aid work in Bosnia (Mattila 1995). Pellonpää was further commemorated in 1996 when Finland's Post Office released a set of stamps on the occasion of the centenary of Finnish cinema: in one of the stamps Pellonpää, as Nikander in *Shadows in Paradise*, looks quietly out into the street. In 1999 the Saarijärvi film society established the Matti Pellonpää Award in recognition of people who have made a positive contribution to film culture (Peltsi 2005).

Sanna Peden

References

Connah, Roger (1991), *K/K. A couple of Finns and some Donald Ducks*, Helsinki: Valtion painatuskeskus.

Kyösola, Satu (1993), 'Shadows in Paradise de Aki Kaurismäki – Un film, un style', Master's dissertation, Paris: Université de la Sorbonne Nouvelle.

Mattila, I. (1995), 'Ystävät ja Ihailijat Muistivat Matti Pellonpäätä Tavastialla', *Helsingin Sanomat*, 10 August.

Peltsi (2005), 'Peltsi-info', http://www.info.uta.fi/kurssit/a9/peltsi/peltsi_info.html#d. Accessed 7 January 2011.

Timonen, Lauri (2009), *Lähikuvassa Matti Pellonpää*, Helsinki: Otava.

YLE (2007), 'Se Minun Töistäni – Matti Pellonpää (1984)', http://www.yle.fi/elavaarkisto/?s=s&g=4&ag=25&t=143&a=3540. Accessed 7 January 2011.

STARS
TAUNO PALO

Tauno Palo (1908–82) was by any standard the most popular Finnish male film star of the classical era. His career spanned from the early 1930s to the early 1960s, starting with the first films with recorded sound and ending with the collapse of the studio system. During these three decades he invariably topped the voting polls by the popular film magazine *Elokuva-Aitta*. Also, he starred in the highest-grossing films of each decade, *Juurakon Hulda/Hulda from Juurakko* (Vaala, 1937), *Kulkurin valssi/The Vagabond's Waltz* (Särkkä, 1941) and *Tuntematon sotilas/The Unknown Soldier* (Laine, 1955), respectively.

Born Tauno Brännäs into a working-class family, he entered the workers' theatre in the late 1920s whilst working at the laboratory of the Ministry of Defence at the same time. In 1932, having caught the attention of the managers of the National Theatre, he finally became a full-time actor, soon changing his last name to Palo. By the end of the 1930s he had his eventual breakthrough as a stage actor, moving up to lead roles. All through his career he stayed at the National Theatre, perceiving himself first and foremost as a stage actor and only secondly as a film star.

As a film star, Palo was born almost overnight. In 1931, the director Kalle Kaarna appointed him to the leading role in *Jääkärin morsian/Soldier's Bride*, an adaptation of a popular musical drama. This sound-on-disc film featured mainly background music, but climaxed with a few songs recorded with direct synchronized sound, two of them notably by Palo. Thus, from the beginning, a crucial part of his star image was his soft tenor voice, later (with the aid of developing recording equipment) achieving somewhat deeper tones.

In 1935, Palo signed with Suomi-Filmi, one of the two biggest production companies. In his first film for the company, urban comedy *Kaikki rakastavat/Everybody Loves* (1935), the dark Palo was cast opposite the blonde Ansa Ikonen. Stealing the show with their duet singing, Ikonen and Palo made top billing in their next film *Vaimoke/Substitute Wife* (Vaala, 1936). From then on Ikonen and Palo were associated as a screen couple, even though they only made twelve films together over the decades. With all probability they would have been paired with each other more often had they stayed with the same studio. Palo, however, never had a long-term contract with any one production company. Such was his popularity that he was able to negotiate ever better terms when changing companies. Studio records show that, for example, in 1943, Suomi-Filmi persuaded him back from the competing Suomen Filmiteollisuus with 25,000 Finnish marks per month; as a point of comparison, the highest-paid female star, Regina Linnanheimo, earned 10,000 marks and the top-director, Valentin Vaala, 9,000 marks per month.

Although Palo is among the few Finnish theatre actors who in his memoirs does not look down on his film career, he does complain about having been somewhat typecast as a romantic hero. True, it is evident that film companies were keen on investing in Palo's romantic image. Whatever the genre – comedy (*Mieheke/Surrogate Husband* [Vaala, 1936]), musical (*SF-paraati/SF Parade* [Norta, 1940]), historical drama (*Helmikuun manifesti/The February Manifesto* [Norta and Särkkä, 1939]) or adventure film (*Rosvo Roope/Rob the Robber* [Leminen, 1949]) – Palo had 'to put his soul into one single phrase: I love you', over and over again. There is, however, more to his star image than that.

It might be argued that Palo's lasting success was built on a certain amount of tension rather than upright all-Finnish appeal. To begin with, there is often a violent undertone in his romantic characters. In *Koskenlaskijan morsian/The Lumberjack's Bride* (Vaala, 1937) Palo's character is a desperate suitor who, after having tried to drown his rival, loses his mind and throws himself into the rapids. In *Hilja maitotyttö/The Milkmaid* (Särkkä, 1953) Palo is, again, a disfavoured rival suitor who, in desperation, rapes the woman he desires. Finally, in *Pimeäpirtin hävitys/Devastation* (Unho, 1947) he is a degenerated nobleman who has an illegal child with a servant and, after the child has grown up, rapes her before being killed by her biblically grim grandfather.

Also, Palo's supposed Finnishness is in fact based on a rather varied and unstable set of characters. A case in point is *'Herra ja ylhäisyys'/The Lord and Master* (Nortimo, 1944), in which Palo plays a Finnish-born high officer of the Mexican army. While being a manifest wartime hero, both physically and mentally superior to the roughly caricatured Mexicans, the explicit sexuality of his character is clearly at odds with any standard conception of male Finnish identity. Not only an active hero, a lover and a seducer, he is also an object of desire, secretly or overtly gazed at by the female characters. Indeed, several contemporary reviewers felt uneasy about Palo being cast as the hero: instead of the Scandinavian type blond hero they expected, having read the series of popular novels the film was based on, they found in the dark and passionate Palo a 'southern' quality, obscuring the assumingly sharp line between 'us' and 'them'.

Further, especially in his postwar films, Palo often portrays characters embodying problematic concepts of masculinity. In general, the 'women's films' – melodramas and urban comedies with active female protagonists – of the late 1930s and the war years gave way to predominantly 'male' genres like war films, crime films, lumberjack films, military farces, buddy films and even Finnish Westerns; all of these were obsessed with the assumed crisis in postwar masculinity and offered different 'solutions', whether it be excessive violence, comic relief or psychological analysis of the male condition.

In contrast to the violent romantic characters, Palo's characters in comedies grew increasingly weak and fragile, gently playing with the expectations of normative masculinity. In, for example, *Hilman päivät/Hilma's Name Day* (Kassila, 1954) and *Kuriton sukupolvi/Wild Generation* (Kassila, 1957), Palo plays elderly men, sophisticated and well-mannered, but reserved and insecure in their romantic endeavours and having lost all authority over the youth.

The third category of Palo's 'problematic masculinity' roles consist of complex and troubled characters, many of whom have a background in the war. Not having been able to get over their war traumas, some of the characters become criminals (*Silmät hämärässä/Eyes in the Dark* [Itkonen, 1952]), some alcoholics (*Mies tältä tähdeltä/A Man from This Star* [Witikka, 1958]), some drug addicts (*Laulava sydän/A Singing Heart* [Laine, 1948]). Such troubled characters culminate in Palo's final screen role in *Tulipunainen kyyhkynen/The Scarlet Dove* (Kassila, 1961). He plays a respected doctor who shadows his wife because he suspects her of having an affair. He ends up being accused of her murder, eventually hiding from the police in the outskirts of the film noirish dark city, and finally suspecting his own sanity. Although revealed as a nightmare in the end – in the manner of Fritz Lang's *The Woman in the Window* (1944) – the happy ending is ambiguous, to say the least: the 'problem' is not external anymore, but rather a psychological manifestation of masculinity in crisis. With his edgy yet subtle performance, Palo's final role embodies the male crisis itself.

Kimmo Laine

STARS
VESA-MATTI LOIRI

Vesa-Matti Loiri is amongst the most popular film comedians in Finnish film history. Born in Helsinki at the conclusion of the Second World War to a family with no background in show business, Loiri got his start when he was cast in Mikko Niskanen's debut feature *Pojat/The Boys* (1962). Loiri was only 17-years-old when he played Jake, a teenager living in northern Finland during the Continuation War but the role would not define Loiri's career, though it won him an honorary Jussi – the subtle and soft-spoken Jake is a big contrast from the image that most Finns have of this versatile talent. Loiri spent some time studying in theatre school before becoming involved in television. He became friends with the comic Spede Pasanen and began to play roles in his popular sketch comedy show, *Spede Show*. It was on the *Spede Show* that Loiri first played the character which consolidated his popularity, Uuno Turhapuro. The character is a stereotypical approximation of the Finnish male – Uuno is ragged and unshaven, clad in a tattered 'wife-beater' vest and missing several teeth. The character came to largely define Loiri's career, a role he reprised through twenty films as well as a television series.

   The first of the Uuno Turhapuro films was self-titled and released in 1973 (dir. Ere Kokkonen). The film offers a much different formula than the more familiar Uuno films to follow. For one, Uuno's father-in-law and arch-enemy, Councilor Tuura, doesn't appear. The film has a familiar style (or a lack of it) with Ere Kokkonen as director, a role he filled in nearly every installment of the *Uuno* series. The film introduces us to a very different Uuno than the character with whom we've subsequently grown familiar: in our introduction, Uuno is well-dressed and groomed as he marries his bride. It is not until immediately after his marriage to this rich woman that Uuno returns to form as the disheveled numbskull familiar to most Finns. The film was a popular success, selling over 600,000 tickets, even if the critics found it less successful.

Though six more Uuno films were made throughout the 1970s, Uuno's stardom was not thoroughly consolidated until 1984's smash hit *Uuno Turhapuro armeijan leivissä/ Uuno Turhapuro in the Army*, selling almost 750,000 tickets. The film revolves around Uuno's return to military service after his father-in-law, Councilor Tuura, discovers he never properly completed his mandatory service time. Thinking the military will break his unruly son-in-law, Tuura has him enlisted, but Uuno quickly ends up being promoted to Major. Befuddling Tuura's best laid plans, Uuno even accidentally causes Finland to declare war on Sweden. The film also keenly employs Vesa-Matti Loiri's talents at billiards (Loiri spent many years as the head of the Finnish Billiards Association). The scene features Uuno characteristically outwitting Councilor Tuura at the game. Tuura is cold and calculating, nearly clearing the entire table with his skilled play. After a missed shot due to Uuno's alcohol induced hiccup, Uuno proceeds to clear the table, stunning his adversary and the spectators with his wide array of talent at complex shots. Through the 1990s, Loiri continued to make Uuno films with Spede Pasanen, and a final film was made in 2004 as a tribute to Pasanen following his death in 2001 with Spede's role constructed from archival footage. The final film is an appropriate final chapter to the Uuno saga, which came to define Loiri's acting career.

Yet, it would be restrictive to only see Loiri as Uuno because his career has traversed more paths than this famed persona. Beginning in the 1970s, Loiri began focusing on his musical career. A talented flautist, Loiri plays a type of Finnish 'Schlager' music, and broke through with *Leino* (1978), which contains his renditions of Finnish poet Eino Leino's work. The album was released to much acclaim, well before his acting career reached the box-office heights of the mid-1980s, and became the second best-selling album in Finnish history. Loiri's fame grew with his competition in the 1980 Eurovision Song Contest, where his performance scored poorly among the European delegates, but was well received in Finland. Loiri continues to record music and today his music career could be considered his dominant preoccupation. His two most recent albums, *Inari* (2007) and *Kasari* (2008), both reached number one in the Finnish album charts.

His success has experienced ups and downs in the past forty years but Loiri will always be remembered for his ability to connect directly with the vast majority of the Finnish population. His widespread success through the better part of forty years led Finnish producer Jörn Donner to call him 'the only Finnish film star'. His highly successful films, managed alongside a best-selling music career, are a testament to his mass appeal and cultural identity. Though comedy and pop music is not always appreciated in high cultural circles, Loiri has received his share of critical acclaim throughout his career. Besides the honorary Jussi given to him for his feature film debut, he won Best Actor Jussi Awards in 1976 (*Rakastunut rampa/Cripple in Love* [dir. Esko Favèn and Tarja Laine) and 1983 (*Ulvova mylläri/The Howling Miller* [dir. Jaakko Pakkasvirta]), as well as a Best Supporting Actor Award in 1982 (*Pedon merkki/Sign of the Beast* [dir. Jaakko Pakkasvirta]). These awards culminated in a lifetime achievement Jussi in 1998, and he was part of the ensemble to win the Best Actor Award at the Brussels International Independent Film Festival in 2003 for the film *Pahat pojat/Bad Boys* (dir. Aleksi Mäkelä). Even today, he continues to command adoration with a documentary on his life directed by Mika Kaurismäki (*Vesku from Finland* [2010]) and a prominent role in Kaurismäki's *Tie Pohjolaan/Road to North* (2012).

John Saari

INDUSTRIAL SPOTLIGHT
THE ECONOMICS OF FINNISH CINEMA PART 1: 1910–1935

The Finnish cinema business was initially based upon touring companies. Some of these were run by Finnish fairground and circus exhibitors, some by foreign companies such as Frères Lumière and there were also those who had their background in photography or other business ventures. Already in 1901, just five years after the first exhibitions, cinematography was so well-known that the local press concentrated on reviewing the quality of the programme instead of introducing the technique itself.

The first cinema theatre was established in Helsinki in the year 1904, and from 1906 onwards the business grew rapidly. Already in 1907 there were three major companies competing with one another: Apollo, Nordiska Biograf Kompaniet and Maat ja Kansat ('The Countries and the People'). They all had an identical business plan: functions were based upon a small chain of cinemas in a couple of cities and the business was supported by film import, distribution and rare film-making. This scheme proved to be very fruitful and provided the basics of Finnish cinema business all through the 1910s, although there were constant alterations in the field. Maat ja Kansat bankrupted and Apollo concentrated on photography and operettas, while rivals for Nordiska Biograf Kompaniet emerged, such as Lyyra, Olympia and Maxim, nourishing from the same basics. There were also a couple of film agencies, such as Finlandia Film and Finska Film Agentur, operating without cinemas and focusing solely on importing and distribution. Each of the big companies had one to five cinemas both in Helsinki and in rural cities. Finland was considered too far away from the big centres of film distribution so no films were leased to the Finnish entrepreneurs. Instead they had to be bought, which gave way to extensive distribution requirements. Already in the turn of the 1910s, the import and distribution were practically in the hands of a couple of companies operating from Helsinki.

Film-making was scarce before the Finnish independency in 1917. Most of the production was non-fiction concentrating on topical issues. No exact number for the non-fiction films made during the era of Russian Grand Duchy exist, but they are estimated to amount to somewhere around 300–400. In any case, it is dozens of times larger than the scale of fiction production: only some 23 feature films reached wider theatrical distribution during the same years. The scarce production numbers can be partly blamed upon technical difficulties especially in the post-production phase. Still the major companies and even a couple of private entrepreneurs persisted in trying to succeed in filming, as it was a part of the competition within the companies. Nevertheless, film-making was only a minor issue in the bigger picture of the cinema economics, and none of the established companies were able or even seeking to solely rely on it in their business ventures.

After Finnish independency in 1917 and the Civil War in 1918, the transformation of the film business started with the field being heavily restructured, especially during the years 1918–1922. Most of the earlier companies had been owned by one businessman – or at least the director solely controlled them. Now the scale of business grew rapidly and most of the new CEOs had no such autocratic powers. Old companies were taken over by groups of investors and the companies were assembled together in bigger corporations. As a result, the competition within the business tightened, and the focus was even more in importing, distribution and exhibition, and production was scarcer than before. The biggest operators were the groups owned by Suomen Biografi Osakeyhtiö, businessmen Gustaf Molin and Abel Adams and German Universum Film AG (Ufa). These four concerns controlled most of the business as, for example, their share of the import and distribution in 1922 was already more than 75 per cent, and two years later it rose to a peak of 95 per cent.

The large companies in Finland were not interested in film production as they saw better business possibilities in the cinemas and distributions and, especially from 1922 onwards, ceased all film-making. This made way for new entrepreneurs to enter the field and establish the first companies focusing solely on film-making. In a period of just a couple of months two competing companies were established because in the newly independent state film production was seen as powerful tool in both nation-building and advertising Finland abroad. The task of the companies was to create a unique form of Finnish film art and to capture the essence of Finnish culture, literature and art. Economic concerns were also important, as domestic production was seen as a way to keep the profits in Finland – in a mercantilist way of thinking cinema was seen as harmful to state economics because large film importation meant that huge amounts of the income went to foreign film companies. Regardless, the potential of domestic production was seen as very modest, almost nonexistent – because there were no traditions of film-making companies and production in its entirety had been minimal for years, there was no base to build upon.

The task of newly established film companies was not easy, and only one of them, Suomi-Filmi, was able to overcome the initial difficulties. An important financial remedy for the first years was the company's secondary field of business – theatre set and prop-making – which provided space for Suomi-Filmi to develop its feature film production capabilities. The quality (and popularity) of feature films grew, the production became stable and the importance of set-making diminished. On the financial side, however, the company faced new difficulties. As it had no theatres, it had to rely on the big cinema companies to distribute its films, resulting in smaller profits. Already after a couple of years of film production, the problem was evident: distribution and exhibition played a crucial role in the economics of film-making.

Suomi-Filmi started to plan on establishing a cinema in Helsinki around 1924, but the scheme proved to be too optimistic when compared with the company's economic status and the heavy competition in the field. Also, Suomi-Filmi arranged to take the company's features to the countryside, which irritated Suomen Biografi Osakeyhtiö with whom Suomi-Filmi had made most of its distribution deals. The next couple of years were very problematic for Suomi-Filmi, as there were constant disputes about the distribution and exhibition contracts – as a counteraction to the strict demands of Suomen Biografi Osakeyhtiö, some of the new features were given to Abel Adams.

1926 was a time of large-scale reforms in film business. The German Ufa withdrew from Finland, not because of any major setbacks, but because of the more general reformation of the company's functions abroad. Gustaf Molin bought all the possessions of Ufa, which meant that his business group grew considerably and he was able to increase his share to more than 40 per cent of the Finnish film distribution. With his assistance a new film company, Komedia-Filmi, was established, whose leaders had earlier worked in Suomi-Filmi but had resigned or were forced out because of disputes with the CEO Erkki Karu. In the spring of 1926, Molin also sought to buy Suomen Biografi Osakeyhtiö, whose investors were planning to give up the business, but instead Suomi-Filmi won the deal. The venture shows how essential exhibition and distribution was for film production as Suomi-Filmi had built up its production functions for more than six years but still needed the distribution companies to support the production. After some years apart, it had become clear that film producers needed distributors/exhibitors and vice versa.

The business deals of 1926 were the origin of the so-called 'Trust War' as both Gustaf Molin and Suomi-Filmi strengthened their status, resulting in a public rift. Most of the smear and slander appeared in film journals *Elokuva* (pro-Suomi-Filmi and -Abel Adams) and *Filmiaitta* (pro-Molin), but it spread to the independent press as well. The rift was characterized by heavy nationalistic tendencies emanating from the so-called 'language-battle'. As a legacy of common history with Sweden, Finland is a bilingual country, and in the 1920s disputes about the status of the languages were intense – Abel Adams and Erkki Karu, the CEO of Suomi-Filmi, were Finnish speakers and Gustaf Molin was Swedish.

In the smear campaign of the pro-Finnish, Gustaf Molin was pictured as an evil outsider, a foreign investor collaborating with the German and American big corporations. The pro-Molin commentators in return noted that he and Komedia-Filmi were opening up the Finnish film and cinema business, seeking to lift the production to an international level and importing the best international films to Finland. The pro-Finnish commentators, or Suomi-Filmi and Abel Adams, were not able to push Molin out of the business or even substantially harm his ventures. The rift dried out around 1928 or 1929, as both sides again concentrated on business instead of mocking the opponent. Instead, Komedia-Filmi folded as the audience did not appreciate its 'international film style', which was a substantial victory for Suomi-Filmi and to the national tendencies of its film production.

The failure of Komedia-Filmi was the biggest economic impact of the Trust War, as cinema companies continued their business as usual. Larger concerns arose a couple of years later when Hollywood production companies such MGM, Fox and Paramount decided to cut off the local distributors and establish their own business for import and distribution. The shares of all the large Finnish cinema companies were cut as most of the Hollywood production no longer went through their hands. The Great Depression and the coming of sound hit Finnish film production hard in the turn of the 1930s. At the same time, Suomi-Filmi fell into poor investments which strained the company's fortunes even more. The first Finnish sound films were made in 1931, and they proved to be technically challenging and so expensive that in 1932 all feature film production paused for almost half a year. The whole industry was stumbling, and by 1933 everybody expected Suomi-Filmi to fall into bankruptcy.

Suomi-Filmi survived the close call due to the support of Kansallis-Osake-Pankki, one of the biggest banks in Finland (with national tendencies) and because of a coup within the shareholders of which many had connections to the bank. CEO Erkki Karu was forced to resign and new directors were recruited to reform the company. The most important of them was Risto Orko, who started as a production manager but eventually became the CEO and the biggest shareholder. Instead, Karu established a new company Suomen Filmiteollisuus ('Finland's Film Industry'). The name consciously imitated the names of both Suomi-Filmi and Svenska Filmindustri, the biggest Swedish film production company.

It took until 1935 for both Suomi-Filmi and Suomen Filmiteollisuus to survive the crisis and establish their new production system. By that time, it was also clear that there would be two major production companies instead of just one. Around the same time, Erkki Karu died suddenly and Suomen Filmiteollisuus got a new leader from Toivo Särkkä. Both companies were, from then onwards, personified by their leaders – Risto Orko and Toivo Särkkä – who used very different business tactics: Suomi-Filmi, which had bought the biggest cinema chain in Finland in 1926, was an 'all-inclusive' cinema house as it produced, imported, distributed and exhibited films; Suomen Filmiteollisuus, instead, focused on production and distribution of in-house films. Differences can be seen in their themes as well: Suomen Filmiteollisuus is seen as a traditional and conservative producer of rural and national stories, whereas Suomi-Filmi is defined as modern, more artistic and focusing on depicting urban life. Both of these definitions are of course generalizations as both companies made all kinds of films, but these tendencies dominated their production.

Jade Warrior, Blind Spot Pictures Oy.

SCORING CINEMA

The art of the film score in Finland has been a severely neglected area of study and popular interest. During the first silent decades of the twentieth century, music was rarely composed for films as they relied predominantly on pre-existing tunes. As film production became more established and industrialized, composers who specialized in films emerged on the scene, of whom Martti Similä and Harry Bergström were perhaps the most prolific. The style of music during the years of the studio era followed the template of Hollywood-influenced scoring. The scores accentuated on-screen actions and favoured melodic profusity over more abstract ideas. The 1950s saw composers such as Osmo Lindeman and especially Einar Eglund contribute a more 'respectable' style to cinema, especially as they infused their scores with modernist idioms from the concert hall. Englund's score for *Valkoinen peura/The White Reindeer* (Blomberg, 1952) is a landmark work for this rare Finnish horror film, expanding the shocking turns of the narrative with music suiting the stunning landscapes. The use of leitmotif techniques and expansive scoring in many of the films action scenes is especially noteworthy and resulted in a much-deserved Jussi Award for the score.

Englund was a neoclassical concert composer first and foremost, and other composers from 'serious music' have devoted their talents to cinema. Jazz pianist and classical composer Jukka Linkola provided large scale orchestral work for his Jussi-winning fantasy music to *Lumikuningatar/The Snow Queen* (Hartzell, 1986) and *Ihmiselon ihanuus ja kurjuus/The Wonder and Misery of Human Life* (Kassila, 1988). Linkola's neoclassical/romanticist concert hall and jazz idioms are adapted to the demands of the films for which they were intended. This fusion of approaches allows the scores to resemble the normative standards established by Hollywood whilst sounding simultaneously entirely original. Linkola has focused mostly on his concert works, but other composers have continued to experiment with combining traditional film scoring techniques with contemporary pop music idioms. The most well-known of these is Anssi Tikanmäki who has provided inventive scores for the films of the Kaurismäki brothers. A notable and oft-commented example is the opening of Mika Kaurismäki's *Arvottomat/The Worthless* (1982), which was one of the first examples of the 1980s New Wave in Finnish cinema. As a part of the new generation emerging in the 1980s, the Kaurismäkis' films rebelled against established conventions of Finnish film culture. Tikanmäki's music is an example of how the films construct this subversiveness as it adapts the canonical 'Finlandia' composed by Jean Sibelius and combines it with a rock band, underscoring our introduction to Helsinki. As we fly across the harbours and enter the cityscape, the aural and visual signs connote alternative visions of nationhood. Tikanmäki has provided music for a range of Kaurismäki productions from the melancholic flow of *Klaani: Tarina Sammakoitten suvusta / The Clan –Tale of the Frogs* (1984) and a combination of classical, folk-inspired melodies and more contemporary idioms for *Juha* (1999), Aki Kaurismäki's experimental 'silent' film which updates Juhani Aho's novel to the late 1990s in an idiosyncratically timeless world filled with elements from the past and the present.

Other Finnish composers have been more traditional in their approach to scoring both dramas and historical epics. Perhaps the most successful of contemporary Finnish composers, Tuomas Kantelinen is renowned for his use of long-lined melodies and string adagios to convey emotion and capture the thematic soul of films by Olli Saarela, such as *Rukajärven tie/Ambush* (1999) and *Suden vuosi/The Year of the Wolf* (2007). Both scores also benefit from well-considered minimalist techniques. Kantelinen has increasingly directed his career abroad, receiving a commission from Miramax for the thriller *Mindhunters* (Harlin, 2004). He also provided the score for the Academy Award-nominated historical epic *Mongol* (Bodrov, 2007) produced in collaboration between Russia, Germany, Kazakhstan and Mongolia, which received a CD release on the Varese Sarabande label. These are all considerable feats for Finnish multimedia composers and Kantelinen occupies a prime position even among the 'A-list' composers for Nordic cinema, providing, for example, a large-scale score for Peter Flinth's epic Arn series (2007–08). Despite his increasing international prestige, Kantelinen continues to keep close ties with Finnish film-makers, scoring the animated feature *Röllin sydän/Quest for a Heart* (Lehtosaari, 2007) amongst others.

While the soundscapes of Finnish films are still largely dominated by pop music 'needle drops', original orchestral scoring is increasingly prevalent. Pop musicians and producers such as Kerkko Koskinen and Leri Leskinen have expanded their repertoire into orchestral music with inspired efforts for *Toinen jalka haudasta/One Foot Under* (Vuoksenmaa, 2009) and *Joulutarina/Christmas Story* (Wuolijoki, 2007), respectively. Samuli Kosmonen and Kimmo Pohjonen composed the score for the Finnish-Chinese co-production *Jadesoturi/Jade Warrior* (Annila, 2006), which combines their unique talents as percussionist and accordionist respectively, and uses many folk sounds and more contemporary idioms in capturing the unique flavour of this film, sounding unlike other fantasy scores yet remaining within its aesthetic realm. The music is a good example of an innovative approach to scoring familiar cinematic tropes, and it settles neither for genre nor conventional musical direction dictated by the Hollywood paradigm.

Towards the end of the 2000s, orchestral scores are once again becoming the norm as many of the larger films of 2008–10 feature full-blown scores presumably to increase the 'technical' values of the films. Simultaneously, these compositions are remarkably free of the temp-tracking that is decreasing the value of the art form in other parts of the world, with new compositions sounding undeniably similar to recent hit scores. Yet, film music as a part of domestic film culture remains severely underappreciated. While publishing of scores on CD are rare, more troubling is the lack of availability of film music as digital downloads. Similarly, events promoting film music in the concert hall have not been successful enough to make this sort of activity sustainable. Thus, a lot remains to be done in increasing the prevalence of Finnish film scoring and deployment of scores in non-orthodox ways. A dynamic film culture must take into account other realms beyond the visual and the narrative if it is to truly thrive and contribute to wider developments in national culture.

To explore some of the dynamics of the globalizing Finnish film music scene, we provide an interview with perhaps the most promising rising star of the current composers, Panu Aaltio. He is a protégé of sorts for Kantelinen, whose music for *Tummien perhosten koti/The House of the Dark Butterflies* (Karukoski, 2008) has garnered substantial domestic and international appreciation, including a Jussi nomination. The score was released on the Swedish label MovieScore Media, which specializes in lesser-known film scores from around world. The score, dominated by a versatile and memorable main theme for solo piano and strings, is seemingly inspired by Michael Nyman-type minimalism and has garnered its young composer plenty of attention.

Pietari Kääpä (PK): You studied at USC with well-known composers such as Christopher Young – do you think it is essential for non-American composers to acquaint themselves with the Hollywood style to succeed in the contemporary marketplace?

Panu Aaltio (PA): I don't think it's essential in an aesthetic sense. In fact it seems European film music has been influential in many ways to American films lately. So, in that way, I think it's a strength not simply trying to do a copy of a Hollywood score.

What is essential though is having the skills to do the music well and efficiently, in whatever genre the film will call for. And in this regard I think Hollywood is a great place to learn, because the process has really been honed and some of the best people in film music work there. USC was a great place to get to see some of that and also get my feet wet on working with real orchestras.

PK: How did you break into the film industry?

PA: I had been doing short films for the University of Art and Design film students in Helsinki for years. It was a great way to get to know a lot of people who work on feature films today, and learn how I as a composer could best serve their films. It's pretty important to approach a film as a film-maker, not just a composer, because those can be two very different priorities.

So in those projects I happened to have worked before with some of the great sound people on *The House of the Dark Butterflies*, who suggested to the director that they should ask me for a demo on that film based on reading the script. I almost didn't do it, because the production company was still considering other people as well, and I had just failed many attempts at getting other projects, and was feeling very pessimistic about it! The demo ended up fitting well enough that it's basically in identical form in the final scene in the film, so that was a good fortunate reminder to never let negativity get the most of me.

PK: Do you think your 'Nordicness' is able to give you an advantage (a sort of unique compositional perspective)?

PA: In an industry with so much competition, I think having a distinct voice is an absolute necessity. So in that regard anything that might help finding fresh angles to your music is great.

Using one's heritage is a good way to bring about some of that, as long as it leads to a natural film music sound and you don't sound just like you're doing a pastiche of Sibelius. So I consider it more as a thing where I let the influences flow freely, but never make them the central thing.

PK: How do you see the state of film music in Finland?

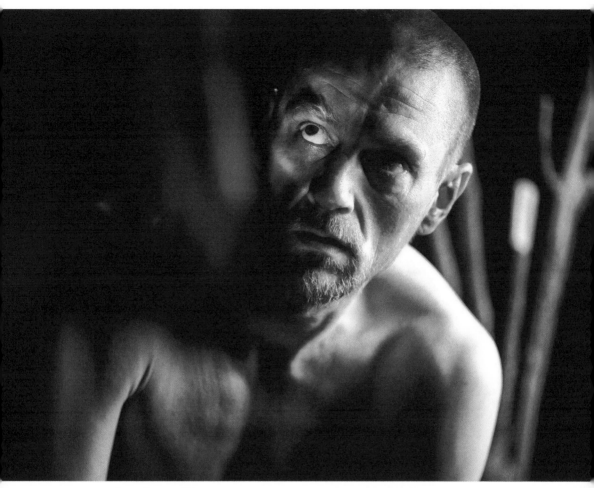

Sauna, Bronson Club.

PA: It seems to be becoming something people take more seriously as a narrative component, not being an afterthought or tacking on pop songs. There's a pretty deep tradition of quiet films in Finland, so that has kept film scoring a more marginal area than it should be. But it seems there's a definite new generation of film-makers that are thinking very openly about it, and I see that as a very positive sign.

PK: How do you see the state of Finnish cinema in relation to commercialism?

PA: Finnish films just had one of the best years in the box office ever so definitely the audiences are finding them more. I think it's largely due to the fact that the technical quality and the variety of Finnish films has increased a lot. There's no longer a preconceived notion of what a Finnish film is like because suddenly there's a lot of different types of movies coming out and they look and sound good enough to compete with their American counterparts.

PK: You scored Antti-Jussi Annila's *Filth/Sauna* (2008) – what are your opinions on scoring Finnish-produced genre cinema?

PA: I've been really happy to see Finnish genre movies becoming more common recently. It really brings variety to the scene, and also provides an outlet to a lot of talented people that really got into film-making having grown up with and loving American genre films. I used to make my own horror films in my childhood liking that genre so much, so it was really great to be able to score *Sauna*.

PK: Your score for *The House of the Dark Butterflies* was released on Mikael Carlsson's MovieScore label – could you describe the importance of record publishing for film composers and the situation in Finland?

PA: It was very fortunate having MovieScore publish the soundtrack because it helped get visibility for the soundtrack that really isn't possible for a Finnish soundtrack normally. Most often Finnish films don't even have soundtrack albums so it's often up to the composer to just do it themselves if they want to. So I was extremely happy with the contribution that Mikael brought into pushing that album forward.

PK: How does the constantly changing landscape of music distribution affect the job of a composer (if at all), and does it provide opportunities for people who may not have the possibility to reside in Hollywood 24/7?

PA: It seems to me that even with the prevalence of working over the Internet on many projects, Hollywood is still one of those places where location is really important. So I find largely the projects that I end up working on in Finland tend to be based somewhere else. But then again, while in Finland I'm able to work on some projects where I probably wouldn't work over the Internet from LA either. So in that regard you can say modern technology hasn't changed everything certainly. People still like to work with other people in the same room a lot of the time.

PK: You provided the score of the video game *Apache: Air Assault* – could you describe the process of creating this score and what you think new media technologies contribute to the art of film scores?

PA: I've really grown up with video games just as much as films, so it's great to be able to compose for them as well. In a game like *Apache: Air Assault* in particular it's a big challenge for a composer, because you only have a very vague idea of how the music will exist in the game. It's not synced to any specific plot points, but is instead divided between suspense and action music and general geographical areas. It's a lot of fun making open-ended music like that, but also pretty daunting, since you're starting off on such an empty canvas compared to films.

Video games are such a young art form that there's very rapid development in the aesthetic and narrative possibilities at the moment. There's definitely a convergence of film and video games happening in that video games are becoming more cinematic experiences. Not in sort of the full motion video, interactive film style of the '90s, but just as a general overall direction that's more natural to the medium. I think it's a very exciting development and I hope to be able to be a part of that area as well.

PK: You record your scores in London – can you give any specific reasons for this?

PA: LA and London are the top places in the world for film music recordings, and especially being familiar with the LA way of working having just returned from there, London felt like a natural choice when I was doing *The House of the Dark Butterflies*.

In Finland there are great players and great engineers, but what's missing is a good studio suitable for film music, and a system for easily booking players and otherwise handling the session logistics. However, we're seeing improvement in all of these areas, so I'm thinking of doing some recordings in Finland as well soon.

Finnish national cinema is often associated with depictions of the countryside and its people. While such spaces are common in Finnish films, their significance should not be overemphasized. First of all the distinctions between nature, rural areas and countryside are somewhat blurry in Finnish cinema. We could define nature as wilderness, rural areas as large isolated areas with low population density and countryside as farming area. This, however, does not get us very far. In the 1920s, as Tytti Soila writes, films were often set:

> [...] on prosperous farms, people worked in the fields and in the grounds, surrounded by traditional wooden houses built on one level with a porch in the middle. The birches would cast shadows over their surroundings and at the rear one could see the woods, not dark and threatening, but as secure domains where cattle could graze and the timber was cut in the winter. (1998: 46)

As this description indicates, the narrative world of such films is clearly delineated and the authorities are in charge in the countryside but not the woods. The character movements in and across these spaces illuminate these ideological tensions, such as in *Pohjalaisia/The Bothnians* (Lahdensuo, 1925), where the main character, Jussi Harri, escapes the Russian authorities, leaving the farming area behind in order to hide in the nearby forest.

Countryside, rural areas and wilderness are spaces that have been explored in numerous Finnish films. It seems that in the 1920s such films were more successful at the box office than those mainly set in urban areas. One reason for the popularity of such films is that urbanization began relatively late in Finland in comparison with most Central European countries. In the silent era, the majority of the population lived in the countryside and rural areas. According to historians Kari Immonen, Katriina Mäkinen and Tapio Onnela, for the majority of Finns, the values of the countryside were nationally valid, while cities were considered alien and even foreign (1992: 13–14).

Considering that characters in Finnish films tend to move between wilderness, rural areas and countryside, the strong emphasis that is often placed on the interrelatedness of Finnish cinema and the countryside is mystifying to say the least. Another important point to keep in mind is that Finnish cinema has not shied away from urban milieus – not even in the silent era. A number of urban crime films were produced in the country already in the 1910s, and in numerous films made in the '20s the action moves between contrasting settings of countryside and urban milieus.

Karl Emil Ståhlberg, the owner of the Atelier Apollo film production company, declared in 1897 that it was his intention to start producing films that would depict the beauty of his fatherland and promote it among Finnish audiences and even abroad (Salmi 2002: 26). Atelier Apollo began its wide-ranging film production in 1906. The company came to produce a number of landscape films, scenics and travelogues, where meadows, forests, lakes and rivers were all captured on camera. The production of landscape films was a nationalistic enterprise in the spirit of the national awakeners of the

Left: The Finnish Mauritz Stiller with Victor Sjöström and Greta Garbo, MGM/The Kobal Collection.

Silent Cinema   73

nineteenth century who had emphasized the interrelatedness of the Finnish people and nature.

The first Finnish fiction film *Salaviinanpolttajat/The Moonshiners* (Puro and Sparre, 1907) told the story of two men producing and selling illegal alcohol in a wintry forest. The film is considered lost, but what we can gather from the synopsis is that the forest was represented as a liminal space where norms and laws of the society were challenged by the moonshiners. As these *The Moonshiners* and *The Bothnians* suggest, the contrast of wilderness and other spaces might well be a lot more important in Finnish cinema (and culture) than previously acknowledged. The first Finnish fiction films set in countryside milieus were *Verettömät/The Bloodless Ones* (1913) and *Kesä/Summer* (1915), both directed by Kaarle Halme. These films introduced significant pictorial, thematic and structural elements that have been explored in various Finnish films, including the mansion setting, the graduate student seducing a naïve country girl, and the divide between the countryside and the city. In *The Bloodless Ones*, the city is a location where the characters are safe from the burning passions of the countryside (Salmi 2002: 179–202). In later films it is almost always the other way around: countryside and its people are associated with high moral standards while cities are places of moral corruption. This is another aspect of Finnish cinema to bear in mind: meanings associated with countryside and other spaces have changed.

After being an autonomous grand duchy in the Russian Empire for over hundred years, Finland became a sovereign state in the aftermath of the October Revolution in late 1917. In early 1918, Finland faced a Civil War of its own which resulted in around 36,000 casualties. The Civil War divided Finnish people for years to come, creating a climate of bitter resentment. Some film historians are of the opinion that the war caused irreparable damage to the development of Finnish film. However, upon closer inspection, the opposite seems to be true. There was a lot of new activity in the field of Finnish cinema right after the war months, including the establishment of a number of new film companies. Moreover, at the turn of the '20s there was increasing talk about the possibility of creating a truly national cinema. It seems that the war strengthened Finnish film production by giving it a mission to unite the divided country into a national film audience. This national project is explicit already in the names of some of these companies, the most important and long-lived of which was Suomi-Filmi Oy (literally 'Finland Film').

The importance placed on interrelatedness of people and individualized spaces in Finnish cinema of the 1920s can be demonstrated with an example. The last episode of Carl Theodor Dreyer's film *Leaves from Satan's Book* (1921) is set in Finland during the Civil War months. This episode was never shown in Finland because local film censorship authorities cut it out. However, a local film magazine published a letter sent by an angry reader who had seen this episode. He argued that in Dreyer's film the representation of 'our people, our religion and manners was as false and unjust as possible' (in *Filmiaitta* 1922b: 35). Finland was not to be depicted like this. What the reader saw as so important were the ethnographic aspects of the film which he found to be unfaithfully represented. Those little details have little to do with the drama of the film, as Dreyer answered in his feedback criticism (in *Filmiaitta* 1922a: 86). Without a doubt he was right, but this did not satisfy Finns who saw cinema as means of making the country and its people known among Finnish audiences and abroad.

The 1920s were crucial formative years for the Finnish national cinema. Shying away from Hollywood practices and using Swedish national cinema as a role model worth following, it was argued that by actor Adolf Lindfors that 'the future of Finnish cinema is the depiction of our nature and our national character' (in *Filmiaitta* 1923: 169). Finnish film-makers began to make extensive use of peasant customs and landscapes in order to create a strong sense of Finnish national identity that drew on memories of an older age. One obvious purpose behind this was to create a stronger impression of a country that was not born yesterday, but could claim deep historical roots. By relying on certain kinds of depictions of Finnish cultural traditions and nature, it was felt that the Finnish national cinema was able to make itself distinct from all other cinemas because it was thought that only Finnish film-makers could properly represent these issues. Moreover, these film-makers knew that it was wise both commercially and culturally to explore the idealized past (or even timelessness) of the nation than to discuss the burning issues of the post-Civil War period.

In the early 1920s, Suomi-Filmi Oy began to specialize in the production of distinctively Finnish films. These adaptations of national literature depict Finnish nature and the character of the people. Broadly speaking, these films are melodramas even though some tend towards tragedy, comedy and action. Here melodrama is best understood as a cluster concept which, as Ben Singer argues, combines pathos, emotionalism, moral polarization, non-classical narrative form and graphic sensationalism (2001: 44–49; 54). In Finnish films of the 1920s, these key features of melodrama appear in different combinations. As Tytti Soila suggests, the typical story 'takes place on a prosperous farm with generation or class conflicts as its central themes, themes which in the melodramatic manner are embodied in the destinies of individual characters' (1998: 38).

The vast majority of popular and critically appreciated Finnish films of the 1920s are faithful adaptations of plays and novels. However, faithfulness did not mean slavish duplication and lazy film-making. Finnish film-makers consciously broadened the narrative world with cinematic means by making use of landscape cinematography, and took great care in expressing and supplanting words with images. For example, they replaced verbal analogies with visual analogies. Just as importantly, films were faithful to the ethnography of the nation they represented. Authentic costumes and artefacts were time and again used in the shooting and scenes were often set on historical locations. When *Anna-Liisa* premiered in 1922 (dir. Teuvo Puro and Jussi Snellman), one critic praised it in these words:

> *Anna-Liisa* is a depiction of the life of the people, where ethnographically correct environment and dramatic coherence are tied together with great care. This film can be offered to foreign audiences without hesitation, saying: take a look; here is a piece of our fatherland, a glance to the life as it was lived in our countryside. (in *Filmiaitta* 1922b: 98)

Alongside *Anna-Liisa* other depictions of Finnish people and nature like *Koskenlaskijan morsian/The Logroller's Bride* (Karu, 1923), *Nummisuutarit/The Village Shoemakers* (Karu, 1923) and *The Bothnians* prospered on the home market.

One common argument in the 1920s was that cinema must be civilizing entertainment. Hence, there was a specific demand for idealized representations of Finnishness. Already in the nineteenth century, national culture had tried to arbitrate the idea of the undivided utopian nation and reality in national romanticism. In national literature, simple and hard-working men both symbolized and defined Finnishness and served as role models for the people. In many popular films of the 1920s, such as *The Logroller's Bride*, village societies show signs of breaking from the inside. It is usually an idealized young Finnish male who comes to save the day and restore the togetherness of the community. Such representations were undoubtedly indirect comments on the contemporary state of affairs. Many films of the day also feature mentally and physically strong female characters. In *The Logroller's Bride*, for example, Hanna (Heidi Blåfield), the daughter of the village chief, comes to save the men who are shipwrecked in the middle of dangerous rapids as all previous rescue attempts by men have failed. One reason for the large number of strong female characters is the fact that various films are based on novels written by pro-feminist authors like Minna Canth.

As Antti Alanen has put it, 'the Finns learned that the Nordic landscape could itself be the supreme production value. The Finns could not compete with the Americans or the Germans in budgets, but nature itself was sublime, incomparable and majestic' (1999: 80). Just as ethnographic information was crucial for the representation of the Finnish people, the depiction of Finnish nature was highly significant as an index of national identity. Landscapes in these films are easily recognisable and provide a sense of place with settings, in many instances, being typical to a particular region of Finland. For example, *The Bothnians* begins with full shots of the well-known flat landscapes of the region of Ostrobothnia where the story is set. In Finnish films of the 1920s, nature is used in significantly melodramatic manner, not merely as something in the background of events, but tied closely to the ongoing drama of the films. In many, nature is used as an indicator of inner emotions of the characters. *Murtovarkaus/The Burglary* (Kivijärvi and Roeck Hansen, 1926) contains a sequence where lovers discuss their relationship on a sunny hill next to running water. The characters are seen in a full shot with the beautiful view behind them signifying their happiness. When the characters come to acknowledge the social realities that keep them apart, the camera takes another point of view as they are now depicted standing in front of thick bushes. Such use of nature was a practical solution in tying the people and the nature closer together, making them effectively inseparable. Some films portray nature as a moral force, which comes to destroy the evil-doers: the villains of both *The Logroller's Bride* and *Murmanskin karkulaiset/Fugitives from Murmansk* (Karu, 1927) drown after hurting others for their own good.

Popular as films depicting the country and the characteristics of its people had been in the domestic film market, they became largely criticized in the late 1920s. Modernist critics were of the opinion that such films were simply bad or at least old-fashioned. It had also become evident that foreign markets were not interested in the recent trends of Finnish national cinema. In the late 1920s, the film-makers tried to remedy this by employing an international style and subject matter in order to both attract Finnish urban audiences and to break through to the global film market. The influence of German and American cinema is evident in international spy films such as *Korkein voitto/The Supreme Victory* (Von Haartman, 1929). Despite the cosmopolitan tone and the emphasis placed on the depiction of Helsinki, the film contains a number of scenes set in wilderness and rural areas. Many of these scenes could be described as exotic as they depict activities unseen in previous Finnish films, such as seal hunting. Ultimately, the attempts to broaden the concept of Finnish national cinema and its audiences failed, evidenced by the troubled reception of *The Supreme Victory* and other cosmopolitan films even on the home market.

At the turn of the 1930s, the tendencies towards greater internationalism foundered on the coming of synchronized sound film, economical depression and extreme right-wing movements. Still, certain privileged conceptions of national cinema held firm. In the 1920s, the essence of national cinema had resided with the representation of the people and the country, and also in the use of adapted literary and theatrical material. The production of synchronized sound offered the possibility of even greater fidelity to the source texts. Depictions of the people and nature like *The Logroller's Bride* and *The Village Shoemakers* were remade in the 1930s. *The Long Drivers*, a comedy about logrollers based on a well-known play, had premiered in 1928 and turned out to be a box office hit. So far melodrama had been the dominant mode of Finnish national cinema, but in the 1930s the comic mode became just as important, evidenced by the popularity of rural films like *Aatamin puvussa ja vähän Eevankin/Dressed Like Adam and a Bit Like Eve Too* (Korhonen, 1931) and *Rovastin häämatkat/The Dean's Honeymoon Travels* (Korhonen, 1931). A fair amount of films set in urban environments premièred in the 1930s as well. Moreover, the so-called studio era of Finnish cinema began in 1933 with the foundation of Suomen Filmiteollisuus (literally 'Finnish Film Industry'). Even though the 1930s came to signify a major change in the discourse of the Finnish national cinema, many continuities are also apparent: one of them being the importance placed on depicting the nature of the country and the characteristics of its people.

References

Alanen, Antti (1999), 'Born Under the Sign of the Scarlet Flower: Pantheism in Finnish Silent Cinema', in J. Fullerton and J. Olsson (eds), *Nordic Explorations: Film Before 1930*, Sydney: John Libbey & Company, pp. 77–85.
Anon (1922a) 'Filmiohjelmistostamme', *Filmiaitta*, 5, p. 86.
Anon (1922b), 'Filmitulkinta Minna Canthin Anna-Liisasta', *Filmiaitta*, 6, p. 98.
Anon (1923), 'Mitä Kotimaiset Filmitähtemme Kertovat: Hetkinen Adolf Lindfordin Luona', *Filmiaitta*, 13, p. 169.
Immonen, K., Mäkinen, K. and Onnela, T. (1992), 'Kaksikymmenluku – oliko sitä', in T. Onnela (ed.), *Vampyyrinainen ja Kenkkuinniemen Sauna: Suomalainen Kaksikymmenluku ja Modernin Mahdollisuus*, Helsinki: SKS, pp. 7–17.
Salmi, Hannu (2002), *Kadonnut perintö: Näytelmäelokuvan synty Suomessa 1907–1916*, Helsinki: SKS & SES.
Singer, Ben (2001), *Melodrama and Modernity: Early Sensational Cinema and Its Context*, New York: Columbia University Press.
Soila, Tytti (1998), 'Finland', in T. Soila, A. Söderberg-Widding and G. Iversen (eds), *Nordic National Cinemas*, London: Routledge, pp. 31–95.
Talvio, Oski (1922), 'Sana Tanskalaisesta Filmistä Jolla On Aiheena Meidän Vapaustaistelumme', *Filmiaitta*, 2, p. 35.

Anna-Liisa

Production company:
Suomi-Filmi Oy

Distributor:
Suomen Biografi

Directors:
Teuvo Puro
Jussi Snellman

Producer:
Erkki Karu

Screenwriters:
Jussi Snellman, from the play by
Minna Canth

Art director:
Karl Fager

Cinematographers:
Kurt Jäger
A. J. Tenhovaara

Editors:
Teuvo Puro
Kurt Jäger

Duration:
78 minutes

Cast:
Helmi Lindelöf
Emil Autere
Einar Rinne
Mimmi Lähteenoja

Year:
1922

Synopsis

Anna-Liisa is a tale of nineteenth-century class and gender politics,
focusing on a female protagonist due to marry Johannes (Autere),
a wealthy and kind landowner. Anna-Liisa (Lindelöf) is harbouring a
dark secret. Mikko (Rinne) had previously wooed the naïve girl and
made her pregnant. But rather than carry on her life with Mikko,
she killed the child and buried him in the forest. Now, Mikko and
his mother Husso (Lähteenoja) try to force Anna-Liisa to marry
Mikko instead of her new fiancé. Anna-Liisa confesses to her past
and Johannes leaves her after rescuing her from drowning herself.
The wedding is still destined to go ahead, with Mikko taking the
place of the groom. Anna-Liisa's guilt and anger at the oppressive
behaviour of her husband-to-be leads her to confess all to the
wedding guests. It seems it is better to go to prison than to remain
in her patriarchal jail.

Critique

Anna-Liisa is one of the canonical masterpieces of Finnish cinema
in both its melodramatic content and its ability to evoke strong
emotions. The film's exploration of class and gender issues is not
uncommon as the majority of the films of the era focused on these
themes, yet the bleak and moral density of the narrative allows the
film to remain powerful even for contemporary audiences.

Tension is built very effectively by the coalescence of the different narrative strands and the fear of revelation of Anna-Liisa's
past deeds. Simultaneously, her confession acts as a catalyst for
emotional relief and convalescence in the narrative. Meanwhile, we
are still very aware that these confessions are not only the acts of
an individual in a fictional narrative, but a wider condemnation of
social mores. As we discover Anna-Liisa's crime, we are made privy
to the silent suffering of women in an ideologically-oppressive society. The film is based on a play by Minna Canth, who was one of
the predominant authors of sociocritical literature in Finnish culture.
Canth's works not only highlighted social divergences, but often
situated them in the context of gender politics, and specifically the
disadvantaged roles of women in nineteenth-century society. Thus,
the acts of Anna-Liisa's men are to be seen as more despicable
than any crime committed by her as both of them only see her as
their property; she can only be possessed as truly virtuous or under
unconditional slavery.

But while these thematic strands provide a strong moral outrage
at the patriarchal mores of the society, they also work to reveal a
set of unassumed, or even axiomatic, contemporary conceptions
of gender difference. Despite its condemnation of patriarchal
oppression, the film portrays women as inherently unstable and
weak. While Husso is depicted as a strong matriarch, she is also
scheming and domineering – effectively embodying most of the
negative characteristics of matriarchs. Anna-Liisa's courage at her
confession is certainly a strong statement of character, but her act

of infanticide shows another side and provides yet another instance of the unstable woman, revealing to us the film's immersion in a regressive and still patriarchally-minded social order. Regardless of these unacknowledged strains of patriarchal thinking, the film must be considered a progressive step in gender politics and a powerful statement about social inequality. The story of *Anna-Liisa* remains a popular narrative and it is frequently performed on stage. Several television and film adaptations have also been received in largely positive terms by audiences, yet the 1922 version remains a respected and canonical text in Finnish film culture. This is a testament to its emotional and ideological power.

Pietari Kääpä

The Village Shoemakers

Nummisuutarit

Production company:
Suomi-Filmi Oy

Distributor:
Adamsin Filmitoimisto

Director:
Erkki Karu

Producer:
Erkki Karu

Screenwriter:
Artturi Järviluoma, based on the play by Aleksis Kivi

Art director:
Karl Fager

Cinematographer:
Kurt Jäger

Composers:
Toivo Kuula
Oskar Merikanto
Selim Palmgren
Jean Sibelius

Editor:
Erkki Karu

Duration:
83 minutes

Synopsis

Jaana (Blåfield) and Eero (Slangus) have been friends since childhood, but things come to a head as Jaana is due to inherit a substantial sum of money from their neighbour, who designated the inheritance to whichever of the two is married first. Jaana is due to get engaged with the local blacksmith Christo (Korhonen), prompting Martta (Suonio), the mother of Esko, to send her son on a quest to find a bride. This sets in motion a complex narrative involving scheming relatives, the return of Jaana's dad, mistaken identities, lots of drinking and even some violence.

Critique

Erkki Karu's adaptation of the Aleksis Kivi play is often credited as one of the most important of early Finnish feature films due to its ability to balance the complex narrative strands and inject them with exquisite humour. The challenge of adapting Kivi's wordy play to the constraints of silent cinema must have been daunting at the time. While this poses some problems for the narrative structure in that much of the back-stories of minor characters remain arbitrary, the formative constraints have also necessitated innovative means to overcome any technological limitations. The standout in terms of inventiveness is the film's visualization of Esko's drunkenness. The camera takes on his perspective as he gets increasingly drunk and out of control, the image at first blurs and then starts to spin wildly. The technique was captured by the crew by situating the camera in a basket hanging from a tree and spinning it while it was descending. The result is an early example of the capabilities of not only Karu the director but also Finnish cinema as a whole.

In addition to its formative innovation, the film is considered canonical in its archiving of national iconography. Throughout, it captures all the hallmarks that have been evoked in national culture before and since – wheat fields, pine forests, lake scenarios, flowing rapids, etc. Amidst all this cinematic innovation and traditionalism is also a story about class conflict (albeit set in a period

Cast:

Axel Slangus

Heidi Korhonen

Kirsti Suonio

Alarik Korhonen

Heidi Blåfield

Year:

1923

when class had different connotations to more contemporary understandings of the term). Class, or more appropriately caste distinctions, are contextualized in relation to the nature/man binary, where the lines between the classes are drawn as sharply as those between the natural environment and humanity. Yet, questioning the absolute nature of this division is one of the most enduring of Kivi's themes, and the film's exploration of the wilderness within the male transcends class divisions. It seems this uncontrollable wilderness is a universal condition amidst all the Finnish men and not only confined to the 'uncivilised and bestial lower classes'. Indeed, Esko's spectacular buffoonery works as a powerful critique of upper-class self-satisfaction, and provides the film with some of its ideological power. Part of this ideological critique is its suggestive exploration of the destructive power of class conflict on communal relations. It is important that the critique emerges in the inter-war period as Finnish society was undergoing fundamental ideological challenges in the wake of the Civil War and the rise of communism in the USSR. Thus, Karu's version can be considered as a contribution to these debates and an important reminder of the significance of community. The story has been remade twice since Karu's version: once in 1938 by Wilho Ilmari and by Valentin Vaala in 1957. These versions have their respective merits, yet they have not managed to penetrate the public consciousness like Karu's version.

Pietari Kääpä

The Bothnians

Pohjalaisia

Production company:

Suomi-Filmi Oy

Distributor:

Suomi-Filmi Oy

Director:

Jalmari Lahdensuo

Producer:

Erkki Karu

Screenwriter:

Artturi Järviluoma, based on his own play

Cinematographer:

Frans Ekebom

Synopsis

Antti Hanka (Rinne) and Maija Harri (Leppänen) are about to get married, but the authoritarian law-maker of the region, Vallesmanni (Bröderman), intervenes. Valdesmanni's corrupt law and unfair brand of justice rule the Ostrobothnian regions with an iron fist, and Antti is thrown into prison for a crime which he did not commit. Due to the shame of the imprisonment, Maija attempts to seek redemption in religious ideas, but the relationship between her and Antti will never be the same. While Antti is imprisoned, Jussi Harri (Soini), the owner of the local mansion, attempts to mend the relationship between his sister and Antti. As he frees Antti, the pieces are thus set for an explosive conflict between the corrupt law and the stern but fair people of the region. While the conflict takes place between individuals, it has resonance for the whole nation and its unequal class structure.

Critique

Jalmari Lahdensuo's adaptation of Artturi Järviluoma's play is a founding contribution in the cinematic canon of Ostrobothnianism. It is one of the first films to attempt to portray *häjy* identity, a term for a long-running film genre focusing on men from this

Duration:

85 minutes

Cast:

Simo Kaario
Oiva Soini
Kaisa Leppänen
Einar Rinne

Year:

1925

south-western part of Finland. The *häjys* are often depicted as extremely stubborn and volatile in their behaviour, while they are also considered as mirroring the national characteristics of the Finn. While *The Bothnians* is not a *häjy*-film as such, the stereotype of the stoic and uncommunicative but perseverant and inflammable identity is certainly strengthened with narratives such as these. The *häjy* genre is inherently connected to the theme of criminality and this early, and thus key, example of the genre is no different. Yet, criminality in *The Bothnians* is not self-serving or a pointless form of anarchism as the film contains a substantial amount of social commentary on contemporary cultural and social mores, showcasing a prevalent strand of anti-authoritarian criticism that pervades the Ostrobothnian master narrative.

The narrative of *The Bothnians* had been immensely popular in its theatre incarnation, and it had also been adapted into opera by Leevi Madetoja in 1924 in another large-scale cultural feat. The roots of the play can be interpreted to lie with the tsarist Russian control of Finland in the early 1910s that had practically enslaved the Finns and caused widespread discontent amongst the population. The play and the film use a typical approach for avoiding explicit criticism of the current authorities by setting the narrative in the mid-1850s and characterizing the authorities as of Swedish origin. Nevertheless, for contemporary audiences the targets of the play's criticism would have been very clear. This applies to the film adaptation as well, though it may be more appropriate to situate its depiction in the context of the post-Civil War period. During the war, the socialist Reds battled the authoritarian bourgeoisie Whites. The conflict, won by the Whites, led to widespread resentment amongst the people. Ostrobothnia especially was a key territory for most of the uprisings as southern Ostrobothnia was controlled by the Whites, and we can see some of the film's conflicts mirroring the Civil War strife. Yet, it would be overstating the case that the film should be seen as some sort of anti-bourgeoisie propaganda as the benevolent presence of landowner Jussi tells us a very different story. Rather, we can understand the ideological implications of the narrative better by focusing on its ideas of national convalescence.

The film's ideological stance suggests that the unity of a people is more important than interpersonal conflicts – the real enemy is the external oppressor. This assertion is supported by the inclusion of a range of cultural factors which underline its sense of nationhood. The spectacular use of the flat Ostrobothnian landscapes strengthens the narrative's emphasis on the inherent ties between the people and the land, and the epic scope of the visuals works well cinematically to emphasize the need for national identification based on shared identity and culture. Despite its mythical sensibilities, the film is not a glamorized depiction of the Ostrobothnian mentality, but one that emphasizes the trials and tribulations of nation-building.

Lahdensuo's film was a significant success at the box office and contributed to the upturn in the fortunes of the production company Suomi-Filmi. The story has thus been able to connect with audiences in all three forms (play, opera, film), demonstrating the substantial appeal the Ostrobothnian myth has for domestic audiences. As an early contribution to the genre of the *häjy* film, *The Bothnians* provides a general framework that has been utilized prolifically since. Films such as *Härmästä poikia kymmenen/Ten Boys from Härmä* (Unho, 1950) provide nostalgic adaptations for postwar audiences. Pekka Parikka's interpretation of Antti Tuuri's novel *Pohjanmaa/Plainlands* (1988) can also be considered as part of the genre in its focus on the Ostrobothnian male psyche. It seeks to reinterpret the genre for the contemporary context of the 1980s, where the rural ways of life are on the verge of disappearance. While anti-authoritative conflict certainly persists here too, the causes of this are not so much to do with ideological class schism, but the wide-ranging exploitation of small business by the ruthless manoeuvrings of investment capitalism.

The *häjy* genre has even received a postmodern reappraisal in Mika Kaurismäki's *Klaani: Tarina Sammakoitten suvusta/The Clan – Tale of the Frogs* (1984). Whereas most of the contributions to the genre continue to strengthen a sense of national identity, *The Clan* consciously interrogates the meanings of Ostrobothnianism. It demystifies the *häjy* lifestyle and emphasizes all its self-destructive urges, providing an antidote to national traditionalism, and thus continues the ongoing dialogue on the constitution of national cinema. Producers have also returned to a more nostalgic and conventional use of the genre in Aleksi Mäkelä's *Häjyt/The Tough Ones* (1999) and *Pahat pojat/Bad Boys* (2003), which self-consciously and often humorously emphasize the stereotypes of the Ostrobothnian male and the conventions of the genre. Both films were immense successes domestically, and their reception emphasizes the persistent fascination with 'häjydom'. Simultaneously, changes in the thematic and narrative conventions of Ostrobothnianism since *The Bothnians* indicate wider patterns of national cultural transformation. From exploring class conflict to emphasizing national homogeneity, from postmodernist interpretations of national fragility to nostalgic reassertions of traditionalism, the ideological role of the genre demonstrates the ongoing variety of Finnish film culture.

Pietari Kääpä

The Highest Victory

Korkein voitto

Production company:
Suomi-Filmi Oy

Distributor:
Suomi-Filmi Oy

Synopsis

Baron von Hagen (Von Haartman) has just got lucky – waking up with a terrible hangover, the baron discovers in a newspaper that he has won a significant prize in the national lottery. Emboldened by this unexpected win, the Baron discovers that an old flame of his, Vera (Nylander), is in town. Showing her the sights of the city, he has no idea that she has in fact become a spy for the Soviets. After a brief affair, he discovers her real aims as she seems all too keen on aspects of Finland's national defence. Yet, there are more thrills to be had as her spy contacts attempt to capture her.

Director:
Carl von Haartman

Producer:
Erkki Karu

Screenwriter:
Carl von Haartman

Art director:
Karl Fager

Cinematographer:
Eino Kari

Editors:
Carl von Haartman
Eino Kari

Duration:
88 minutes

Cast:
Carl von Haartman
Kerstin Nylander
Aku Korhonen
Ellen Sylvin

Year:
1929

Critique

The Highest Victory is an international-style thriller from director Carl von Haartman, produced at the end of the silent era. Von Haartman was from an elite background and had trained as an officer. He ventured to Hollywood in the 1920s to gain experience in the film industry. During his time there, he had a notable role in one of the key films of the era, William Wellmann's *Wings* (1927), for which he acted as the military consultant. These experiences were to prove very useful when he returned to Finland and began working for Suomi-Filmi as a director. For *The Highest Victory*, von Haartman focused on the genre of the romantic thriller, and he succeeds admirably. One of the first aspects one notices is the film's dynamic style with plenty of camera movement and prolific use of close-ups. Von Haartman's film provides a sense of visual splendour and spectacle in its creation of an appealing image of a northern cultural capital, almost as if it was designed for international consumption. Similarly, the genre of the spy thriller provides the film with a very entertaining narrative drive, further strengthened by the inclusion of substantial humorous elements.

The glamorous depiction of Helsinki is in many ways a precursor to the city's role during the Cold War as a space of international politics. Indeed, the politics of the film are intriguing as it reflects Finland's then-contemporary relations with the Soviet Union despite its narrative setting in an ambiguous historical past. The deep mistrust of the Soviet enemy and fears over infiltration of not only the national population but interpersonal relationships as well is part of its strengthening of nationalist rhetoric suggested by Kangasjärvi (2002). Vera's shameful conversion to a Soviet spy is appropriately punished as she is incarcerated for her crimes and stripped of her rank. When she is ultimately released from prison, Vera has now become a truly patriotic individual as conveyed in her words: 'Darling, we have now both achieved the highest of victories'. The strength of Finnish patriotism is so powerful that it can cure a Soviet spy and remould her into a moral, righteous individual. Thus, the film can be considered part of the cinematic nation-building project to strengthen patriotic feelings and a sense of unity. While the film is typically patriarchal in its gender depictions of the fallible woman in need of correction by the male protagonist, its nationalist rhetoric is distinctly problematic in its depiction of Vera's Jewish spymaster. Portrayed by Aku Korhonen, this Leninesque character is caricatured by many negative stereotypes of Jewishness, and thus exemplifies much of the problematic ethnic racism of the era. Despite these problems in its representational methodology, von Haartmann's film remains an important if still neglected part of Finnish cinema history.

Pietari Kääpä

References

Kangasjärvi, Jukka (2002), 'Carl Von Haartman – 20-luvun Järvi Laturi', http://www.film-o-holic.com/1998-2003/palsta/artikkelit/carl_von_haartman_20_luvun_jarvi_laturi.htm. Accessed 17 April 2011.

WAR

Finnish cinema maintains a paradoxical relationship with war – the theme of war provides key source material for many important and successful films throughout its history. Meanwhile, both material scarcity and loss of key personnel has occurred due to the conflicts, causing substantial problems for the continuation of national cinema production. The four key wars – 1918, the Winter War, the Continuation War and the Cold War – all play a different role in the development of the Finnish film industry and impact its cultural-political functions. Finland's relationship with the Soviet Union lies behind the majority of these conflicts. Strategic proximity, geopolitical allegiances, tsarist history and empire-building all play a crucial role in this antagonism. During the Civil War in 1918, the battles between the socialist Reds and the bourgeoisie Whites transformed into a confrontation between allegiance to the Soviets and the fascist Germans. Once WWII erupted, the Finns were fully aware that they would get the worst of a straight confrontation with the Red Army as the Soviet Union was intent on annexing Finland as a protectionist method against Nazi Germany. After the Finnish government rejected the Soviets' ultimatum of exchanging the city of Viborg for the North Karelian region, the Red Army attacked Finland without a declaration of war. The war encompasses the so-called Winter War (1939–40), which was followed shortly by the Continuation War (1941–44).

Since then, the subject has provided an exceptionally rich source of thematic material for numerous Finnish films. War maintains a key role in the Finnish film industry, gaining interest in international markets as well as holding the unconditional interest of the domestic audiences. Curiously enough, the subject of the Winter War appears in fewer films than the Continuation War – this regardless of the notion that the Winter War is largely perceived as an honourable war, a battle between a righteous Finland defending her borders from an external aggressor. In contrast to this narrative of David facing Goliath and succeeding, the Continuation War arouses more mixed feelings amongst the domestic public, and provides a source for more complex thematic material. There are many reasons for this, including an uneasy alliance with Nazi Germany and aggressive Finnish expansionism into Soviet territory.

As is often the case with cinema and war, an overflow of propaganda films ensued as a reaction to WWII, both as a contemporaneous means to unite the national population, and a retroactive means to explore the nation's history. This type of production was highly biased as befits their propaganda origins: Russians are often portrayed with racist overtones – they rape women in churches, they are constantly drunk, dumb and lazy (*Helmikuun manifesti/The February Manifesto* [Norta and Särkkä, 1939]; *Aktivistit/The Activists* [Orko, 1939]; *Isoviha/The Great Hate* [Kaarna, 1939]). Partly due to Soviet diplomatic pressure, the production of propaganda soon subsided. Another explanation for the waning of propaganda films was a clear audience antipathy towards the topic of war. As Finland was concurrently engaged in the fighting, it did not seem appealing to relive the harsh realities of everyday life in the cinema.

This does not, however, imply that war themes were completely ignored during the Second World War. Risto Orko's documentary

Taistelun tie/Our Fight (1940) deals with the story of the Finnish negotiators in Moscow and discusses the results of Soviet bombing and aggression as it illustrates the most important of battles – the one being waged in the realm of politics. Orvo Saarikivi's *Tyttö astuu elämään/Girl in Grey* (1943) approached war from a novel perspective – a feminine one. The main character is Elli Arho who joins a group of women in uniform (the Lotta Svärd women organisation) who performed many vital functions during the conflicts, from nurturing the wounded to helping the troops communicate. They took part in practically everything except the fighting proper, providing a solid support structure which enabled the men to fight in the front lines.

Ilmari Unho's *Kirkastettu sydän/A Woman's Heart* (1943) contrasts the difficulties of war with the importance of family ties. The father who leaves for the front explains to his children with enthusiasm that Russians are the curse of nature (they use the patronizing phrase 'ryssä') and every Finnish man must fight with them, standing up for their country. The year 1943 was a productive one for Finnish war cinema, as even Risto Orko produced a war comedy (*Jees ja just/Yes and Just* [1943]) based on Armas J. Pulla's novel series. The film's protagonists (Kalle Ryhmy and Ville Romppainen) are instructed to blow up an ammunition depot on the enemy's side. Kalle and Ville let themselves get caught by the Russians because this is the easiest way to get close to them – the film obviously parodies the reputation of the Winter War, and its message is that two brave Finnish soldiers are more than enough to defeat an entire Russian army. In contrast to the vivid range of works made in the subsequent years, this is not a standard war film as we do not see any specific killing or brutality. Here, the sharpest weapon is the human tongue itself.

The 1940s are often considered the golden age of Finnish cinema, with substantial audience attendance welcoming even the flimsiest of products. Perhaps understandably, few productions dealing directly with war were released during this era. It was not until the early 1950s that war films gained resurgence with the release of Väinö Linna's novel *Tuntematon sotilas/The Unknown Soldier* (1954), of which Edvin Laine almost immediately produced arguably Finland's most important war film. *The Unknown Soldier* (1955) was Finland's most expensive production and one of its highest grossing films ever with over 2.8 million viewers (more than half of the Finnish population saw it on its extended release). The nearly three-hour long film cost 50 million Finnish marks, yet this financial investment paid off as it had within a year made a profit of 200 million marks. The narrative of the film starts in the summer of 1941 and tells the story of the Continuation War between Finland and the Soviet Union from the point of view of ordinary Finnish soldiers, a novel approach for its time. Laine's creation resonates as a whole chapter in its own right in Finnish film history, as it more or less defined the war film genre and became an instant classic, a position it maintains through, for example, domestic television screening every year on Independence Day (6 December).

Following *The Unknown Soldier*, war films demonstrated ambiguous methods for dealing with the politics of conflict, something especially apparent in two war-themed films: Hannu Leminen's *Ratkaisun päivät/Decisive Days* (1956) and T.J. Särkkä's *1918* (1957), which was screened at the 7th Berlin International Film Festival. A new wave of war films began in the 1960s, and specifically, a number of documentaries brought an alternative perspective on war: (*Taistelujen tie/Finland's War* [Mikola, Orko and Salokangas, 1960]), as did television films and talk shows (*Kirjeitä itärintamalta/Letters from the Eastern Front* [Sipilä, 1968]) and even television series (*Yhdeksän miehen saappaat/The Boots of Nine Men* [1969]; *Kun maailma paloi/When The World Burned* [af Grann, 1969]). Among the feature films, one example of this new approach stands out: Mikko Niskanen's *Pojat/The Boys* (1962). The film is based on Paavo Rintala's novel of the same title in which the war is approached from the perspective of children for whom the war is just a big adventure. Niskanen continued to explore war in *Sissit/Commando Assault* (1963), using it to highlight the destructive effects war has on the human psyche. By this time, it was quite obvious that reliving war events can have a therapeutic effect on both the film-maker and the viewers, and Edvin Laine continued to be actively involved in producing films which explored historical conflicts (*Täällä Pohjantähden alla/Here, Beneath the North Star* [1968]; *Akseli and Elina* [1970]). Both adaptations of Väinö Linna's novels explored the causes and consequences of the civil war from a perspective that attempted to come to terms with these still painful memories.

The production of war films fell out of favour in the 1970s, primarily due to two developments: a wave of small-scale socio-realist cinema met with increasing support from the Finnish Film Foundation, and the popularity of domestic films was at an all-time low at the box office. As war films often require substantial investment and large-scale production resources, the genre was largely marginalized. As the 1980s dawned, and the Foundation found it increasingly necessary to support different types of cinema, war films began to make a resurgence. Jaakko Pakkasvirta's *Pedon merkki/Sign of the Beast* (1981) reminisces about almost forgotten memories in an occasionally abstract manner. It cannot be called an anti-war film, although it occasionally feels like one as it predominantly leaves the moralizing to the viewer. In 1985, Rauni Mollberg produced a new version of *The Unknown Soldier*, and in 2009, directors Kristian Smeds and Mikko Kuparinen adapted Smeds' controversial theatrical version for television, though its controversies were somewhat diluted in television form. Linna's novel has withstood the test of time as the quintessential Finnish war tale, both as a result of these reinterpretations (it is also frequently performed in theatre) and through the frequent screenings Laine's film received on television. Mollberg's version also proved to be an extraordinary success at the Finnish box office in 1986 and it was even screened at the Cannes Film Festival's *Un Certain Regard* section.

The Second World War has remained popular throughout the latter parts of the twentieth century, acting as the theme of many large-scale domestic 'blockbusters'. Pekka Parikka produced what would become the most successful film of the 1980s with *Talvisota/The Winter War* (1989), based on Antti Tuuri's novel of the same title and Olli Saarela's *Rukajärven tie/Ambush* (1999) was a substantial part of the resurgence of Finnish cinema after the troubled 1990s. *The Winter War's* battle scenes are extremely realistic, especially in the violent impact warfare has on the human body and the natural environment. Whereas Mollberg's *The Unknown Soldier* aims for a realist effect (handheld cameras, naturalistic acting), *The Winter War* recreates the war as a spectacle of horror. Saarela's film follows this pattern in its battles, though it also contains a more lyrical side: instead of focusing only on the men fighting the war, it centres on a romance between a lieutenant and a member of the Lotta Svärd. No longer only a source of national pride or shame, both films showcase the wide range of thematic applications through which war films reflect the ever-changing and unpredictable patterns of Finnish history.

The constant reinterpretation of war continues in the new millennium as some of the genre products are realistic and honest as they draw on testimonies from actual participants in these conflicts (Åke Lindman's *Framom främsta linjen/Behind Enemy Lines* [2004] and *Tali-Ihantala 1944* [with Kirjavainen, 2007]). They also rely on verisimilitude with the events, seeking to recreate the milieu and activities of individual soldiers as closely as possible. Others are more melodramatic as they tackle sensitive themes to do with the role of women in the conflict (*Lupaus/Promise* [Vanne, 2005]), or they explore the Civil War from both sides of the conflict (Lauri Törhönen's *Raja 1918* [2007]), reflecting a desire to interrogate dominant views of the events and the political affiliations of the conflict. This political rethinking continues in films such as Jörn Donner's *Kuulustelu/The Interrogation* (2009), which focuses on Soviet spies in Finland, and which is unusual in its attempts to humanize the 'enemy'. The ongoing focus on war highlights a troubling and sad fact: the passing of time has not been enough for the Finns to process and bury the memories of war for good. This is made clear in Markku Pölönen's *Koirankynnen leikkaaja/Dog Nail*

Clipper (2004), which explores post-traumatic stress disorder amongst the soldiers who fought in the war. No longer seen as simply an honourable duty of every Finn, the war is shown for what it really is – a destructive and dehumanizing activity. Yet, paradoxically, it continues to supply Finnish cinema with some of its most persevering and popular thematic material. Recently, a large-scale two part version of *Here, Beneath the North Star* (2009–10) premiered in the cinemas. While its reception was mixed, it underlines the need for new generations to reinterpret the national past for the contemporary present. What happened more than half a decade ago is not something we can merely bury – it is something that shapes the development of Finnish culture.

Emőke Csoma

Soldier's Bride

Jääkärin Morsian

Production company:
Suomi-Filmi Oy

Distributor:
Suomi-Filmi Oy

Director:
Risto Orko

Producer:
Matti Schreck

Screenwriters:
Ilmari Unho
Risto Orko, based on the
musical play by Sam Sihvo

Art director:
Hannu Leminen

Cinematographer:
Marius Raichi

Composer:
Sam Sihvo
Pekka Attinen

Editor:
Risto Orko

Duration:
95 minutes

Cast:
Tuulikki Paananen
Kullervo Kalske
Ritva Aro
Tauno Palo

Year:
1938

Synopsis

Finnish soldiers underwent training and service as *yaghers* (soldiers) in the German army in the 1910s. *Soldier's Bride* takes place in 1916 as the villainous Baron Lichtenstein encounters a group of honourable *yaghers* preparing for national defence in the Baltics. Yagher Martti (Kalske) falls in love with Lichtenstein's (Erkki Uotila) companion Sabina (Paananen), but he is arrested for confronting Lichtenstein. It turns out that Lichtenstein works for the Russians, supplying information on the number of troops and their movements via a Jewish spy named Isak (Sasu Haapanen). Lichtenstein's lover Sonja (Aro) finds out about his betrayal through her husband's demise on the front, caused indirectly by the information Lichtenstein supplied. As Martti and Sabina try to undo Lichtenstein's plans, Sonja is shot accidentally during a struggle. Martti is briefly imprisoned for the murder, but his commanding officer soon releases him. Martti sets out to rescue Sabina, now being held by Lichtenstein. As Lichtenstein is captured, the heroes are awarded in a grand ceremony and the film culminates in a spectacular scene involving thousands of cavalrymen charging to battle amidst explosions and gun fire. The final words of the film spoken by the commander are 'Long live a free and independent Finland!'

Critique

The two adaptations of Sam Sihvo's musical plays demonstrate developments in Finnish cinema throughout its formative years in the 1930s. First of all, the invention of sound technology had a fundamental impact on the film industry and the ways it organized its narratives, and increased the necessity to produce films in the indigenous language. Kalle Kaarna's 1931 version was one of the first experimentations in synchronized sound in the Finnish cinema. Notably, it provided the chance for audiences to hear Tauno Brännas' (later Palo, one of the biggest stars of Finnish cinema) post-synchronised songs. When Orko's 1938 version was released, much of the narrative remained the same, but the ways it was told differed crucially; partially because of the advanced capabilities of the technicians, partially due to international geopolitical developments. The spectacle of synchronized singing was now the norm, necessitating that productions would focus on more elaborate musical numbers and visual splendour. Both versions culminate with visually impressive and patriotically inspiring scenes. In Kaarna's version, the *yaghers* land in Vaasa aboard an icebreaker titled *Sampo* (a mythical urn in the national epic *Kalevala*). A number of national signifiers thus coalesce in a scene that leaves no ideological uncertainty as to the patriotic aims of the product. The Orko version manages to surpass this in its patriotic fervour as it culminates in what many still see as the most spectacular scene in Finnish cinema history – the charge of the *yagher* brigade set to Jean Sibelius' 'Jääkärinmarssi' ('Yagher's March'). The use of 3000 cavalrymen and 2000 foot soldiers provides the scene with a sense of authenticity rare in epic cinema, and some even still hold it alongside real-life spectacles such as the 'Ride of Valkyries' scene from Francis Ford Coppola's *Apocalypse Now* (1979).

Both versions of *Soldier's Bride* are also important reflections of contemporary politics. Geopolitical manoeuvrings were altering political allegiances Europe-wide, and inflamed political relations between Finland, Germany and the Soviet Union necessitated constant dialogue on Finland's allegiance. While Finnish independence was already achieved in 1917, pressure from the Soviet side escalated throughout the 1930s. Thus, it was no coincidence that two films about *yaghers* preparing to battle for the independence of Finland were released. While they are both set in the past, as is common in political cinema at times of conflict, both versions urge Finland to strengthen its ties with Germany. They also seem to suggest that the Finnish-German war against the Soviets is also to do with the independence of the Baltic regions as the setting of the narrative in the region establishes a sense of fraternity between the nations. Poland's position in the ideological mapping of the films is, however, more difficult as Sabina is from Warsaw in the 1931 version, yet this connection is obscured in Orko's film (potentially reflecting contemporary events). An even more distasteful yet revealing turn comes through in the anti-Semitism that pervades parts of the film as the Jewish spy is a clear racist caricature, depicted as an outcast and an enemy of the nation. There is a clear 'whitist' bias pervading much of the film as the moral righteousness of the *yaghers* and their honest officers are validated by the narrative, indicating the prevalent tensions that still echoed years after the events of 1918.

Both versions of *Soldier's Bride* were successful, and Orko's version recouped its massive investment multiple times on its initial cinema-run, making it one of the largest successes of Finnish cinema up to that point. While both films have managed to gain substantial critical and commercial success in Finland, they both faced problems in sustaining their audiences. The negatives for the 1931 version were thought to be lost in a fire, and the film remained unavailable until a partial copy was discovered in a basement in Helsinki. Later, a pristine version was found amidst Finnish migrants in the US (albeit still with one reel missing) and the film received its restored premiere in 2001. The Orko version met with a similarly troublesome fate as it was banned in 1949 for being too patriotic and demeaning in its image of the USSR. Due to this external political pressure, it remained largely unseen until 1986 when it received a rerelease with the thawing of the Cold War. Both films are thus emblematic of Finland's geopolitical relations with the Soviet Union as they function as contemporaneous propaganda and exhibit some of the more dubious ethnopolitics of the time. That both films have successfully retained a substantial standing in the canon of Finnish cinema tells us something of the ways in which they remain important historical documents as well as evocations of nationalist sentiment.

Pietari Kääpä

The Unknown Soldier

Tuntematon Sotilas

Production company:
Suomen Filmiteollisuus

Distributors:
Finnkino
Suomen Filmiteollisuus

Director:
Edvin Laine

Producer:
T. J. Särkkä

Screenwriters:
Juha Nevalainen, based on the novel by Väinö Linna

Art director:
Aarre Koivisto

Cinematographers:
Pentti Unho
Osmo Harkimo
Olavi Tuomi
Antero Ruhonen
Kalle Peronkoski

Composer:
Ahti Sonninen

Editors:
Osmo Harkimo
Armas Vallasuvo

Duration:
170 minutes

Cast:
Åke Lindman
Tauno Palo
Matti Ranin
Pentti Siimes

Year:
1955

Synopsis

The narrative of *The Unknown Soldier* follows a machine gun platoon throughout Finland's participation in the Second World War. Though the narrative is action packed, the majority of the film focuses on the conflicts between the soldiers' get-the-job-done attitude and their commanding officers' stern Prussian-style discipline. Following heavy marching and a decisive victory, the platoon is ordered to move out with minimal rest. The platoon voices its anger, and two men are executed for insubordination. The conflict heats up as Rokka (Tolvanen [1955] and Liski [1985]) and his old friend join the regiment. Older than the commanding officers, the two soldiers are veterans of the Winter War. After several heroic actions by Rokka in battle, he is caught carving a lamp stand while on guard. The officer orders him to decorate the officer camp paths with rounded stones, a task that Rokka refuses. That night, he kills two enemy soldiers who had snuck into the trench and takes an officer prisoner. Rokka characteristically attends his court marshal, prisoner in tow, and jokes that if he's going to prison, they might as well take the two of them at the same time. In their final battle, the platoon is forced to retreat and act in insubordination to the commanding officer. Yet the film validates the soldiers; they retreat listening to the Finnish President's declaration of the end of the war over the radio.

Critique

Uncritical use of the term 'war film' is ill-advised for both Edvin Laine's original (1955) and Rauni Mollberg's later (1985) adaptation of the Väinö Linna novel *The Unknown Soldier*. Exempting period references, there is little for the history buff to correlate to actual events of the Continuation War. The films instead focus on the large cast of characters whose heroism and cowardice, perseverance and stubbornness, camaraderie and disillusion, embody the war experience. Laine's 1955 version of the film is the highest-grossing Finnish film of all time with nearly half of Finland's population seeing it in theatres when it was first released. The popularity of the original extends to the 1985 remake, which was the most expensive Finnish production to date and is one of the highest-grossing Finnish films of all time. The action and most of the dialogue is preserved between the 1955 version and the remake. Mollberg uses a much more gritty style, and curbs much of the original's comedy to achieve its effect. The effectiveness of Mollberg's alterations and minor additions is questionable, a fact given credence by the enduring audience preference for the original. The central conflict between the strict officers and the earthy soldiers turns from a celebration of the Finnish character in the original to a condemnation of war's absurdities in the remake.

Rokka, an officer from the Winter War, is the heart of Laine's film. An officer who serves as a regular soldier as there were no leadership openings, Rokka is totally irreverent toward military tradition. He is not a man preoccupied with his own glory or Finland's for that matter – he never gripes about the conditions or the food, he

The Unknown Soldier

Tuntematon Sotilas

Production company:
Arctic Film

Distributor:
Kinosto

Director:
Rauni Mollberg

Producer:
Rauni Mollberg

Screenwriters:
Veikko Aaltonen
Rauni Mollberg, based on the
novel by Väinö Linna

Art director:
Ensio Suominen

Cinematographer:
Esa Vuorinen

Composer:
Heikki Valpola

Editor:
Olli Soinio

Duration:
187 minutes

Cast:
Risto Tuorila
Mika Mäkelä
Pirkka-Pekka Petelius
Paavo Liski

Year:
1985

is there to get the job done. In many ways, Rokka embodies the Finnish *sisu* (loosely translated as 'strength of will') as he effectively becomes a mouthpiece for the Finnish character. Rokka's *sisu* manifests itself in his skilled fighting and his conflict with the superior officers. In his first battle of the film, Rokka advances with a private, borrowing his gun as he orders the private to bombard the trench ahead with grenades, which Rokka will then clean up; methodically, Rokka takes the whole trench. When he is approached for his bravery and skill, he dismisses the admiration, stating that victory is not a matter of bravery or talent, but simply keeping your head down, aiming well and not hesitating. *Sisu* isn't a philosophy that lends itself to moral ambiguity or existential doubt; it lives through perseverance and guts. Yet Rokka's heroism is his doom as he is wounded while carrying a fellow soldier while retreating. Though the film ends in Finland's loss, Finland will persevere because it is Rokka, not the Red Army, who is the film's true victor.

The remake of *The Unknown Soldier* is a much more brutal experience, where there are no winners, just varying degrees of failure. The central comparison between criticism of Finland's misled war effort and the heroic soldiers' *sisu* resolves itself on a much less celebratory note. The humour that floats through Laine's film is largely absent in Mollberg's gritty war film. Mollberg predominantly uses amateurs and young actors, much as in his critically acclaimed debut *Maa on syntinen laulu/The Earth is a Sinful Song* (1973), as well as visceral handheld camerawork to cast off any semblance of Hollywood glamour. Much like his debut, Mollberg's camerawork and visual style is more profound then the human narratives it contains. The style is suited to his larger thematic reach as well as the film's darker tone.

The depiction of the final battle and the concluding retreat is emblematic of Mollberg's take on Linna's novel. The soldiers retreat, with the lieutenant who sanctioned the retreat being scolded by his officer, who doesn't acknowledge the folly of trying to defend against the upcoming onslaught. The central platoon is not the only faction retreating; the entire brigade falls back, while officers proclaim that all traitors will be shot. Eventually, an officer shoots and kills a soldier. The soldiers continue to march home, ignoring the commands of the officers. While a horse-drawn cart gets stuck in the mud, the retreating soldiers do not bother to stop and help. An officer tries to help the driver of the cart, but the man dismisses any help from this officer. As he sets the horse free, the metaphor is clearly encapsulated in the dialogue: 'torturing poor dumb beasts, as though they've done someone harm'. The line compares the Finnish soldier to the horse, condemning the officer's use of capital punishment for insubordination as insensible and unproductive as torturing a work horse for doing nothing other than its job. The film asks: if the Finnish people have never done anyone harm, why does the military brass insist on driving the Finnish soldiers into Russian territory to die there? The film's vilification of the officers answers its central question: the officers are out of touch with the Finnish spirit. The victory of the common soldier over the officers' folly is celebrated in the original, but here there are no such easy answers. The film's concluding image of a faceless

The Unknown Soldier, Suomen Filmiteollisuus.

dead body with its dog tag flipped over is also the film's concluding message; there are no victors – what was lost is something more ambiguous, more profound than the lives of individuals.

John Saari

The Boys

Pojat

Production company:
Suomen Filmiteollisuus

Distributor:
Suomen Filmiteollisuus

Director:
Mikko Niskanen

Producer:
T.J. Särkkä

Synopsis

A group of teenage boys in northern Finland spend their days during the last months of WWII scavenging for goods to sell to the passing German troops. The activities are harmless enough, just a way for children to pass the time. Occasionally, darker realities intrude on the boys' games as large numbers of wounded soldiers and even a train carrying dead soldiers passes by. Soon, their harmless infatuation with the Germans takes a darker turn. The boys spend a lot of time spying on local girls who sneak off to the bushes with the soldiers. It turns out that Jake's (Loiri) mother is seeing a German officer, while his father is away at the front. One day, Jake comes home to find it deserted. Shattered at this betrayal, he chases after them to the train station but it is too late as the train has already departed, leaving a despairing Jake behind

Screenwriters:

Mikko Niskanen, based on the novel by Paavo Rintala

Art director:

Reino Helkesalo

Cinematographer:

Olavi Tuomi

Composer:

Einar Englund

Editor:

Armas Vallasvuo

Duration:

100 minutes

Cast:

Pentti Tarkiainen
Vesa-Matti Loiri
Uti Saurio
Kauko Helovirta

Year:

1962

Critique

Mikko Niskanen's *The Boys* is a seminal film in Finnish cinema. It is by no means 'children's cinema' (a limiting and potentially derogatory term). *The Boys'* main contribution is its provision of an accessible way to deal with the memories of the war and especially Finland's collaboration with Germany. The collaboration took place during the Continuation War against the Soviet Union, where German assistance was deemed to be necessary. The strategy was successful for a while, but resulted in catastrophe for Finland as their relations with Germany cooled and the Germans started losing the war, resulting in the soldiers rampaging through Finnish Lapland. Taken metaphorically, the film can be understood as a reflection of the honeymoon period between the two nations and its disastrous culmination. As in the best of the children's film, real horrors take place just outside of the frame, as can be seen in the deportation of prisoners and the death train scenes. The dawning realization of the realities of the war is beautifully conveyed through spectacular child's perspective camerawork and the performances of the child actors. The film was the cinematic debut of Vesa-Matti Loiri, one of the domestic cinema's long-standing and brightest stars. His performance as Jake is heartbreaking, especially the astonishing tracking shot as Jake tries to grasp for the train, fails and falls on the tracks. It is an impressively mature performance and one that showcases the considerable range and talent that would make him a household name. Niskanen's film is exemplary 'children's cinema' as it functions on multiple levels as an adventure film, a drama, a story of war, and a wider depiction of a national crisis.

Pietari Kääpä

The Winter War

Talvisota

Production company:

National Filmi Oy

Distributor:

Finnkino

Director:

Pekka Parikka

Producer:

Marko Röhr

Screenwriters:

Pekka Parikka
Antti Tuuri

Synopsis

The Winter War is an examination of the fates of several Finnish soldiers engaged in the harsh battles between Finland and the Soviet Union during WWII. The main character of the film, Martti Hakala (Mäkelä), is a typical Ostrobothnian male: he does not talk much as he is focused on getting the job done. The Soviet onslaught intensifies throughout the war, but the soldiers mostly succeed in rebuking them through tactics and sheer perseverance. Throughout the war, the different characters we follow die in often heroic actions, though some of them meet a senseless end. The soldiers get momentary respite from the horrors of war as they are sent to recuperate at the home front. Yet, they must soon return to the front to continue the national defence. Seeing his younger brother blown in half by the enemy grenades makes Martti Hakala realise the absurd horror of war, but he has no choice but to fight on. The film culminates in a ceasefire, but any sense of victory is defeated by our knowledge that the men would soon be back at the front for the Continuation War.

Cinematographer:
Kari Sohlberg

Composer:
Juha Tikka
Jukka Haavisto

Editor:
Keijo Virtanen

Duration:
195 minutes

Cast:
Taneli Mäkelä
Vesa Vierikko
Timo Torikka
Esko Salminen

Year:
1989

Critique

The Winter War remains one of the most successful Finnish films of all time with 650,000 spectators domestically. While it was also touted for international success, this breakout never materialized. This is not entirely surprising as the real power of Parikka's film lies in its status as a national monument. At the time of its release, *The Winter War* received almost unchallenged critical and popular acclaim, not only for its successful contribution to Finnish cinema, but also for the way in which it reflected Finland's current political situation.

In the late 1980s, the prevalence of Glasnost, Perestroika and the collapse of the Berlin Wall had decreased the Soviet Union's political influence over Finland, allowing *The Winter War* to transcend considerations of external political pressure. As a 'neo-nationalist' depiction, *The Winter War* provided an account of the war where the emphasis is strictly on the sacrifices made by Finland, defending itself righteously against the onslaught of the mighty Soviet Union. A crucial part of this nationalist mission is its examination of the Finnish male character and the significance of nature in Finnish mythology. While *The Winter War* shares the focus of Rauli Mollberg's *The Unknown Soldier* (1985) on the relentless horrors of war and the toll it takes on human life, it also embellishes the significance of the ancestral *patrie* ('fatherland'). The film's opening mirrors that of Parikka's previous Antti Tuuri adaptation, *Pohjanmaa/Plainlands* (1988) with a helicopter shot over the plains of Ostrobothnia, which both sets up a connection with their shared protagonists, the Hakalas, and establishes the importance of defending the *patrie*. Whereas *The Unknown Soldier* has a distinctly claustrophobic feel, despite large-scale battle scenes with numerous extras, *The Winter War* expands its scope to the vastness of the landscape with a number of the battles fought over expansive plains. The fatherland is represented as something inherent to the nation, a material element with ideological connotations, where the sacrifice of one's life is rewarded by the prospect of assimilation into the immortal nation.

The characters of *The Winter War* are mirrored by the surrounding landscape, where the stoic features of the archetypal Ostrobothnian men are reflected in the prototypical images of nature. The mirroring of the character and the *mise-en-scène* culminates in a juxtaposed display of the absurdity of war in a lengthy montage, intercutting scenes of destruction with Martti's mental degradation. Blood and soil become connected in a juxtaposition of scenic landscape shots and the visual starkness of chaos and destruction, as the purity of the white snow is corrupted by the dark mud and the redness of spilled blood and body parts. *The Winter War*'s climax takes place during the announcement of ceasefire, as the soldiers emerge from various tunnels and potholes, safe from enemy fire. The film's final image is not a celebratory one, however, but a close-up of Martti's face, frozen in a grimace that displays anger and confusion in the face of such abject destruction of human life.

The Winter War's final scene evokes the question: do the film's loyalties lie in a neo-nationalistic depiction of the glory of defending one's nation or a rejection of the nationalistic cause in the name of universal moral values? The ambiguity is underlined by the audience's knowledge that the ceasefire that ended the Winter War would not last and, within just over a year, these men would be back in the trenches for the Continuation War. It therefore seems somewhat misguided to read *The Winter War* as an unquestioning neo-nationalistic embrace of the national cause. Rather, the film is perhaps more accurately understood as a sceptical examination of the cost of defending the nation, where loyalties become divided by attachment to the nation and to boundless humanism. While it has not achieved the canonical status of Edvin Laine's *The Unknown Soldier* (1955), it remains a respected emblem of its time and a key indicator of the political liberation of the era as it meant the previously taboo Winter War was now a topic free for reassessment. Yet, whether the film can become something more than a Glasnost-era reflection of external geopolitical relations remains to be seen.

Pietari Kääpä

Friends, Comrades

Ystävät, toverit

Production companies:
Filmi-Molle
Finnish Film Foundation
Finnkino
Svenska Filminstitutet (SFI)
Yleisradio (YLE)

Director:
auni Mollberg

Producer:
Rauni Mollberg

Screenwriters:
Joni Skiftesvik
Rauni Mollberg

Art directors:
Tom Hamberg
Aatto Hongisto

Cinematographer:
Kjell Lagerroos

Synopsis

Arno Jurmala (Mikiver) is an international arms dealer residing in the Finnish part of northern Lapland. We are first introduced to his flamboyant lifestyle during his birthday party as luminaries from around the world gather to greet him. Especially welcome are ambassadors from Russia and Germany who both hope to benefit from their long ties with Jurmala. As this is during the cessation period between the World Wars, Jurmala plays both sides against each other. He also discovers that one of his adjutants has betrayed him and the adjutant is swiftly executed publicly. Jurmala's wife, Lisa (Ekblad), meanwhile, is estranged from her husband who is both controlling and abusive to her. He makes enemies as often as he makes friends, and as the Second World War ends, changes in the balance of power await him. Yet, even in the circumstances of changing global powers, Jurmala is able to benefit by selling weapons to whoever needs them. But remaining open to everyone's offers with no ideological loyalty or direction leaves him hopelessly alone and vulnerable.

Critique

Rauni Mollberg is well-known for his epic heritage films and his earthy sense of realism. While his films have always been controversial, they have also managed to be consistently successful domestically; for example, both *Maa on syntinen laulu*/*The Earth is a Sinful Song* (1973) and *Tuntematon sotilas*/*The Unknown Soldier* (1985) feature amongst some of the all-time box office champs. Thus, expectations were high for this epic tale combining corporate

Composer:

Kari Rudman

Editor:

Kaie-Ene Rääk

Duration:

118 minutes

Cast:

Mikk Mikiver
Stina Ekblad
Hannu Lauri
Paavo Liski

Year:

1990

greed and national history. When the film failed at the box office, Mollberg's career was at an end and resulted in only one more feature *Paratiisin lapset/The Children of Paradise* (1994).

Despite its reputation as a confused misfire, *Friends, Comrades* is an intriguing and atmospheric epic. In many ways, it follows the conventions of a rise and fall narrative, yet it concludes in ambiguous fashion. At times, the film plays like a story focusing on the villain of blockbuster entertainment, including complex plays with power and even a remote lair for their villainy. *Friends, Comrades* does not allow the audience any respite from the nastiness and corruption. Even seeing the events from Jurmala's innocent wife's perspective does not help matters as she soon descends into drug addiction and despair. To contrast its bleakness, the film makes ample use of its lavish surroundings and the landscapes of northern Lapland. This contrast helps summarize its problematic status well – by presenting an epic narrative but refusing any point of identification leaves it to occupy a curious liminal perspective with no real chance of audience identification. Arguably, such complexity is to be commended, but one can question the wisdom in producing what effectively amounts to an art house film with the scope and budget of a European heritage epic.

While its commercial chances are thus meagre, its ideological perspectives require further interpretation. The film can be read in multiple ways: for example, as a historical exploration of Finland's conflicted status or as a critical interrogation of contemporary business politics. As a historical metaphor, the film's title is an apt summary of its thematic centre and Finland's geopolitical and socio-economic status between the West and the East. The need to maintain friends in Germany and comradeship with the socialist USSR necessitates his constantly shifting alliances. As Jurmala's geopolitical connectivity and business empire extends to all the neighbouring countries and even beyond, we can see the necessity to sustain links to the West while expanding operations to the East. But simultaneously, in the dirty game of the arms race, there are no real friends, only fleeting acquaintances and potential enemies.

The film's rich ideological tapestry allows us to read it in multiple ways in addition to its historical and geopolitical commentary. It can also be interpreted as a play on the socio-economic and geopolitical situation of Finland in the late 1980s. Jurmala's war profiteering sets its targets on the irresponsible and individualistic capitalist exploitation that was increasingly becoming the norm in the era of 'casino economics' in Finland. During this period, governmental policies on inflation rates and free market principles enabled the rise of yuppie culture and gambling on the stock markets. Jurmala effectively acts as the embodiment of the irresponsible and even misanthropic tendencies of the era, providing the most critical condemnation of the banking system and the government that enables it.

On its release, *Friends, Comrades* was perceived as a disappointment with critics suggesting we never connect with the protagonists on any emotional or even conventional narrative level. Whereas Mollberg's previous films are well-known for their naturalistic, down-to-earth qualities, they too maintain a certain theatrical distance in their attempts to provide different visions of familiar material. Mollberg's cinema is a paradoxical combination of intense naturalism and sweeping epic tapestries and *Friends, Comrades* is no different. Yet, the film tones down the naturalism for its political scope and perhaps loses something in the process. There is something very Slavic about the film's world both in terms of morality and its brooding reliance on the formalist and bureaucratic nature of business enterprise. The sprawling qualities of the narrative provide it with a certain weighty tone which occasional flashbacks to happier times are not able to alleviate, resulting in a film with limited commercial potential.

Domestic audiences were largely disappointed with the film on its release and its international reception was not much better. While 1990 was a difficult year for Finnish cinema, Pekka Parikka's *The Winter War* had broken box-office records the previous year and the advertising campaign for *Friends, Comrades* made extensive use of shots of carnage and war. Yet, the film is not the type of straightforward historical narrative that had been advertised. The film's intentional duality of capturing both Jurmala's humanity and uncontrollable destructiveness, and the corrupting nature of business and its essential role in national defence, results in a conflicted product. Ultimately, the film was seen in some critical circles as a further example of the stagnant nature of Finnish cinema. For others, the internationalism on the level of both production and narrative also brought it dangerously close to the disparaged 'euro-pudding' productions (films produced in collaboration with several European nations, which often ended up as banal products only offering surface glimpses of each culture). In many ways, this is a shame as while the film is certainly not a lost masterpiece, it does showcase a deft eye for expansive internationalism. It also provides a uniquely dark and expansive contribution to the fictional biography genre, where we gaze on powerful, corrupt men weaving their empire and ultimately crafting their doom.

Pietari Kääpä

The Butterfly from Ural

Uralin perhonen

Production company:
Osuuskunta Camera Cagliostro

Distributor:
Yleisradio (YLE)

Director:
Katariina Lillqvist

Synopsis

The late C.G.E. Mannerheim brings a man with him to Finland as his valet after extensive travels in Russia and the Far East beyond the Ural Mountains. Mannerheim's wife, Anastasia Arapova, is not pleased when she hears about the men's homosexual relationship. Mannerheim takes the valet, called the 'Butterfly of the Urals' to the town of Tampere, where the dramatic events of Finland's Civil War (1918) are taking place. Mannerheim executes the socialist Reds, the losing party in the war after their captivation, departs Tampere and leaves his Kyrgyz valet there alone. Even though elderly public sauna keepers and washerwomen take care of the valet, he finally commits suicide. The final scene presents the old and lonely Mannerheim, who ends his life sad and alone.

Producer:

Jyrki Kaipainen

Screenwriters:

Katariina Lillqvist

Hannu Salama

Animator:

Alfons Mensdorff-Pouilly

Cinematographer:

Miloslav Spála

Composers:

Hannu Kella

Alec Kopyt

Editors:

Katariina Lillqvist

Tatu Pohjavirta

Duration:

27 minutes

Cast:

Jotaarkka Pennanen (voice)

Aliisa Pulkkinen (voice)

Year:

2008

Critique

The puppet animation film *The Butterfly from Ural* represents Carl Gustaf Emil Mannerheim (1867–1951), former President of Finland, as a butcher of the socialist Reds, the losing party in the Civil War. The film suggests that as commander of the triumphant nationalist Whites, Mannerheim is to blame for thousands of field executions of captured Reds. What is more, the film represents Mannerheim as a homosexual and a transvestite. Mannerheim dresses in a purple corset and has sexual intercourse with his male servant, the Butterfly of the Urals. In these two tropes, the ones of the 'Butcher Marshal' and the 'Gay Marshal', Lillqvist makes use of culturally ambiguous and contested images of President Mannerheim: the first reminds audiences of the social revolution and counterculture movement of the 1960s and 1970s that challenged the largely unquestioned public image of Mannerheim as a national hero by turning him into a right-wing butcher; the second refers to a less public image, drawing on obscure Finnish folklore according to which Mannerheim was actually homosexual, or rather, bisexual.

Both of these narrative elements of *The Butterfly from Ural* created controversy and upset many people in Finland. The animation was said to insult the memory of the 'Greatest Finn' and continue a brand of Soviet wartime propaganda as latter-day Red Army spin. According to some commentators, the film instigated a 'new Civil War' in Finland. Before even seeing the film, some Finnish politicians, representatives of the army and veterans declared war on Lillqvist in the media. They argued the film to be insulting, its eligibility for financial support was disputed and the officials who approved its production were chastised due to the fact that it presents Mannerheim 'as "a corset-wearing homosexual", who finds pleasure spending time with his male orderlies' (Karkulehto 2011).

The media war surrounding the animation was not an accident or a surprise, especially as journalists energetically scandalized the film's depiction by pursuing the matter with a range of authoritative pro-conservative sources. However, one can not diminish the fact that the film rewrites and revises the dominant historical narrative of the Finnish Civil War, telling a story of the 'Butcher Marshal' that differs from traditional and publicly acknowledged national narratives, and brings to light the long-term silence surrounding issues concerning the legacy of the Civil War that have most often remained ambiguous in public discourses. It is also political from the viewpoint of the history and politics of gender and sexuality, illustrating the previously concealed and silent history of non-normative, or queer, sexualities (cf. Juvonen 2002). This history is made public through Mannerheim's personal relationships, which, regardless of intention, became a topic of debate in media headlines (Karkulehto 2011).

Sanna Karkulehto

References

Juvonen, Tuula (2002), *Varjoelämää ja Julkisia Salaisuuksia*, Tampere: Vastapaino.

Karkulehto, Sanna (2011), 'The "Greatest Finn" Meets the "Gay Marshal": Foucault's Cycle, National Narratives and *The Butterfly from Ural*', *Journal of Scandinavian Cinema*, 2, pp. 177–97.

CONTEMPORARY FILM
AND LITERATURE

Literature has played a significant role in the history of Finnish cinema since Minna Canth's *Sylvi* (film directed by Teuvo Puro, 1913), Aleksis Kivi's *Nummisuutarit/The Village Shoemakers* (film directed by Erkki Karu, 1923) and Väinö Linna's *Tuntematon sotilas/The Unknown Soldier* (film directed by Edvin Laine, 1955). Especially since the 1970s, this picture of Finnish culture has become increasingly diverse, fragmented and individualized both in literature and film. Films such as *Maa on syntinen laulu/The Earth is a Sinful Song* (Mollberg, 1973), *Lampaansyöjät/Sheep Eaters* (Huunonen, 1972), *Jäniksen vuosi/The Year of the Hare* (Jarva, 1977) and *Aurinkotuuli/Solar Wind* (Linnasalo, 1980), based on novels written by Timo K. Mukka, Veikko Huovinen, Arto Paasilinna and Kullervo Kukkasjärvi respectively, depicted Finland and Finns that differ from, for example, the more explicitly collective post-independence and postwar national narratives represented in *Täällä Pohjantähden alla/Here, Beneath the North Star* (Laine, 1968) and *Akseli and Elina* (Laine, 1970), adapted from Väinö Linna's canonical novels. From this perspective, the union between literature and film has not only worked as a means of constructing a unified, intact picture of Finland and its citizens, but also as cultural challenger of these very ideas and ideals of a unified Finnish nation, nationality and national identity.

Adaptations from literature to film have decreased during the past decades as almost half of Finnish films had their origins in literature in the 1950s, whereas during the most recent decades only a quarter of films are based on literary texts. Regardless, literature is important for contemporary Finnish cinema as, out of the approximately 15–20 films produced in Finland annually, 3–5 are based on a (Finnish) literary work. These contemporary works seem to continue their aims at presenting a picture of diverse and multi-layered Finland rather than a unified nation.

National narratives have not, however, entirely vanished. Even today, films focusing on, for example, significant historical events and notable national figures are produced, such as Timo Koivusalo's adaptation of *Here, Beneath the North Star* (2009–10), and Hannu Kahakorpi's biopic of the esteemed writer Kalle Päätalo, *Päätalo/The Novelist* (2008). In addition, humorous tales originally authored by writers such as Veikko Huovinen and Heikki Turunen, the famous humorists and sympathetic depicters of the Finnish countryside and wildlife, provide an alternative type of national narrative, which is also a powerful aspect of national cultural memory in their use of local vernacular and depictions of their *idiot savant* characters as some sort of prototypical authentic Finns. In contrast to these narratives aiming for the construction of a broad and wide-spectrum national audience, stories produced in and by the margins and the marginalized (often defined in ethnic terms), as well as women, children and Swedish-speaking people, have largely been presented as contradictory to the unified national project in mainstream film production.

When it comes to the study of Finnish film adaptations of literature it is intriguing to notice that, as a matter of fact, the process of adaptation itself is able to reveal many of the complex processes in which film adaptations contribute to and shape Finnish cultural

Left: *The Geography of Fear,* Blind Spot Pictures. Photo: Nauska

history. In the theorization of adaptations, adaptation does not refer only to a certain work that has been adapted and versioned from another, already existing work, but also to the process of adaptation itself. As translations, adaptations are always also processes of creating and interpreting something new. In literature and film this is crucial, especially due to the difference between their forms of expression. Furthermore, adaptation is automatically intertextual, which inevitably refers least to the object of adaptation but usually also to other works, periods, mediums and genres. Thus, for example, *Päätalo* (2008) could not be interpreted only as an adaptation of Kalle Päätalo's autobiographical works, as it also resembles previous Päätalo films: for instance, the actor Pirjo Leppänen performed the role of Kalle's mother already in Mikko Niskanen's *Elämän vonkamies/Life's Hardy Men* (1986) and *Nuoruuteni savotat/Lumberjacking* (1988). Through this the film can be considered both within the mode of realism and the conventions of biographical films about nationally important culture figures as it faithfully concentrates on the pivotal moment of the protagonist's life and career – his literary breakthrough in Finland.

In conventional adaptation research much of the work is devoted to assessing the faithfulness of the adaptation to the original work. This is not, however, the most productive or the only angle on thinking about the process of adaptation. Recent methodologies in adaptation studies have sought to categorize other modes of adaptation, where verisimilitude with the original text is only one concern among many (Bacon 2005: 138–46). There are, of course, many Finnish adaptations that try to preserve the characters, events, emphasis and plot of the original, and whose very reason for existence is their resemblance to the original text. Typical examples of these are adaptations of canonical texts such as Timo Koivusalo and Edvin Laine's *Here, Beneath the North Star* adaptations. This process of adaptation emphasizes mimicry, which takes many forms. From more canonical films working from texts by authors such as Arto Paasilinna and Veikko Huovinen, films such as *Ulvova mylläri/The Howling Miller* (Pakkasvirta, 1982) and *Havukka-ahon ajattelija/Backwood Philosopher* (Väänänen, 2009) seek to recreate the vernacular of the texts in cinematic form. The depiction of 'authentic Finns' as the sort of *idiot savants* of marginal regions works to capture something essential about national identity present in the prose of the original text. Simultaneously, verisimilitude plays a key role in alternative histories of the nation, often focusing on the perspectives of infrequently presented protagonists of historical films such as children: *Näkymätön Elina/Elina: As If I Wasn't There* [Härö, 2002] from Kerstin Johansson i Backe's novel); *Populäärimusiikkia Vittulajänkältä/Popular Music* [Bagher, 2004] from Mikael Niemi's novel; *Äideistä parhain/Mother of Mine* [Härö, 2005] from Heikki Hietamies' novel). It is once more important that the cinematic world captures not only the sense of history adequately, but also the mind-worlds created by the author. Through this, they continue to contribute to the ongoing dialogue on Finnish culture.

Another form of adaptation takes a looser approach to the original work, striving to mould the content of the text or comment on it in one form or another. While adaptation of course always involves changes to the original work, the freer, self-reflexive form of adaptation may change the plot structure or narrative conventions or excise lengthy story strands. An example of this type of adaptation is Aku Louhimies' *Käsky/Tears of April* (2008), based on the Civil War-set novel by Leena Lander (2003). The initial scene of the novel features its protagonist Miina (played by Pihla Viitala in the film) already captured by the Whites, and regresses to unravel the events in flashback form. In contrast, a battle scene opens the film, showing Miina's capture, and the story progresses in linear form from there. The characters and the basis of the events are thus the same, but the process of adaptation brings substantial changes to the content of the story. For one, a relationship between Miina and her capturer *yagher* Aaro (Samuli Vauramo) forms early on in the film as we see them stranded on an uninhabited island. Thus, the dynamic between them and the judge Hallenberg (Eero Aho) interrogating Miina changes entirely as the relationship between the two is gradually revealed through the interrogations, discussions and the suspicions of Hallenberg. Furthermore, Miina's character is painted in entirely different colours as she is depicted as a hardened fighter, which differs from the novel which has no battle scenes (C.f. Hatavara 2010: 163–77).

A third form of adaptation concerns so-called analogue adaptations, where the original text provides only raw material or a basic inspiration for the cinematic work. Aki Kaurismäki's *Rikos ja rangaistus/Crime and Punishment* (1983), *Hamlet liikemaailmassa/Hamlet Goes Business* (1987) and *Juha* (1999) use this mode of adaptation to create films that more resemble the idiosyncratic world of the director rather than the original novels. In *Juha*, all that remains of Juhani Aho's original novel (1911) is the love triangle between Juha (Sakari Kuosmanen), Marja (Kati Outinen) and Shemeikka (André Wilms). But even this is represented in different shades in the film version. Juha and Marja are initially depicted as content, and Marja goes with Shemeikka voluntarily. Other changes are more substantial: the events are set in the present – or at least closer to the present in the typically undefined timeless world well-known from Kaurismäki's films, comprised as they are of a range of signifiers from different periods in postwar history. Furthermore, Shemeikka has now become a city-based Lothario, and the city is depicted as a haven of sin – something that provides an entirely new thematic twist to this tale.

Another example of an analogical adaptation is Neil Hardwick's musical comedy *Jos rakastat/If You Love* (2010). The topics of adaptation in the film are both well-known Finnish pop and rock songs and Sakari Topelius' fairy tale 'Adalmiina's Pearl' (published originally in *Läsning för barn*, 1865–96). The film is set in contemporary Finland, where multiculturalism is an increasingly vital part of the society. The protagonist of the film has been changed from Princess Adalmiina to a minister's daughter, Ada (Elli Vallinoja), who falls in love with the dark-skinned Toni (Chikwe Ohanwe). The process of adaptation changes the original material to make a politicized contribution to contemporary societal debates on multiculturalism. This is especially evident in the adaptation of Eppu Normaali's 'Joka päivä ja joka ikinen yö', a song which has established itself as a well-known part of contemporary shared national culture. Hardwick's film makes a pointed comment on what this shared culture means in contemporary Finland as the topic of longing is now Toni, and the background dancers create a collage of the ethnic diversity of Finnish society. Here, the intertextual connotations of the adaptation are one of the ways in which the film envisions new ways to depict the process of cultural change and the problematic questions of race and ethnicity in the globalized world without resorting to simplistic caricatures or stereotypes, or demeaning the existing differences between diverse cultural groups.

The division of the methods of adaptation into these aforementioned three groups does not mean that all adaptations follow the same logic. The striving for absolute faithfulness and seeking mere inspiration in the original are total opposites, and most adaptations fall somewhere in between. In addition, it is very important to remember that adaptations consist of a range of different source texts beyond the fictional works. For example, the past few years, have seen adaptations of non-fiction works such as *Rööperi/Hellsinki* (Mäkelä, 2009). This crime epic is based on Harri Nykänen and Tom Sjöberg's interview-based work *Rööperi. Rikoksen vuodet 1955–2005* (2005). Other example is *Putoavia enkeleitä/Falling Angels* (Kujanpää, 2008), which adapts two different types of source texts: the first is Aila Meriluoto's biographical work on her husband, *Lauri Viita – Legenda jo eläessään/Lauri Viita – A Legend in His Own Time* (1988); the second is Harri Kujanpää's theatrical play of the same name.

Adaptations have also been made out of several collective works, with examples such as Olli Saarela's war film *Rukajärven tie/Ambush* (1999), based on a series of novels by Antti Tuuri and Päätalo, which combines autobiographical elements from several of the author's works. This is an especially common method in children's films which are often based on novel series. Both *Uppo-Nalle* (Rusto, 1991) and *Urpo & Turpo* (Rimminen, 1996) as well as the more recent hit films *Heinähattu ja Vilttitossu/Hayflower and Quiltshoe* (Rastimo, 2002) and the *Risto Räppääjä* series (Rantasila, 2008–12) have been adapted from the popular children's novels. A recent popular culture phenomenon is the adaptation of single novels of a long-running series based on fictional detective characters. Solar Films' adaptations of Reijo Mäki's downbeat Vares character have to date provided material for five theatrical films (2004–11), all of which have been extremely popular at the domestic box office. Another recent phenomenon is the adaptation of entertainment based 'women's romantic novels', which have met with substantial enthusiasm by audiences. Adaptations of material such as Katja Kallio's *Kuutamolla/Lovers & Leavers* (Louhimies, 2002) and Kata Kärkkäinen's *Minä ja Morrison/Me and Morrison* (Hellstedt, 2001) tell us of important changes in popular Finnish culture and the central role played by female audiences. In contrast to these more conventional tales, novels such as Anja Kauranen's *Pelon maantiede/The Geography of Fear* (1995) (and its film adaptation by Auli Mantila, 2000), provide a much more controversial version of explicitly feminist politics.

Films can also be based on poems and songs, which was a particularly popular form in the entertainment and ballad films of the 1950s, or on comics as Pekka Puupää films in the 1950s, and short stories, novel extracts or unpublished prose manuscripts: Matti Ijäs' *Räpsy & Dolly/Dolly and Her Lover* (1991) is grounded on an excerpt from the only novel written by a Finnish poet Arto Melleri; Minna Virtanen's *Levottomat 3/Addiction* (2004) is said to be based on an unpublished short story written by a Finnish feminist detective story author Leena Lehtolainen; and *Paha maa/Frozen Land* (2005), directed by Aku Louhimies, has made use of the Russian realist Leo Tolstoy's short story. Furthermore, a typical contemporary form of adaptation is built on a humorous character born first on television: Uuno Turhapuro is the best known and the most long-lived manifestation of this type, and others, such as the Kummeli group, have continued this tradition in contemporary media culture. All in all many popular contemporary films – as well as bestseller books – are nowadays often multi-layered media phenomena, and it may be difficult or counterproductive to attempt to name the original version that enabled the breakthrough. Besides, the phenomenon is not new – even Aleksis Kivi's *The Seven Brothers* (1873) and Armas J. Pulla's *Ryhmy and Romppainen* (1940–1967) have lived their lives both in novels, on stage, on performance tours, in films and on the radio.

However, one can certainly say that some forms of multimediated productions have become more common and more systemized, especially in the last two decades. The majority of Finnish full-length films receive funding partly from television, and almost as many times a separate, longer version of the film is made for television distribution. What is more, certain contemporary authors such as Kari Hotakainen and Hannu Raittila have even been rebuked for writing novels that resemble ready-made theatre scripts or screenplays. Multimediality is also a part of the widened life-cycle of a book, especially if it has become a bestseller as popularity in one medium has selling potential in other mediums as well. Thus, great successes such as Kari Hotakainen's *Juoksuhaudantie/Trench Road* (2002) and Sofi Oksanen's *Puhdistus/Purge* (2008) find their way faster and faster both to the radio, the stage and screens. Adaptations from literature to film strengthen the cultural status of both the literary works and the films. These examples are important reminders that literature adaptations unavoidably take part in the ongoing redefinition of national culture and the historical past, even though they may use new methods to do so: *Trench Road* by depicting its protagonist's obsession with a certain wartime ideal of masculinity; *Purge* by reflecting the subjugation of women with the historical status of neighbouring Estonia – a country that, unlike Finland, lost its independence during WWII and only regained it with the Soviet Union's final dissolution in 1991.

By Sanna Karkulehto, Kimmo Laine and Pietari Kääpä

Juha

Production company:
Aho & Soldan

Distributor:
Adams Filmi

Director:
Nyrki Tapiovaara

Producer:
Heikki Aho

Screenwriters:
Heikki Aho
Björn Soldan
Nyrki Tapiovaara, based on the
novel by Juhani Aho

Art director:
Hannes Närhi

Cinematographers:
Björn Soldan
Olavi Gunnari

Composer:
Helvi Leviskä

Editors:
Heikki Aho
Björn Soldan

Duration:
101 minutes

Cast:
Hannes Närhi
Wille Saikko
Tuulikki Paananen
Aino Haverinen
Ida Kuusela
Irma Seikkula

Year:
1937

Synopsis

An isolated croft in eastern Finland in the distant past. An older man, Juha (Närhi), who does not speak much but works hard, has married orphan Marja (Seikkula) despite his mother's wishes. One day Shemeikka (Saikko), a travelling tradesman from further east, from Karelia, arrives. With eloquent presents and smooth talk, he woos Marja and finally takes her by his boat towards Karelia. They stop on their way and make love. Near home, Shemeikka leaves Marja in a fishermen's lodge, which he visits occasionally. His previous conquests are now maids in his house and the same fate awaits her too. Shemeikka's mother gives Marja permission to return, but she has to leave her child behind. Marja returns, Juha takes her back, and after finding out that she has a child, they go together to claim the baby. Juha almost kills Shemeikka, but when he finds out that Marja had voluntarily left him for Shemeikka, he lets the river take him to his death.

Critique

Juhani Aho's novel *Juha* was published in 1911 and proved its cinematic adaptability almost instantly. The first adaptation of the novel was made in 1921 by the Swede Mauritz Stiller. After Nyrki Tapiovaara's adaptation in 1937, the novel has been filmed twice. T.J. Särkkä produced a studio era *Juha* in cinemascope and colour in 1956, and Aki Kaurismäki directed his 'revisionist' take as a silent black-and-white film in 1998.

Juha was Nyrki Tapiovaara's debut feature, which was offered to him by Juhani Aho's sons, Heikki Aho and Björn Soldan. They had a production company, Aho & Soldan, which had previously focused on documentaries and photography inspired by Bauhaus stylistics, an influence which can also be found in the poetic visual style of *Juha*. Tapiovaara, only 25-years-old when *Juha* was made, directs with a firm hand and a clear aesthetic vision. Aho's book is determinately translated into the visual language of cinema. The dialogue is reduced to a bare minimum, and the film is narrated poetically using visual symbolism of the natural environment.

Juha and Marja live in harsh conditions in the remote eastern parts of Finland in an undefined distant past. Juha tames the nature by cutting down woods and carrying heavy stones from his fields. Putting the nets on the tranquil lake in the evening is his way of relaxation, which brings food to the table as well. Juha is a person who adapts quietly to the demands of his surroundings as well as to a loveless marriage and the nagging of his monstrous mother who occasionally visits them.

Shemeikka is the polar opposite of Juha. He is a talkative tradesman always on the move and the film associates him with quick physicality and the wild rapids. Instead of Juha's solitary environment, Shemeikka's home is a lively meeting place for his male friends and his ex-girls, now maids in the farm run by his mother. It is easy for Marja, already unhappily married with an older man, to fall for this exotic stranger. The transitory scene involving Shem-eikka rowing his conquest towards Karelia allows the film to attain an almost fantastical touch in the vein of Charles Laughton's later *Night of the Hunter* (1955). The camera points to the top of the trees, picks glimpses of sunlight and follows the waters' play slowly. It captures the moment of unrestrained freedom experienced by Marja for the first time in her life. Besides using nature for poetic effects and as a reflection of the characters' emotions, *Juha* also obeys nature's cyclical time. The film begins in the summer, Marja spends the autumn and winter in Karelia and she returns back to Juha for the spring. In the final scene, strong spring currents at the rapids swallow Juha.

   Juha was difficult to make in the harsh conditions in northern Finland. In addition, a fire in the post-production phase destroyed some of the negatives. Thus, the sound and picture quality of the existing prints varies and in some cases does not even meet the standards of mid-1930s.

Pasi Nyyssönen

The Song of the Scarlet Flower

Laulu tulipunaisesta kukasta

Production company:
Teuvo Tulio

Distributor:
Suomi-Filmi

Director:
Teuvo Tulio

Screenwriters:
Yrjö Kivimies, based on the novel by Johannes Linnankoski

Art director:
Kosti Aaltonen

Cinematographer:
Fred Runeberg

Composer:
Toivo Lampén

Editor:
Teuvo Tulio

Synopsis

The Song of the Scarlet Flower follows Olavi (Oksanen), the son of a prosperous landowner, whose sense of entitlement leaves him to abandon the women in his life without hesitation. His first love, Annikki (Kuosmanen), pushes aside his sexual advances, but Olavi soon sets his targets on his next love, Elli (Mäkinen). She, however, does not meet his parents' approval and Olavi is driven out of his home by his father. Soon making a living as a lumberjack, Olavi turns lustily towards a local brunette peasant (Birgit Nuotio), whom he abandons at the culmination of the logging season. He soon returns home and falls for the fair-headed Pihlajanterttu (Ranius) before discovering that she is married. Kyllikki (Linnanheimo), a warm-hearted daughter of a wealthy farmer, provides Olavi a chance to settle down. Olavi's confession of his past liaisons and admittance of jealousy of Kyllikki's stability unravel the inner turmoil with which Olavi must wrestle before being able to accept his past and move on with Kyllikki. Winning over the approval of Kyllikki's father (Veikko Linna), the film concludes as Olavi becomes a father, signalling a new future for Olavi and his wife.

Critique

The popular novel by Johannes Linnankoski, written in 1905 and based largely on his experiences as a lumberjack, has been produced twice for cinema in Sweden, with Mauritz Stiller's 1919 adaptation especially influential for the development of Finnish cinema as well as the 1938 Finnish version. The social themes that drench the novel reflect many of the social ills Linnankoski found in the lumber industry; a suggestion given further credence by the author's work

Duration:

110 minutes

Cast:

Kaarlo Oksanen
Rakel Linnanheimo
Mirjami Kuosmanen
Maire Ranius
Nora Mäkinen

Year:

1938

for a reformist newspaper and his active defence of women's rights. It can be interpreted as a bourgeois romp, where the disparity between Olavi's chance at redemption and the fates of his many lovers becomes the crucible of the film's themes. The Finnish master of melodrama Teuvo Tulio made his name directing 'fallen women' pictures, a genre that went out of style in the 1950s, and his approaches makes a perfect pairing with Linnankoski's social themes. Olavi's role as a log runner serves as a metaphor for the social relations that construct the thematic crux of the film. Olavi is a free spirit with little desire to settle down. He doesn't contemplate the result of his actions, and is much like the flowing river in service to his profession: Olavi does not only break up log jams, but also the hearts of the women he conquers.

Tulio's film is widely renowned for its cinematography, which takes advantage of the natural beauty of its locations. Tulio uses the patterns of nature in a range of ways: for example, a change in weather cues the film's dramatic turning point. The film's moral ponderings are enhanced by the expressionistic camerawork that unsettles and reflects the characters imbalanced way of life. Yet, all its artistic skill at rendering Finnish landscape scenery serves to highlight the disparity between Olavi and the women of his life. A characteristic exchange that highlights Tulio's melodrama and its social message is when Olavi re-encounters Elli, whom he would have married were it not for his parents' disapproval. She had been resistant to Olavi's sexual advances, but did not hold to her principles as shrewdly as his first love Annikki. When Olavi first realizes that Elli is now a 'common whore', a career choice necessitated when Olavi abandoned her, Olavi is shocked. Elli puts the final moral nail in the coffin, referring to her state by announcing to Olavi, 'Here I am, just the way you wanted me'. Elli's directness is shocking and the moral message is clear to Olavi: from now on, he needs to be responsible for how his actions may affect others. While Olavi's role may be clear, Tulio's argument is more subversive. The film highlights women's limited choices and how their future is often dictated by the men with whom they choose to keep company; a reality which puts greater social responsibility on men for the role they've malignantly created for women. The message fits within the biographical framework of Tulio's melodramas as well as the original source novel by Linnankoski. Inspired in part by Eisensteinian montage editing, but also enthusiastic in its mimicry of Hollywood conventions, Tulio's film highlights the social position of Finnish women and encourages social change that would bring greater respect and rights for them. Simultaneously, it is a dynamic summary of Tulio's own melodramatic focus on disparaged women.

John Saari

The Vagabond's Waltz

Kulkurin valssi

Production company:
Suomen Filmiteollisuus

Distributor:
Suomen Filmiteollisuus

Director:
T.J. Särkkä

Producer:
T.J. Särkkä

Screenwriter:
Mika Waltari

Art director:
Hannu Leminen

Cinematographer:
Felix Forsman

Composer:
George de Godzinsky

Editor:
Armas Vallasvuo

Duration:
104 minutes

Cast:
Tauno Palo
Ansa Ikonen
Elsa Rantalainen
Ida Appelberg

Year:
1941

Synopsis

Count Arnold (Palo) gets embroiled in a duel over a woman in Russia and has to leave the country to escape the authorities. As he is originally from Finland, he decides to flee to this autonomous region. On the way, he falls in with a band of circus entertainers and a group of gypsies. In both the camps, Arnold charms the women of the groups and gets into trouble with their leaders. Finally, he ends up in a mansion in Finland where he woos Helena (Ikonen), the daughter of the mansion. Arnold pretends to be a vagabond and thus gets into trouble with Eric (Jorma Nortimo), the fiancé; Helena refuses to marry either of them, but soon she falls for the count. Complications arise as she catches Arnold with the maid and she decides to marry Eric. Arnold recruits his gypsy and circus troops and rides to her rescue. Soon, all parties discover that he is of noble blood and the film ends with the declaration of love from his mother and the kiss of the couple.

Critique

The Vagabond's Waltz is one of the most important films completed during the cessation period between the Winter War and the Continuation War. Inspired by the hit song of the same title, the head of Suomen Filmiteollisuus T.J. Särkkä hired novelist Mika Waltari to adapt the story to the screen. The result was what many describe as the ultimate escapist romantic film, a perfect way of avoiding the daily, dark realities of the era. Two of the biggest stars of the period, Tauno Palo and Ansa Ikonen, were the ideal pair to capture the passionate romance of the story. They also contributed their musical voices to create a package of supreme entertainment. As audiences were in need of escapism, this story was exactly what the struggling film industry needed. Almost 1.5 million Finns went to see the film during the war, and it has endured as one of the cornerstones of popular Finnish cinema. Even critics were largely fond of the film and paid attention to its success in creating its fantastical world and providing entertainment. It paved the way for the massive domestic re-emergence of cinema as a real and viable force to entertain the nation. For example, on its television broadcast in 1981 it reached half the population of Finland (approximately 2.5 million people).

While some of the contemporary critics interpreted the film as nothing more than mere entertainment aimed to alleviate the pain and trauma of the Winter War, there are still many interesting ideological themes in the film. *The Vagabond's Waltz* has endured as a vital research topic as it captures many of the prevalent tendencies of the time, as well as communicating a snapshot of idealistic patriotic Finnishness. Harkening back to an unspecified time in the 1800s, the film constructs a fantasized but nostalgic image of the past. Yet, its focus on class differences gives away some of the contemporary concerns over class identity as the typical narrative of the prince in disguise allows the film to strengthen its fairytale tropes. Similarly, the awkward and lingering unease with the neighbouring Soviet Union is reflected in the narrative. Not only is Count Arnold's nemesis in Russia, Lord Avertsejev (Uno Wikström), depicted as an aggressive scoundrel, but Arnold makes it very clear that he considers the Russians inferior and has no need for their 'dirty' money. As with many of the similar entertainment films of the period such as Risto Orko's *Jääkärin morsian/Soldier's Bride* (1938), the propagandistic elements are conveyed in the manner of entertainment. It is this combination of spectacle, nationalist sentiment, vilification of the enemies, and loyalty to the traditions of musical epic narratives that makes the product appealing. Särkkä's film has become a true classic of Finnish cinema as it touches on many of the well-known themes of the rural adventures and the class-based plots so common in the pre-war cinema. It is not only a reflection of contemporary mores, but a trendsetter for the next decades of Finnish cinema.

Pietari Kääpä

Cross of Love

Rakkauden risti

Production company:
Tuxan Film

Distributor:
Väinän Filmi

Director:
Teuvo Tulio

Producer:
Teuvo Tulio

Screenwriters:
Filmimies (a pseudonym of Nisse Hirn), based on Alexander Pushkin's 'Stationmaster' (1831)

Art Director:
Kosti Aaltonen

Cinematographers:
Uno Philström
Pentti Lintonen

Composer:
Tauno Marttinen

Editor:
Teuvo Tulio

Synopsis

Riitta (Linnanheimo) has lived all her life on a small island with her father (Tengström), a lighthouse keeper. A storm washes a castaway, a consul (Salminen), to the shore. He soon sets his sights on Riitta who longs to see the world outside the island, especially as the consul offers to show her the sights of the city. She stays the night at the consul's place, where he rapes her. Dishonoured, Riitta cannot return home and sinks into prostitution. An idealistic artist (Tuomi) sees Riitta and wants her to model for his painting 'Cross of Love'. They become lovers and intend to marry. The arrival of Riitta's suspicious father, however, reunites Riitta and the consul, who in turn arranges a fake wedding with Riitta and himself. Riitta's glad father attends the wedding and returns home. But Riitta's real fiancé accidentally finds out about her past and furiously abandons her, leading her to stay with the consul and eventually shoot herself.

Critique

Latvian-born Teuvo Tulio (originally Theodor Tugai) is one of the few masters of melodrama in Finnish cinema. Before the war, until the 1940s, his films took place in the countryside and revealed the tensions beneath the surface of the idyllic agrarian environment. After the war, Tulio's fierce rural melodramas were relocated to the urban environment, which allowed them to stress the opposition between the countryside and the city. The former is seen as an idealistic *topos* of black and white morality, while the later is a place of sin, which is especially corrupting to women who are usually driven to prostitution.

In *Cross of Love*, Tulio elaborates on the thematic concerns he established with *Sellaisena kuin sinä minut halusit/The Way You*

Runtime:

99 minutes

Cast:

Regina Linnanheimo
Oscar Tengström
Ville Salminen
Rauli Tuomi
Pentti Viljanen
Senja Soitso

Year:

1946

Wanted Me (1944). Both are stories of a young girl from a small seaside community. She is forced (*The Way You Wanted Me*) or she goes voluntarily (*Cross of Love*) to the city where her morality is decayed in the blink of an eye, and she ends up selling herself in the harbour, the smoky bars and the dark streets. The fallen girl in *Cross of Love*, Riitta, pines for the anonymous city just like her 'hot-blooded' mother who has left and never returned. Tulio shows Riitta as a typical paradigmatic character of the melodrama, a victim-hero woman whose victimisation is doubled. She is, first of all, a victim of men. For the vicious consul Riitta is just another innocent conquest as the photo collection of his previous women proves. The tragic night at his home drives her into prostitution and Riitta, who has believed in goodness, becomes a tragic hero. Familial and moral obligation towards her father is another form of victimization facing Riitta. She loves her father, but suffers from not being able to fulfil his demands. The father's domination over her is established firmly in the early parts of film. Indeed, the symbolic implications of the recurring images of the erect lighthouse are rather obvious.

Cross of Love, as almost all of Tulio's films, can be criticised for sensationalism, overacting, repetition of key scenes, use of the same overdramatic music, stock images and borrowed material from his own and other's films. However, the narrative consistency and logic is a secondary aspect in *Cross of Love* as in other works by Tulio. Instead, he strives for maximum emotional impact with every means available. Instrumental in conveying its messages is the flashback narrative structure employed throughout *Cross of Love*. It begins dramatically in a dark and stormy night when old lighthouse keeper Kalle tries to shoot a castaway washed on the island's stony shore. His younger colleague saves the poor man and tells him the story of Kalle, who always loses his mind when the storm hits the island. The rest of the film tells the tragedy that has caused his insanity. Finally, the epilogue shows Kalle on his daily visit to Riitta's grave wishing soon to be joined with his daughter again. Tulio directs and edits with pure creative instinct making almost surreal connections between people and visual tropes, usually with obvious erotic associations. *Cross of Love* started the intensive ten-year collaboration between Tulio and actress Regina Linnanheimo who plays Riitta. Her captivating eyes and increasingly more mature manic intensity matched perfectly with Tulio's strive for melodramatic excess.

Pasi Nyyssönen

People in the Summer Night

Ihmiset suviyössä

Production company:
Suomi-Filmi Oy

Distributor:
Suomi-Filmi Oy

Director:
Valentin Vaala

Producer:
Risto Orko

Screenwriters:
Lea Joutseno
Valentin Vaala, based on the
novel by F. E. Sillanpää

Art director:
Ville Hänninen

Cinematographer:
Eino Heino

Composer:
Taneli Kuusisto

Editor:
Valentin Vaala

Duration:
66 minutes

Cast:
Eila Pehkonen
Martti Katajisto
Emma Väänänen
Eero Roine
Matti Oravisto

Year:
1948

Synopsis

People in the Summer Night intertwines four stories and several perspectives to depict one summer day and night in the idyllic Finnish countryside just before the harvest time. A husband tries to find a midwife or a doctor for her wife who is in labour; a young couple falls in love; and a man violently dies after heavy drinking and fighting. Although the film deals with questions of life and death, the topics are not the main focus of the film. Instead, the Finnish nature comes to play the leading role in the film.

Critique

People in the Summer Night is based on a novel written by Nobel laureate F. E. Sillanpää. Appropriately for a story taking place on one night in Finnish countryside, there is only one real protagonist in the story – the summer night as Sillanpää himself has characterized it. However, the title of the novel and the film emphasizes people for a reason. The story is not only a thorough examination of nature, but also human nature and the course of human life. The story is based on basic elements of human life, including birth and death, as well as strong emotions and passions such as love and hate; crime and punishment also play a role, not to mention the Finnish 'elixir of life' – alcohol.

Both the novel and the film create an idyllic, Finnish rural utopia where even hard alcohol consumption and homicide are framed in glamorous ways. The novel was written in 1934; in other words, many years after the Civil War (1918), as people began to have faith in national ideals again, and the forthcoming horrors of the Second World War were still a distant and unimaginable threat. Valentin Vaala's *People in the Summer Night*, for its part, premiered in 1948, four years after the end of the Continuation War, when depressed, disappointed and disillusioned Finns needed new hope in a better future, as well as the type of collective comfort that national cinema could offer.

Vaala's version of *People in the Summer Night* is surprisingly loyal to Sillanpää's original novel. The narrator's leisurely, poetic and occasionally extremely detailed depictions of the environment, especially of nature, have influenced the camerawork as the camera is allowed to freely and calmly capture the national romantic atmosphere of the bloomy fields, delicate flowers, sturdy trees, silvery lakes and the clear sky that stays bright even at night in as northern a country as Finland.

There are four parallel storylines in the film. Firstly, in the Syrjämäki farm, the always energetic mistress Hilja (Väänänen) finalizes the farm work for the day before getting ready for the imminent childbirth. Hilja's sluggish husband Jalmari (Roine) is sent to find a midwife from the village. Meanwhile, the bold and beautiful Arvid (Oravisto) arrives at the Teliranta manor where he meets the similarly bold and beautiful Helka (Pehkonen). The couple gets to know each other better, and while admiring the summer night together their mutual admiration gradually extends and they fall in love. Simultaneously, a group of drinking men is hosted by Santra (Kaisu Leppänen) at the Mettälä croft, who awaits her drunken lumberjack husband to come home. As the husband never arrives, Santra enjoys the comfort and affection she receives from one of the patrons. Finally, young and restless lumberjack Nokia (Katajisto) lethally stabs Santra's drunken husband Jukka (Matti Lehtelä) after a fight caused primarily by alcohol. During the night, Nokia's frantic defiance and pretension transform into almost as fierce remorse and despair. The dawn brings forth the inescapable punishment.

People in the Summer Night occupies one of the key roles in Finnish film history. First of all, this film, directed by the productive Vaala, is a representative of the successful years of the Suomi-Filmi production company. For example, it received half of the Jussi Awards given out by the Finnish film industry in 1949. From the perspective of its critical success it is intriguing to note that it represents female characters as active, independent, highly capable and upright subjects, whereas many of the men are either inefficient or uncontrollable creatures driven by their passions – a characteristic traditionally reserved for women. In addition, Nokia's passionate character is said to be the first homosexual representation in the Finnish film industry. Even if Nokia's anxiousness and distress, as well as his relation to death and punishment, hit relatively well-known stereotypes of closeted homosexuality, and the possibilities for political agency are still limited for the women characters, one can say that the film reveals considerable ambiguity and diversity in its representations of gender and sexuality. It is noteworthy that this happens at a time in film history that has often been criticized for its purely masculinist and heteronormative bias.

Sanna Karkulehto

The Niskavuori Saga

Niskavuoren naiset/Women of Niskavuori

(dir. Valentin Vaala, 1938)

Loviisa – Niskavuoren Nuori Emäntä/Louisa

(dir. Valentin Vaala, 1946)

Niskavuoren Heta/Heta from Niskavuori

(dir. Edvin Laine, 1952)

Niskavuoren Aarne/Aarne from Niskavuori

(dir. Edvin Laine, 1954)

Synopsis

The *Niskavuori* saga tells the epic tale of the battles over the Niskavuori estate through the end of the nineteenth century and first half of the twentieth century. It begins with the marriage of Loviisa to Juhani, who is a womanizing and unreliable character. From a kind and naïve girl emerges a strong and stern matriarch, and a key theme of the saga – that of the trials and tribulations of strong women. Loviisa's daughter Heta has been forced into marriage with Akusti, whom she perceives to be of a lower class. Aarne, the son of the family, is married to strict Martta. Yet, Aarne falls in love with local school teacher Ilona and struggles with his sense of loyalty to his family. Ultimately, he makes the decision to elope with Ilona to the big city and leave the mansion to the women. The next instalment in the saga sees Aarne making only occasionally secretive visits to the mansion. Meanwhile, Loviisa is increasingly agitated as the now-divorced Martta rules the mansion in an even stricter manner than her. She is also having an affair

**Niskavuori taistelee/
Niskavuori's Battles**

(dir. Edvin Laine, 1957)

**Niskavuoren naiset/Women of
Niskavuori**

(dir. Valentin Vaala, 1958)

Niskavuori

(dir. Matti Kassila, 1984)

with the estates head and has been made pregnant by him, yet
she considers him ineligible for marriage due to his lower-class
status. Loviisa conspires to reinstate Aarne as the head of family
and entices him back to the farm. Complicated negotiations ensue
to oust Martta from the farm. Eventually, Aarne gains back his farm
and Ilona takes the seat of the matriarch at the head of the table.
The final instalment of the saga, *Niskavuori's Battles* chronicles the
events of Juhani returning to the farm. The year is 1944 and the
war has taken most men to the front. He is an illegitimate son of
Loviisa's deceased husband and the maid Malviina, so Juhani's existence is kept secret. Yet, nothing stays concealed too long in this
world and Juhani's heritage is soon revealed. The once great estate
is left for Juhani and Ilona and finally, in the postwar era, son Paavo
inherits the remains of a diminished estate.

Critique

The *Niskavuori* saga originated in plays by novelist Hella Wuolijoki,
initially under a male pseudonym. The historical scope of the
plays spans more than half a century, as do the production of
their cinematic incarnations. They thus provide exemplary material to explore the development of Finnish culture through crucial
periods in its history. They also provide substantial contributions
to both gender and class politics as they focus on the wealthy
landowner family and its strong female protagonists who dominate
the house. A strong sense of a changing gender order permeates
both Wuolijoki's plays (published between 1936 and 1953) and the
films (from 1938 to 1984). Certainly, some of the saga's narrative
reflects the wartime demands placed on women as they were to
take over the roles of farmhands whilst the men were engaged
at the front. While the focus on strong female characters is a vital
part of the enduring legacy of the plays and the films, there are
also some more problematic aspects to these matriarchs who are
often depicted in stereotypical terms as *pirttihirmus* (a matriarch
of an excessively domineering nature). Similarly, many of the other
female characters are depicted as gossipers or floosies, and do
not leave much room for more stable depictions of femininity. This
somewhat reductive characterization is perhaps a consequence of
their abidance with conventions of the rural melodrama, a genre
that dominated Finnish cinema through the golden age of the
studio system.

Simultaneously revolutionary in their gender politics while resorting to some of the worst stereotyping, gender considerations in
the *Niskavuori* saga allow us to unravel the narrative depictions of
social order and class politics. They emphasize the value of rural
labour and the need to maintain the strict order of a matriarchal
society where most men fracture the protestant work ethic by
being restless creatures of impulse. This authoritarian suggestion is
consistently questioned through the hardships the women endure.
While the women may be depicted in excessively austere terms,
it is made clear that such authoritarian measures are necessary for
social order. Yet, even this authoritarianism is compromised as the

women are still bound by the rules of the society and its patriarchal norms (ownership of the estate is consistently passed down from male heir to male heir). Tytti Soila and Anu Koivunen suggest the key conflict of the narratives concerns the fulfilment of one's duties and the sacrifice of one's own happiness, which underlies the hard exteriors and the difficult choices the matriarchs are forced to make. Thus, the story is once more the narrative of female hardships – a notion which persists in the rural melodrama up to the contemporary present. Furthermore, land ownership and the need to retain control over one's estate contrasts with human fallibility and builds another thematic paradox of the saga. Private property is the essence for what the protagonist fight, but it is ultimately those that desire capital the most that fare the worst and suffer the most in terms of human loss.

The *Niskavuori* saga is in many ways a canonical exploration of the national psyche. The relationship between the natural environment and the national character is constructed through the lengthy shots of landscapes and labour. Mirroring one in the other, the natural environment embodies the hard but vital task of nation-building, which we see in *Heta from Niskavuori* (1952) and its distinctly cinematic attempt at national reconstruction in the postwar context. Similarly, Laine's final *Niskavuori* transforms the back story of the son's crime from being a member of the *käpykaarti* (a leftist faction during the Continuation War) to a more politically innocuous rebellion at the authorities' treatment of war casualties. This form of consolidation is a typical postwar strategy conducted in popular culture to create a sense of national cohesiveness.

These strategies have persisted until the 1980s, when the *Niskavuori* saga was once more unearthed to assure a population reeling from the still-ongoing Great Migration. The depletion of the rural ways of life is keenly felt in Matti Kassila's adaptation of the (chronologically in terms of narrative) third and the fourth play into *Niskavuori* in 1984. The 'reimagining' was part of a heritage boom in the early 1980s cinema as several film-makers re-engaged with rural stories for the post-Great Migration audience. While not quite as revisionist as Mika Kaurismäki's 'anti-heritage' *Klaani/ The Clan – Tale of the Frogs* (1984), Kassila's film is a much grittier examination of rural life than its predecessors. In fact, its approach is closer to Mikko Niskanen's adaptations of Kalle Päätalo's novels such as *Nuoruuteni savotat/Lumberjacking* (1988) in their examination of the hardships of rural life. The rest of the saga was adapted for television in the late 1980s and, in combination with the 1984 cinema release, comprises a reinterpretation of the *Niskavuori* cycle for the contemporary period. The saga thus persists as a cornerstone of Finnish culture, providing an invaluable archive to understand gender and class relations throughout the decades. They are also a significant barometer for wider conceptualizations of Finnish national identity in cinema. Yet, the saga does not end there. Juha Wuolijoki produced a film on his great-great aunt Hella Wuolijoki, the author of the original *Niskavuori* plays, titled *Hella W*, which was released in early 2011. The reviews for the film have been mixed, but most of the critics focus on the centrality of its strong female protagonist. Appropriately then, in contrast to the 'great man' pictures that dominate much of Finnish cinema, *Hella W* continues the narrative of the 'great woman' that the *Niskavuori* saga has sustained throughout Finnish cinema history.

Pietari Kääpä

Reference

Koivunen, Anu (2007), 'Niskavuoren Heta', in Tytti Soila (ed.), *The Cinema of Scandinavia*, London: Wallflower Press, pp.119–29.

Here, Beneath the North Star (aka Under the North Star)

Täällä, Pohjantähden alla

Production companies:
Yleisradio (YLE)
Fennada Film

Distributors:
Adams Filmi
Fenno-Filmi

Director:
Edvin Laine

Producer:
Mauno Mäkelä

Screenwriters:
Edvin Laine
Juha Nevalainen
Matti Kassila
Väinö Linna (based on his novel)

Art directors:
Ensio Suominen
Jukka Salomaa

Cinematographer:
Olavi Tuomi

Composer:
Heikki Aaltoila

Synopsis

'In the beginning, there was the swamp, the hoe – and Jussi'. So starts the canonical novel by Väinö Linna, which tells the history of Finland from 1880s to the 1950s from the point of view of the residents of one village, Pentinkulma. Part 1 begins with Jussi, a tenant farmer of a vicarage, clearing marshland. It is the beginning of his croft, called Koskela, which becomes home for Jussi and his wife. Despite hardships, the croft grows and the family expands with three sons, Akseli, Aleksi and August. At the beginning of the twentieth century, socialist ideas gain popularity among the crofters who toil under the rule of landowners. Akseli, now married with Elina, becomes a key member of the movement. During the battles for Finland's independence, class differences escalate to a civil war in 1918. The war ends with the defeat of the Reds. Several socialists are executed, including Aleksi and August. Akseli is saved but sentenced to prison. After some years of incarceration he is pardoned and returns to Pentinkulma.

Part 2 continues with Akseli returning from prison and settling to a quiet life of farming with his wife and five children, while being under the surveillance of the authorities and meeting disdain from some of the villagers. At the end of the 1920s the rise of the right-wing movement is exemplified by the arrival of a new teacher to Pentinkulma. Socialists are kidnapped and beaten in the woods, and the upper-classes call for national uprising with the help of Germany. However, when the war against Soviet Union begins, political disagreements are forgotten and all men leave to the front. In the war, three of Akseli and Elina's sons are killed but life must go on.

Critique

Väinö Linna's novel trilogy *Here, Beneath the North Star* (1959–62) is one of the key works of Finnish literature, and holds a canonical position in national culture in general. The sheer length and the time span of the trilogy, from 1880 to the 1950s, poses substantial challenges to film-makers. The background of Linna's books

Editor:
Juho Gartz

Duration:
186 minutes

Cast:
Aarno Sulkanen
Titta Karakorpi
Risto Taulo
Anja Pohjola

Year:
1968

Akseli and Elina

Production company:
Fennada Film

Distributors:
Adams Filmi
Fenno-Filmi

Director:
Edvin Laine

Producer:
Mauno Mäkelä

Screenwriters:
Edvin Laine
Juha Nevalainen
Juho Gartz
Georg Korkman, based on the
novel by Väinö Linna

Art director:
Ensio Suominen

Cinematographer:
Olavi Tuomi

Composer:
Heikki Aaltoila

Editor:
Juho Gartz

Duration:
137 minutes

Cast:
Aarno Sulkanen

concerns crucial events in recent Finnish history and they deal with difficult topics, including the persecution that erupted with the Red uprising, the hatred and mistrust sown by years of class oppression between people and families, the treatment of captured Reds by the death squads of the Whites and, finally, conflict with the invading Soviet Union which helped restore unity to the nation during WWII. The scars of the Civil War still persist, and the novel and the films are important for continuing public dialogue and memory work on it.

Linna's novel was commended upon publication for its focus on the Civil War from the perspective of its losers, the Reds. Whereas history is conventionally written by the winners, Linna's work provided an important alternative perspective on these conflicts. Crucially, it remains unbiased enough not to be mere socialist propaganda, but also to critically consider the actions of the Reds. Thus, the work is able to act as a locus for the Finnish population to reassess their past in the popular form. As with the film adaptation of Linna's *The Unknown Soldier* (1955), Edvin Laine would mould the work for the screen. He adapted the first two installations of the novel for the first part, released in 1968 and the third for *Akseli and Elina* which received its premiere in 1970. The first instalment was a huge success and remains one of the most popular films in Finnish cinema history. This was at a time when the domestic film industry was in crisis as the golden years of the studio era had come to a close, and the emergence of television into household status had decreased interest in theatrically-distributed fare. Laine's grand epic was brought to life with a sizeable budget and epic scope. As was the case with many of the Hollywood epics of the 1960s, it proved to be sufficiently spectacular and 'important' enough to draw the audiences back to the theatres.

Timo Koivusalo's adaptation of Linna's work in 2009 met with less unanimous appreciation. According to its critics, the adaptation was a professional and well-made film with due attention to historical veracity and national sentiment. Both ...*North Star* films are easy to criticize (as contemporary reviews have frequently done) especially concerning the common problem facing cinematic adaptations of literature: films are not able to reach the subtlety of the original text as they condense the narrative too heavily or just settle for illustrating the key themes and dramatic situations of the books. Laine's first film (1968) especially was criticized as an old-fashioned historical epic at time of its release when the Finnish New Wave was already in vogue. The most stiffening aspect is Laine's use of voice-over narration throughout his film. For example, the biblical beginning of Linna's trilogy – 'In the beginning there was the marsh, the hoe – and Jussi' – is in Laine's film version presented both visually and in the narrator's words. For most of his film, however, Laine puts his experience in the theatre in good use with his actors who manage to create memorable characters using vivid language. In his recent adaptation, Koivusalo (2010) has dropped the narrator, as Laine did also in his second part *Akseli and Elina*.

Ulla Eklund
Risto Taulo
Anja Pohjola

Year:
1970

Here, Beneath the North Star

Täällä Pohjantähden alla

Production companies:
Artista Filmi Oy, Yleisradio (YLE)

Distributor:
Walt Disney Studios Motion Pictures Finland

Director:
Timo Koivusalo

Producer:
Timo Koivusalo

Screenwriters:
Timo Koivusalo, based on the novel by Väinö Linna

Art director:
Markku Myllymäki

Cinematographer:
Pertti Mutanen

Composer:
Jaakko Kuusisto

Editors:
Jyrki Luukko
Timo Koivusalo

Duration:
193 minutes

Cast:
Ilkka Koivula
Vera Kiiskinen
Risto Tuorila
Ritva Jalonen

Year:
2009

Koivusalo's version was criticized for its close resemblance not only to Linna's novel but also to Laine's adaptation, motivating many to question the reasoning behind another version of this canonical tale. Adapting a work of fiction is never an easy task, and providing a film which resembles a literal illustration of the novel was hardly sufficient for many of the critics. Koivusalo's version looks good enough, with handheld chaos for battles and a sweeping epic tapestry, yet it never rises above an almost shot-for-shot remake of the original or a theatrical restaging of the novel. The romantic scenes especially are hastily made and resemble kitsch versions of the old Finnish countryside dramas. It is also distracting to see the same actor (Ilkka Koivula) play Akseli Koskela from a teenager to an old man, especially as little effort is made to indicate the spanning fifty years on the actor's physique.

To fully understand the implications of the ...North Star adaptations in Finnish culture, we must also explore other depictions of the Civil War, which remains a contentious issue in Finnish cinema. Only recently producers have started to tackle the wounds of the topic in any sufficient numbers. Films such as Lauri Törhönen's Raja 1918/ The Border (2007) and Aku Louhimies' Käsky/Tears of April (2008) are some of the recent explorations of the topic, both with substantially different takes on representing the conflict. The former is more traditional in its approach to the conflict, featuring protagonists from both the Whites and the Reds, all conveyed in the traditional framework of epic historical cinema. Tears of April on the other hand prefers a more artistic and unconventional approach to depicting the conflict. As revisionist depictions of war, both films interrogate the ideological confusion on the side of the victors by featuring yagher lieutenants who come to question their role in the war and the justification of their cause. As with all versions of ... North Star, they argue that they do not take sides but reflect the realities of the circumstances by focusing on the war crimes committed by both sides. Yet, all of these narratives can be seen to fall on the side of the Reds – the ... North Star adaptations because of their focus on proletarian protagonists, and The Border and Tears of April due to the ways their White protagonists question their cause.

Simultaneously, Tears of April uses a range of subversive devices to undermine the traditional trajectory of depicting the Civil War. Most of the more traditional epic narratives focus on heterosexual romance as a way of instilling ideological conformity. In Tears of April, the lieutenant protagonist is enforced into a homosexual relationship with his commanding officer to save the Red female soldier with whom he is infatuated. While this is, of course, a 'sacrifice' problematically suggested as similar to giving one's life for a cause, in challenging the heterosexual normativity of epic war narratives it forces us to question our spectatorial role. This is especially relevant as heterosexual romance often functions as an ideological tool to ease viewers into watching and even accepting historical arguments. This is certainly the case with the other Civil War films as, even though they show the complex motivations behind the war, heterosexual relationships carry the emotional weight of the films. By challenging these norms, we are made to

Here, Beneath the North Star II (aka Under the North Star II)

Täällä Pohjantähden alla II

Production companies:
Artista Filmi Oy
Yleisradio (YLE)

Distributor:
Walt Disney Studios Motion
Pictures Finland

Director:
Timo Koivusalo

Producer:
Timo Koivusalo

Screenwriters:
Timo Koivusalo, based on the
novel by Väinö Linna

Art director:
Markku Myllymäki

Cinematographer:
Pertti Mutanen

Composer:
Jaakko Kuusisto

Editors:
Jyrki Luukko
Timo Koivusalo

Duration:
138 minutes

Cast:
Ilkka Koivula
Vera Kiiskinen
Risto Tuorila
Ritva Jalonen

Year:
2010

question ourselves as spectators of entertainment about a nation turning on itself.

The narrative of *Here, Beneath the North Star* also reconciles its conflicts through the Winter War – while it shows the conflicts that erupted within the nation, it enables the protagonists to forgive and coalesce in harmony. In contrast, the recent explorations of the Civil War leave this conflict more open. While historical facts support the coalescent effects of the Winter War, why do such resolutions disappear from *Tears of April* and other more recent films? One explanation may be the lack of external political pressure to unite against a common foe – during the production of Linna and Laine's work, Finland was still encased in the Cold War. But the more global context of twenty-first century enables critical assertion and reflection on the past in less ideologically obvious terms. But this, of course, makes it intriguing that Koivusalo's film does not provide any substantial alterations to the ideological content of the original text.

Indeed, Laine and Koivusalo's films share the same problem: utmost respect towards a literary classic and its cultural status, which leads to too faithful an adaptation of the written text. This lack of innovation is best illustrated by the outdated gender politics of both films. From a contemporary point of view, the absence of central roles for women is striking. Both adaptations strengthen a distinctly male-biased view of the world which, as many of the articles in this collection note, are a constant topic of concern in Finnish cinema. Women act as brides and wives tied to their homes, or ones with loose morals. The only active woman is the priest's strong-willed wife, who is portrayed in a negative light. She has a major influence on her husband's decisions, which often ends up being unfavourable to tenant farmers, and her actions are integrally tied to right-wing politics of the 1930s. This point of view is a remnant from Linna's books which the film-makers have not dared to touch or update to meet more egalitarian standards of their contexts of production. While altering the content of Linna's novel substantially would also be problematic, critics seem to agree that a measure of adaptation to meet contemporary standards is relevant. All in all, the diversity of interpretations of the Civil War showcases the ways in which national solidarity is an ongoing issue and a form of critical debate.

Pietari Kääpä and Pasi Nyyssönen

Plainlands

Pohjanmaa

Production company:
National Filmi Oy

Distributor:
Finnkino

Director:
Pekka Parikka

Producer:
Marko Röhr

Screenwriters:
Pekka Parikka, based on the novel by Antti Tuuri

Art director:
Pertti Hilkamo

Cinematographer:
Kari Sohlberg

Composer:
Antti Hytti

Editor:
Keijo Virtanen

Duration:
129 minutes

Cast:
Esko Salminen
Taneli Mäkelä
Esko Nikkari
Vesa Mäkelä

Year:
1988

Synopsis

Plainlands's narrative takes place on a fateful day in the lives of the Hakala family, who have gathered for the wake of their grandfather. The eldest son, Veikko (Salminen), has lost the family bindery in a corrupt deal and faces the imminent repossession of their farm. As the day progresses, feelings of frustration and anger build up, abetted by the consumption of increasing amounts of homebrewed alcohol, resulting in explosive and destructive consequences. The brothers are arrested for the possession of illegal firearms, resulting in the death of Veikko in his cell.

Critique

Plainlands continues the tradition of 'häjy-films', which focused on Ostrobothnian men, who have a negative reputation for alcohol-induced violence and knife-fighting. The image of these 'authentic Finns' is present throughout Finnish cinematic history in films such as *Pohjalaisia/The Bothnians* (Lahdensuo, 1925) and *Härmästä poikia kymmenen/Ten Boys From Härmä* (Unho, 1950), with a variety of genres devoted to Ostrobothnians, Härmä-ruffians, lumberjacks and folk heroes, reproducing a 'mythic Ostrobothnianism' (Toiviainen 2002: 248). Parikka's film updates the traditional Finnish character and the omnipresent agricultural theme into the context of late 1980s Finland, where the traditional rural way of life has lost most of its past significance as a means of livelihood, and has come to connote a bygone era.

Plainlands offers an update of the blissful representations of the pre-1960s rural films, metamorphosed through the grim angst of the politicized cinema of the 1960s and the 1970s. The traditional provider role of the male is threatened by the declining rural way of life, and this compensation and momentary escape is found in homebrewed alcohol. Themes such as uncertainty, male-centeredness, anger and drunkenness at their most destructive are explored in the film, while the female characters are sidelined to secondary roles as housewives and mothers. This continues a long line of obsession with 'the male odyssey' (Koivunen 2003), where women act as mere catalysts for the action. The women in *Plainlands* receive slightly more attention than these previous depictions as they act as an important backbone, a grounding in reality for the men's often juvenile escapades. The relationship between the genders is, somewhat ironically, encapsulated in the words of the brothers' mother: 'In Ostrobothnia, all wisdom lies in the old women – in the men lies insanity'.

The opening helicopter shot over the Ostrobothnian plains establishes not only the setting but also the tone of the film, creating an impression of the intertwined relationship of the people and the natural environment. The landscape of the plains takes on mythic connotations as a material signifier of the nation where it surrounds, reflects and provides a point of identification for the characters. Significantly, the landscape is not a fetishized, idyllic vision, but rather bleak and grey-toned, underscored by a string elegy, a tone which haunts the whole film. Man, nature and the contemporary social context are bound together in the character of Veikko Hakala. He represents a facsimile of the authentic Finn, embodying several of the stereotypical characteristics of the Finnish male – he is stubborn, stoic, prone to alcoholism and insanity, and last but not least, full of self-pity. *Plainlands'* denouement exemplifies the troubled state of the nation, where traditions are in danger of becoming extinct. As Veikko, the symbol of authenticity, collapses in his cell from a heart attack brought on by extreme drunkenness and physical exhaustion, the impression is of the passing of an era.

Plainlands, then, ties into contemporary concerns about the state of the nation, where the past is unravelling and the future looks even more uncertain. By positioning its approach as quintessential national cinema, the film was able to create the sense of a significant national epic. On its release, it was met with a largely favourable critical reception and success at the box office with over 200,000 spectators. *Plainlands* can be considered as the culmination of the revisionist heritage genre of the 1980s when Mikko Niskanen's adaptations of Kalle Päätalo's work and Matti Kassila's *Niskavuori* adaptation contributed their gritty takes on rural heritage epics. The genre would recede from the domestic cinemas until its revival with Markku Pölönen's nostalgic trips in the 1990s.

Pietari Kääpä

Dog Nail Clipper

Koirankynnen leikkaaja

Production company:
Fennada-Film

Distributor:
Buena Vista International Finland

Director:
Markku Pölönen

Producer:
Kari Sara

Screenwriters:
Markku Pölönen, based on the novel by Veikko Huovinen

Art director:
Minna Santakari

Synopsis

Mertsi Vepsäläinen (Franzén) is shot in the head during the Winter War and a comrade, Eetvi Manninen (Reimaluoto), carries him to a hospital. Mertsi's life is saved but he is left brain damaged and mentally handicapped. He finds employment as assistant to a carpenter named Ville (Kuoppala) and, entranced by Ville's stories of his dog, Sakke, and its troublesome claws, resolves to travel to Ville's home to trim them. He leaves in the middle of the night but soon forgets who he is. Eetvi recognises Mertsi on a train and, with Eetvi's help, Mertsi is given various logging jobs. He fails at all of them and, once again, leaves unannounced to find Ville's home. When he arrives, Ville's wife takes him in and encourages him to cut Sakke's claws. When Sakke bites him, he suffers serious blood poisoning and, once again, Eetvi must race to get Mertsi to hospital to save his life.

Critique

The winner of Best Film, Director, Actor, Screenplay and Cinematography at the 2005 Jussi Awards, *Dog Nail Clipper* is the kind of production that, had it been made in America, would have won the equivalent Oscars: a spectacularly photographed drama

Cinematographer:

Kari Sohlberg

Composer:

Vesa Mäkinen

Editor:

Jukka Nykänen

Duration:

99 minutes

Cast:

Peter Franzén

Taisto Reimaluoto

Ahti Kuoppala

Ville Virtanen

Year:

2004

that showcases a brave simpleton's efforts to be useful to, and find a place in, society whilst examining a period that is a source of both great pain and great pride for its nation. This should not suggest, however, that is an over-serious or self-consciously worthy film. Its strange story – of a mentally handicapped man's long and meandering journey through the snow to find a dog he has never met and clip its nails – ensures it always feels both fresh and unusual.

Peter Franzén's central performance has the same effect, and he should be celebrated for taking a character that is a mass of quirks and tics – forever fidgeting, Mertsi seems perpetually on the point of either crying or laughing – and creating from it a coherent and believable person who seldom seems a construct. Because of Mertsi's instability, the audience is often made uneasy – watching a character whose actions we cannot predict, and whose mind we know to be abnormal is always disquieting – and this prevents the film from descending into sentimentality and becoming simply a cheering tale of strangers being kind to a likeable invalid.

As enthralling as Franzén's acting is, however, it is Kari Solberg's cinematography that captivates most. There are several short but exquisite shots of a steam train slicing through white landscapes that, in their grandeur and precision, are reminiscent of Freddie Young's work with David Lean; and the final pan across an undulating and apparently endless expanse of snow immeasurably heightens the impact of the final scene.

Though the film deals with a war hero who is wounded defending Finland, and those who aid him out of selflessness, gratitude and pity, national pride is seldom verbally expressed. There is a patriotic speech from an army commander in the first minutes, which is soon offset by the unpleasant scene in which Mertsi is wounded, and after that there is silence on the subject. When Mertsi drains a mug of beer and breaks into an old army song extolling Finland's prowess, he is quickly silenced by Eetvi, who treats him as an embarrassed adult would treat a child who suddenly starts swearing. 'We have different songs now,' he says. Instead of verbal expression of nationalism, there are images. Pölönen's wide shots seem sometimes to be taken from a government-sponsored documentary designed to capture the majesty of the Finnish landscape; and his scenes of hearty workers felling trees and gutting fish, and of fluttering Finnish flags, are visual odes to the nation.

Dog Nail Clipper is a simple and subtle film that often looks like other films but never quite behaves like them. The aforementioned final scene is, when considered out of context, exceptionally odd – but, considered in context, it provides a remarkably moving climax to a remarkably moving film that deserved far more than to barely break even at the box office.

Scott Jordan Harris

The Year of the Wolf

Suden vuosi

Production company:
Matila Röhr Productions (MRP)

Distributor:
Nordisk Film Theatrical
Distribution

Director:
Olli Saarela

Producer:
Ilkka Matila

Screenwriters:
Mika Ripatti, based on a novel
by Virpi Hämeen-Anttila

Art director:
Päivi Kettunen

Cinematographer:
Robert Nordström

Composer:
Tuomas Kantelinen

Editor:
Benjamin Mercer

Duration:
95 minutes

Cast:
Krista Kosonen
Kari Heiskanen
Johanna Af Schulten
Ville Virtanen

Year:
2007

Synopsis

Sari (Kosonen) studies at the Faculty of Literature at the University of Helsinki – women are jealous of her because she is beautiful and intelligent, and boys admire her for the very same reasons. However, Sari is not as perfect as it may seem: she has epilepsy and a beast is lurking inside her, appearing as a wolf when she has a seizure. Sari never speaks about her disease at the university, and feels like an outsider. Her literature professor, Mikko Groman (Heiskanen), does not fit in either: he enjoys the company of his books much more than his wife and daughter. Sari and Mikko become friends, and later even more, although other people do not like the idea of their relationship. *The Year of the Wolf* is mostly about forbidden love, perseverance, environmental pressures and overcoming one's own fears, but it also addresses other themes like marriage, faith, illness and craftsmanship in its thematic range.

Critique

Olli Saarela's fifth feature film, *The Year of the Wolf*, is based on the book of the same title by Finnish writer Virpi Hämeen-Anttila. Saarela does not believe in direct, literal book adaptations, so the film only follows the basic plotline of the novel. Yet, he keeps its original message and its themes in this stunning character study of two soul mates discovering the existence of one another. The focus on two individuals who seem transcendent from the rest of the world allows Saarela to address themes of social alienation and the pressure to conform. While Sari and Mikko may seem even too pure and sincere in their behaviour to be 'real' individuals, this is precisely the point of the film – how we perceive normal behaviour is largely a social construct. It is not surprising that Mikko is a docent of literature as it is his job to rethink social norms and conventions. But, occasionally, such preoccupations may become too much and the very act of deconstruction may ultimately extend to one's real life. While such extensive critical thinking is necessary for the betterment of culture and society, it may not be acceptable in a society still predicated on long-established standards and codes of behaviour.

While Mikko's problems are to do with his mind literally working overtime; Sari's condition manifests itself in her body. Just as the professor is not able to control his overarching mind, Sari is not able to stop the epileptic attacks. Thus, the film seems to suggest that both conditions are entirely natural, despite what mainstream society forcefully dictates. In this way, it becomes an argument about social pressures on 'disabilities' which may not, in fact, be disabilities. The social theme of the film resides in these arguments for tolerance. In the contemporary Finland, where appearances seem to matter the most, what takes place inside the individual does not seem to matter – unless these internal movements take the form of physical illness as is the case with Sari's condition.

In its exploration of the social effects of difference, the film inter-rogates a diversity of themes. Social alienation and peer pressure is not only to do with one's peers, but it is also about expectations that the wider public seems to create. No-one explicitly condemns Sari or Mikko for their difference, but the fear of alienation, of being seen as the 'Other', manifests in their own minds. Thus, the film demonstrates the extent to which individuals may be aware of the negative impact of prejudice and injustice. Fortunately, these two alienated Others discover one another and sustain their own understanding. This can, of course, be interpreted from an alternative angle as the film emphasizes that both Sari and Mikko are emphatically different from 'normal' society. In this way, the film seems to reinforce normative conceptions of society, despite all its arguments for tolerance and permissiveness. In fact, why should we be asked to tolerate these individuals? Why do we not imme-diately accept their individual conditions as a natural part of the societal fabric? The fact is that prejudice exists in society and this is something that needs to be overcome, even if this is done through cinematic education.

Saarela's films are well-known for their expressive visual style and *The Year of the Wolf* is no different, even to the extent that the spectacular cinematography and aural world often distances the viewer from the main narrative. Here, Robert Nordström's expres-sive cinematography combines harmonious colours and shapes to capture the ways Sari's seizures manifest like bad dreams that take place underwater, capturing the ways they distance her from the 'real world'. Tuomas Kantelinen's score brings a further expansive quality to the proceedings, occasionally complementing the tran-scendent isolation of the protagonists, and at times threatening to overwhelm them.

Pietari Kääpä and Csoma Emőke

Falling Angels

Putoavia Enkeleitä

Production company:
Blind Spot Pictures Oy
Yleisradio (YLE)

Distributor:
Sandrew Metronome
Distribution

Director:
Heikki Kujanpää

Synopsis

The story of two of the most respected authors in Finnish litera-ture, Lauri Viita (Korpela) and Aila Meriluoto (Knihtilä), is told from the perspective of their daughter, Helena (Leeve), who idolizes Viita and blames Meriluoto for their break-up. The film provides an occasionally romanticized, occasionally harrowing explora-tion of the travails of artistic production. Viita is an alternative thinker and something of a rebel amongst the Finnish literature elite. He meets his match in Meriluoto, whose poetic literature is even more revered and successful than his. Together, the pair would provide substantial modernist contributions to the canon of Finnish literature. Under this harmonious surface things are not well as Viita suffers from schizophrenia and his attacks take

Producers:

Tero Kaukomaa

Petri Jokiranta

Screenwriters:

Sami Parkkinen

Heikki Kujanpää

Heikki Huttu-Hiltunen, based on the novel byAila Meriluoto

Cinematographer:

Harri Räty

Composer:

Timo Hietala

Editor:

Jukka Nykänen

Duration:

101 minutes

Cast:

Elena Leeve

Tommi Korpela

Oiva Lohtander

Elina Knihtilä

Year:

2008

increasingly bizarre and paranoid turns. Meriluoto perseveres by his side as he grows increasingly volatile. As the past is revealed, Helena discovers the real reasons why her father had to move away from the family, which leads her to rethink her relationship with her mother.

Critique

Falling Angels is a frequently touching, at times harrowing exploration of the travails of artistic writing and family angst and fear. The film works as a passionate love story between the two writers and, ultimately, as a tragic tale of persevering love in the face of all adversity. Part of the film's success is Tommi Korpela's performance, which captures the exuberance of creativity as well as the despairs of his mania. As Aila Meriluoto has famously remarked, Lauri Viita was a force of nature, and Korpela's performance captures this intensive and inspirational insanity. As an exploration of insanity, *Falling Angels* keeps us guessing on perceptions of reality as Helena reassesses past events. Her idolization of her father leads her to highlight the inherent genius of Lauri Viita. Thus, the film works as a conventional artist biopic for most of its duration, following the rise to fame and the eventual fights with the cultural authorities. But as her selective memory is unravelled, we are made to reconsider not only flaws in this sort of idolization, but also to understand artists as real human beings. Transcending the confines of the biopic, it becomes a film about the creation of art and the myth of being an artist.

A large part of this artistic exploration lies in *Falling Angels'* visual style, which works as a sort of neo-heritage film. It constructs important elements from the national past and re-examines them in a critical, yet never just condemning light. We are led to reassess the role of national icons, while we are encouraged to respect their substantial contributions to the national culture. The visual style is situated somewhere between the stylized fantastical Finland of Aki Kaurismäki's postmodernist nostalgia, and the socio-realist films of the Finnish New Wave of the '60s and the '70s. The recreation of the 1950s as a fantasy land of deep colours and the more banal everyday-like 1970s allows the film to combine fantasy and reality into a singular experience. This transcendence of the normative conventions of the genre is also created by the focus on a fictional daughter (compendium of all four daughters of Viita and Meriluoto). Helena's behaviour contributes a rather unexpected oedipal trajectory to the film, especially as young Aila is portrayed by Elena Leeve (the actress who plays Helena). Thus, lines between reality and fiction are blurred in a way that would have surely made Viita, the modernist synergist of genres, very proud. Avoiding conventionality and producing a complex narrative that transcends its genre (and metaphorically also comments on that genre) enables the film to differentiate itself from many biopics common in Finnish cinema. The film was met with a good level of critical success, and all three main actors received Jussi Awards for their performances. *Falling Angels* is thus exemplary of the creative directions film producers take in their attempts to rethink the national past and the genres through which it is conventionally represented.

Pietari Kääpä

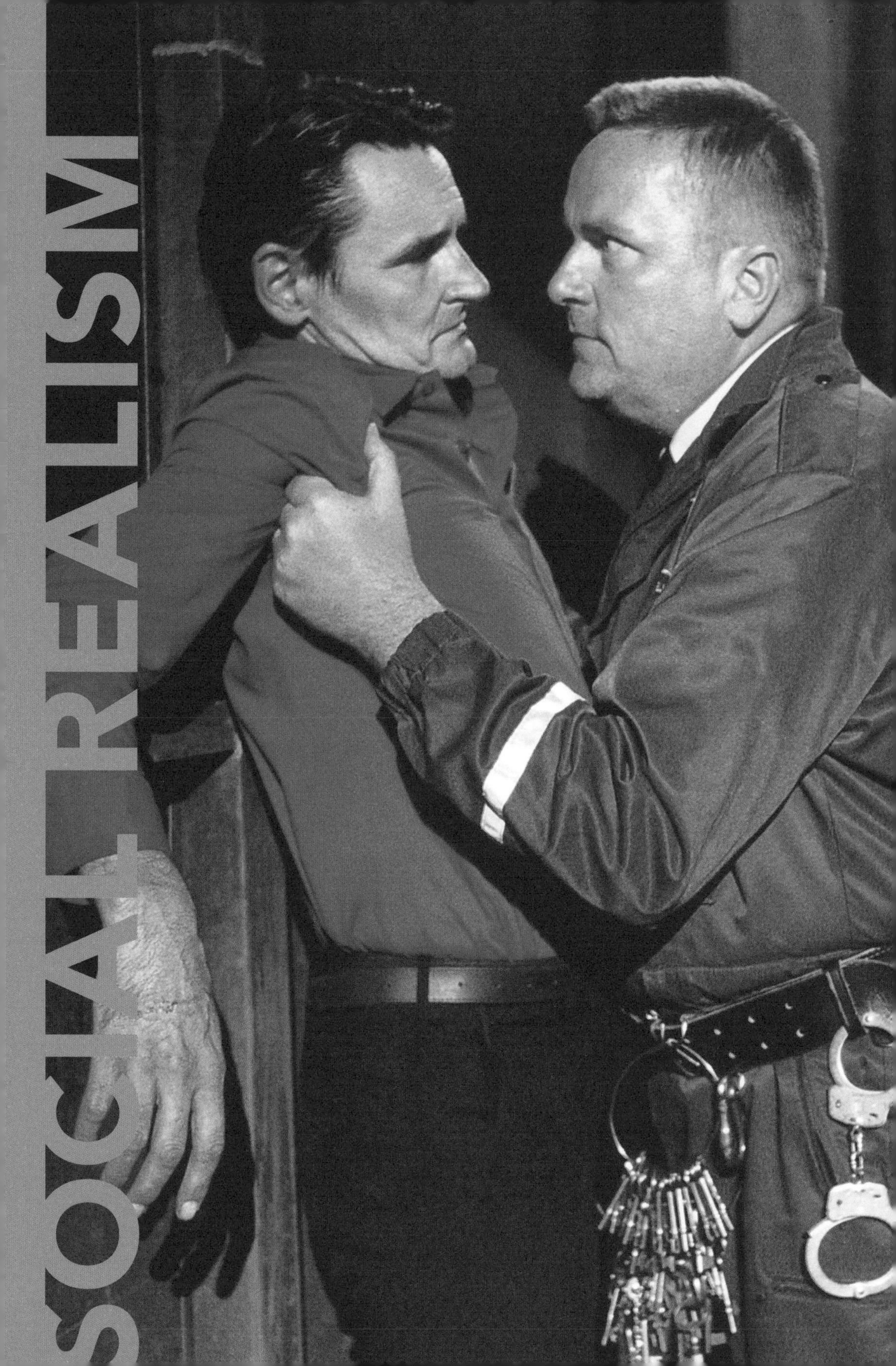
SOCIAL REALISM

If one were to enquire about predominant impressions of Finnish cinema from international audiences, social realism would unavoidably feature centrally. The reasons for this are largely to do with pervasive national stereotypes and the popularity of directors such as Aki Kaurismäki and Aku Louhimies. This section discusses some of the predominant examples of the 'genre' (if it can be called a genre), and their relevance in different historical contexts. The films discussed in this section, first of all, focus on contemporary problems which are relevant to the context of the films' production. These may comprise concerns such as welfare, injustice, class divisions, labour markets and the conditions of immigrants. These concerns have certainly been present from early on in Finnish cinema history. Even the first feature length film, *Salaviinanpolttajat/The Moonshiners* (Puro and Sparre, 1907), addresses many class- and gender-based concerns. Though the film is now considered lost, cinema's responsibility of addressing social problems clearly exists already in films of the autonomy era (discussed in the section on silent cinema).

With post-WWII restructuring of societal order and the substantial war reparations demanded by the Soviets, Finnish cinema producers had plenty of cause to focus on urgent social issues amidst more commercial cinema. Additionally, cycles such as the *Trümmerfilme* ('rubble film') in Germany and Italian neorealism represented social problems in vivid and gruelling terms, gaining international recognition in their wake. Inspired by these developments, film-makers such as Edvin Laine and Matti Kassila emerged at the forefront of a burgeoning wave of Finnish social realism with films such as *Laitakaupungin laulu/The Song of the Streets* (1948), a depiction of the criminal underworld, and *Sininen viikko/Blue Week* (1954) depicting class divisions and infidelity. While the formative and narrative choices of these films hardly qualifies them as the type of hard-hitting social realism produced in Germany or Italy, gritty aesthetics and downbeat narratives of ordinary people became increasingly acceptable. Moralizing depictions of alcoholism or the threat of emerging youth culture made for popular themes through the 1950s and early in the '60s in social problem films such as Jack Witikka's *Mies tältä tähdeltä/A Man from this Star* (1958) and Åke Lindman's *Jengi/The Gang* (1963).

Cinema's responsibility to society became a more urgent issue during the 1960s and 1970s. The establishment of the Finnish Film Foundation was designed to promote and support quality products, with quality to be defined by the film's social value or its artistic merit. The Finnish New Wave emerged out of these considerations with films by directors such as Risto Jarva and Mikko Niskanen. Their films took issue with the structural changes of the Great Migration and its individual costs. Key films such as Jarva's *Työmiehen päiväkirja/The Diary of a Worker* (1967) and Niskanen's *Kahdeksan surmanluotia/Eight Deadly Shots* (1972) chronicled the disappearing countryside and the meagre opportunities available in the development zones of the urban centres. Subsequently, films of this 'participating movement' explore unemployment or claustrophobia in urban spaces where both men and women find their traditional roles challenged. Critics labelled these films '*arkirealismi*' ('banal realism'), which provides an appropriate condensation of their focus on ordinary individuals while condemning the structures of wider society. Many of the films of the era culminate in pessimistic scenarios with the protagonists having to abandon Finland or facing imprisonment for their actions against the authorities.

These themes continued to be explored throughout the 1980s in the films of the Kaurismäki brothers, who took a different angle on the implications of social realism. Films such as *Arvottomat/The Worthless* (Mika Kaurismäki, 1982) and *Ariel* (Aki Kaurismäki, 1988) feature all the hallmarks of social realism, including unemployed protagonists struggling against a bureaucratic welfare state that is increasingly more attuned to neoliberalist concerns rather than the provision of equality. Yet, it would be difficult to describe these films in the typical cinematic vocabulary of social realism as they are influenced by international pop culture, the aesthetic of the previous New Waves, contemporary realism and a heightened sense of irony. While they are perhaps best described as postmodernist takes on social realism, they regardless take part in contemporary sociopolitical debates and contribute alternative perspectives on these issues.

As may be becoming evident from the above, any attempt to constrict these films in the category of a singular genre runs into problems with the very breadth of the films included. Thus, this section will also focus on youth films alongside the gender polemics of *Tuomari Martta/Judge Martta* (Leminen, 1947) and yuppie tale *Insiders* (Törhönen, 1989), which are in no way social or realist, but which function as important barometers for contemporary developments in the nation's self-conceptualization. Social realism does not, of course, have to be about urban estrangement: for example, *Maa on syntinen laulu/The Earth is a Sinful Song* (1973), Rauli Mollberg's adaptation of Timo Mukka's novel, could be considered sociorealist in its naturalistic approach. The use of amateur actors, the focus on everyday activities, unflinching depictions of carnality and critical views of governing social structures all fall in with the realist tradition. Extending the category of social realism to the rural areas is a necessity in Finland's case as the Great Migration lurks behind most socially-committed films. It is not difficult to find rural realism in many of the films of the early 1980s as they focus on young males who feel constrained by their social confines and lash out in violent ways against the system. Films such as Mikko Niskanen's *Ajolähtö/Gotta Run!* (1982) and Jaakko Pyhälä's *Jon* (1983) feature protagonists who wander the dilapidating countryside in an alcoholic haze. While they often see migration as the only option, life in the city is rarely any more amiable. Building from Mikko Niskanen's youth film *Käpy selän alla/Skin, Skin* (1966) to Tapio Suominen's *Täältä tullaan, elämä!/Right on Man!* (1980), as well as other key films of the era, demonstrates the ongoing conceptualizations of the city as a claustrophobic space. But perhaps more tragically, whereas previous generations could always return to the countryside, the 1980s generation has no such option. For many of these youngsters the countryside has never existed in its idyllic form.

Many of the social realist films of the 1980s focused on these concerns, leading critics to suggest that the division between rurality and the city dominates Finnish film culture. And while this dichotomy still remains at the centre of Finnish self-conceptualization, many emergent directors have taken alternative approaches to depicting social problems. Directors such as Auli Mantila and Aleksi Salmenperä centralize gender and body politics in their criticism of the welfare state. Mantila's feminist explorations *Neitoperho/The Collector* (1997) and *Pelon maantiede/The Geography of Fear* (2000), and Salmenperä's focus on male identity and family dynamics in films such as *Miehen työ/ Man's Job* (2007) and *Paha perhe/Bad Family* (2010) provide a wide-ranging and devastating critique of the failures of the welfare state, and the ways these failures are often ignored in mainstream media. Similarly, films about contemporary youth culture function as barometers for assessing the nation's perspectives on its own development. Moving on from the city-countryside dichotomy still evident in the works of Suominen and the Kaurismäkis, other youth films such as Jarmo Lampela's *Sairaan kaunis maailma/Freakin' Beautiful World* (1997) and recent films such as Marja Pyykkö's *Run Sister Run!* (2010) focus on rebellious teenagers who now inhabit a cosmopolitan and thoroughly globalized information society, no longer preoccupied with the obsessions of antecedent generations of youngsters. Pyykkö's film is especially noteworthy for its female centred exploration of social rebellion as it provides a viable alternative to this male dominated 'genre'. It is also another indicator of the increased respect and success female film-makers have received domestically. Other directors such as Kaisa Rastimo and Saara Cantell have made critically successful films in a still largely male-dominated industry. Cantell's *Kohtaamisia/Heartbeats* (2009) is especially remarkable for its simultaneously small-scale and complex narrative and formative construction. Built around seven stories all featuring women at different points in their lives, it achieves a remarkable intensity and also tells us a lot about the state of contemporary Finland. It is not surprising that Cantell's film is the recipient of several significant international festival awards, and has met discussion of the next great Finnish auteur.

Other films about troubled teens, for example Dome Karukoski's *Tummien perhosten koti/The House of the Dark Butterflies* (2008) and Zaida Bergroth's *Skavabölen pojat/Last Cowboy Standing* (2009), focus on fractured families, dark secrets and reassessment of individual memories. The maintenance of a harmonious façade is a part of contemporary Finland's self-conceptualization, and these films seem to suggest that there is something darker lurking inside the self-image of a prosperous welfare state. *Last Cowboy Standing*, for example, follows the story of two boys growing up through the transforming society of the 1970s and early '80s. We initially see the world from the children's perspective where everything seems like an innocent childhood game. As events from the past are revealed, the boys come to terms with the death of their mother and the alcoholism of their father. *The House of the Dark Butterflies* also relies on reassessment of repressed memories in the lives of a group of troubled teens undergoing treatment in an isolated island's rehabilitation centre. Again, it transpires that parental angst and insanity has led to deaths in the family and betrayal of the parent-child relationship. These depictions can be interpreted as key indicators of a society where isolation and suicides are not uncommon, and where recently teenage angst has manifested in catastrophic school shootings. They are symptomatic of the sense of betrayal and abandonment in a society that tells itself that everything is fine, whilst angst and depression lurk beneath the tranquil surface.

While these works are too stylized to qualify for the type of social realism discussed here, other directors have taken up the mantle of social criticism. Aku Louhimies has proven to be an especially apt interpreter of social estrangement in Finnish 'feel-bad' cinema. *Paha Maa/Frozen Land* (2005), especially, is almost heightened in its depiction of social angst. It features representatives from all classes of Finnish society, thus providing a distilled impression of the illnesses gnawing away at the welfare state. *Irtiottoja/Takeoffs* (2003), a television mini-series, and *Valkoinen kaupunki/Frozen City* (2006), an adaptation of some of its narratives into feature-length format, continue this project. Critics have taken issue with Louhimies' films due to their recycling of stereotypes of Finnish angst and depression. The emphasized focus on these tropes functions almost as a type of self-exoticization designed to cater for international markets by playing up foreign preconceptions of Finnish identity. Meanwhile, these ideas are also repeated in more 'magical realist' settings in Aki Kaurismäki's *Kauas pilvet karkaavat/Drifting Clouds* (1996) and *Mies vailla menneisyyttä/The Man Without a Past* (2002), and to a lesser extent in Mika Kaurismäki's *Kolme viisasta miestä/Three Wise Men* (2008) and *Haarautuvan rakkauden talo/ The House of Branching Love* (2009).

The Ministry of Foreign Affairs has criticized the image of Finland these films create internationally. And while we should not relegate cinema to cultural promotion, the Ministry has a point to make in that these sociorealist films are still the prime cinematic export from Finland, even if some more explicitly commercial films have also gained substantial attention. The Kaurismäkis, Louhimies and their compatriots continue to receive not only festival success but also commercial releases in cinema and on DVD. This is not surprising as commercial films from small nation cinemas are rarely able to compete with Hollywood product in their foreign circulation. Thus, the impression of authenticity inherent in any sociorealist film provides them the necessary cultural capital to differentiate them in the marketplace. In an appropriately ironic twist, these seemingly lo-fi and anti-commercial film-makers become the most popular representatives of Finnishness internationally. Implicit in this success is the suggestion that they also consciously mobilize these tropes to reach success, resulting in a paradox where socially-committed critical film is utilized for, if not explicitly commercial success, then consciously for gaining international recognition. While this contributes to fostering stereotypical conceptions of Finnish cinema, it also contributes to the diversity of global film culture. Meanwhile, they also act as important ways to measure contemporary social developments and transformations. Thus, social realist films have their role to play in both domestic and international film culture, and work as important indicators of the ways cinema engages with its commitment to society.

By Pietari Kääpä

Judge Martta

Tuomari Martta

Production company:
Suomen Filmiteollisuus

Distributor:
Suomen Filmiteollisuus

Director:
Hannu Leminen

Producer:
T.J. Särkkä

Screenwriters:
Martti Larni, (based on the play by Ilmari Turja)

Art director:
Hannu Leminen

Cinematographer:
Felix Forsman

Composer:
Martti Similä

Editor:
Hannu Leminen

Duration:
91 minutes

Cast:
Helena Kara
Unto Salminen
Elsa Rantalainen
Uuno Laakso

Year:
1943

Synopsis

Martta (Kara) is an aspiring judicial candidate who fails the final graduation test of her studies. She is also engaged to be married to the son of the professor who failed her, largely due to her gender. When this is revealed to the old judge, he warms to her despite his misgiving about career women. His wife is a dentist and spends most of her time outside of the home and he fears Martta will go down this way too. Martta gets an opportunity to advance her career by acting as the district judge in a remote community overseeing a case involving the violent murder of a landlord by the lover of his son. Martta takes over the role of judge and soon convinces all the sceptical menfolk on the jury. But soon she hears that her son has fallen down the stairs back home and now it is for Martta to blame herself for not being there with her 'maternal' gaze. Facing crisis on both fronts, Martta decides to carry out her duties as a judge and subsequently returns to home with promises of prioritizing family over her career.

Critique

Hannu Leminen began his career as a set designer for Suomi-Filmi, but he soon graduated to feature film directing and went on to create a lengthy prosperous career. *Judge Martta* is a key contribution to debates on gender politics in the Finnish cinema and stars Leminen's cinematic muse and wife, Helena Kara. The film makes a strong case for women's emancipation and entry into the workforce. It is especially relevant for its time as many of the men were engaged in the war effort at the front while women were left to take care of societal affairs. While gender politics in the film make a strong case for allowing women a productive role in society, the film still reflects many of the often unacknowledged patriarchal mores of its time. The mother of Martta's new family is depicted as a strong but inherently selfish matriarch who has more or less abandoned her family for her own career aspirations. A similar trajectory occurs in Martta's life as she struggles against the commands of her husband and insists on participating in the judicial hearings to further her career. Once the hearing is finished, she rushes to the hospital where she is sternly reprimanded for her lack of feminine caring. Her final words are done straight to the camera (albeit in a parodic fashion, according to director Leminen), imploring the women of Finland not to abandon their children. Martta has learnt her lesson – while women's emancipation is all well and good, they have a biological duty to their families.

Similarly conflicted and problematic gender dynamics are present in other films by Leminen: *Vain sinulle/Only For You* (1945), for example, focuses on an innocent and naïve country girl Elina (Kara) lost in the big city, where she longs for Lauri (Tapio Rautavaara), a civilized forestry researcher and is being looked after by his doctor acquaintance, Matti (Olavi Reimas). A clear distinction is made between the educated classes and the farmers from the countryside who are depicted as uncivilized alcoholics who would only use and abuse Elina. In contrast, the 'better' side of the society provides her with chances to fulfil her needs and eventually publish a book. The book sells well but she overhears two male critics describe it as typically melodramatic female literature. Even the publisher is more interested in her physical attributes rather than any philosophical qualities she may possess. Despondent due to her mistaken impression that Matti has left her, she returns to the countryside and is stricken with pneumonia. She returns to the city to die and her memoirs are published posthumously to huge success.

The portrayal of women protagonists as conflicted mothers or suffering archetypes (other women in the film are either superficial usurpers or matriarchs) are normative roles for women at the time of the films' production. Simultaneously, they indicate the contemporary realization that transformations in gender roles are inevitable. Feminist politics thus come through in the films but they are cast in caricatured or even regressive light, reflecting the uncertainty felt by men in their roles in contemporary society. Leminen's films nevertheless remain important contributions and reflections of the wider social changes in Finnish society during the 1930s and '40s. Much of their enduring value must go to his skills in capturing social milieus and Kara's ability to embody her conflicted roles. The films are thus very much products of their time: well-made if melodramatic and ideologically dubious forms of entertainment.

Pietari Kääpä

Blue Week

Sininen viikko

Production company:
Suomen Filmiteollisuus

Distributor:
Suomen Filmiteollisuus

Director:
Matti Kassila

Producer:
T.J. Särkkä

Screenwriters:
Matti Kassila, based on the short story by Jarl Hemmer

Art director:
Aarre Koivisto

Synopsis

As the urbanization of Finnish society increased throughout the early parts of the twentieth century, weekends away at island resorts became a common way to unwind from the monotony of the factory and reconnect with the natural environment. Factory labourer Usko (Oravisto) gets carried away on Sunday night and decides to sleep in next morning, but his initial plan for a 'Blue Monday' soon extends. Siiri (Sandkvist) has also stayed behind on the island. They soon meet and start a passionate affair. She keeps insisting on her loving and happy relationship with her older husband, who she calls 'Daddy' (Mäkelä). There is very clearly something wrong with her, and her quick willingness to elope with Unto underlines this sense of unhappiness. Uuno and Siiri spend a passionate week together, but soon the next weekend and the return of husband Bertel looms. She pretends that nothing has happened, but it soon becomes apparent that she has been unfaithful and Bertel finds use for his gun.

Critique

Kassila's adaptation of Jarl Hemmer's short story about social mores and the turmoil forming underneath the placid surfaces of

Cinematographer:
Osmo Harkimo

Composer:
Matti Rautio

Editor:
Armas Vallasvuo

Duration:
79 minutes

Cast:
Gunvor Sandkvist
Matti Oravisto
Leo Jokela
Toivo Mäkelä

Year:
1954

Blue Week, Suomen Filmiteollisuus.

urbanizing Finland is a widely esteemed masterpiece of Finnish cinema. The need to transcend everyday life, even if it is only for a brief moment, provides the starting point for an analysis of hedonism and guilt. Usko and Siiri seem superficially very different as Usko's working-class background is in sharp contrast to his upper-class counterpart. Yet, they are both lost in their own ways: Usko due to the impersonality of factory labour and Siiri as part of the constraints that traditional patriarchal values impose on women. The collision of these two lost individuals who begin a relationship they know is only temporary is given extra weight due to their need to believe in its meaningfulness. Patriarchal structures (she has been a child bride) and class roles still upheld by society coalesce in the claustrophobia and their desperate need to escape their conventional roles in the surrounding world.

The film's recreation of this temporary break with social reality can be usefully analyzed through Mikhail Bakhtin's conceptualization of the carnival, and its abilities for subverting conventional norms and morality. As with Bakhtin's carnival, these transgressions critically illuminate the conventions on which contemporary social life is built, and allows us to visualize alternative modes of existence. Yet, carnivals are not indefinite and they all have to come to an end. The conclusion depicts what happens when carnivalesque morality intrudes on real life. Bertel's return to the island brings with it a sense of impending doom as Kassila begins to use a number of techniques more at home in a Hitchcockian thriller. While we do not see the husband until later, the rolling of small rocks down a hillside and glimpses of something unseen just outside of the corner of the eye becomes a sign and admission of Siiri's guilt. Transgression is punished as Siiri's 'Daddy' kills himself due to the shame she has brought on them. Conventional morality must be upheld and any excessive subversion of these norms can only be destructive for the social core. The suicide introduces a moralistic tone to the film, which was refreshingly missing from the earlier sections of the film.

Much of this overwhelming guilt can be seen as a critical indictment of postwar consumerism and the structural changes that resulted in the foregrounding of leisure activities. In fact, the whole of the 'Blue Week' is effectively like an out of control leisure binge where no concern for social structure or morality can be found. As this anti-consumerist critique is also contextualized with class concerns, the film's ideological stance becomes even more problematic. *Blue Week* plays out like the typical noir narrative of the working-class man (carnal Usko) and the upper-class wife (loose Siiri), while vindicating the more 'civilized' perspective of the upper-class male. This is certainly a method that linearizes what is largely a complex and ambiguous ideological dissection of social mores.

And perhaps it is this unusual pairing of social moralizing and ideological ambiguity that led to critics expressing confusion over the purpose of the film, though some recognized its innovative cinematic and narrative tone as indicating the emergence of a new sort of film language. Indeed, many of the film's formative innovations and its thematic ambiguity would surface again with the New Wave ten years later. The risqué, sensational tone of the film was also unusual for its time, featuring nudity and infidelity as its key theme with Kassila's taut direction and impressionistic 'Herrmann-esque' score strengthening the disquieting atmosphere. *Blue Week* is nowadays recognized as a classic of Finnish cinema, which is not surprising considering its cinematic and thematic innovations and reflection of contemporary social and cultural mores.

Pietari Kääpä

Skin, Skin

Käpy selän alla

Production company:
FJ-Filmi

Distributor:
Suomi-Filmi

Director:
Mikko Niskanen

Producers:
Kyösti Varesvuo
Arno Carlstedt
Jörn Donner

Screenwriters:
Robert Alfthan
Marja-Leena Mikkola

Cinematographer:
Esko Nevalainen

Composers:
Henrik Otto Donner
Kaj Chydenius

Editor:
Juho Gartz

Duration:
91 minutes

Cast:
Eero Melasniemi
Kristiina Halkola
Pekka Autiovuori
Kirsti Wallasvaara

Year:
1966

Synopsis

Four youths, the couples of Santtu (Melasniemi) and Riitta (Halkola) and Timo (Autiovuori) and Leena (Wallasvaara), take a trip to the countryside to camp out in the forest. Santtu and Riitta make out openly in front of the others, building frustration between Leena and Timo. While Santtu and Timo explore the nearby countryside, the girls discuss their relationships. Santtu decides that Leena's traditionalist attitudes complicate her relationship with Timo and that she needs to be liberated. As Timo is taking care of the daughter of a nearby farmhouse, Santtu and Leena have sex. Upon returning to camp, Riitta senses that something is wrong and shuns Santtu. That night, the foursome goes out to a village dance and get increasingly drunk. All secrets are exposed and the trip and the couple's lives together come to an end. The film culminates with Leena packing her bags and leaving for the city.

Critique

Mikko Niskanen's seminal New Wave film came out in the midst of the burgeoning sexual revolution and the emergence of a rebellious generation of young people for whom the mores of their parents meant little. The tale of sexual and ideological awakening in the countryside is a key part of the Finnish New Wave movement, itself inspired by the *nouvelle vague*. The film uses conventions already seen in the films of Risto Jarva and Maunu Kurkvaara to create an ideological/artistic condensation of the attitudes of the contemporary generation. The formative qualities of the film are very innovative and brought a style of cinema to large audiences which they had not encountered previously. The jump cuts, the frequent breakings of the fourth wall, 'shaky cam', and existential monologues are complemented by impromptu agitprop songs and rants about the state of society. In one particularly iconic instance, Santtu climbs atop a farmhouse standing for the Helsinki Cathedral to demonstrate his rebellion against everything that national traditions and conventional societal mores represent.

The film's rebellious qualities are not only to do with explicit speeches like Santtu's climb. In many ways, the sexual politics of the film reflect the wider disillusionment of the generation. While commitment and the notion of free love are evoked as polar opposites, these youths are not able to find value in either. They cannot trust their relationships with their own partners, nor do they know if they want to exist outside of such relationships. This uncertainty is also to do with the issues against which they protest as their rebellions seem distinctly uncertain. From one perspective, they are individuals coming to terms with a legacy of complacency. They rebel at the confines of the postwar society in all ways, ranging from their style of dress to their vernacular expressions. This final point comes through in the various on-screen songs of the film which use unusual harmonies and lyrics to establish the point of dissatisfaction and the need to rethink the conventions of the previous generation. Simultaneously, these are the children of the postwar generation who grew up in relative political and economic stability. While certainly the threat of the Cold War and the constant presence of Soviet control meant uncertainty for the nation, these concerns seem to be almost entirely absent from the lives of the new generation. Uncertainty and the problems of identity are captured in the final scene of the film. Using jump cuts to give us different perspectives on Leena, the film concludes on an intriguing note. What is the identity of this generation, it seems to ask. Thus, the rebellion of this generation needs to be understood as identity politics in a society of recognizable comfort, but a rebellion which is nevertheless important for intellectual developments and social equality.

Skin, Skin was a huge success on its release, playing to over half a million viewers in cinemas. The success indicates that it managed to make a connection with domestic audiences and indeed speak for the generation. It also encapsulates concerns which were keenly felt in a society undergoing not only socio-economic structural changes, but also ideological transformations. The contributions of Niskanen's film are not only important for assessing gender relations and political changes, but also the ways in which Finnish cinema embraced international genres and produced its own cinema of social importance. Following this successful connection, it would take almost fourteen years before a similar seismic shift would occur in Finnish film culture with Tapio Suominen's *Täältä tullaan, elämä!/Right on Man!* (1980).

Pietari Kääpä

Eight Deadly Shots

Kahdeksan surmanluotia

Production companies:
Yleisradio (YLE), Käpy-Filmi

Distributor:
Finnkino

Director:
Mikko Niskanen

Producer:
Mikko Niskanen

Screenwriter:
Mikko Niskanen

Synopsis

Pasi (Niskanen) supports his family of four children and one baby in late 1960s countryside Finland through seasonal work on his small farm and by doing forest work during the winter. He is a hard-working man, but the tough circumstances frequently lead him to seek escape in heavy drinking and to earn a few pennies by illegally distilling moonshine with his neighbours. This leads to confrontations with the law, as well as putting stress on Pasi's marriage. When the police surround Pasi's house, the drunken man opens fire with his hunting rifle and kills four of the officers.

Critique

Mikko Niskanen's seminal film starts with its climax: we see a family escaping in the snow, a drunken man in a house, the police surrounding the house, the eight shots that kill four officers. The film then backs up to the roots of the events, and gradually we get to understand Pasi, and the frustration he and the likes of him go through. The news about a poor farmer killing four policemen in a village in central Finland shocked the nation in 1969. Soon

Art director:
Jorma Lindfors

Cinematographers:
Kimmo Simula
Juhani Voutilainen
Seppo Immonen

Composer:
Erkki Ertama

Editors:
Jyrki Rapp
Jörn Donner

Cast:
Mikko Niskanen
Tarja-Tuulikki Tarsala
Tauno Paananen
Elina Liimatainen

Duration:
145 min (theatrical version), 316 min (TV version)

Year:
1972

after the event, director Mikko Niskanen, who was from the same region, started developing a film based on the events. He saw in the project a possibility to depict the Finnish countryside and the concerns of small farm owners during a time when the government was actively promoting a shift from small farms to a more profitable factory farming model, thus effectively putting small farms in a dire situation. Debt to banks, unemployment and the gap between the Helsinki-based decision makers and the ones whose life these decisions affect are the main themes of the film. For Niskanen, the film was also a return to his roots, to the type of life he had grown amongst, and this is where the filming took place, in Konginkangas in central Finland. According to his own words, he did not choose the topic – instead, the topic chose him.

Eight Deadly Shots situates the characters tightly against the social circumstances that affect them. In this sense of realism, the film is perhaps one of the most remarkable social problem films ever produced in Finland, and here Niskanen comes close to such working-class centred directors as Ken Loach. At the same time, Niskanen and his cameramen caught the poetic moments in Pasi's life by placing him and his work against the four seasons in the village. The film contains several memorable and affecting scenes, such as those of Pasi working in the woods with his horse in wintertime, and extensive depictions of summertime farm work, which do not so much advance the story, but lend to its poetic heroism, in which influences from Niskanen's film training in the Soviet VGIK film school are visible.

Niskanen is well-known for his skilful use of amateur actors, and in this film Helsinki-based professionals are seamlessly matched with local amateurs from central Finland, including the four children and Sulo, Pasi's moonshine partner in crime, played by Sulo Hokkanen. Niskanen himself took on the main role of Pasi, and effectively immerses himself in the character. Indeed, it is hard to imagine any other actor getting so deeply, almost maniacally embodied in the role. Appropriately, the film received the top industrial award – the Jussi – for Best Film of 1972, with Niskanen also collecting the Best Actor Jussi for his searing performance.

Eija Niskanen

One Man's War

Yhden miehen sota

Production companies:
Filminor

Distributor:
Finnkino

Synopsis

Erik Suomies (Rinne) is one of the many Finns who decide to move from the countryside to the city in search of a better life. Taking up the promise of private enterprise and class ascension, he sells his parents' farm, takes out a bank loan and purchases a Caterpillar. Setting out to operate on the many construction sites that permeates the now-booming margins of the Finnish cities with his wife (Nyman), daughter (Maarit Rinne) and friend Pete (Hautaniemi) in tow, Erik finds it difficult to find permanent employment. Occasionally, they find work and it seems that there is a future to

Director:
Risto Jarva

Producer:
Kullervo Kukkasjärvi

Screenwriters:
Jussi Kylätasku
Risto Jarva

Art directors:
Antti Peippo
Matti Kuortti

Cinematographer:
Antti Peippo

Editor:
Risto Jarva

Duration:
115 minutes

Cast:
Eero Rinne
Tuula Nyman
Tauno Hautaniemi
Martti Pennanen

Year:
1973

Erik's enterprise. Mostly, the work is very fragmentary and liable to the unpredictability of the capitalist market. On several occasions Erik is left destitute as the firms he works for go bankrupt, leaving him with no means of getting compensation. Meanwhile, relations between Erik and his wife, and Erik and Pete, inflame due to the external pressures. Finally, Erik has to sell his Caterpillar and move to Sweden in search of a more sustainable life and the promise of the welfare state.

Critique

Risto Jarva's bleak exploration of the structural transformations of the Finnish welfare state during the 1970s makes for challenging but important viewing. As tens of thousands of individuals and families moved from the countryside to the city to find employment and more prosperous ways of life, rural communities began to slowly die. In contrast, infrastructural developments in the cities demanded labour, but this was no longer a communal, welfare state driven enterprise. Capitalist principles and the promise of private enterprise lured individuals to commit to the system and provided them little in return. The process was collectively known as the Great Migration as it fundamentally altered the socio-economic structure of the Finnish nation. As opportunities in the cities were meagre and the conditions of labour worse, thousands left for Sweden in search of a more sustainable life.

Jarva's film captures these despairing times in almost documentary fashion as it chronicles the desperation of the Suomies family. It continues many of the processes initiated by the *nouvelle vague*, which emphasized formative innovation and political commitment. Shots of the emptying countryside open the film as we hear the hymn 'Oi Kaunis Kotimaa' ('Oh, Beautiful Homeland') over the very grainy monochrome shots. The intended connection of depicting a dystopian image of the nation is rather obvious but also very effective in its irony. It is clear that any promise the welfare state held is on the verge of collapse. In comparison to earlier depictions of the countryside, rural imagery does not signify national belonging but the fundamental schisms emerging in its structures. Alongside other extremely critical films such as Mikko Niskanen's *Kahdeksan surmanluotia*/*Eight Deadly Shots* (1972), *One Man's War* provides a diagnosis of a truly dysfunctional society – it is critically-motivated national cinema at its best.

The film's focus on private enterprise instead of victimization of individuals loyal to the socio-democratic system provides us with an unexpected though entirely appropriate perspective on the travails of the nation. Instead of providing simplistic attacks on the victimization of the labourer in the capitalist system, Jarva's film shows us individuals who believe in the system and its promises. Thus, its rhetorical perspective is a lot more powerful than simple attacks on capitalism as it provides a dialectical analysis of the necessities of modernization. Jarva is realist enough not to blindly argue against industrialization and the need for social development. Accordingly, the film lulls the spectators into a false sense of comfort by providing the protagonists with all the necessities to expand into private business that is currently reconstructing the nation. Yet, it pulls the rug from underneath them (and by extension, us the spectators) by refusing to fulfil the promise in which the Suomies have believed. This makes the film not only the type of socially-committed cinema for which the participatory movement was renowned: it also puts it into the category of truly challenging films that aims to undermine our basic conceptions about social justice and equality in a capitalist welfare state.

Considering its intentionally difficult nature, it was not entirely surprising that *One Man's War*'s financial returns were catastrophic and resulted in substantial losses for Filminor. The film was initially delayed by almost a year on its release as its distinctly uncommercial approach was deemed unsuitable for the cinemas. Even the supporter of quality cinema, the Finnish Film Foundation, refused it support during its production. Eventually, the film did garner a unanimously positive reception with critics interpreting it as a vital contribution to national cinema. When it was broadcast on the national television in 1975, it garnered over 1.5 million viewers (a huge contrast to its box office). This, and its esteemed place in film culture, confirms that the film managed to establish an eventual connection with the domestic population.

Pietari Kääpä

Home for Christmas

Jouluksi kotiin

Production company:
Filmityö Oy

Distributor:
Suomi-Filmi

Director:
Jaakko Pakkasvirta

Producer:
Jaakko Pakkasvirta

Screenwriters:
Jaakko Pakkasvirta
Väinö Pennanen
Esa Vuorinen

Cinematographer:
Esa Vuorinen

Synopsis

Urho Suomalainen (Pentikäinen) is a construction worker with a dream – he intends to build his own house. He aims to do most of the work on his own though he organizes a collective transport for the trees from his home region. Urho has been living in the city for two decades but still longs for the security and fairness of the countryside. Taking loans and working on the house in his spare time starts to take its toll on Urho. He explodes at his wife (Martinkauppi) and alienates his children, while developing the first signs of pneumonia. Yet, he insists on working. Fragments of his past are revealed to us where we get to know his stubborn and perseverant character. These are contextualized with an exploration of the Civil War of 1918. As Urho is a supporter of leftist politics, the conflict seems to become one between the left and the right, with Urho's house as the battlefield. As with the Civil War, the right wins the fight as Urho insists on working on his house despite his deteriorating condition. Urho dies at the front (the construction site of his house) and at his funeral a manifesto of socialist politics is read.

Critique

Jaakko Pakkasvirta is another key director of the Finnish New Wave movement. He is a long time collaborator with Risto Jarva at Filminor, where he had served as actor, co-director, screenwriter

Composer:

Henrik Otto Donner

Editor:

Jaakko Pakkasvirta

Duration:

85 minutes

Cast:

Paavo Pentikäinen
Irma Martinkauppi
Selma Miettinen
Jari Erkkilä

Year:

1975

and occasional producer. *Home for Christmas* is his third solo feature film and it was produced for his own film company, Filmityö Oy. Alongside other important 'participating' films such as *One Man's War* (Jarva, 1973), these films provide an impression of a society where structural transformations have already taken place and the past ways of life have disappeared. Pakkasvirta explores the life of a worker who wants to regain the promise made to him in the postwar society and the welfare state, which is that of private property (own home). Private enterprise has two functions here. Firstly, it is not depicted as something vain and improper, a sign of embourgeoisement; instead, it is seen as something that belongs to all individuals in this society. But it is also made very clear that this aspiration is only an impossible dream and thus a sort of mirage, something which the working-classes will never be able to reach. *Home for Christmas* condemns the machinations of a capitalist society where exploitation and individualistic greed are covered up by false illusions to make individuals behave and contribute.

According to film historian Peter von Bagh, the film works more as a theorem than an involving narrative. It is not difficult to see how Von Bagh would come to such a conclusion. The final coda of the film culminates in what can only be described as a heavy-handed manifesto against social injustice. The speech, with its calls for socialist equality, works in tandem with the flashbacks to the Civil War. It constructs a sort of cine-socialist manifesto by contextualizing the contemporary struggles of the worker with the fights of the past. The worker is once more defeated by bourgeoisie forces and history repeats itself. Now, instead of a tangible enemy it is the general conditions of the society that prove infatigable. Thus, the bourgeoisie condition has been normalized and the status of working-class marginalized.

While many of the politicized films share the film's political agenda and even its formative understated qualities, they also conducted their rhetoric in a more nuanced way. *Home for Christmas* is too obvious in its rhetoric, coming across more like a manifesto than an effective piece of cinematic politics. Whereas other participatory films achieved a sense of identification and even affect through their characters, the film is too cold and preachy to get its message across. While there is a need for explicitly political statements in the cinema, manifestos often fail to connect with the audiences. Only a few thousand viewers saw the film in the cinemas, which is not entirely surprising as most of the participant films failed to make a connection with audiences. While television figures are more respectable, it remains something of a swan song for the movement.

While sociorealist explorations were still released in the early 1980s, they increasingly moved away from austere, political contributions to more playful or youth-oriented forms. Film-makers such as Tapio Suominen and Anssi Mänttäri contributed naturalistic explorations of social conditions, but it was increasingly clear that leftist politics were increasingly shunned by the mainstream. Even when film-makers such as the Kaurismäki brothers included the rhetoric of the working-class in their works, these would be conveyed in distanced or ironic terms. Cinematic radicalism thus found new ways to express dissatisfaction with contemporary society and the most explicit methods of the participating cinema were abandoned. Pakkasvirta would still continue to contribute to Finnish cinema, building from the best director Jussi he received for his work on *Home for Christmas*. He has had a prolific career up to the mid-1980s and has produced more inventive yet less explicitly politicized cinema, which has also met with public interest. Films such as *Runoilija ja muusa/Poet and Muse* (1978) are very different from these early examples of political cinema. But true to his artist roots, the films are formatively innovative, with complex flashbacks and experimentation with sound and image. His final production, appropriately, is an adaptation of *Linna/The Castle* (1986) by Franz Kafka, about an individual struggling against an overwhelming bureaucratic state apparatus that has succeeded in normalizing its oppressive procedures with the population.

Pietari Kääpä

Right on Man!

Täältä Tullaan Elämä

Production company:
Sateenkaarifilmi Oy

Distributor:
Kinosto

Director:
Tapio Suominen

Producers:
Jorma Virtanen
Tapio Suominen

Screenwriters:
Pekka Aine
Yrjö-Juhani Renvall

Cinematographers:
Pekka Aine
Juha-Veli Ärkäs

Composers:
Pelle Miljoona
Maukka Perusjätka

Editor:
Tapio Suominen

Synopsis

Jussi (Niemelä) is one of seven misbehaving teenagers sent to a target class for troubled students. The teacher (Yrjö-Juhani Renvall) is able to keep them under control through an understanding perspective, but it is more evident that the broken families from where most of the students come from cannot be substituted by enforced schooling. The students play a range of pranks on the stern headmasters of the school and Jussi is expelled for it. He lashes out at the world and robs a woman giving him a ride. Going out on a wild night on the town, he spends all the money with his mate and ends up sleeping in a school yard. Feeling as if he has been pushed outside of everything he knows, he turns to the self-appointed outcast of the class Lissu (Outinen) to help him collect his belongings from home. Feeling a spark between them, Jussi sets a date for the evening. As he sees Lissu debark from her bus, a security guard with whom he had conflicted before sets chase and drives him to the top of the shopping mall. Cornered by the vicious guard dog, Jussi jumps.

Critique

Right on Man! is one of the key texts in Finnish cinema as it emerged at a crucial turning point in Finland's cinematic history. As urbanization was increasingly becoming the norm, films were no longer only about the disappearing ways of life in the countryside. Now, depression and a sense of claustrophobia were keenly felt in the spaces of the city. This film captures this sense of hopelessness of a generation of young individuals for whom the rural ways of life have never been an option, yet no real or stable sense of place has

Duration:

118 minutes

Cast:

Esa Niemelä
Heikki Komulainen
Tony Holmström
Kati Outinen

Year:

1980

emerged to replace them. Focusing on young teenagers who go to a designated class for misbehaving individuals, the film emphasizes all the aspects of this generational angst. The roots of the social rebellion in Suominen's film lie in Suomen Kansan Teatteri's performance of the play *Pete Q*. The play is an argument against totalitarian ideology and social complacency and these issues play a key role in Suominen's film. It is made very clear that the current predicament of the youth is to do with the uncaring system created by the adults. School teachers are repeatedly overheard exclaiming their conceptions of morality, condemning anything they find strange. Punk culture and aggressive behaviour are repeatedly used as weapons to battle social conventionality and societal stagnancy. Yet, this rebellion is ultimately futile as their club house is torn down unceremoniously and the misbehavers are locked up in their windowless classroom.

Often in youth films social rebellion is explained by an uncaring parental system. This is also the case here, but Lissu, the only one of the students truly out of sync with conventionality, is not given an excuse of a broken and inhospitable family environment. This is an important indicator that not all social problems are answered by easy categorizations or blaming parental authorities. But, ultimately, the film is the sad story of one individual, Jussi, who is let down by the elders of the society. We are repeatedly shown how Jussi loves animals and wants to be taken seriously, but the rejection of his father daunts every one of his attempts at connection. Futility also characterizes his jump at the end as it seems he has chosen to commit suicide instead of continuing to live on in this world. Questions resonate in the end as to what kind of a welfare state can leave its innocent and fragile subjects to commit suicide.

Right on Man! was a real watershed for Finnish cinema on its release as it was seen by over 400,000 spectators, making it one of the top domestic attractions since the golden age. The film's music also heralded a new form of popular culture with post-punk bands such as Sielun Veljet emerging to provide a voice for the voiceless youth. Finnish cinema was concurrently stagnating in populist comedies and large-scale but impotent historical dramas, and Suominen's contribution was significant in giving it a breath of life that helped start a 'new' New Wave in cinema. Much as the work of film-makers such as Jarva and Niskanen had rethought post-studio-era cinema, another shift had occurred. Contributions to this cycle were made by established film-makers such as Mikko Niskanen (*Ajolähtö/Gotta Run* [1982]) and the Kaurismäki brothers, who were to ultimately emerge as key figures in the second New Wave of Finnish cinema.

Pietari Kääpä

The Worthless

Arvottomat

Production company:
Villealfa Filmproduction Oy

Distributor:
Finnkino

Director:
Mika Kaurismäki

Producer:
Mika Kaurismäki

Screenwriters:
Aki and Mika Kaurismäki

Cinematographer:
Timo Salminen

Composer:
Anssi Tikanmäki

Editor:
Antti Kari

Duration:
118 minutes

Cast:
Matti Pellonpää
Pirkko Hämäläinen
Juuso Hirvikangas
Aki Kaurismäki

Year:
1982

Synopsis

Manne (Pellonpää), Harri (Hirvikangas) and Ville Alfa (Aki Kaurismäki) are rootless twenty-somethings in search of a purpose for their apparently banal lives. The loose narrative revolves around a priceless painting stolen by Manne from a group of petty criminals. Manne and Harri flee from the gangsters across Finland, while Ville goes to Paris. On the road they meet Veera (Hämäläinen), an old girlfriend of Harri's, and try to avoid the gangsters in pursuit. They hide in a circus called the Oriental Express and eventually elope to an old farmhouse. But soon, the police and the gangsters catch up and things end violently.

Critique

The Worthless was Mika Kaurismäkis' first full-length feature film, and it received substantial press coverage building on the expectations created by his debut, the short film *Valehtelija/The Liar* (1981). *The Worthless'* title sequence is iconic in its pointed attempt to rewrite the conventions of Finnish cinema: the film opens with a re-orchestrated version of Jean Sibelius' 'Finlandia' with electric guitars and drums accompanying a helicopter shot approaching Helsinki from its harbours. 'Arvottomat' means the 'worthless' (or 'valueless', as the term 'arvoton' in Finnish can mean both a person of no worth and a person without any moral values). In the film, the 'band of the worthless' are cosmopolitans suffocating in the restrictive, traditional society surrounding them. They cannot identify with any of the norms and conventions by which the society around them is bound, rather preferring an outsider existence modelled on an approximation of the cinematic lifestyles of gangsters and bohemians.

As the protagonists flee the city, *The Worthless* transforms from a city-bound gangster thriller into a road movie, a genre traditionally focused on outsiders who rebel against dominant norms. The sweeping landscape shots and travel montages examine Finland from the marginalized perspective of the protagonists who see little of value in them. For example, Manne meets Harri at a village dance hall, where the camera assumes their disillusioned point of view and lingers on the performers of a traditional tango and the people dancing to it. Matti convinces Harri to leave behind his rural existence, to which Harri replies: 'The most important thing is leaving'. What matters is not necessarily where they are going, but the very act of liberating oneself from the stagnant confines of the traditional nation. *The Worthless* looks forward to the invigorating new challenges and possibilities that increasing transnational interaction provides, which is what interested Mika Kaurismäki about the project. For him, it reflects his return to Finland after studying in Germany – the aim was to 'examine what Finland was and how it had changed or was in the process of changing'. The creation of a globalized perspective of Finland is not a one-way process, but the result of a complex set of negotiations, where global and national elements function as equal parts of individual identity. But crucially, *The Worthless* also hints at the increasing global aspirations of its protagonists by emphasizing the loosening of the hold that the national has on them. For example, in Manne and company's attempts to escape the police and the gangsters by hiding out in a cabin by an idyllic lake, *The Worthless* reinterprets the traditional Finnish landscape. This is a prolific part of the national cultural imagery, but here it is presented as desolate, obsolete even, as the cabin is a run-down shack with punctured walls and broken windows. For the protagonists, such idyllic scenarios hold no potency, but exist only as further signifiers of their isolation from the surrounding society.

The Worthless shows us a social space where the national is challenged and replaced by new subjective life-worlds imagined through transnational cultural flows. The film uses cultural elements foreign to the Finnish context, such the intertextual games the film plays with film noir and other genre conventions and the injection of foreign cultural elements into the seemingly banal, urban *mise-en-scène* (cadillacs, cowboy hats, French and American film posters, foreign beverages, etc.). The vision of Finland that the film provides is a reflection of the cosmopolitan, bohemian mindset of the protagonists, where conventional national iconography loses its ethno-symbolic meanings. Manne's flat, for example, is a sub-bohemian hideout, where a picture of President Urho Kekkonen hangs on the wall. The picture, with its connotations of formality, is out of place in Manne's messy, casual, book-littered abode. Similarly, Manne's favourite haunt, BaariBaari, a local, seedy bar-cafeteria, serves Calvados in the morning whilst Shostakovich's 'Symphony no. 7' plays in the background. Helsinki may be portrayed in conventionally recognisable terms, but this mishmash of cultural experiences allows cosmopolitanism to seep into the frame through visual and narrative means.

The cityscapes and townscapes of the film are constantly shifting, porous environments. The images of urbanity emphasize the monumental quality of the architecture, but this stability is constantly undermined by the presence of elements that emphasize and foreshadow the ways that the national capital is slowly becoming subsumed by the advances of capitalism and neoliberalism. By emphasizing the neon slogans of various banks, contrasted with the bleakness of darkened urban backgrounds and the Cadillacs and Volgas driven by the protagonists (signs of western capitalism and eastern Communism, respectively), the images project the state of flux in which the Finnish nation found herself in the 1980s. The theme of change is even more prevalent in the images charting the effects of the Great Migration and the ways that the rural townscapes – the 'authentic' homes of the national imaginary – are changing in the face of urbanization. This is evident in the depiction of small rural towns. In some cases, the *mise-en-scène* highlights the ways traditional architecture is being replaced by more modern, urban buildings. In others, the images foreground symbols of global capitalism. Thus, the traditional wooden architecture of rural shops and cafés is infiltrated by the signs of Esso or

Pepsi or of bank slogans, providing us with a metaphoric picture of the constantly changing face of Finnish society, where only momentary stability is achievable.

In contrast to the all-pervasive realism of *Right on Man!* (1980), *The Worthless* works on a slightly altered level of reality, which necessitates we consider its politics metaphorically: 'We should not think of reality as it is, but what it is like in our dreams,' suggests Manne. This fantasized abandonment of strict notions of the real is a key factor in deciphering how the film appropriates the ideological perspectives of the protagonists. The characters often make seemingly absurd comments that reflect their transnational perspectives: Ville Alfa tells Manne that he bought the painting in Istanbul, to which Manne replies that Ville has never been in Istanbul; Ville responds that this is exactly his point. Harri sings American blues music at a country dance hall and answers the phone by identifying himself as 'American Express'. To further indicate Manne's outsider imaginary, we might note that he responds to an accusation of running away from reality by stating that 'Reality runs away from me'. *The Worthless* displays the nation as a multifaceted sphere, in which competing voices converge in disharmony.

In addition to unravelling the myth of the nation, all aspects of the film point towards Finland's global connectivity, especially as the protagonists flee to Paris during the climax. While Finland may be a part of Europe, the protagonists still inhabit a world structured along the lines of nation-states and very little hope of stability can be found in such restricted confines. Accordingly, the protagonists are left staring at empty space, wondering what to do – or where to escape to – next. This poses more of an existential dilemma of what happens after you transcend the societal confines of the nation. If the dream worlds of the cinematic imagination are not real, we are left with a troubling, open-ended look at contemporary social existence – a sign of the changing status of the national in times of increasing globalization. The film was a critical hit on its release though it failed to meet the box office standards set by *Right on Man!*. Yet, this was not entirely surprising considering the occasionally surreal, occasionally esoteric ways in which its arguments are conveyed. The Kaurismäkis would become leading figures in Finnish cinema and, crucially, *The Worthless* is a significant contribution to the increasing globalization of Finnish film culture.

Pietari Kääpä

References

Kääpä, P. (2010) *The National and Beyond: the Globalisation of Finnish Cinema in the Films of Aki and Mika Kaurismäki*, Oxford: Peter Lang.

Shadows in Paradise

Varjoja Paratiisissa

Production company:
Villealfa Filmproduction Oy

Distributor:
Finnkino

Director:
Aki Kaurismäki

Producer:
Mika Kaurismäki

Screenwriter:
Aki Kaurismäki

Art director:
Pertti Hilkamo
Heikki Ukkonen

Cinematographer:
Timo Salminen

Editor:
Raija Talvio

Duration:
75 minutes

Cast:
Matti Pellonpää
Kati Outinen
Sakari Kuosmanen
Esko Nikkari

Year:
1986

Synopsis

Shadows in Paradise tells the awkward love story of garbage truck driver, Nikander (Pellonpää), and supermarket checkout operator, Ilona (Outinen). A connection forms between them as Ilona tends to Nikander's injured hand mid-transaction, taking the opportunity to have a cigarette break at the same time. Their first date, however, is a disaster: Ilona does not appreciate the romance of a bingo hall and a bunch of carnations.

Nikander's life is briefly shocked by the sudden death of an amicable older colleague. Having expressed his mourning through drunken violence, Nikander finds himself in a jail cell. There he befriends Melartin (Kuosmanen), who joins the ranks of the garbage collectors and advises Nikander in his pursuit of Ilona. Ilona, meanwhile, takes her revenge on a callous employer by stealing the supermarket's cash box. Nikander finds a way to return the stolen goods and saves Ilona from prosecution. Still, as their lives are marked by transience, Ilona and Nikander struggle to find happiness in their marginal social positions. Ilona in particular has difficulty adjusting to a stable relationship, aspiring to something better than being the girlfriend of a garbage collector. However, she finally agrees to join Nikander on a honeymoon to Estonia, the couple's eastward departure being an ironic take on the happy endings of more conventional romances.

Critique

Shadows in Paradise is the first part of what has been referred to as the 'Loser', 'Worker' or 'Proletarian Trilogy': the later parts Ariel and Tulitikkutehtaan tyttö/The Match Factory Girl appeared in 1988 and 1990 respectively. Shadows in Paradise won the Finnish national film award, the Jussi, for Best Film and Best Director in 1986 and it was featured at the Cannes Directors' Fortnight in 1987. In her dissertation on the film's critical reception in Finland Giedrė Andreikėnaitė (2003: 5–6) describes Shadows in Paradise as an incomparable phenomenon of Finnish cinema, one that both baffled and pleased critics by its mix of fantasy, realism, national content and understanding of international cinematic aesthetics. While it was not the director's first film, Shadows in Paradise was integral in increasing Aki Kaurismäki's profile both nationally and internationally.

The film has become iconic in Kaurismäki's oeuvre. It is slow, measured: the acting, pacing and mise-en-scène are admirably restrained. Yet, a bleak, anarchic humour marks the work. 'The classic night: cinema, bar, shitfaced,' insists Melartin. Graffiti on the jail cell wall responds to Nikander's question – 'Where am I?', 'Here, in the slammer, fuck!' Ilona decides not to go to Florida: reportedly there are only Finns and Donald Ducks there. 'Humour' is perhaps the wrong word. There are no jokes, but the ridiculousness of life is laid bare.

The film begins with the blue doors of an industrial hall. The doors slowly open, resembling curtains at the start of a play, or a film in old-fashioned cinemas. A powerful dialectical image, the curtain-doors announce the start of a narrative, and simultaneously draw attention to the constructed and artificial nature of the process itself. The doors open, and workers dressed in blue overalls walk into the hall. The men appear as if emerging from among the audience, entering the screen to play their part in the filmed narrative. Once the men have collected their rosters, garbage trucks begin filing out of the hall to start their rounds. The dawn scene is dominated by blue tones, from the trucks themselves to traffic signs. Although the colours evoke those of the Finnish flag, they do not express an unproblematic, romanticized Finnishness. The trucks, while painted 'Finnish', are of Swedish manufacture, and the blue-grey tint of large garbage bins underscores the idea of an unromantic national identification. Indeed, filmed in the years of glasnost and economic scheming, and only a few years before the phenomenal geopolitical shifts of 1989 and the subsequent economic crisis of the early 1990s, the film raises questions regarding the realities and myths of Finnishness at a time of relentless commercialism and irreversible social change.

While the curtain-doors foreground the start of a narrative, the workers symbolically breaking the fourth wall by moving from without to within the narrative does not indicate a disruption of the narrative, but rather a conscious decision to take part in the storytelling process. That the start of the film so explicitly claims narrative agency for a group of uniformed workers emphasizes the collective mode of the story. The subsequent focus on one of these uniformed workers suggests Nikander's story is not personal but social. Just as the garbage collectors come to represent the conflicted, unromanticized nation by stepping forward from the audience, Nikander is a further focused symbolic representative of the collective of Everymen.

Narrative processes are similarly foregrounded throughout the film. Nikander's older, unnamed colleague suggests Nikander join him as a foreman in a soon-to-be operational private garbage disposal company. After offering him a drink, Nikander's colleague addresses the protagonist by name before proposing the venture: 'Listen, Nikander'. In her analysis of the film, Satu Kyösola (1993: 36) suggests that the positioning of the colleague's bottle of alcohol recalls a microphone in an interview situation, and so underlines the beginning of a story. Kyösola also argues that the inducement to listen applies as much to the audience as it does to Nikander. It is this latter connection in particular that further emphasizes Nikander's role as an Everyman, a representative of the nation. Having already been shown as emerging from among the nation-as-audience, Nikander's naming coincides with him 'returning' to this position: he is an audience to the older colleague's narrative. However, the presence of the bottle-as-microphone also suggests a dialogic interaction, implying that Everyman Nikander will have some say in the direction of the story. The use of the bottle also plays with perceptions of Finnish men only being able to 'express themselves' with the help of alcohol.

Pietari Kääpä (2006) discusses locations in Kaurismäkian films, such as the rubbish collection route, as corresponding to Michel Foucault's 'heterotopias', or 'counter-sites': buildings and delimited areas that somehow code social transition or transgression. Shadows in Paradise is mainly set in such places which by their existence expose the compulsion to control society and imagine the nation. Garbage collection, featured throughout the film, is a normalizing and controlling heterotopian task. As a garbage collector, Nikander adjusts and corrects the capital cityscape, and is an integral part of keeping both the margins and the centre of the city ordered and respectable: in the introductory sequence he is seen emptying a bin near the empire-style centre of the city, the iconic Uspenski church and the Helsinki cathedral in the background, as well as in inner-city courtyards and back alleys. Although in his working life Nikander ritually creates an ideal cityscape, he is excluded from some levels of society precisely because of this function: a maitre d' will not let him and Ilona dine in an upmarket restaurant, and Ilona's employer refers to him derogatively as the 'shit collector'. Nikander's presence reveals that a place has to be dirtied before it can be cleaned, that national authenticity cannot exist without invention, editing and make-believe. His heterotopian identification leads Nikander to being associated not with order and cleanliness, but with the refuse of society: whilst in the cinema with the Melartins, Nikander does not even look up at the screen until a character calls out 'you're trash!' Nikander is indeed trash: not only is he a marginal social figure associated with rubbish in his daily work, in this particular context he has been rejected by Ilona, in effect 'dumped'. The fact that the only person to have genuine interest in the serially-dismissed Ilona is a garbage collector of course marks her as equally heterotopian 'trash.'

The film-within-a-film also draws attention to the act of spectating. The film reflects the audience back at itself, again emphasizing Nikander's collective and representative function. The film's theatrical release, the auteur's well-known cinephilia and the diegetic depiction of cinema-going in the film itself suggest that the intended, ideal audience is, aside from being Finnish, specifically a theatrical one. It is only the cinema-going viewership of Shadows in Paradise that can feel part of the same collective as Nikander: only a cinema-going audience can experience the same ironic detachment from that single line shouted to Nikander from The Good, The Bad and The Ugly (Leone, 1966). Like the curtain-doors at the start of the film, the line reflects on Nikander's 'heterotopianness' and exposes narrative practice, while reinforcing Nikander's and the audience's existence within the same collective.

The foregrounding of narrative practice emphasizes the role of the film itself as the first in a trilogy; a point of departure from more common depictions of Finland on-screen. As all of Aki Kaurismäki's films, Shadows in Paradise deals with universally applicable themes of urban belonging, alienation and friendship. The film also sets itself up as an alternative perspective on the national imaginary, all the while acknowledging and revelling in its own artifices.

Sanna Peden

References

Andreikėnaitė, G. (2003), 'Aki Kaurismäen Elokuvan *Varjoja paratiisissa* Lehdistövastaanotto Suomessa', Masters dissertation, Turku: University of Turku.

Elonet (n.d.), Varjoja paratiisissa, http://www.elonet.fi/title/ek2ar8/. Accessed 22 December 2010.

Kääpä, Pietari (2006), '"Displaced Souls Lost in Finland": the Kaurismäkis' Films as Cinema of the Marginalised', *Wider Screen*, 2.

Kyösola, Satu (1993), '*Shadows in Paradise* de Aki Kaurismäki – Un film, un style', Paris: Université de la Sorbonne Nouvelle.

Insiders

Production company:
Fantasia Filmi

Distributor:
Finnkino

Director:
Lauri Törhönen

Producers:
Asko Apajalahti
Tapio Suominen

Screenwriters:
Asko Apajalahti
Michael Baran
Tapio Suominen
Lauri Törhönen

Cinematographer:
Timo Heinänen

Composer:
Johnny Lee Michaels

Editor:
Olli Soinio

Duration:
107 minutes

Cast:
Mikko Reitala
Ilkka Heiskanen
Niina Nurminen
Katja Kiuru
Markku Mustonen

Year:
1989

Synopsis

Reporter Saaristo (Mustonen) aims to do a piece on the upper-class yuppie culture of mid-to-late 1980s Finland for his tabloid paper. Invited to a party for high rollers by Lasse Fjält (Reitala), a CEO of an investment company, Saaristo captures all the excesses of this culture. He leaves a tape recorder in the bathroom of the mansion, which in turn captures explosive material on illegal insider trading. The tight group around Fjält is implicated in blackmail and corruption as they turn on each other following the revelations. Their conflicts escalate until a member of the group is found murdered.

Critique

The 1980s were a tumultuous era in Finnish society. The liberalization of regulations on financial investments abroad and gambling on loans and stocks had become a way of life for the young elite of the nation. As risk and gambling on financial assets was valorized, the period came to be known as the era of 'casino economics'. Part of this emergent culture was the need to show off one's wealth, which enabled one to enter the social circles of the elite. *Insiders* is a depiction of this culture from a perspective that initially seems critical of the shallowness of the lifestyle. But much as Oliver Stone's *Wall Street* (1987) had provided a cornerstone for yuppie identification, so *Insiders* was appropriated by the very social group it seemed to criticize. Both films highlight the corruption and violence lurking beneath the civilised surface, but they are simultaneously enamoured by the hypercapitalism on display. Perhaps to highlight the sleaziness of the lifestyle, perhaps to revel in its lack of morality and marketable value for cinematic consumers, the film's focus on muscle cars, parties fuelled by cocaine and booze, designer clothes, early mobiles, etc., provides an appropriately flashy surface, complemented further by its excessive focus on female nudity and fornication which takes place at the parties. The excessive and narratively redundant lesbian sex scenes and orgies especially drew the ire of the critics. Many suggested the film exploited the sensationalism caused by its sex scenes and drugs to provide the film with more publicity. Ironically, then, it seems the film actually became an embodiment of the lifestyle it aimed to depict.

Another frequent accusation was directed at Törhönen's attempts to emulate international conventions and produce cinema that transcended the nation, while relying on these very confines for its thematic material. Törhönen's previous production had been the spy thriller *Jään kääntöpiiri/Tropic of Ice* (1987), which clearly emulated the conventions of the popular Cold War spy genre. This film had been criticized widely for its crass attempts at achieving international production standards and for its superficial narrative. Similar criticism met *Insiders*, though critics went even further here as some suggested it was catastrophical in its wide-eyed look at yuppies and its inability to create a believable narrative. The film has since gained a substantial cult following and was indeed embraced at the time of its release by the group it nominally criticizes. *Insiders* was not the only contemporary film to criticize the casino economics era, but it was certainly the only one with enough superficiality and glamour to make it a hit in the yuppie circles. For example, Kaurismäki's *Hamlet liikemaailmassa/Hamlet Goes Business* (1987) provides a hard-hitting and wide-ranging criticism of the era, often working allegorically and refusing any sort of idolization of capitalism. Törhönen's work is more easily identifiable as commercialist in its aspirations, which leaves it open for intense criticism. While the film is by no means a traditionally commendable effort, its life philosophy and style are true testaments of an era and thus integral parts of national cultural history.

Pietari Kääpä

The Well

Kaivo

Production companies:
FilmTeknik
Kino Finlandia
Metronome Productions
Nordisk Film- & TV-Fond
Nordvision
Svenska Filminstitutet (SFI)
Yleisradio (YLE)

Director:
Pekka Lehto

Producer:
Pekka Lehto

Screenwriter:
Outi Nyytäjä

Synopsis

A farmhouse family in rural southern Finland meets the worst of the worst tragedies, as the mother kills her three children by drowning them in a well.

Critique

The Well is a family tragedy, based on a true story that took place in rural southern Finland in the 1980s. Anna-Maija (Larivaara) drowns her three children in a well in the yard of the family house and is later convicted for murder. The tragic death of the children is, however, only the tip of the iceberg in the entire story of the unfortunate family. The family is despotically ruled by the mother-in-law, Taimi (Laaksonen), who throws her own discontent, frustration and self-hatred on her daughter-in-law's face. Anna-Maija's husband, a second- or more likely third- or even fourth-generation farmer, lets his mother poison the family atmosphere, as he does not know anything better. The husband closes his eyes, leaves his wife alone in the house with his mother and escapes to the fields and hard farm work, as well as wallowing in his distressing silence.

Cinematographer:
Esa Vuorinen

Composer:
Anssi Tikanmäki

Editor:
Arturas Pozdniakovas

Duration:
110 minutes

Cast:
Merja Larivaara
Liisa-Maija Laaksonen
Katariina Kaitue
Auvo Vihro
Martti Suosalo
Otto Hakala
Dick Idman

Year:
1992

Taimi's malevolence and mordant words gradually drive Anna-Maija towards mental disorder – her psychological and behavioural system does not last the pressure she is under in her own house, and the pressure is released in the most dramatic and irreversible manner, as she carries her children one by one to the well on a beautiful summer night.

Outwardly the family in *The Well* is a model example of a hard-working and successful Finnish rural family, whose estate and livestock is grand and in precise order. The family at its best is representative of Protestant values and the Lutheran work ethic highly valued in Finland, although beneath the surface the emotions and family dynamics are not as ideal. The values and work ethic that are shown to the outside world do not exist in that form in the inner family life, and they are highlighted in Anna-Maija's daily habit as she washes all the cows of the farm every single day. This daily routine offers her some mental support and illusion of control over her deep depression and helpless situation, despite the fact that the cows do not need such regular treatment. It seems obvious, however, that finally there is only one way to counteract the resentful rule of he controlling and vicious mother-in-law; that is her desperate act of murder, acting in her mind as a form of euthanasia on her own children. Through this depiction, *The Well* provides a deconstruction of the rural idyll and the value system it supposedly embodies – a theme often depicted in utopian terms in domestic cinema.

Merja Larivaara and Liisamaija Laaksonen were both awarded Jussi Awards by the Finnish film industry for Best Actress in a Leading Role and the Best Supporting Actress, respectively, in 1992. The intensity between the two actresses is indeed tangible and prepares the audience to accept the inevitability of the forthcoming tragedy. The power relation between the two women dominates the whole film and plays a prominent part of the whole tragedy. Explaining the tragedy through the wickedness of an elderly woman and the irresponsible and emotional coldness of the 'slayer mother' could be interpreted as misogynist, no matter how artistically ambitious and successful the film itself is.

Nevertheless, it can be argued that *The Well* is certainly one if not the best of Pekka Lehto's films. Lehto is a film-maker with a career spanning a lifetime of working with many Finnish long-term professionals such as Jörn Donner, Pirjo Honkasalo, Ere Kokkonen, Maunu Kurkvaara, Claes Olsson and Pertti 'Spede' Pasanen. In addition to full-length fiction films, he has made documentaries, and appropriately a key characteristic of his films is a passion for mixing fiction and real life. On the one hand, the most recent full-length fiction films such as *The Real McCoy* (1999), *Tango Kabaree/Tango Cabaret* (2001) and *Game Over* (2005) walk a tightrope between fact and fiction, but they do not reach the severe emotional trauma of *The Well*. On the other hand, many of his documentaries such as 'biographical' films of Jussi Parviainen (*Yksinteoin/Going it Alone* [1990]), Ior Bock (*Temppeli/The Temple*

[1991]) and Alpo Rusi (*Epäilyksen varjossa/In the Shadow of Doubt* [2010]) undoubtedly cement his esteemed position not only in the Finnish film industry, but also in Finnish cultural history.

Sanna Karkulehto

The Collector

Neitoperho

Production company:
Gnu Films

Distributor:
Finnkino

Director:
Auli Mantila

Producer:
Tero Kaukomaa

Screenwriter:
Auli Mantila

Cinematographer:
Heikki Färm

Editor:
Riitta Poikselkä

Duration:
98 minutes

Cast:
Leea Klemola
Elina Hurme
Robin Svartström
Rea Mauranen

Year:
1997

Synopsis

Mentally disturbed Eevi (Klemola) is both psychologically and physically dependent on her sister Ami (Hurme). As Ami wants to move together with her new girlfriend, she arranges an own apartment to her sister and makes her move out. Feeling rejected, Eevi's already alarming outsiderness, social exclusion and loneliness dramatically explodes. Eevi steals the sister's car and flees. On her aimless road trip Eevi fails in seducing a hitchhiker who is on his way to meet his girlfriend. Eevi's misfortune in love drives her to deeper mental destruction and she maliciously kills the hitchhiker, finds her way to the girlfriend's house and captures her. The lady is a butterfly expert and Eevi wants her to fix a damaged specimen, called the Collector Butterfly. The lady attacks Eevi with a knife and after a fight between the two women, Eevi kills her too. Ami finds her way to the house after Eevi's phone call, as do the police.

The Geography of Fear

Pelon Maantiede

Production companies:
Arte
Blind Spot Pictures Oy
Eurimages
Finnish Film Foundation
Norddeutscher Rundfunk (NDR)
Nordisk Film- & TV-Fond

Distributor:
Finnkino

Director:
Auli Mantila

Producer:
Tero Kaukomaa

Screenwriters:
Auli Mantila, based on the novel by Anja Kauranen

Cinematographer:
Heikki Färm

Original music:
Hilmar Örn Hilmarsson

Editor:
Kimmo Taavila

Duration:
95 minutes

Cast:
Tanjalotta Räikkä
Leea Klemola
Eija Vilpas
Anna-Elina Lyytikäinen

Year:
2000

Synopsis

Psychiatrist Oili (Räikkä) is raped on her way home from work, and she is left in a state of shock and helplessness with no assistance or significant help forthcoming from the police. She meets a group of vigilante women who specialize in abducting and molesting criminals. Initially, the activities provide her with the necessary outlet to lash back out at people who abuse others. Soon, it is increasingly evident that the group's activities border on fanaticism and Oili has to make a real choice between group loyalty and her sense of morality.

Critique

Auli Mantila is one of the few female directors in Finland who has managed to carve out an idiosyncratic body of work. Critics often suggest that her work provides a feminist interrogation of contemporary society, introducing Finnish audiences to the international theme of explicitly aggressive women who are not victims of (male) violence, but become violent themselves. Tarja Laine convincingly argues that in *The Geography of Fear*:

> Mantila shows how women's fear of violence is so pervasive in general attitudes and norms that they have learned well to control the threats to their safety and freedom by adjusting their behaviour, rather than changing their environment. Mantila's women instead take that fear and use it to teach men where their boundaries of personal space lie by re-mapping the geography of fear. (Laine 2000)

In Mantila's perspective, the control over the female body is something that not only operates in the more conventional sense of objectification associated with the male gaze. This also involves concrete domination of social space, reliant on what is best described as a Foucauldian sense of the panoptic. The panoptic is premised on the notion that surveillance and behavioural control are acknowledged as the social norm by the very people who are objects of this control. In other words, especially the relationship between women's fear of male violence and their perception and use of space becomes relevant in contemporary society in which equality between genders remains somewhat ostensible. According to human geographer Gill Valentine, 'women's inhibited use of space is a spatial expression of patriarchy' (1989), and it is this argument in particular that turns into flesh in Mantila's work. Thus, social conditioning constructs a geography of fear which restricts women's movements and behaviour in this 'egalitarian' society. What is more, Mantila's women do not submit to this gendered conception of the controlled and gender-regulated use of space, but fight back. Through its depiction of the violent extremes the vigilante group in *The Geography of Fear* takes, Mantila's film seeks to point out the ways in which women break out of the patriarchal framework that justifies and normalizes their subjugation.

While feminist discourse is certainly a key to understanding Mantila's films, it would be limiting to their scope to insist on inspecting them only in this light. Mantila is an intensely private person, whose perspective on life inevitably filters into her films. She does not allow any photography of herself and does not give interviews for television. Private space was the theme of her debut film *The Collector* (1997) as it focused on an individual, Eevi, who is unable to understand the need for such space as she repeatedly and violently enters private spaces without permission. The film begins with Eevi peeping at people's private photographs while working in a photography laboratory. She does not understand her sister's need for privacy either, and when learning that the hitchhiker she picked up does not let her enter his private space, she becomes violent against him. Eevi's will for controlling other people's personal space reaches its peak when she breaks into the house of the hitchhiker's girlfriend, imprisons her into her own cellar and, despite her morbid control, tries to make the woman her trusted mental support.

The theme of people's right for private space continues in *The Geography of Fear* where space is recontextualized more explicitly in gendered terms. Yet, patriarchal oppression is only a symptom of the wider suffocation engineered by a society which increasingly values profit and dehumanization of its subjects:

> Increasing capitalism has made the human being a simple resource, something like a renewable natural commodity, which has no inherent meaning in itself. The fact that human worth is not recognized and individuals are not respected just because they have been born increases fear and violence in the society. (Mantila 2000)

In these remarks, Mantila gets close to the ideas of Slovenian philosopher Slavoj Žižek on the relationship between capitalism and violence. Žižek talks about 'systemic violence' that makes use of people, and sees it as 'the catastrophic effects of economic and political systems', violence as a way of life ingrained and accepted as part of societal infrastructures (Žižek 2009: 1–2; 9–13). Both *The Collector* and *The Geography of Fear* could be seen as manifestations of these ideas as, according to Mantila, the lack of privacy in society during a capitalist information age is an interpersonal and societal concern, a symptom of wider social malaise. As explorations of social problems and the lack of equality, *The Collector* and *The Geography of Fear* remain important landmarks not only in feminist, but also socially-committed Finnish cinema.

Sanna Karkulehto and Pietari Kääpä

References

Laine, Tarja (2000), 'Body Horror and the Gender of Space and City', http://www.kinoeye.org/03/08/laine08.php. Accessed 4 May 2011.

Rosenqvist, Juha (2000), 'Auli Mantila ja Pelon Maantiede', http://www.film-o-holic.com/haastattelut/auli-mantila-pelon-maantiede/. Accessed 4 May 2011.

Valentine, Gill (1989), 'The Geography of Women's Fear', *Area*, 21: 4, pp. 385–90.

Žižek, Slavoj (2009), *Violence: Six Sideways Reflections*, London: Profile Books.

Restless

Levottomat

Production companies:
Solar Films
Nelonen

Distributor:
Buena Vista International
Finland

Director:
Aku Louhimies

Producer:
Markus Selin

Screenwriters:
Aleksi Bardy
Aku Louhimies

Cinematographers:
Mac Ahlberg
August Jakobsson

Composer:
Leri Leskinen

Editor:
Samu Heikkilä

Duration:
110 minutes

Cast:
Mikko Nousiainen
Laura Malmivaara
Irina Björklund
Petteri Summanen

Year:
2000

Synopsis

Ari (Nousiainen) is a 27-year-old ambulance doctor whose human relationships are based on superficiality and momentary pleasure. For him, a one-night stand is as profound as it gets, but soon he discovers that all this skin-based shallowness has left him with an empty void inside. Tiina (Malmivaara) provides him with a challenge as she seems different from the other women he has dated. But soon she wants to get serious and Ari self-destructs the relationship in spectacular fashion by sleeping with her friends. But his past soon catches up and he is left alone to ponder his life.

Critique

Restless is something of a zeitgeist film, taking up the fashionable topic of exploring the casual relationships of young professionals. Co-produced by Solar Films, Markus Selin's commercial production house, the film explores the increasing sense of detachment of individuals in a society based on material gain and interpersonal transience. The film has often been mentioned as a spiritual successor to Lauri Törhönen's *Insiders* (1989) in its examination of a group of young professionals who are more interested in money than maintaining human connections. And as *Insiders* was very much a product of its time, so *Restless* captures the attitudes of individuals from Generation X gaining access to the employment world. And as was the case with Törhönen's film, the final product is very much a part of the culture it aims to criticize. It tries to tell us of the empty lives of its protagonists, but there is also a pervasive sense of sensationalism to all aspects of the film, from its theme to its production and marketing. While one could argue that individual self-gratification and lack of any ideological mooring is the critical theme of the film, it also seems to celebrate this lifestyle. Indeed, the film was a massive success on its release and acts precisely as the type of cinematic therapy that allows spectators to justify their lifestyles by criticizing how bad other people have it. Accordingly, we see Ari return to one of his former loves for redemption in the ambiguous conclusion. This is of course a typical tactic for films which explore hedonistic lifestyles. Thus, it can work both ways as a sexually explicit tale of contemporary relationships, and a condemnation of the lifestyles on which it relies.

Restless accumulated close to 300,000 viewers at the domestic box office so it was not surprising that it was to result in two sequels, the first of which was only tangentially connected to the narrative of the film. Lenka Helstedt's *Minä ja Morrison/Me and Morrison* (2001) depicts the relationship between Milla (Björklund) and single dad Aki (Samuli Edelmann). Both protagonists are aloof in the world: Milla due to a personal inability to settle with anyone and Aki because he acts as a drug smuggler. It is a less confrontational film than its predecessor as the narrative provides less caricatured individuals as surrogates for audience identification. It was also very successful at the domestic box office reaching over 200,000 spectators. It benefitted substantially from the marketing provided by Solar Films including auxiliary products such as hit singles and sensational coverage of its controversial themes. As with its predecessor, *Me and Morrison* is still most well-known for its explicit sex scenes rather than any merit in its narrative.

Minna Virtanen's *Levottomat 3/Addiction* (2004), the third film in the series, also focuses on a career-motivated individual who is addicted to extramarital sex as her married life is not enough to fulfil her physical or emotional needs. The film is extremely sensationalist in both its narrative and its adjacent publicity. While the theme of the film in its own right could be used for a more level-headed exploration of female sexuality, the film aims for simplistic user gratification. Appropriately, its publicity and marketing reflects its shallow thematic content as the producers aimed to generate serious debate in the national press over female identity and sexuality. Unfortunately, much of this was conducted in tabloids and only focused on the most superficial and seemingly shocking aspects of the theme. Pre-publicity for the film focused on a reality television show, *Do you want to be a film star?*, with the intention of casting the winner in the film. The winner of the competition did not become a film star as her role was to be the secretary of the protagonist, amounting to only a minute of screen time. While all these tactics provoked criticism after criticism for the production, it truly puts the idea of 'there's no such thing as bad publicity' to the test. Unsurprisingly, the film met with extremely negative critical reception domestically. Yet, it received over 130,000 spectators domestically, qualifying it as the fourth most successful domestic release of that year. Whereas the other two instalments of the series were considered a bit more seriously in the press, the third one was outright panned. It also has the dubious distinction of being the only Finnish film in the bottom 100 list on imdb.com, yet it remains one of the most widely downloaded Finnish films of all time.

In the 1980s, Selin had already suggested the need to utilize publicity and auxiliary products for franchising purposes, and with the *Restless* trilogy he had his franchise. In utilizing the means of multimedia generated publicity, *Addiction* is truly a product of its time. It is both naïve in its perception of domestic audiences and exploitative in its ability to manipulate the reality television craving audiences. The *Restless* film series is an intriguing indication of the ways Finnish cinema develops throughout the early parts of the 2000s. While sensationalism has always been profitable for domestic producers, this series fully embraces its commercial potential without recourse to superficial moralizing. It is both highly successful domestic cinema and an indicator of some of its contemporary fallacies.

Pietari Kääpä

The Man Without a Past

Mies Vailla Menneisyyttä

Production companies:
Bavaria Film
Pandora Filmproduktion
Pyramide Productions
Sputnik Oy
Yleisradio (YLE)

Distributor:
Untied International Pictures,

Director:
Aki Kaurismäki

Producer:
Aki Kaurismäki

Screenwriter:
Aki Kaurismäki

Art director:
Markku Pätilä

Cinematographer:
Timo Salminen

Editor:
Timo Linnasalo

Duration:
97 minutes

Cast:
Markku Peltola
Kati Outinen
Sakari Kuosmanen
Juhani Niemelä
Kaija Pakarinen

Year:
2002

Synopsis

An anonymous man, M (Peltola), is beaten on arrival in Helsinki. Having been declared dead in hospital, he suddenly awakes and leaves. He is taken in by the Nieminen family living in a village of disused shipping containers, and begins to forge a place for himself in this marginal society, even while he cannot remember his name or anything about his past life. He becomes involved with the Salvation Army as a manager for the group's musicians, and begins a cautious romance with Irma (Outinen), one of the officers. M's witnessing of a bank robbery acts as a catalyst for officialdom to find out his true identity, and eventually M does learn his real name and some details about his past, for example the fact that he was recently divorced. Having reached some closure about his past life, M returns to the shanty town in Helsinki to commit to a life with Irma.

Critique

The Man Without a Past is the most successful of Aki Kaurismäki's films. In addition to winning almost all feature film Jussis in 2003 – Best Editing, Script, Cinematography, Actress, Film and Director – it won the Grand Prix at the Cannes Film Festival, where Kati Outinen was also awarded Best Actress. The film won a host of other awards at festivals around the world, and was also the first Finnish film to have been nominated for a foreign language Oscar. The international successes of the film elicited much public discussion in Finland: on the one hand the film's successes were reported as national victories (Pajala 2003), on the other hand there was significant unease over the popularity of a film which depicted poverty and homelessness in Finland – 'What if the foreigners think it's all true?'

Having made the silent black-and-white film *Juha* in 1998, Kaurismäki returned to film-making with his most sumptuously coloured film to date. The richness of colour in *The Man Without a Past* reflects the density of emotion at play: love is pure and true, loss hits the protagonists hard, and melancholy, longing and hope shape their experiences. The highly stylised diegesis, from the settings to the speech patterns, is full of affection for its inhabitants.

There are frequent references to different periods of national challenge, linking M's wanderings on the margins of society in the twenty-first century to earlier periods of national transition: for example, some scenes recall nationally significant paintings from the nineteenth and early twentieth century; other scenes suggest the post-Second World War era of rebuilding; and others remind the viewer of more recent events, such as the financial crisis of the 1990s. The film also features cameo appearances by high-profile Finns, whose public personas enhance the sense of national negotiation in the film text. For example, the head of the Salvation Army flea market is played by Annikki Tähti, a popular postwar performer. The sight of Tähti singing her own nostalgic hit 'Do You Remember Mon Repos?' bestows the closing scene of the film with a heightened sense of nostalgia, as the song's lament for ceded Karelia and the 'wondrous land' of youth combines with the sight of Tähti's aged, weathered face and the sound of her weakened voice (Koivunen 2006: 142). There is a similar nostalgic effect in casting Anneli Sauli, a popular actor famous for her sensual roles in postwar film, as a sympathetic cafeteria owner.

Throughout the film M is confronted with reminders that he as himself is not enough to be taken seriously: he needs a bank account and a social security number at the very least to belong in society. Attempting to open a bank account, he witnesses a bank robbery. He is taken into police custody and interrogated, not as a suspect of the robbery, but as a person whose inability to remember his name seems suspicious to the core, profoundly un-Finnish and worthy of further investigation. One of the police officers justifies the jailing simply with 'You could be a foreigner'. When M points out that he does speak Finnish, the officer does not change course: 'You people are fast learners'. M is finally released from police custody following intervention by the celebrated human rights attorney Matti Wuori: the absurd duel of expertly-delivered legalese between Wuori and the police chief serves as a critique of a system that chooses to interpret M's misfortunes as malicious, instead of directing its energies to helping him.

Shortly afterwards, M comes across the bank robber (Esko Nikkari) in a bar. The robber, a bankrupted builder, explains he took money from his own frozen account to pay the wages he owes to former workers. He describes his bankruptcy as a result of unscrupulous banks exploiting small business owners, finishing his tale with 'as you know'. The comment implies the builder's situation is a typical one, recalling the large-scale economic crisis of the 1990s. The scene is shot in the Kaurismäki-owned Moskva-bar, which has been furnished with items the director has collected over the years for his film sets. The scene further emphasizes the internal consistency within Kaurismäki's oeuvre by including a tribute to a deceased former cast member. On the wall behind M and the bankrupted builder is a picture of Matti Pellonpää, who has a similar moustache to the builder. The physical similarity of Pellonpää and Nikkari visually connects the two characters, and recalls in particular the first film of Kaurismäki's proletarian trilogy: Varjoja paratiisissa/Shadows in Paradise (1986). In the film, the same two men play garbage truck drivers about to start their own business. Nikkari's character in Shadows in Paradise states that starting a company should not be too difficult. He announces that the government supports businesses, and 'it's easy to get a loan', an aspect which has been identified as one of the causes for the

The Man Without a Past, Sputnik Oy.

economic downturn in the 1990s. The tribute to Pellonpää, then, highlights the continuing causal relationship between the economic boom of the 1980s, the crisis of unemployment in the 1990s and Kaurismäki's more contemporary critique of social marginalization (Peden 2009: 92–93).

Having received confirmation of his true identity and an absolution of sorts from his past – his ex-wife has a new partner – M's return to Helsinki is an optimistic one, and holds the promise of belonging and successful adaptation. On the train back, M is served a plate of sushi and some sake, which he calmly consumes as a Japanese song plays in the background. M's aptitude at using chopsticks suggests he has been able to adapt to new challenges, and can take advantage of signs of globalization for his own needs. The attendant's polite way of addressing M, even referring to him as 'good sir', indicates that M has become an accepted and integrated part of society.

When he arrives in Helsinki, M comes across the same gang who attacked him, but a group of homeless men appear from behind M and proceed to chase the attackers. The sudden display of solidarity among the community emphasizes a sense of continuity between M's nameless state and his new, socially more acceptable identity: he is a 'good sir' to the train staff, yet the homeless community still considers him one of them. The bridging of different identifications is made more explicit with the arrival of the guard Anttila (Kuosmanen). Anttila tells M that the three have beaten up 'many of us'. M seems surprised, assuming Anttila means security guards. Anttila corrects him by repeating 'many of *us*' indicating he considers M and himself to belong to the same group of people. As Anttila has earlier in the film asserted himself as an unsympathetic authority figure of the community, his acceptance of M and the other homeless men as equals signifies a shift in identity. M has been able to bring a new sense of unity into the marginal community by merging his official bureaucratic identity and his self-made shanty town persona.

Sanna Peden

References

Koivunen, Anu (2006), '"Do You Remember Monrépos?" Melancholia, Modernity and Working-class Masculinity in *The Man Without a Past*', in C. C. Thomson, (ed.), *Northern Constellations: New Readings in Nordic Cinema*, Norwich: Norvik Press, pp. 133–48.

Pajala, M. (2003), 'Suomalainen Voittaa Aina', *Lähikuva*, 3, pp. 3–7.

Peden, Sanna (2009), 'Still in the *Shadows*: Reconsidering History through Intertextual References in Aki Kaurismäki's European Films', in H. Radner and P. Fossen (eds), *Remapping Cinema, Remaking History*, Dunedin: University of Otago, pp. 85–95.

Frozen Land

Paha maa

Production company:
Solar Films
Yleisradio (YLE)

Distributor:
Birch tree Entertainment
ICA Projects (UK)

Director:
Aku Louhimies

Producer:
Markus Selin

Synopsis

Frozen Land could be characterized as an avalanche of sin centred around a €500 note. The plot commences with a teacher's distress after he finds out that due to some 'reorganizing', he is no longer needed in the school. To wallow in his misery, he gets drunk and takes his anger out on his lazy teenage son, Niko (Pääkkönen), and throws him out of the apartment. Niko wanders the streets penniless, but soon meets one of his old friends Tuomas (Leppilampi), who is organizing a wild party with his girlfriend Elina (Tola) in their home. At the party, Niko gets bored and goes through some files on the young couple's computer, where he finds pictures of 500 notes, and prints one for himself. Later in the pawnshop he pays with the fake banknote – this is where the vicious circle of the false money starts, always changing hands, always bringing misery to its owners.

Screenwriters:

Paavo Westerberg

Jari Rantala

Aku Louhimies, based on a story
by Leo Tolstoy

Art director:

Sattva-Anna Toiviainen

Cinematographer:

Rauno Ronkainen

Editor:

Samu Heikkilä

Duration:

130 minuntes

Cast:

Jasper Pääkkönen

Mikko Leppilampi

Pamela Tola

Petteri Summanen

Year:

2005

Critique

Aku Louhimies has emerged as one of Finland's most talented directors in the last few years. *Frozen Land* is loosely based on Leo Tolstoy's drama, whose main theme is the pessimistic perception that individual sins are so contagious that they can contaminate unrelated individuals in unnoticed ways. This is not the first time that Louhimies has drawn inspiration from literary works – his first film *Levottomat/ Restless* (2000) was inspired by Albert Camus' debut novel, *L'Etranger/The Stranger*. Although it was a relative international success, the reception of *Frozen Land* was decidedly mixed in Finland. Finns either loved or hated it, while foreign audiences seem to have enjoyed it the most. This is potentially a result of the film using a range of familiar cultural tropes about the Finnish society and the 'national character': for example, the use of the drunk Finnish stereotype was often criticized domestically, while foreign audiences seem to find such characteristics endlessly fascinating – see the popularity of Aki Kaurismäki's films in the international markets.

Although the roots of the story were conceived a hundred years ago, it still relates to the powerful problems of our contemporary society: they may be clichés, but unemployment, alcoholism, drug addiction, family conflicts, murder and theft appear in every minute of the film, sometimes in parallel, sometimes in combined scenes. The film's title literally translates as *The Bad Land*, which emphasizes that the Nordic welfare state of Finland can be just as a terrible as any other country in the world with miserable and unemployed people whose acts and feelings affect their society as a whole.

The idea of a sinful city is not a brand new concept in film history, but the way the film connects all these fates is somewhat unique for Finland. Continuing from the work of Jarmo Lampela in the multi-narrative *Joki/The River* (2001) (in itself inspired by Robert Altman's *Short Cuts* [1993] amongst others), Louhimies' film provides a bold and often austerely humorous portrayal of modern life and human frailty. Individual citizens, all people unknown to each other, are connected through a chain reaction caused by a fusion of personal problems. As Peter Tattersall notes, the film also deals with the Heideggerian concept of being 'thrown into the world': the tragedy of the characters can be attributed to the fact that they fail to recognize the opportunities offered by their lives. They largely react passively against a world they perceive to be bad, whereas reality is often a more complex combination of societal malaise and individual failure.

Frozen Land fits perfectly in the line of sociorealist Finnish cinema, capturing the difficulties of everyday life. This is complemented by a distinct strive for realism, almost if the film was a documentary. Rauno Ronkainen's cinematography and Samu Heikkilä's editing strive to maintain this effect with grainy and handheld camerawork which emphasizes extreme close-ups, reinforcing the sense of immediacy and realism. Violence, sexual and verbal abuse are constantly present, which creates a package of feel-bad angst and social oppression. All in all, this is a fascinating continuation of a key genre in Finnish cinema.

Emőke Csoma

References

Tattersall, Peter (2005), 'Heidegger's Resoluteness in the Film Paha Maa', *Mustekala*, 9:3.

Man's Job

Miehen työ

Production companies:
Blind Spot Pictures Oy
Yleisradio (YLE)

Distributor:
Sandrew Metronome
Distribution

Director:
Aleksi Salmenperä

Producers:
Petri Jokiranta
Tero Kaukomaa

Screenwriter:
Aleksi Salmenperä

Art director:
Markku Pätilä

Cinematographer:
Tuomo Hutri

Composer:
Ville Tanttu

Editor:
Samu Heikkilä

Duration:
97 minutes

Cast:
Tommi Korpela
Maria Heiskanen
Jani Volanen
Konsta Pylkkönen

Year:
2007

Synopsis

Aleksi Salmenperä's psychological family drama takes place in Finland's developed information age society and tells a story about the world's oldest profession – prostitution – in this case perpetrated by a man. Juha (Korpela) is an average middle-aged man who has a family and a job; in short, everything's going well for him (except for his wife who is taking antidepressants). One morning, Juha gets laid off and, as he is too afraid to tell his wife the truth, he tries to make a living by offering his services as a handyman to private customers – unsuccessfully. He gets hired by an older woman who is more interested in his body rather than his construction skills. In less than two hours he has made more money than he used to get for a week's work as a construction worker. Despite the warnings of his friend Olli (Volanen), he continues with his new job and finds himself in increasingly bizarre situations. The money helps him cope with the downsides of his new work, but he is unable to resolve the growing tension in his family.

Critique

Aleksi Salmenperä's second feature shows important details of the dark side of everyday life, and about the responsibilities and obligations of a family man in the transforming welfare society. Juha fails to do what he believes is expected of him, thinking that money is more important in the family than his presence at home. Thus, the film becomes a study of masculinity and the challenges men face when their lives are governed by traditionalist thinking. In this film, prostitution not only symbolizes sexual liberalism, moral decay and family breakdown, but everything that is wrong with the existing social order; it is the culmination of broken social structures. In a patriarchal society, men occupy more high-status roles than women because they are expected to be the breadwinner of the family – and because they are expected to do this, they are offered more chances. This cannot be said about Juha as he faces an ironic role-reversal, a doubled emasculation by first losing his job and then taking on the 'usual' woman's work. In this way the film interrogates gender roles that are nowhere near as stable as they are often perceived.

Despite the consistently gloomy realism of the film, its climax is not pessimistic. Juha overdoses on pills and lies unconscious and naked on the couch, while his wife smashes his ankle with a hammer. While he is being pushed to the ambulance, his motionless face shows a mysterious smile and his wife's hand reaches out for him, showing that there is hope for a second chance. By forgiving each other, they will be able to overcome the negative effects of the events, which will help them reinstitute their social ties. The strength of *Man's Job* is in its emphasis on humanity in the face of insurmountable challenges. Visually it does not show off as the cinematography goes for an invisible, seamless and smooth look. While the story revolves around massive changes of character in its protagonist, the realistic environment and modest presentation allow it to maintain a down-to-earth feeling. Neither does it go for easy moralizing as it does not represent sin as an exotic, desirable matter but something which may be a necessity, a constant part of the human experience. The director moves his actors well: the protagonist's usually lethargic, motionless face and constant expressionless gaze is able to explore the deepest depths of the human soul. Salmenperä subtly and sensitively illustrates prostitution, the conflict between traditional and modern gender roles in society, attitudes to mental illness and family responsibility.

In many ways, the film is highly ironic of the profit-oriented worldview of information-age Finland. Juha accepts the women's wishes and takes everything without questioning: it does not matter what he does for money as it only matters that he can buy a new car, a washing machine; that he can take his family out for a nice trip and everything seems relatively idyllic. In this society, individuals are mostly judged by what they do and what they earn, which is why Juha desperately tries to keep up the appearance of a strong and modern man who is able to support his family without any help. But ultimately, this is shown to be unsustainable as it is the wife that has to physically handicap the man to get him out of this vicious circle. The culmination of the film thus leaves the roles of men and women open – it is entirely unclear what a man's job is in the contemporary society.

Emőke Csoma

Thomas

Production companies:
Silva Mysterium Oy
Yleisradio (YLE)

Distributor:
Pirkanmaan Elokuvakeskus (PEK)

Director:
Miika Soini

Synopsis

Thomas (Pöysti) is an old man who once had a great career as a doctor, but who now lives a simple and isolated life in his apartment. He climbs on a wooden crate to gaze outside his small window, watching people pass by, invisible to the whole world. His flat is furnished moderately, everything is in great order and nothing seems to be very personal except for a photo of his wife. All his old friends are dead, and he feels painfully alone in his little apartment as even his daughter does not want to see him anymore. He does not go out very often and when he does, he wants to return home right away. Everything outside reminds him of his loneliness,

Producers:

Mika Ritalahti

Nico Ritalahti

Janne Wrigstedt

Screenwriters:

Miika Soini, based on short stories by Kjell Askildsen

Art director:

Antti Nikkinen

Cinematographer:

Daniel Lindholm

Composer:

Lasse Enersen

Editor:

Jerem Tonteri

Duration:

70 minutes

Cast:

Lasse Pöysti

Mauri Heikkilä

Visa Koiso-Kanttila

Pentti Siimes

Aarre Karén

Year:

2008

his old age and despondency. One day, while strolling in the park, he meets a fellow older gentleman who recognizes him from the past. This meeting uncovers the repressed memory of Thomas' past mistakes, which may be why he lives alone.

Critique

Miika Soini's debut feature film is a touching story about aging and loneliness, compassion, forgiveness and atonement. It also deals with the delicate topic of euthanasia. *Thomas* is based on short stories focusing on old age written by Kjell Askildsen, a Norwegian writer who is known for his minimalistic style. The director preserved this minimalism, and although this is an extremely sad story, he turned it into a wonderful visual and spiritual experience. Daniel Lindholm's cinematography greatly contributes to the film's calmness, as it often uses pastel colours which illustrate the hollowness of being alone. Lasse Pöysti (born 1927), who plays the title character, is a respected legend in Finland and, despite his old age, he is active in the film business and provides a very authentic portrayal of the protagonist. His tired, motionless face combines comedy and tragedy. Pöysti became a well-known performer in Finland when he was 14-years-old with the role of Olli Suominen in *Suomisen perhe/ The Family Suominen* (Särkkä, 1941), a role he became associated with for a long period of time. While he has covered a wide range of work in his cinematic and television performances, it is intriguingly appropriate to see this legend culminate his lengthy career in this way, almost as if we see the unfolding and conclusion of a life on-screen

Finland has a considerable problem with older people, as depression and even suicide are not entirely uncommon amongst the elderly. Research findings show that about a third of older Finnish people suffer from loneliness and emotional isolation, causing pain and suffering. Feelings of loneliness increase with age as it is related to living alone or even becoming widowed, and not feeling like one plays any meaningful role in society. A further significant contributor to this alienation is urbanization, which has had a major influence on the living conditions of older people. This not only involves the lack of a steady communal support structure in society, but also changes the role of the elderly in society – they are often expendable in the contemporary social order, just bodies that are waiting to perish. They become a statistic, a medical problem, something that is a burden on a thriving and dynamic society. This marginalization is coupled with the long, dark winters, which increase the chances of depression, alcoholism and suicide in young people as well.

By addressing the pervasive nature of social negligence and injustice that most people are aware of but which are rarely discussed in mainstream media, Soini's film makes us reflect on our social mores and behaviour. *Thomas* is a very intimate and touching film as it shows us that there are hidden lives behind every window, someone is always in pain in the crowd. Life and its eccentric twists make an appearance at every level of this film. Yet, this film is not a fable nor is it an explicit attack on society. Rather, it functions as a warning sign as it attempts to involve the spectator emotionally, ultimately coming to emphasize that something must be done about this injustice.

Emőke Csoma

Forbidden Fruit

Kielletty Hedelmä

Production companies:
Helsinki-Filmi Oy
Yleisradio (YLE)

Distributor:
Sandrew Metronome
Distribution

Director:
Dome Karukoski

Producer:
Aleksi Bardy

Screenwriter:
Aleksi Bardy

Art directors:
Antti Mattila
Antti Nikkinen

Cinematographer:
Tuomo Hutri

Composer:
Adam Nordén

Editor:
Harri Ylönen

Duration:
105 minutes

Cast:
Amanda Pilke
Marjut Maristo
Joel Mäkinen
Jani Volanen

Year:
2009

Synopsis

Raakel (Maristo) and Maria (Pilke) receive the chance of a lifetime – to leave their Laestadian religious community for summer in the city. Upon arrival, both girls start to experiment with their newly found freedom. As they come from a close-knit community where ties with next of kin are highly emphasized and where the youth occupy distinctly subservient roles, the freedom of the city results in both girls losing their bearing. Eventually, leaders from the community come to take them back, but by now the girls have grown into independent women and make their own choices.

Critique

The central theme of *Forbidden Fruit* is the age-old separation between the city and the countryside, and the corruptive influence the big city has on innocent outsiders. In many ways, Dome Karukoski's film is a refreshing take on this topic as it explores these well-worn concerns through Laestadians experiencing urban life. As rural communities had by the 2000s become increasingly integrated into the information age society of modern Finland, isolated communities such as those of the Laestadians occupy the familiar role of rural communities in more traditional depictions. In this way the film works as a contemporary interpretation of the city/country dichotomy, where its narrative themes seem entirely familiar, while they are also suggestively updated for the contemporary society. The conservative and authoritarian Laestadians are often criticized or even scandalized in the media for their refusal to acknowledge social equality and the rights of women and sexual minorities. Karukoski's film is refreshing in that it refuses to fall into easy condemnation or rejection of the Laestadian way of life. Instead, it constructs a relatively unbiased look at the conventions of the community, especially the willingness of individuals to be a part of it. But in many ways, the patriarchal and restrictive qualities of the movement still come through as it is clear that Raakel and Maria have never been given the choice for other ways of life. This is the reality they have grown up in and thus it is not entirely unexpected that one of the girls chooses to return to the community.

Simplifications are also present in the film's depiction of the city as a place of corruption and vice as the girls are inundated with parties and alcohol. Karukoski does his best not to condemn this part of the society either as is often the case with these rural/city films. Rather, the need for independence as a key part of becoming an adult is enabled by the choices the girls have to make in the city, which all contribute to the process of growing up. All in all, a refreshingly and unexpectedly mature sense of criticism pervades Karukoski's film in its refusal to condemn either mode of life.

This collision between traditional forms of culture and society and emergent ideas is something that Karukoski has explored in many of his films. If one were to characterize an overarching theme to his works, it would be the ideological transformation of society as seen through the eyes of its youth. From his debut film *Tyttö sinä olet tähti/Beauty and the Bastard* (2005) onwards, he has focused on alternative lifestyles within the mainstream society. The film's central romance between a DJ and a singer creates a narrative of two individuals offbeat (literally) with society. Youth culture and its conflicts and coexistence with traditional culture are themes continued in *Napapiirin sankarit/Lapland Odyssey* (2010). Here, the lingering persistence of tradition is explored through the changing gender roles of contemporary Finland.

These themes come through most effectively in the gender politics of *Forbidden Fruit* and its predecessor *Tummien perhosten koti/The House of the Dark Butterflies* (2008). A key theme of *Forbidden Fruit* is female liberation from the patriarchal oppression of the Laestadian community, where the Laestadian elders are depicted in stern but largely benevolent terms. While they may hold a protective shield for the unprepared youngsters, *Forbidden Fruit* ultimately places social responsibility on the shoulders of its young female protagonists. Yet, the structures of society, at least in their home community, remain very much male centric, something also established in *The House of the Dark Butterflies*. In this touching drama, the leader of the community for young offenders (played by Tommi Korpela) is a stable figure onto whose care the troubled teens are sent for social rehabilitation. It seems that such a force can undo the destruction caused by the protagonist Juhani's unstable and suicidal mother who drowned his sister in an extreme state of depression. It is thus crucial that *Forbidden Fruit* rethinks the patriarchal benevolence and the male-centred space of *The House of the Dark Butterflies*. Though Karukoski has only produced four films, we can already observe the construction of a complex body of work on changing gender relations from a multitude of critical perspectives. It remains to be seen if the prevalence of strong female characters and his professional partnership with actress Pamela Tola will allow for the emergence of films which explore gendered politics in more complex ways than merely focusing on the challenges strong femininity presents for patriarchy. After all, these depictions of masculinity in crisis can be argued to only sustain existing relations and gender inequalities.

Pietari Kääpä

Letters to Father Jacob

Postia pappi Jaakobille

Production companies:
Kinotar
Yleisradio (YLE)

Distributor:
Nordisk Film Theatrical
Distribution

Director:
Klaus Härö

Producers:
Lasse Saarinen
Risto Salomaa

Screenwriter:
Klaus Härö

Art director:
Kaisa Mäkinen

Cinematographer:
Tuomo Hutri

Composer:
Dani Strömbäck

Editor:
Samu Heikkilä

Duration:
74 minutes

Cast:
Kaarina Hazard
Jukka Keinonen
Heikki Nousiainen

Year:
2009

Synopsis

Letters to Father Jacob takes us back to the 1970s through an immaculate visualization of the period. The starting point of the film is almost evangelical: the blind Father Jacob (Nousiainen) takes Leila (Hazard), an ex-convict, into his home as she is pardoned from serving life in prison for murder. Initially, Leila seems to be a harsh person both physically and psychologically, in whom the life and sight of this vulnerable old priest only arouses annoyance. Father Jacob gets many letters from people who have all sorts of spiritual and sometimes financial problems. Leila becomes Father Jacob's secretary, a writer and reader to aid the priest in his life and work. Living together actually subverts their lives more than they would ever think: the priest faces the fact that his correspondence serves his own spiritual needs more than any sort of philanthropic religious communality, and Leila realizes that she has much more to do with God than she ever considered or even wanted to have – she is a lamb disguised as a wolf.

Critique

Klaus Härö's work to date is like a puzzle: each of the pieces fit together in very subtle ways, creating a sense of an enchanting emotional journey. His fourth feature film, *Letters to Father Jacob*, is no exception as its thematic focus and sensitive approach perfectly continues the topics of the director's previous films (*Näkymätön Elina/Elina: As If I Wasn't There* [2002]; *Äideistä parhain/Mother of Mine* [2005]; *Den nya människan/The New Man* [2007]). In Härö's sophisticated dramas, human relations and loneliness consistently take central place. While they often represent sadness, pain and suffering through simple images, the authentic and committed acting and the well-developed screenplays allow these dramas to leave a resonant impression with the viewer. Härö has been called a cinematic poet, and has received the Ingmar Bergman Prize in 2004, which is significant as winners were chosen by Bergman himself. *Letters to Father Jacob* was originally made for television, but it was a surprise success on its theatrical release, and it was ultimately submitted for consideration for the Best Foreign Language Film Oscar at the 82nd Academy Awards.

The film's essence does not necessarily reside in the story itself, but rather in its combination of the work of a great director and a wonderful cinematographic style. Härö prefers simplifying his plots to their purest emotional core, which he uses to capture a sense of empathy for the human condition. The combined intensity of Leila and Father Jacob creates an extraordinary tension: among the minimalist scenery they consume their tea mostly in silence, and they feed themselves with the simplest of dishes under the most modest of circumstances. The breathtaking landscapes emphasize the loneliness of these two people, and broaden the gaping sociocultural edge between them (which disappears by the end of the film). In Härö's film, an optimistic impression of the world comes to life and breaks through the austerity of the protagonists' surroundings.

Although Jacob's blindness has isolated him from other people, he has found a meaningful way to connect with the outside world. For Leila, there is also an opportunity for second chances, as even the most despondent cases can change for the better if you have enough faith. While Härö is a devout Christian, he emphasizes that his films are not about the dissemination of religious ideology. Rather, by faith he does not necessarily mean religious faith, but faith in oneself as sometimes that is more than enough.

The robust-statured masculine Hazard brilliantly assails the oppressive Leila, whose inherent humanity constantly hides behind her angry veneer, while Nousiainen captures both the fragility of the elderly blind priest and the substantial strength that lies inside him. As Jacob represents the goodness of the world and Leila is the embodiment of human disbelief, the duo's harmonious acting is helped by Tuomo Hutri's cinematography: the grim altering of natural light and deep shadows fluctuates between hope and despondency. The ragged but expansive nature and Dani Ström- bäck's music also supports this duality, turning the most bitter thoughts into the most caring and sincere love.

Emőke Csoma

Run Sister Run!

Sisko tahtoisin jäädä

Production companies:
Solar Films
Nelonen

Distributor:
Nordisk Film Theatrical Distribution

Director:
Marja Pyykkö

Producers:
Markus Selin
Jukka Helle
Piia Nokelainen

Screenwriters:
Laura Suhonen
Maria Pyykkö

Art director:
Antti Nikkinen

Cinematographer:
Konsta Sohlberg

Synopsis

Emilia's (Kukkonen) life seems perfect on the surface – she is a conscientious student and effectively a surrogate mother for her sister. Yet, all is not as perfect as it seems. When she meets wild and rebellious Siiri (Melleri) at a party, the two hit it off. In Siiri, she sees independence and unconventionality in ways she aspires to be. Soon, her increasingly aggressive and outrageous behaviour causes major problems not only at school but also in her personal life. Both girls need each other in different ways, but something will eventually need to give in their mutually destructive relationship.

Critique

Pyykkö's Run Sister Run! is part of a long cycle of teenage rebel- lion films that have chronicled Finnish society from the perspective of its alienated youth. Simultaneously, it is part of a wider trend in Nordic film culture, where the seeming contentedness and egalitarianism of the welfare state is critically interrogated in films such as Lukas Moodyson's Fucking Åmål/Show Me Love (1998) and Lilja 4-ever (2002). The emergence of these symptoms at the heart of the Finnish welfare state system continues the work of seminal films such as Käpy selän alla/Skin, Skin (Niskanen, 1966) and Täältä tullaan, elämä/Right on Man! (Suominen, 1980). These are all films with very specific cultural-historical concerns – the counterculture generation had its own politicized modes of engagement with societal traditions, and the urbanized post-Great Migration genera- tion expressed their rebellion in the claustrophobic confines of the cityscapes. Run Sister Run! is set in a seemingly stable social con-

Composer:

Antti Lehtinen

Editor:

Mikko Sippola

Duration:

113 minutes

Cast:

Ada Kukkonen
Sara Melleri
Roope Karisto
Seppo Pääkkönen

Year:

2010

text which more than anything resembles teenage life in the US. The school is a bright and invigorating space full of multicultural students, and the classroom layout and teaching methodology is clearly inspired by conventions seen in mainstream American youth film culture. Certainly, it is very unlike the usual depictions we see in Finnish cinema. According to the stylistic choices of the film-makers, it seems that Finland has become a space that increasingly resembles global (read US) standards.

Yet, a more troubling drama about teenage angst emerges from under this MTV-style harmonious surface. This is a film about exploring boundaries, experimenting with drugs and alcohol, petty criminality, sexual relations, and the very real consequences these have not only on individuals but their families. While the outward sheen of the film may be distinctly about a global Finland, many of its cultural references are specifically Finnish. Thus, parties on the commercial ferries between Finland and Sweden and prominence of the music of the singer Vicky Rosti, well-known in the 1970s, feature prominently. The balancing between domestic cultural references and its more universal themes of teenage alienation and rebellion tell us a lot about contemporary Finland. In earlier youth films, such as the Kaurismäkis' *Arvottomat/The Worthless* (1982) or Jarmo Lampela's *Sairaan kaunis maailma/Freakin' Beautiful World* (1997), the use of imported popular culture and film style high-lights international connectivity. Here, any stylistic influences and thematic concerns to do with internationalism are thoroughly inte-grated into the film's overall structure. No longer a source of stylis-tic or thematic excess (in that they draw attention to themselves), global influences are part of the lives of the film's protagonists and thus part of the normative vernacular of Finnish cinema.

Pietari Kääpä

GENRE

Commercial genre production has been a controversial topic of debate throughout the existence of Finnish cinema. A large part of the discussion relies on the widespread understanding of national cinema as an indigenous art form that expresses the specific cultural values of the nation. This has been especially the case since the early 1960s with the establishment of the Finnish Film Foundation. With its power to designate governmental bursaries to finance domestic cinema, the Foundation's role has been that of a gatekeeper for national cinema. Up until the 1990s, Finnish films were rarely popular genre films as most of the funds were devoted to art films or heritage epics. Consequently, popular forms of cinema have often met with substantial resistance from funding bodies and cultural authorities. Furthermore, any aspirations to produce commercial genre fare has had to rely on government subsidies due to the small size of the domestic audience, effectively making any sort of competitive genre production distinctly problematic. Thus, commercial fare has been shunned in favour of 'artistically experimental' production.

Commercial genre production in Finland has not always been controversial as domestic audiences frequented the cinemas on a regular basis to view a range of commercial product from comedies to melodramas during the studio era. Other genres have also been popular with directors producing plenty of war films, musical comedies, films noir and even the occasional horror film. Out of the latter, *Valkoinen peura/The White Reindeer* (Blomberg, 1952) is especially significant. This tale of a Sami woman who transforms into a reindeer to protect herself against hostile forces was not only a domestic success, the film also won accolades in Cannes and received international distribution in commercial cinemas. Yet, it was not followed by additional contributions to the genre. Whereas genre production was often cyclical during the studio era with popular hits followed by similar titles, *The White Reindeer* falls into more complex ground due to its merging of the popular with more artistic, difficult elements. Thus, 35 years would pass before the horror genre was revitalized, albeit only momentarily, with *Kuutamosonaatti/The Moonlight Sonata* (dir. Olli Soinio) in 1988, an attempt to rework the currently popular slasher film genre to the Finnish confines. The film takes advantage of the Finnish environment with the snowy expanses and the isolation of the log cabin in the woods playing on fears familiar from films such as the *Friday the 13th* series or the expansive plains of Texas in the *Texas Chainsaw Massacre* films. The film was a moderate success and received a sequel, *Kadunlakaisijat/Street Sweepers* (Soinio, 1991), which resurrected the villains of the first film and moved them to the cityscapes of Helsinki. The result was an entirely different animal from the original text. Whereas its predecessor was a Finnish version of the slasher genre, the sequel is more appropriately considered a part of the slapstick splatter genre of the late 1980s (such as Peter Jackson's *Bad Taste* [1987]). While both films have distinct ideological arguments to make and generated much debate over the lack of populism in Finnish cinema, they remain isolated spots in the Finnish cinematic landscape.

Children's films have also attempted to utilize commercial genre tropes, especially in the early parts of the 1980s. Integrating elements from fantasies and fairy tales into films such as Heikki Partanen's *Pessi ja Illusia/Pessi and Illusia* (1984) and Päivi Hartzell's *Lumikuningatar/The Snow Queen* (1986) were met with respectable critical reviews and box office, though they did not manage to create a sustainable genre. This was partially due to their large budgets, but also competition from imported fantasies and domestic low-budget comedy. While blame can be laid on the content of the films, the lack of a sustainable industrial and exhibition structure has proven to be the real downfall of domestic genre production. Similar problems faced Renny Harlin and Markus Selin who collaborated on producing a Finnish version of the popular action film genre with *Born American* (1986) (alternatively known as *Arctic Heat*). It proved to be the most expensive production in Finnish cinema history and effectively bankrupted its producers. The film was the topic of much controversy on its release due to its distinct anti-Soviet rhetoric, and the film was banned for almost a year. In its genre context the film is a successful replica of the muscular action hero genre with plenty of explosive action and gunplay. Unsurprisingly ignored by the domestic critics and audiences, its director has since forged a very successful career in Hollywood while Selin continues to produce commercial domestic genre cinema through his production company Solar Films.

The resurgence of Finnish cinema at the turn of the millennium has been attributed to a range of factors, such as viewing habits and developments in exhibition. Key among these has to be policy changes and embracement of genre conventions by the Finnish Film Foundation. Solar Films continues to act as the predominant innovator in combining Finnish-specific thematic concerns with imported genre frameworks. Aleksi Mäkelä is the company's prime in-house director and also one of the most critically divisive figures in contemporary Finnish cinema. Mäkelä's films have been consistently successful in the twenty-first century, including such blockbusters as the crime epic *Pahat Pojat/Bad Boys* (2003) and the biopic of the ski-jumping superstar Matti Nykänen *Matti* in 2005. These films combine traditional national cinema frameworks with embracement of well-established genre frameworks. For example, the ensemble detective thriller *Vares: Private Eye* (2004) is modelled after the films of Guy Richie, whereas gangster epic *Rööperi/Hellsinki* (2009) seems inspired by Martin Scorsese. Mäkelä got his start by aligning forces with producer Spede Pasanen (well-known for his efforts in popular comedy) to produce the 'first' Finnish action film, *Romanovin kivet/The Romanov Stones* in 1993. Whereas *Born American* was in English with only minor parts for Finnish actors, Mäkelä's production emphasized its Finnishness in most areas. Meanwhile, the film wears its Hollywood inspirations on its sleeve with car chases and gun fights erupting at well-timed intervals. Mäkelä's film was relatively successful at the domestic box office, but constituted by no means a breakthrough. The critical reception is another story as it was widely despised, especially for its adherence to American-inspired commercialism. Yet, he was not deterred by the critical drubbing, but moved on to produce *Esa ja Vesa: auringonlaskun ratsastajat/Sunset Riders* in 1994. Mäkelä's first collaboration with Selin, it is a youth-oriented adventure film following road movie conventions. The genre is not uncommon in Finnish cinema as directors such as Mika Kaurismäki have produced road movies with a distinctly existential bent, but Mäkelä's version undoes all subversive trappings in favour of straightforward entertainment.

Genre has certainly been a key feature in Finnish film production throughout its history, but it has never achieved the status it enjoys in many other national industries and especially in Hollywood – and perhaps it should not either. War, comedy, detective thrillers and heritage cinema are all enjoying massive success at the domestic box office as these 'universal' genre frameworks are contextualized with distinctly national themes and cultural elements. We are also seeing more unusual combinations emerge such as A-J Annila's Finnish-Chinese *wuxia* film (historical epic combining sword-fighting with *Kalevala*-inspired material) *Jadesoturi/Jade Warrior* (2006), and follow-up horror film *Filth/Sauna* (2008). Both films combine elements from hitherto unexplored genres in the

Finnish context (*Jade Warrior* and kung fu, *Sauna* and J-Horror) with national history and mythology. Previously, when we see attempts in commercial genres, critics have commented on the lack of production values and the films' inability to achieve international standards. Annila's productions have met with more favourable criticism, especially for their production values, though their domestic success has been limited. Recently, there have been more successful attempts to fuse genre with nationally-specific concerns such as Jalmari Relander's *Rare Exports* (2010), which was also the recipient of ample support from the Foundation. Meanwhile, children's films demonstrate the increasing variety and capabilities of the film industry (see p. 150). Moreover, attempts to combine new media technology and distribution with commercial genre has resulted in some burgeoning successes, which may pay off in the years to come (see p.177).

Pietari Kääpä

North Express

Pikajuna Pohjoiseen

Production company:
Fenno Film

Distributor:
Fenno Film

Director:
Roland af Hällström

Producer:
Yrjö Norta

Screenwriter:
Viljo Hela (pseudonym for
Roland af Hällström)

Art Directors:
Eero Levä
Kosti Aaltonen

Cinematographer:
Esko Töyri

Composer:
Tapio Ilomäki

Editor:
Tapio Ilomäki

Duration:
91 minutes

Cast:
Ansa Ikonen
Tauno Majuri
Aku Korhonen
Leif Wager

Year:
1947

Synopsis

An express night train is leaving northwards. A colourful group of people gather in the same sleeping car. They are comprised of newlyweds on a honeymoon, a veteran streetwise journalist, a young man acting suspiciously, a beautiful young nurse, two swindlers posing as businessmen, a haughty rich lady, and Maire (Ikonen), along with her middle-aged lover (Majuri) who suddenly wants to accompany her home. A separate drama is going in the locomotive between the engine driver and a fireman. During the journey the young man and the nurse become attached to each other and the journalist exposes the swindlers' card tricks. Maire is struggling with the decision of her life: should she give up resisting her lover's passionate courting and leave her husband and her small daughter? Everybody becomes suspects of a crime when the old lady's valuable antique watch is stolen. During the investigation, the train crashes at the very station where Maire's husband (Kaipainen) works as a station master. The journalist manages to deliver his last story before dying, Maire's lover passes away too, and after some hesitation she unites with her husband and her daughter.

Critique

North Express was produced in 1947 by a minor production company Fenno-Film, which had begun operations a few years back, during the war, with clever and timely spy films. At the time, *North Express* was regarded as one of the better films during a generally weak period for Finnish cinema. The narrative gets to a start at the Helsinki railway station, where people busily rush through the platform to board the northbound train. As the happy newlyweds say goodbye to their relatives, Maire, the wife of a pedantic station master in an aptly named northern region, Perämaa ('hinterland'), and her cultured and travelled cosmopolitan lover Mauno from the capital Helsinki, step on board the train. Through this parallel, the film is already introducing its contrast between young untarnished love and marriage in crisis. The illicit couple have had one of their regular rendezvous in the big city and it is time for her to return to the quiet life in the countryside. Unexpectedly, Mauno follows Maire to the train. He has decided that it is time for Maire to choose between him and her husband. Maire is played with tragic elegance by one of the most admired actresses in Finnish cinema history, Ansa Ikonen.

The story of a woman between two men is the melodramatic core of *North Express*. But the film is much more complex in its construction as multiple narratives and even conventions from different genres intertwine around its thematic core. The other storylines which develop gradually point towards tragedy (young man falling in love with nurse with a fatal disease), crime (the petty swindlers as card swindlers), and thriller (the theft of the watch). Finally, with the climactic train crash and a train station transformed into a temporary first aid centre, the film provides a twist on the disaster film genre – a rare breed in Finnish cinema.

The train is a conducive setting for a film of this complexity. It is a natural motivation for a narrative where people of all ages and life situations meet, and constitutes effectively a sort of microcosm of life. However, some of the storylines are better developed than others and some are simply confusing. The aging journalist who gently follows, or in some cases even steers the people and their individual narratives, is intended as a connective character. However, it is not a sufficiently powerful device as the abundance of characters and different unconnected storylines are easily the weakest aspect of *North Express*. The script, written by director Af Hällström under the pseudonym Viljo Hela, echoes the uncertainty of the lives of the people slowly recovering from the war. Dreams and reality clash most visibly in the final scene where optimism for the future, symbolised in the travel posters for exotic destinations, are contrasted with the victims of the train accident.

Pasi Nyyssönen

The White Reindeer

Valkoinen Peura

Production company:
Junior Filmi

Distributors:
Adams-Filmi
Suomi-Filmi Oy
Coronet Film (USA)

Director:
Erik Blomberg

Producer:
Aarne Tarkas

Screenwriters:
Erik Blomberg
Mirjami Kuosmanen

Art director:
Osmo Osva

Cinematographer:
Erik Blomberg

Composer:
Einar Englund

Synopsis

Pirita (Kuosmanen) is a newlywed wife in a northern Lapland village, married to a herder (Nissilä) who has to go on lengthy deer drives as part of his job. She gets bored and lonely and seeks the help of a local shaman (Arvo Lehesmaa) to give her the power to entice all men to her. In return for this, she has to sacrifice a deer to the spirits. The ritual goes wrong and Pirita is cursed to change into a white reindeer periodically to entice men and slaughter them. Local men from the village try unsuccessfully to capture and kill her and one day her husband takes on the task with fateful consequences.

Critique

The White Reindeer is one of the most oft-discussed classics of Finnish cinema. It is also a rarity as it is a horror film in an industry where such productions are distinctly few. The film received considerable acclaim on its release, going on to win the Golden Globe for Best Foreign Film and a prize in the Cannes Film Festival. It is not surprising that Blomberg's film met with this success. It is an intriguing and ambitious film with a range of thematic strands that yield fruitful analytical exploration. The theme of feminine oppression manifesting in uncontrollable animalistic urges is nothing new as these had been explored before, for example in Jacques Tourneur's *Cat People* (1942). But setting the film in the northern periphery of the snowy Lapland provides the film with an atmosphere seldom if ever truly equalled. The visual spectacle of the expansive landscapes is captured by Blomberg in his role as cinematographer, providing a cinematically striking but also morally ambiguous backdrop for the narrative. Utilizing a lean narrative constructed by

Valkoinen Peura, Junior-Filmi.

Editor:

Erik Blomberg

Duration:

68 minutes

Cast:

Mirjami Kuosmanen
Kalervo Nissilä
Åke Lindman
Jouni Tapiola

Year:

1952

the husband-wife duo of Blomberg and Kuosmanen, the film never lags in suspense. Kuosmanen's performance has also been widely commended – and for good reason. She embodies the conflicting emotions and animalistic urges of the metamorphosing woman, providing a key performance in Finnish cinema.

Gender politics in horror films are often criticized for their problematic depictions of patriarchal relations and uncontrollable female sexuality. *The White Reindeer* is not exempt from this. The film generates substantial sympathy for the 'monster' as she tries to evade the curse. Indeed, it was the patriarchal division between the active man and the docile woman that led her to seek help from the shaman in the first place. As she is finally put down by her husband, the film maintains these divisions and castigates the woman to a secondary social status. Her transgressive behaviour must be punished despite any alleviating facts that may have resulted in her condition. The fear of female sexuality and empowerment is thus negated by the narrative structure, challenging any sense of female empowerment or emancipatory social transformation in postwar Finland. Similarly, the anthropocentric qualities of the film rely on a problematic dualism. On one hand, Pirita's lack of control over her animalistic side challenges the usual human supremacy over the natural environment. Yet, the domesticating and controlling need for strong masculinity not only establishes dominance over women but also over nature. These limitations are also evident in the film's ethnographic qualities. While we certainly should not mistake it for any sort of authentic depiction of Sami culture, it is novel in depicting these largely culturally marginalized people. But this is also problematic as the emphasis on mysticism and Otherness only recycles stereotypes of the Sami culture. Of course, the exoticism of the film has played a crucial role in its success in gaining international and domestic interest abroad. Thus, the film has its share of cultural myopia much in line with general norms of the time of its production, but it can also be considered progressive in its attempts to provide refreshing genre and ideological material.

Pietari Kääpä

Eyes in the Dark

Silmät Hämärässä

Production company:
Adams-Filmi

Distributor:
Suomi-Filmi

Director:
Veikko Itkonen

Producer:
Veikko Itkonen

Screenwriter:
Juha Nevalainen

Art director:
Osmo Osva

Cinematographer:
Veikko Itkonen

Composer:
Heikki Aaltoila

Synopsis

This 'Finn noir' is an episodic tale of four shady characters holed up in a hotel room, hiding from the police and observed by a mysterious stranger in the street. Through flashbacks, we discover the secrets of each individual and what drove them to their current despairing state. It seems that they were all involved in a heist of some sort, a caper that involves a mysterious femme fatale. The narratives of these individuals are bookended by the tale of a desperate writer (Salminen) holed up in a hotel room, who writes his way out of his predicament through his four fictional protagonists.

Critique

Eyes in the Dark is an exemplary case of the inventiveness of postwar Finnish cinema. First of all, the film can be understood as part of the widespread 'problem film' genre, which focuses on a range of social diseases. Thus, all the protagonists are suffering a typical ailment (broken marriages, betrayals, corruption, alcoholism). Most prominently, the film is a Finnish contribution to the film noir genre. The film mobilizes many well-known genre conventions from unreliable narrators to hardboiled protagonists, from its chiaroscuro *mise-en-scène* to its tough dialogue. In addition to these genre conventions, its world includes many disorienting surrealistic elements that complicate its basic narrative. One of the more iconic moments of the film involves a group of dancing girls, outlined against the window of a nightclub, contrasted against two of the

Editor:

Veikko Itkonen

Duration:

71 minutes

Cast:

Tauno Palo
Uuno Laakso
Ekke Hämäläinen
Vilho Siivola
Unto Salminen

Year:

1952

protagonists scheming their way out of their predicament. The contrast is an effective method to portray the multi-layered moral uncertainty of the world.

The different modes of morality between public and private spaces are constantly contrasted, especially through the trope of the insecure hotel room. The film plays expertly with red herrings, such as our assumptions that the put-down husband (Siivola) has robbed the bank he visited, or the complicity of the sportsman (Hämäläinen) in the death of his fiancée. As these frequent invitations to make moral judgments about the characters based on stereotypes familiar within the genre prove to be often wrong, the film is engaged in self-conscious plays with genre conventions and narrative tropes, implicating the audience in its metanarrative on fictional criminality constructed through its framing device. Perhaps its key element of subversion is the casting of the iconic star Tauno Palo in the role of the criminal who sets the plan in motion. As we associate him with morally righteous and occasionally misunderstood heroes (despite a history of playing villainous characters), his subversive presence forces us to ponder our knowledge of the events.

This preoccupation with illusionism and flaws in our subjective perspectives is made explicit as the mysterious observer in the street is revealed to be a blind man (Oiva Sala) awaiting his guide. The framing metanarrative of the writer constructing the main narrative based on his impressions of the characters he glimpses in the opposite window provide an alternative commentary on the ways individual preoccupations with surfaces can lead to misleading impressions and conceptions of the world. While this preoccupation with surfaces does admittedly lead the film to work more as a gimmick than a fully fledged narrative, it still works as a key example of Finnish film noir. It is something of a shame that the director Itkonen never attempted anything on this scale of cinematic inventiveness subsequently.

Pietari Kääpä

Inspector Palmu's Error

Komisario Palmun erehdys

Production company:
Suomen Filmiteollisuus

Distributor:
Suomen Filmiteollisuus

Director:
Matti Kassila

Synopsis

The Inspector Palmu series is based on the novels of esteemed writer Mika Waltari and spans the length of the 1960s. The first film adaptation directed and adapted by Matti Kassila *Inspector Palmu's Error* (1960) revolves around the murder of Bruno Rygsack (Jussi Jurkka), a spoiled heir to a large fortune. Palmu (Rinne) and his team of detectives Toivo Virta (Ranin) and Väinö Kokki (Jokela) set out to solve the complicated network of blackmail and familial relations.

Kaasua Komisario Palmu/Gas, Inspector Palmu (1961) provides a similar narrative of murder and destructive interpersonal relations. The murder of Ms. Scrof (Henny Valjus) sets in motion a dirty battle for the inheritance involving her nephew (Kaarle Lankela),

Producer:

T.J. Särkkä

Screenwriters:

Matti Kassila, based on the
novel by Mika Waltari

Art director:

Aarre Koivisto

Cinematographer:

Olavi Tuomi

Composer:

Osmo Lindeman

Editor:

Elmer Lahti

Duration:

101 minutes

Cast:

Joel Rinne
Matti Ranin
Leo Jokela
Leo Riuttu

Year:

1960

stepdaughter (Elina Salo), a judge (Toivo Mäkelä) and an evangelist (Risto Mäkelä). It seems that the old lady had planned to
manipulate her nephew to marry her stepdaughter but the two
had refused the advances. Meanwhile, the evangelist has been
scheming to get the heritage for himself. But perhaps most dubi-
ously, the nephew has a live-in 'friend', Kuurna (Pentti Siimes), who
is entangled in the affairs. The nephew seems to be the most likely
suspect, yet Palmu can see behind the complex façades of passion.

*Tähdet kertovat, Komisario Palmu/It Is Written in the Stars,
Inspector Palmu* (1962) features the by-now familiar narrative of
murder, complex and destructive family affairs, blackmail and
greed. Nordberg (Vilho Kekkonen) is found murdered in a park on
Observation Hill and all signs point to the boyfriend of his niece,
Virtanen (Maija-Leena Soinne). Palmu however discovers a connection between Nordgren and retired general Vadenblick (Helge
Herala), who has a bad reputation as people generally tend to die
if associated with him.

Vodkaa Komisario Palmu/Vodka, Inspector Palmu (1969) is the
last film of the series and differs somewhat from the earlier films
as it is less of a whodunit and more of a political parable. Palmu
is recommissioned from retirement due to the murder of reporter
Tohko (Turo Onho). Embroiled in these affairs are the envoys of the
Soviet Union, who are negotiating the construction of a pipeline
with Finnish politicians. Palmu clashes with the police as they take
an authoritarian approach to solving the murder. Meanwhile, the
broadcasting company behind Tohko, YLE, is increasingly frustrated
by the cover-up and secrecy and turn to Palmu to unravel the political façades and the personal connections underlying the crime.

Critique

The Inspector Palmu series runs from 1960–69, providing a
dynamic cultural landscape through which to explore the nation's
social and political transformations. The first film was produced by
the ailing Suomen Filmiteollisuus under the tutelage of T. J. Särkkä.
Matti Kassila took the directorial reins and provided a film that still
endures nowadays as a modernist masterpiece and a key depiction of Helsinki. Focusing on the secrets of a family of blue bloods,
the film provides an incisive dissection of upper-class corruption.
While this is all relatively typical thematic material for the period,
the tone of the film makes it a real standout. Mixing elements of
comedy with scenes that would fit in more with the most intense
of expressionist horror, the film sustains its erratic yet entertaining
mood. Complemented by Osmo Lindeman's disturbing and quirky
score, *Inspector Palmu's Error* provides an indelible introduction to
a character that would become an icon of Finnish cinema.

Gas, Inspector Palmu continues the series' fascinating exploration of contemporary Finland. While the focus on wealthy individuals and their misdeeds is by now a very familiar theme, its sexual
politics provides it with a unique approach. The relationship between
the nephew and Kuurna is implied to be a homosexual one as the
two share their bedroom and Palmu frequently comments about

their lifestyle. Pentti Siimes' performance as the bohemian Kuurna is camp theatricality at its best, and while his love for the niece is blamed for his murderous actions, the target of his adoration is clearly the nephew. While gay villains are not unusual in Hollywood cinema, the caricaturing of the murderous homosexual panders to negative stereotypes prevalent in popular culture. Furthermore, the subtextualisation of the relationship indicates both the taboo status of homosexuality and its marginalization in popular Finnish culture.

The theme of disobedient youth is also central to the third film in the series, It Is Written in the Stars, Inspector Palmu. As with the previous entries, it captures essential aspects of the era in its focus on clashes of tradition and modernity. The emphasis on new communications methodology and generational clash are the prime contributors to the theme. The decreasing morality and increasing superficiality of the press is largely played out for humour, especially through the sleazy reporter character played by Pentti Siimes. Simultaneously, its depiction of youth culture has unfortunate implications of moral panic with emphasis on the gang culture behaviour of the lättähatut (the hats) and nahkarotsit (the jackets). Sointu Angervo's attempts to seduce the hapless Toivo Virta are clearly both part of this moralizing and a somewhat paradoxical intention to provide the film with steamier, controversial content. The subtext of the film also includes a range of suggestive material to do with the potential incest between uncle and niece and her problematic pregnancy. Regardless, the depiction of the era is astute as not only an archive of the changing cityscape of Helsinki but the changing mores of its culture. In many ways, the film exemplifies a grudging acceptance of modernization. In contrast to many Finnish films which highlight the binary between the rural countryside and the cityscape, Inspector Palmu seems to have already moved beyond them as it depicts a thoroughly urbanized world.

The film's villain, the neo-Nazi Carl Gustaf Valdenblick, is also an intriguing figure as he is portrayed as a fascistic and psychotic individual with connections to the problematic right-wing politics in Finnish history. Geopolitical connections are also a central theme of the final Palmu film Vodka, Inspector Palmu. The first of the series in colour, the film was criticized on its release for its 'Finlandizising' approach to the Cold War. Traditionally, Finlandization has involved an increasing acceptance of Soviet control over domestic social and political issues; certainly, the latest of Palmu's adventures begins with his trip to Moscow, where he acts both as a consultant and a tourist. This surprising collaborationist attitude can be explained by the increasing pre-eminence of leftist attitudes in the public sphere and the media of the decade as cultural authorities reassessed Finland's geopolitical relations. The film also works as a love letter to the power of the mass media. The national broadcasting corporation YLE and press freedom are key aspects of the narrative and even Palmu aligns with their side against the authoritarian police. This is a somewhat unexpected role reversal from the media criticism and anti-authoritative power politics of the earlier films in the series. Simultaneously, plenty of subtextual indicators imply an undercurrent of alternative ideological rhetoric that allows audiences to use the films for multiple purposes, including criticizing the prevalence of pro-Soviet propaganda. Their complexity and ability to act as the locus for multi-levelled interpretations allows the Inspector Palmu films to maintain their persistent relevance in the annals of Finnish cinema, alongside their exemplary positions as archives of cultural knowledge about the era.

Pietari Kääpä

A Time of Roses

Ruusujen Aika

Production company:
Filminor

Distributor:
Filminor

Director:
Risto Jarva

Producer:
Risto Jarva

Screenwriters:
Risto Jarva
Jaakko Pakkasvirta
Peter von Bagh

Art directors:
Lauri Anttila
Antti Peippo
Juhani Jauhiainen
Kullervo Kukkasjärvi

Cinematographer:
Antti Peippo

Composers:
Henrik Otto Donner
Kaj Chydenius

Editor:
Risto Jarva
Jukka Mannerkorpi
Lasse Naukkarinen

Duration:
107 minutes

Synopsis

It is the year 2012 and social leaders tell us that the world has become a thoroughly liberal and democratic entity, a utopian place of harmony. Television researcher Raimo Lappalainen (Tuominen) intends to produce a programme exploring the society of the past through the memories of an individual who died in the late 1960s. He focuses on recreating the life of model Saara by enlisting his researcher Kisse (Vepsä) to act as a substitute for her. As reality and identities begin to blur, the purpose of the project becomes questioned, and with it, the notion of social harmony.

Critique

A *Time of Roses* is perhaps the first real science fiction film produced in Finland, taking place in a future utopia-dystopia, in what is a sterile and seemingly harmonious society. Jarva's approach is still ingrained with the thematic preoccupations of the New Wave, despite its genre trappings. According to its screenwriter Peter von Bagh, the film was full of 'neo-leftist ideas about the power of communications. It shows everything about then-contemporary knowledge and cognitive comprehension'. A *Time of Roses* is indeed cerebral sci-fi, a complex meditation on social power and the construction and manipulation of public and private reality through media communications. The meritocratic society of the film and the complacency of its citizens is a prophetic look at the postmodern consumer society, reflecting many of the fears of technological dependency and Big Brother-style control at the time.

The film's focus is on a seemingly liberal society where most sources of social discontent and inequality have been erased. The countercultural movements and social rebellion endemic of the 1960s have been erased, but with them individual identity also faces erasure. If one is not able to express criticism or challenge social complacency, what sort of identity do they hold? The media plays a key part in this control of identity as the powerful manipulate and alter reality and individual cognition to suit their purposes. Ideological divergence certainly exists under the surface as is evident in the constant strikes and the violent death of a power plant manager. But as these events are erased from the public eye by tools of media manipulation, maintenance of power and the shaping of collective reality in a mediated society is revealed in all its dystopian omnipotent ways.

Cast:

Arto Tuominen
Ritva Vepsä
Kalle Holmberg
Unto Salminen

Year:

1969

The film is thus a critical view of the contemporary moment, explaining and even elaborating on many of the concerns of the leftist ideologies of the decade. The bourgeois utopianism of the future is a reflection, or more accurately a warning, of the ideological direction of society in the wake of the disappointment of 1968. As part of the participatory cinema of the New Wave, the film finds new means of commenting on sociopolitical realities. Indeed, the use of science fiction tropes allows it to achieve this without remaining too stuck in realist verisimilitude. While many of its concerns are to do with media culture in Finland, its explorations of dystopian themes are part of international politically-engaged cerebral science fiction. Yet, upon its cinematic release in Finland, the film was a financial disappointment and met with decidedly mixed reviews by media commentators.

Science fiction remains a marginal genre in Finland with only a handful of examples using its tropes and conventions. The majority of these films are ecocritical explorations of future dystopias such as in Timo Linnasalo's *Aurinkotuuli/Solar Wind* (1980), Juha Rosma's *Huomenna/Tomorrow* (1986), Mika Kaurismäki's *The Last Border* (1993), and Jari Halonen's *Lipton Cockton in the Shadows of Sodoma* (1995). These films have all been financial disappointments domestically – indeed, most of them do not try to be commercial in orientation and instead focus on explicitly experimental themes and means of cinematic expression. While they are now sadly largely forgotten, they all have plenty to contribute to the development of Finnish cinema in terms of social relevance and cinematic innovation. Jarva's *A Time of Roses* thus remains an anomaly in that it still merits wide critical attention and discussion, and seems to be even more relevant in the contemporary information age society than at the time of its production.

Pietari Kääpä

References

Toiviainen, Sakari (1998), '1968 Suomalaisessa Elokuvassa', *Filmihullu*, 5–6, p. 2.

Born American

Jäätävä Polte

Production companies:

Cinema Group Ventures
Larmark Productions
Man & Gun Film
Videogramm

Synopsis

Three American tourists foolishly cross the border from Finland to Russia and get embroiled in the Cold War animosity between the nations. They first enter a village where they are accused of an attack on a local girl and get into a firefight with the locals. They are soon pursued by Soviet forces, who have been alerted to their presence. Captured and interrogated by the army, the Americans are thrown in a Soviet jail with no contact to the outside world. Each of them copes with the dystopian conditions in their own ways: Savoy (Norris) attempts to plot an escape with the help of a

Distributors:

Finnkino
Cinema Group
Continental Video

Director:

Renny Harlin

Producer:

Markus Selin

Screenwriters:

Renny Harlin
Markus Selin

Art director:

Torsti Nyholm

Cinematographer:

Henrik Paersch

Composer:

Richard Mitchell

Editor:

Paul Martin Smith

Duration:

95 minutes

Cast:

Mike Norris
Steve Durham
David Coburn
Vesa Vierikko

Year:

1986

Renny Harlin, Tri Star.

girl he met in a village; Simon (Durham) breaks down and eventually perishes in the inhuman conditions; Coop (Coburn) turns to illegal fights to cope but is psychologically scarred beyond recognition by the battles. Savoy eventually succeeds in breaking out and heads for freedom at the Finnish border.

Critique

Renny Harlin and Markus Selin initiated the production of *Born American* as a response to what they perceived as the stagnancy of contemporary Finnish cinema. Both producers had grown up on Hollywood action and adventure films and aspired to produce an indigenous version of the genre. The Finnish Film Foundation was largely opposed to funding strictly commercial films during the 1980s, resulting in a lack of financial support for the film.

The producers had to look abroad for potential production allies and financed most of the production on their own. They initially courted Chuck Norris to star in the film and even received tentative acceptance. However, complications with schedules resulted in him pulling out of the production. Harlin and Selin were set on an international name and turned instead to his son, Mike Norris.

This was not to be the only problem of the film as its explicitly anti-Soviet content run afoul with the domestic censors. Indeed, the film makes no qualms about its political orientation. It is fervently patriotic, but not about Finland, the country of its producers, but America. This is not entirely surprising considering the genre precedents for the film, which range from Cannon productions like *Invasion USA* (Zito, 1985) to the Rambo quadrilogy (1982–2008). The Soviets are depicted as backwards and immoral, the enemies of freedom and liberty. In contrast, the Americans are innocent bystanders drawn into the murky world of Cold War politics. The narrative also makes it clear that the Soviet Union is truly an empire where American intervention is necessary. For example, its rural villages are immersed in inbreeding and unquestioned rampant violence, while its administrative and judicial system are at best bureaucratic, at worst absolutely corrupt, demonstrating the lack of common sense morality of the CCCP. The film was unsurprisingly banned before its release for political reasons. This was still the tail end of the Cold War, but a Finnish-produced explicitly anti-Soviet film was perceived to have potential to upset the fragile geopolitical balance. As Harlin and Selin had invested their own funds into the project and taken substantial bank loans to cover the production, the banning in their native country was a major blow. The film was eventually released in severely censored form towards the end of 1985, though its controversy did not equate to box office success in Finland. While the film left both Harlin and Selin destitute, it proved to be a key indicator for both of their careers.

Finnish cinema has often been berated for the producers' inability to 'do action' (despite plenty of incidental large-scale spectacle in films ranging from Risto Orko's *Jääkärin morsian/Soldier's Bride* [1938] to Edvin Laine's *Tuntematon sotilas/The Unknown Soldier* [1955]). Harlin's bombastic directorial style certainly undoes any such concerns as slow motion shootouts and large explosions combine with rampant violence. *Born American* truly demonstrates that international standards are achievable with the industrial confines of Finland. Yet, this was a large part of the problem according to contemporary critics. Rampant pro-US patriotism and emulation of Hollywood standards situates the film in a problematic position. Neither part of the Hollywood machine nor exotic enough to appeal to international art house consumers, the film met with a largely indifferent international reception. *Born American*'s unabashed commercialism would land Harlin in Hollywood where he graduated to directing such blockbusters as *Die Hard 2* (1990) and *Cliffhanger* (1993). Selin fell on hard times, but would soon rebound as he formed Solar Films in the early 1990s, which was to become a leading force in Finnish cinema of the 2000s. These career trajectories indicate some of the patterns in which Finnish cinema would play a more prominent role globally: with Harlin, assimilating Hollywood's technical and ideological tropes provided a good example of the capabilities of Finnish professionals; with Selin, a more commercial national cinema with franchising potential would emerge by combining genre products with national themes in films such as *Vares: Private Eye* (Mäkelä, 2004) and *Pahat pojat/Bad Boys* (Mäkelä, 2003).

Pietari Kääpä

The Final Arrangement

Tilinteko

Production company:
Villealfa Filmproduction Oy

Director:
Veikko Aaltonen

Producer:
Aki Kaurismäki

Screenwriters:
Veikko Aaltonen
Aki Kaurismäki

Cinematographer:
Timo Salminen

Composer:
Leo Friman

Editor:
Juha Jeromaa

Duration:
72 minutes

Cast:
Juhani Niemelä
Esko Nikkari
Kaija Pakarinen
Seppo Mäki

Year:
1987

Synopsis

Kalervo Mäkinen (Niemelä) and Timo Varjola (Nikkari) hijack a delivery truck containing a substantial cash deposit. The heist is a success but in the aftermath Varjola shoots Mäkinen and leaves him for dead. While Mäkinen languishes in prison, Varjola uses the money to ascend in society, becoming the mayor of a small city. When Mäkinen is released, he immediately sets his sights on bringing Varjola down. As his old sins return to haunt him, Varjola gets increasingly distraught and soon their cat and mouse game ends in explosive fashion.

Critique

The Final Arrangement is a true Finnish noir and an underappreciated taut thriller. The debut film of its director Veikko Aaltonen, the film provides a model lesson in economic, minimalist film production. Constructing homages to film noir and the Western, it builds an oppressive mood as the past comes to haunt the now seemingly respectable mayor. As is the case with most of its genre antecedents, the game of politics acts as the fundamental locus for corruption. Capitalist greed is another key vice that enables one's ascension in the social pecking order. But despite this focus on corruption, the film is refreshingly free of explicit moralizing. The characters are more like suggestive metonyms of the wider social conditions rather than real or fleshed-out protagonists. They act as way for the film to deliver its equation of the dirty world of business and politics with criminality and violence. It is not surprising that Aki Kaurismäki was the co-writer and producer of the project as it resembles his early stripped-down works both in its formative minimalism and moral ambiguity. Thus, the dialogue is kept minimal as only brief instances of communication convey the plot and all unnecessary exposition or activity is exterminated.

The Final Arrangement established many of the key themes that Aaltonen would expand upon in his subsequent work. Predominant amongst them is the focus on men struggling to come to terms with their transforming roles in contemporary society: 'This fracture, that I have also explored in my documentary films, is the dispersal of our society in the postwar era, in which the search for masculine identity or feeling lost are just some key symptoms,' states

Aaltonen. The films are explorations of a constantly transforming society, where economic and social movements create constantly shifting roles for individuals. These themes are foregrounded in films such as *Tuhlaajapoika/Prodigal Son* (1992) and *Juoksuhaudantie/Trench Road* (2004). Both films focus on male crises, but they also concern a search for stability in a world out of balance. The psychological and even physical damage sown by these changes manifest in the twisted family relationships of the films where trauma grows out of domestic abuse and violence.

As families in these films are fragmented by physical and emotional disturbance, they point out the illusionary power of the family unit as a cornerstone of society. For example, the protagonist of *Trench Road* is separated from his wife after an outburst of violence. He sees an old house for sale which he thinks will solve his problems. This is a house provided to war veterans (*rintamamiestalo*) and indicates the nation's gratitude to her 'sons'. But any sense of national or communal loyalty is being corrupted by familial relations as the son is now selling the house from under his father. The plan to heal this communal rift by placing a new generation of family into the home is compromised by both the escalating insanity of the protagonist and market forces. If society is meant to be like a large family, then such a society is an internally destructive, self-immolating constellation. Thus, the depiction of Finnish society in these films is fundamentally despairing and diseased. Aaltonen remains an underappreciated director who shares a focus on social crisis and conflicts within the nation with the more well-known Aki Kaurismäki. While not as thematically or visually idiosyncratic as the films of his former collaborator, Aaltonen's works are regardless as important in their pessimistic diagnoses of the state of the nation.

Pietari Kääpä

References

Passoja, Teemu (2004), 'Veikko Aaltonen ja Juoksuhaudantie', http://www.film-o-holic.com/haastattelut/veikko-aaltonen-juoksuhaudantie/. Accessed 20 July 2011.

The Moonlight Sonata

Kuutamosonaatti

Production company:
Filminor

Synopsis

Anni Stark (Björkman) journeys to a faraway cabin in the countryside to escape the paparazzi and the fashion industry. Upon arrival, she runs afoul of the neighbouring Kyrölä family, especially their son Arvo (Sorvali). The matriarch of the family, Äite (Soli Labbart), keeps Arvo under her belt, while brother Sulo (Mikko Kivinen) is a deformed giant locked in the basement. Arvo's obsession with Anni takes unhealthy dimensions as he starts to harass her. Anni's brother (Gunell) comes to join her from the city, but proves no

Distributor:

Finnkino

Director:

Olli Soinio

Producer:

Heikki Takkinen

Screenwriter:

Olli Soinio

Art director:

Tikke Tuura

Cinematographer:

Kari Sohlberg

Composer:

Antti Hytti

Editor:

Irma Taina

Duration:

85 minutes

Cast:

Tiina Björkman
Kim Gunell
Kari Sorvali
Ville-Veikko Salminen

Year:

1988

match for the confrontational Arvo. Meanwhile, Sulo escapes from his basement and locks Äite outside to freeze. Anni has to confront Arvo and his tractor as he chases them down snowy paths. This leads to a final siege at the cabin, where things come to an explosive end. Yet, not all of the Kyröläs have perished as Sulo still prowls the wilderness.

The sequel – *Kadunlakaisijat/Street Sweepers* (Soinio, 1991) – picks up almost immediately after the original as Sulo resurrects Äite and Arvo in the sauna. Arvo has to leave for the big city to find employment, but instead finds his real calling in producing spirits. Äite and Sulo follow him to the city, but Arvo and Sulo escape her to hit the town. To further complicate matters, the swamp at the farm belches out an old regiment of the Red Guard, who also leave for the city to take back the country from the bourgeoisie capitalists.

Critique

Olli Soinio's *The Moonlight Sonata* works well as a Finnish contribution to the horror genre. As much as *The White Reindeer* adapted the shapeshifter monster movie to Lapland, so *The Moonlight Sonata* takes conventions and shapes them through 'authentic' Finnishness. The inbred predatory families of *The Texas Chainsaw Massacre* (Hooper, 1974) are here situated in the snowy frozen landscape of northern Finland. Lonely isolated women fighting against an almost supernatural foe find its Finnish equivalent in some of the slasher scenes of Arvo peeking on the undressed Anni. The film makes great use of its indigenous landscape as it not only isolates Anni, but Arvo uses it as a weapon to stalk Anni – the environment is truly a culturally-specific milieu that expands the film's genre aspirations.

Soinio's direction is largely successful in avoiding the more obvious tropes of the genre as he focuses on making Arvo and his outrageous behaviour the main attraction of the film. Thus, character interaction and the almost surreal inescapable atmosphere of the countryside, rather than prolonged scenes of stalking, ratchet tension. The action of the film is also well-handled, especially a chase through the snow with Arvo's tractor. While the film may not be high art, its professional and efficient production is a substantial contribution to the development of Finnish cinema. It was relatively successful with the critics on its release, with many of them commenting on its novelty value. The film even received two Jussis; one for Sorvali's performance as Arvo, and the other for editing. While genre fare was still largely shunned during the 1980s, this critical acclaim demonstrates the extent to which cultural tastes and barriers were transforming.

Whereas the first film was more of an earnest attempt to construct a Finnish horror film with occasional instances of satire of the media world and yuppie culture, the sequel goes for a full-blown comic carnival. It starts out as a satirical look at the misadventures of country boy Arvo in the big city. Left to his devices, he chases girls with his street cleaning machine and cooks homebrew that blinds his customers. As is often the case with such narratives, the city is portrayed as a corrupt and superficial space dominated by commercialist ideology and capitalist individuals. The stylish, controlled visual look of the original is replaced by garish lighting that resembles cheap genre products from the 1980s and early '90s. The diegesis is bathed in primal red and green, and much of the production resembles an overdone music video. Furthermore any sense of narrative linearity found in the original collapses here with its kitchen sink approach, liberally dispersing multiple narrative strands and critical targets. One such instance is the inclusion of the Red Guard resurrected from their Civil War grave. This inclusion makes little narrative sense and seems to function only to provide the film-makers the opportunity to provide a haphazard rant against capitalist vice.

To underline the unsubtle carnivalesque atmosphere, the majority of the action actually takes place in the Linnanmäki amusement park. But this obviousness is exactly what is wrong with the film as it seems to feel the need to compensate for its flights of surreal fancy with the most overemphasized of connections. The first film provided superficial digs at celebrity culture, but it also forced us to ponder the horror spectator's objectifying male gaze. Following along these lines, the sequel seemingly critiques the fashion industry, but it feels the need to include a ten minute, narratively redundant Miss Finland competition to its already overflowing thematic concerns. Of course, most of the camera angles selected to capture the half-clad competitors are from below, thus bordering on exactly the type of obsessive glamorization it seemingly parodies. The result is a product much like the sketch shows that populate the national television channels, comprised of loose ties between each segment. Of course, from another critical angle, the film can be understood as a grand, large-scale deconstruction of the Finnish psyche. Here, obsessions with irrelevant television programming, national history, traditional stereotypes of masculinity and the wounds of urbanization all come to connote a postmodern parody of the national mentality. While the film has to be commended for its originality, its chaotic and carnivalesque approach remains unrefined and barely comprehensible. *Street Sweepers* effectively put a halt to any attempt to produce Finnish horror films until the more genre friendly context of the 2000s when lampooning was no longer a necessary part of mainstream domestic cinema.

Pietari Kääpä

Star Wreck: In the Pirkinning

Production company:
Tuotantoyhtiö Energia

Distributors:
Tuotantoyhtiö Energia (Finland)
(DVD)
Revolver Entertainment (UK)
(DVD)

Director:
Timo Vuorensola

Producer:
Samuli Torssonen

Screenwriters:
Samuli Torssonen
Rudi Airisto
Jarmo Puskala

Cinematographer:
Sami Aho-Mantila

Composer:
Tapani Siirtola

Editors:
Atte Joutsen
Samuli Torssonen

Duration:
105 minutes

Cast:
Samuli Torssonen
Atte Joutsen
Timo Vuorensola
Antti Satama
Karoliina Blackburn
Janos Honkonen

Year:
2005

Synopsis

After travelling into the past, Captain James B. Pirk (Torssonen) and the crew of the starship Kickstart are stranded in the twenty-first century. Tiring of their lives there, they decide to accelerate history and build a fleet of spacecraft, which they use to conquer the world and install Pirk as Emperor. Pirk takes his ships – known as P-Fleet – through a 'maggot hole' to a parallel dimension, hoping to conquer the planets in it. This brings a battle with the inhabitants of the Babel 13 space station, led by Captain Joni K. Sherrypie (Joutsen) and, when Babel 13's defence fleet is largely destroyed, Sherrypie surrenders. Pirk and half his followers 'beam' aboard the station for shore leave but are surprised when Sherrypie leads a revolt as reinforcements arrive. Pirk is captured but eventually escapes and returns to the Kickstart, from where he leads the P-Fleet in a colossal battle against the reinforced enemy fleet.

Critique

The first feature-length work from the group of amateur film-makers and science fiction fans behind Star Wreck Productions, *Star Wreck: In the Pirkinning* has had an astonishing impact. Because it is distributed at no charge over the Internet, and because it spoofs subjects as iconic as *Star Trek* and the tropes of science fiction, the film has reached an enormous audience, much of it well outside Finland. Indeed, by many estimates, it is the country's most watched film. Consequently, and as unlikely as it seems, it is perhaps the most influential of all modern Finnish films.

It is fortunate, then, that *In the Pirkinning* is largely excellent – albeit in unconventional ways. Its comedy is simple and broad, but considered and superbly observed, and its screenwriters make admirable efforts to avoid the most frequently parodied elements of *Star Trek*. For example, instead of clichéd jokes about how the one character not played by a main member of *Star Trek*'s cast is the one who is always killed by aliens when a landing party travels to an unchartered planet, there is a far funnier sequence in which an officer 'beams down' to a planet without breathing apparatus, as characters in *Star Trek* always do, and dies instantly because he cannot survive in its atmosphere.

In the Pirkinning makes irrelevant most of the criticisms that could be made of it and is, paradoxically, often enhanced by its flaws. A critic could note that its actors are not especially fine actors and that its special effects are not especially special; but because it is difficult, if not impossible, to encounter the film without knowing that is not a professional production but ultimately an offshoot of Internet 'fan fiction', its audience has no expectation that its production values or performances will be of a professional standard, and could even be disappointed if they were.

Furthermore, though *In the Pirkinning*'s acting is often awkward and its special effects do not match those of its theatrically-released US contemporaries, they are no worse than the acting and effects in many of the (far older) television programmes and films it parodies. Samuli Torssonen's jarring overemphasis of every line he delivers as James B. Pirk, for instance, serves only to make his parody of William Shatner's jarring overemphasis of every line he delivers as James T. Kirk more exact and, therefore, more effective.

The obvious affection for the material that inspired *In the Pirkinning* displayed by those who made the film mirrors the inspiration behind many, ostensibly more 'legitimate', Hollywood blockbusters. In America, many of most popular science fiction and comic book franchises are being remade by film-makers who grew up obsessed with their original incarnations. Those films, however, are not marketed as what they ultimately are – large budget 'fan films' – and so, compared to them, the unpretentious *In the Pirkinning* seems both more honest and more vibrant. Because of this, it is something very rare: a film of wide and unchallenging general appeal, and a work of great interest to academics.

Scott Jordan Harris

Vares: Private Eye

Vares – Yksityisetsivä

Production company:
Solar Films

Distributor:
Buena Vista International Finland

Director:
Aleksi Mäkelä

Producer:
Markus Selin

Screenwriters:
Pekka Lehtosaari, based on the novel by Reijo Mäki

Art director:
Sattva-Anna Toiviainen

Cinematographer:
Pini Hellstedt

Composer:
Kalle Chydenius

Synopsis

Downbeat private detective Jussi Vares (Veijonen) finds himself embroiled in a complicated mystery involving Eeva (Malmivaara), a woman with whom he had a brief fling. Her husband-to-be has just escaped from prison and is seeking the millions a fellow con stole from the Russian mafia. Vares escapes with Eeva as private hitmen, a crooked cop, her husband and the Russian mafia are in merciless pursuit. The shifting loyalties between the criminals enable Vares to play all sides against one another, while he develops a plan to get out of this mess.

Critique

'The toughest movie thriller ever made in Finland' – Solar Films.

Jussi Vares is a private detective created by Reijo Mäki for his long-running series of popular crime novels, a character optioned for franchising purposes by Solar Films. The result is a flashy and entertaining cocktail of visual and verbal fireworks. The combination of Finnish-specific content and stylistic 'homages' to the works of Guy Ritchie or Quentin Tarantino in the genre works surprisingly well. While the story in itself is largely forgettable, the film's aesthetic and narrative style distinguishes it amongst similar Finnish thrillers. The multi-character plot is handled relatively well, but resemblance to gangster films such as *Lock, Stock and Two Smoking Barrels* (Ritchie, 1998) is occasionally jarring. Similarly, the profuse, profane banter between the assassins clearly emulates the verbose and pop culture-infested dialogue by Tarantino.

While the ways in which the images are composed, and the editing, the characters and the narrative constructed are clearly inspired or copied from elsewhere, *Vares* is emphatically Finnish in its content

Editor:

Kimmo Taavila

Duration:

91 minutes

Cast:

Juha Veijonen
Laura Malmivaara
Jorma Tommila
Pekka Valkeejärvi

Year:

2004

and industrial origins. For one, both Vares and his compatriot poet/ drinking buddy are emphatic caricatures of Finnish masculinity. Similarly, all of the imported cultural elements are contextualized with Finnish references both in terms of slang or milieu.

This combination of different cultural elements in interactive ways allows the film to exist as a good example of the globalization of film culture. Imported elements provide the film with commercial viability, while its domestic content allows it to distinguish itself from the imported productions dominating the multiplexes. In this combination, the national does not have to exclude the international or vice versa. Thus, *Vares* indicates one dominant pattern in which contemporary small national cinema can survive and even thrive, at least domestically. This is in direct contrast to productions such as Renny Harlin's *Born American* (1986) which used conventions from Hollywood cinema and was criticized accordingly for being 'supranational' rubbish. It seems that critics and domestic audiences do not want carbon copies of the Hollywood model as combinations like *Vares* tend to be more successful.

V2 – Dead Angel (dir. Aleksi Mäkelä) followed three years later with more or less the same team as Vares' cinematic debut. The sequel was less successful as it was criticized for being too excessive in its violence and profane humour. The series was rebooted in 2010 (dir. Anders Engström) with a new production team, though the production was still carried out under Selin's Solar Films banner. The reboot has been very successful with over 100,000 viewers and Solar Films is making the series a biannual cinematic event. More intriguingly, the new version is clearly intended for the international markets, presumably to capitalize on the Nordic detective craze initiated by Mankell's *Wallander* and Larssen's 'Millenium' series. It remains to be seen if this newly internationalized version of this Finnish detective can make it in the 'big world'.

Pietari Kääpä

Black Ice

Musta Jää

Production companies:

Making Movies Oy
Schmidtz Katze Filmkollektiv

Distributor:

Sandrew Metronome
Distribution

Director:

Petri Kotwica

Synopsis

Saara's (Mäenpää) husband, architecture professor Leo (Suosalo), is having an affair with his student, Tuuli (Kataja). Fed up with his lies, Saara is close to exploding and only maintains a façade of civility. Tracking Tuuli down, she impulsively takes part in her karate class and the pair strike up an uneasy friendship. Having established confidence with Tuuli, Saara manipulates Tuuli and Leo into a variety of uncomfortable and dangerous actions. Things soon get out of control as Saara's obsession intensifies when it appears Tuuli is pregnant and Saara's true identity is revealed.

Critique

Black Ice can be considered a genre production that deftly combines elements from horror and thriller genres into a uniquely

Producer:
Kaarle Aho

Screenwriter:
Petri Kotwica

Art director:
Sattva-Anna Toiviainen

Cinematographer:
Harri Räty

Composer:
Eicca Toppinen

Editor:
Jukka Nykänen

Duration:
107 minutes

Cast:
Outi Mäenpää
Ria Kataja
Ville Virtanen
Martti Suosalo

Year:
2007

oppressive and traumatic experience. The 'erotic thriller' genre has been prolific in Hollywood throughout the 1990s, but no clear Finnish emulations have been produced. *Black Ice* takes these conventions and builds a distinctly slow-burn narrative drive, which strives for realist, unhistrionic plot elements. Through this, the film is able to achieve a grounded sense of dread that differentiates it from similar, perhaps more explicitly commercial, products. Synergising conventions from esoteric art productions to commercialist frameworks allows the film to work both as a commercial product and the type of national cinema which gets recognized abroad.

The conflicts of the film emanate from a class-based examination of contemporary Finland. From its early moments, the upper-class open spaces of Saara and Leo's large designer house contrasts with the 'ordinary' apartment Tuuli inhabits. There is a clear sense of class criticism in Saara and Leo's patronage of Tuuli as they both effectively use her to get to their own goals. This patronizing attitude is challenged by the film's depiction of Tuuli, who is a distinctly stronger character than either her female or male opposites. Class politics thus tie in with gender politics where any sense of ideological certainty is kept at a distance due to the power dynamics between the two women. While the stalker narrative provides most of the power to Saara, the film constantly refuses to see her as a monster. In Kotwicka's restrained hands, the need to understand Saara as a hurt human being only adds to the film's feminist criticism of patriarchal social power relations. Instead of vindicating the construction of the nuclear family and the capitalist superstructure of the patriarchal system (as takes place in films such as *Fatal Attraction* [Lyne, 1987]), *Black Ice* does not let the man get away with his infidelity. Instead, he dies in a largely undramatic fashion off-screen as the two women try to come to terms with their new relationship. While both the female protagonists are certainly strong characters, their roles in society are still depicted as the second sex to the alpha male prowess of Professor Leo. But by sidelining him, and focusing on the power games between the two women, it reveals the lack of available roles for women in such a society.

The use of familiar gender roles was criticized on the release of *Black Ice* as this arguably undermines the growing tension the film otherwise sustains. And while it certainly flirts with sensationalist aspects, the dramatic but controlled performances by the leads help it to avoid too much excess. For example, while the explicit sexual tension between the women could also be used for lurid thrills, it refuses this spectacle and twists the scene of intimate contact to a horrifying attempted abortion. While criticism of the film's gender and sexual politics are certainly understandable, they are substantially ambiguous and contradictory and allow for multiple readings. *Black Ice* won several Jussi Awards including Best Director and Best Film. Outi Mäenpää's performance as the increasingly unhinged Saara was also honoured with the Best Actress Jussi Award. Enhancing the bleak tone of the film is the score by Eicca Toppinen from the metal band Apocalyptica. The use of a minimalist cello-driven score allows the film to create a unique aural experience, which compliments the blue and white, 'metallic' visuals of the film perfectly. *Black Ice*'s domestic and international success at festivals indicates some of the ways in which Finnish film producers can put well-known genre conventions to work. By combining them in with novel thematic approaches, they can produce films which are both nationally-specific and populist enough to succeed in the international markets.

Pietari Kääpä

Dark Floors

Production company:
Solar Films

Distributors:
Nordisk Film Theatrical Distribution
Metrodome Distribution

Director:
Pete Riski

Producer:
Markus Selin

Screenwriter:
Pekka Lehtosaari

Cinematographer:
Jean-Noël Mustonen

Composer:
Ville Riippa

Editors:
Antti Kulmala
Joona Louhivuori
Stefan Sundlöf

Duration:
89 minutes

Cast:
William Hope
Leon Herbert
Philip Bretherton
Noah Huntley

Year:
2008

Synopsis

Ben (Huntley) takes his autistic daughter, Sarah (Skye Bennett), to hospital as she is suffering from an unspecified attack. They enter the hospital elevator with a group of token strangers including a security guard and a businessman. Upon reaching their destination, they find that the whole hospital has been abandoned. To make everything worse, a group of monsters seems to be preying on the humans. It is soon made clear that Sarah's autistic condition has something to do with confronting the monsters, and the two groups face off to escape the haunted hospital.

Critique

Dark Floors was conceived as a Finnish attempt to produce an international-standard horror film in the tradition of the *Saw* (2004–10) or the *Nightmare on Elm Street* (1984–2010) franchises. Produced by the Markus Selin's Solar Films, the film was directed by the Finnish music video director Pete Riski and featured a predominantly English and American cast. The heavy metal (or glam rock) band Lordi, who star in the film, had just won the Eurovision contest and gained substantial international notoriety. (The band's lead singer, Mr. Lordi, had worked with Selin years before as a storyboard artist and Riski had directed many of Lordi's music videos). As the production language was English, it was very clear that domestic markets were not the prime consideration of producers. Thus, the film was not only targeted at horror fans, but also consumers who had been taken in with the outrageous but widely-appealing extravagance of the band. *Dark Floors* was thus an in-house production which allowed the band to branch out into cinema and Selin to produce a film with real international appeal. Yet, the film was a gigantic flop upon its Finnish release and has only received sporadic international distribution.

While the professional qualities of the film are not to be dismissed, it is not difficult to speculate on the reasons behind the failure of the film. For one, 'hard rock' bands seldom cross over into mainstream success, especially ones who have won the Eurovision contest – not exactly a contest renowned for its geek credibility. Indeed, it seems the film-makers misconceptualized Lordi's brand

Dark Floors, Icelandic Film/Kisi Productions/Solar Films/Yle.

value, which is more to do with camp value, at least outside of Finland. The decision not to have the monsters of the band communicate verbally or even perform any songs was also brave as keeping them as an undulating force increases their threat quota and can also work to deter any sort of camp reaction to the band. But this also detracts from one of their more immediate attractions – the music. Not allowing the band to communicate makes them relatively anonymous and strips away most of the potential to capture their originality and character. While each monster is well-known in Finland, covered as they were in the popular press, internationally they are just another set of latex-covered monsters. Superficial verisimilitude with the horror genre was thus not enough to succeed in either the domestic or the international markets saturated with similar products.

According to its director, there is no sense of shame in considering *Dark Floors* a Finnish film. The confidence of the producers is refreshing, especially for a cultural context where financial and infrastructural support for popular genre film is lacking. Meanwhile, critics questioned the use value of producing national films with no nationally-specific content, especially when the film does not even have a Finnish name. *Dark Floors* is still useful as a measure of the Finnish film industry's increasing development as it functions as an effective calling card for the production standards that can be achieved. Audience familiarity with 'global' (i.e. Hollywood) genre conventions and standards of production make it no surprise that producers would attempt to cater to these tastes. While critics understandably argue against the wholehearted embrace of such conventionality, the increasing respect that the audiences are gaining not only from producers and organizational bodies implies changing standards. Simultaneously, the film functions as an effective warning sign for those commentators that suggest that outright assimilation of the Hollywood standards can benefit the film industry in the long run. As is becoming increasingly evident with hits such as *Rare Exports* (2010), genre conventions are clearly part of Finnish cinema and its audiences. But it seems the audiences crave a balance of the domestic and the foreign in their genre products. Indeed, the main problem with *Dark Floors* is its lack of cultural specificity – there is very little to identify with in the film. Selin had had a similar problem with *Born American* (1986) nearly 25 years before as the ability to produce lookalike Hollywood reproductions does not indicate its automatic acceptance by audiences favourable to the original products. *Dark Floors* thus remains something of a curious footnote in the history of Finnish cinema: it emphasizes both the problems and the potential of embracing commercialist modes of production.

Pietari Kääpä

Filth

Sauna

Production companies:
Bronson Club, Etic Pictures,
Yleisradio (YLE)

Distributor:
Sandrew Metronome
Distribution

Director:
AJ Annila

Producers:
Jesse Fryckman
Tero Kaukomaa

Screenwriter:
Iiro Küttner

Cinematographer:
Henri Blomberg

Composer:
Panu Aaltio

Editor:
Joona Louhuvuori

Duration:
80 minutes

Cast:
Ville Virtanen
Tommi Eronen
Viktor Klimenko
Rain Tolk

Year:
2008

Synopsis

In 1595, the long war between Russia and Sweden has ended in the peace treaty of Teussin. The representatives of both countries are signposting the new border in Karelia, a current border zone between Russia and Finland. Sweden is represented by Finnish brothers, Knut (Eronen), an educated geographer from Stockholm, and tough soldier Eerik (Virtanen). Towards the beginning of their journey, Eerik suspects a peasant of loyalty to the Russians and kills him. Meanwhile, Knut locks his daughter in a dark cellar. After the incident, they meet the Russian delegation and proceed with their task of setting the border. They come face to face with a large swamp which they need to cross. Upon venturing into the swamp strange things start to appear. They find a dog with pierced eyes, the peasant girl seems to appear to Knut, and finally they discover a previously unknown village with a few quiet inhabitants and a strange construct called a sauna.

Critique

Sauna is director AJ Annila's second feature film. The debut *Jadesoturi/Jade Warrior* (2006) was an unusual love story mixing Finnish folklore and kung fu set both in modern Finland and ancient China. The ambitious reworking of genres characterises *Sauna* as well, as Annila takes an original approach to horror – a genre that Finnish film-makers have rarely touched. *Sauna* is a disappointment for those horror fans who expect blood and gore. Instead of explicit horror effects, Annila relies on a meditative approach and uncanny atmosphere of the historical context and strange territory. Annila's horror film has a touch of the gloomy gothic as it centres on unexplainable incidents, the eeriness of the swamp location, and finally on the enigmatic sauna. However, the evil and horrific-looking monster, the key element of the traditional horror film, is missing. Instead of using explicit horror tropes, *Sauna* leans more towards Tarkovski's cine-philosophical meditations about human morality and existence.

Despite these Tarkovskian overtones, *Sauna* is loyal to the traditional patterns of gothic horror: the pure protagonist (in this case Knut) enters into the magic territory – the swamp – where normal natural laws cease to apply and difference between the living and the dead, the natural and the spiritual world, seems to blur. The film does not rely on the old dark gothic house or the castle filled with vampires, but the sauna carries the same function. The sauna – a white, straight angled building surrounded by water at the outskirts of the village – is a mystery. It seems to attract people and have a profound effect on those who enter it. The sauna is a place where forces otherwise hidden reign.

As is often the case with the horror genre, the narratives often contain heavy political and religious overtones and Annila's film is no different. The border is drawn between the eastern and western monarchies, tsarist Russia and the kingdom of Sweden. The Russians are Orthodox and the Swedish rule, represented by the brothers, means the growing influence of a new religion, Protestantism. The swamp and the village in the midst of it is a space where these contrasting ideologies meet. It is a liminal space of transformation, where antecedent customs and spaces become horrific sites of fears and uncertainties of the future.

The story of *Sauna* is told in a relatively straightforward manner, except the inserted flashback scenes which gradually reveal more and more about the incidents in the farmhouse. The film's tagline, 'Wash Your Sins', connects the sauna's traditional function of refreshing the mind and cleaning the body to the film's thematic preoccupation with spiritual and moral purification. The protagonists have things in their consciousness which do not bear daylight. The elder brother, Eerik, has a bloody past as a callous soldier, having killed 73 individuals. This also happens to be the number of the people in the village found in the middle of the swamp. Knut on the other hand is filled with remorse due to leaving the girl to die in the farmhouse's cellar.

The major problem and, simultaneously, the strength of *Sauna* lies in its persistently restricted narration and refusal to give the film a clear explanatory ending. Many reviewers expecting a more traditional horror film were puzzled and considered *Sauna* a confusing experience. The skilled low contrast cinematography creates haunting visual spaces, and careful framing adds the threatening otherworldly quality to key scenes. In addition to the professional technical qualities, the actors complement the intriguing tone of the film. A special delight is an appearance by stone-faced Viktor Klimenko, a famous Finnish entertainer, 'a singing Cossack' of the 1970s, later turned evangelist, who plays Semenski, the tranquil and charismatic leader of the Russian delegation.

Pasi Nyyssönen

If You Love

Jos Rakastat

Production companies:
Juonifilmi
Yleisradio (YLE)

Distributor:
FS Film Oy

Director:
Neil Hardwick

Synopsis

Ada (Vallinoja) has grown up into a spoiled 'princess' as she has been raised without her mother, while her politician father has fulfilled her every whim. On her graduation night, she steals a car and crashes it into Toni's (Ohanwe) father. Ada loses most of her memory and starts rebuilding her life in the hospital where Toni comes to visit his comatose father. Toni and Ada gradually fall in love, but her dark secret haunts her. Meanwhile, she is able to reassess her life and her priorities, but all her secrets will eventually be revealed.

Producer:
Jarkko Hentula

Screenwriters:
Katja Kallio, based on the fairy tale by Sakari Topelius

Art director:
Kaisa Mäkinen

Cinematographer:
Pini Hellstedt

Composer:
Leri Leskinen

Editor:
Harri Ylönen

Duration:
121 minutes

Cast:
Elli Vallinoja
Chike Ohanwe
Minttu Mustakallio
Taneli Mäkelä

Year:
2010

Critique

If You Love is a rarity in Finnish cinema – it is a musical comedy set in a largely realistic contemporary world. Directed by the expat Neil Hardwick, it also provides something of a rarity for Finnish cinema – a competent exploration of multiculturalism. In a film culture where previous examples either play on ethnic stereotypes or scream about the need to overcome ethnic differences, it is distinctly refreshing that the racial differences between the two leads of If You Love are not an issue. This sort of strong multiculturalism provides a comparatively mature approach to a vital social theme which needs balanced analysis. While one could suggest that ignoring racial differences and dis-crimination that still exists in some parts of the nation is ignorant of its realities, adopting approaches that only problematize race hardly contribute any substantial innovations that can overcome discrimination.

The format of the musical allows the film to address these concerns in inventive ways as it adapts well-known pop songs to the narrative of the film. As an adaptation of Sakari Topelius' mid-nineteenth century fairy tale 'Adalmiina's Pearl', the film has its share of fantastical qualities, yet Leri Leskinen's musical arrangements ground it in everyday reality. Refusing the explicitly outlandish choreography of much of the genre, the film plays out in a recognisable Finnish society and contributes to debates on multicultural Finnish identity. For example, the song 'Joka päivä ja joka ikinen yö' by the band Eppu Normaali is interpreted by Afya (Sarah Kivi), who has a crush on Toni. The performance fascinat-ingly merges traditional Finnish culture with updated interpreta-tions of it by second generation immigrants. This is a concrete example of the film's contributions to the ongoing development of Finnish culture, where constant dialogue shapes its contempo-rary form.

Most reviews of If You Love were positive with several critics commending it for its novel approach and its mature take on multicultural Finland. Yet, the film was criticised for its stilted dance choreography and its inability to 'let loose'. This was often equated with a problematic stereotype of Finnish identity, emphasizing well-worn conceptions of stoic uncommunicative Finns. In contrast, Hardwick argues that If You Love should be considered as both Finnish and British (he is originally from Brit-ain) as it combines ideas in ways that refuse categorization into the simplistic framework of national culture. Indeed, he has a long history of exploring Finland from an insider-outsider perspec-tive and his feature debut continues that project. It was seen by a respectable 84,769 spectators, though this did not make it a commercial success. This is a substantially lower number than those for the Risto Räppääjä musicals which have garnered mas-sive success with over 200,000 spectators each. Of course, these films are also children's cinema based on existing books, which enables them to target a more specific audience group. While If You Love was not a breakthrough in commercial or artistic terms, it provides a good example of the Finnish Film Foundation's strive to produce films that take issue with contemporary society. It is a film with a political message done in an inventive style, and it is to be commended for that.

Pietari Kääpä

References

Lehtonen, Sakari (2010), 'Neil Hardwick ja Jos Rakastat', http://www.film-o-holic.com/haastattelut/neil-hardwick-jos-rakastat/. Accessed 20 July 2011.

COMEDY

Comedy films are perhaps the most enduring and perseverant type of cinema produced in Finland. They are also substantially varied in both the form of their humour and the topics of the films. Early films, starting with the first Finnish feature length film *Salaviinanpolttajat/ The Moonshiners* (Puro and Sparre, 1907), have ample comedic elements. In these early films, comedy often emanates from class conflicts and gender politics. Alcohol also frequently plays a key role in creating comedic chaos and narratives of mistaken identity. Many of the comedies to emerge from the early decades of Finnish cinema focus on negotiating differences between the country and the city, differences which are ideologically connected to debates on class, gender, ethnicity and international politics. For gender conflicts, classics such as Valentin Vaala's *Kaikki rakastavat/Everybody Loves* (1935) and *Vaimoke/ Substitute Wife* (1936) explore the changing gender roles in ways that often maintain and repeat stereotypes under their progressive surfaces.

Important directors all made contributions to the comedy genre throughout the early studio years. Nyrki Tapiovaara produced essential contributions to the farce genre with *Kaksi Vihtoria/Two Victors* (1939) and the music comedy *Herra Lahtinen lähtee lipettiin/Mr. Lahtinen Takes Off* (1939). Valentin Vaala produced farces (*Juurakon Hulda/Hulda from Juurakko* [1937]), urban explorations (*Gabriel, tule takaisin/Gabriel, Come Back* [1951]; *Omena putoaa/The Apple Falls* [1952]) and contemporary commentaries on social mores (*Varaventtiili/Spare Vent* [1942]). Even 'prestigious' directors working for the studios during the golden age produced comedies alongside their more dramatic work, including Edvin Laine with *Vihaan sinua – rakas/I Hate You Darling* (1951). Hannu Leminen was another master of genre-hopping and produced such class-based explorations as *En ole kreivitär/Countess for a Night* (1945) alongside his more acknowledged melodramas. The farcical exploration of contemporary norms in these studio comedies have been recognized by historians as presenting vital archival material for sociological analysis.

Comedy franchising had already begun in the 1940s with the Family Suominen adventures (six instalments from 1941 to 1959) and the army farces *Ryhmy ja Romppainen/Ryhmy and Romppainen* (Orko, 1941) and *Jees ja just/Yes and Just* (Orko, 1943). The most successful of the franchises in the studio era was Suomen Filmiteollisuus' adaptation of Ola Fogelberg's comic character Pekka Puupää (Blockhead Pete) for the film series 'Pekka ja Pätkä' ('Pete and Runt'). The series is comprised of thirteen films between 1952 and 1960, and they provide an important snapshot of contemporary cultural mores in Finnish society. The films can be loosely considered as part of the *rillumarei* tradition, a genre of comedy which focuses on folk heroes who best authoritarian figures with their commonsensical and down-to-earth thinking. The films were mostly scripted by Reino Helismaa, who was a key figure in other aspects of *rillumarei* culture from the 1940s to the end of the 1950s. Comedies such as *Rovaniemen markkinoilla/The Markets of Rovaniemi* (Nortimo, 1951) were disparaged at the time by critics, but loved by audiences. As with the more 'legitimate' comedies of the era, the *rillumareis* have risen in appreciation retroactively both as forms of art history and popular culture. As this brief discussion of the diversity of the comedy genre

Left: *Leningrad Cowboys Go America*, Villealfa Productions.

throughout the first fifty years of Finnish cinema demonstrates, comedies function as an essential barometer for assessing the state of the national society.

Finnish cinema encountered many problems throughout the 1960s as urbanization dispersed traditional viewing communities and the increasing prevalence of television challenged the predominance of the cinematic experience. Comedy production also faced difficulties throughout the decade as many of the key film-makers of the era such as Risto Jarva and Mikko Niskanen focused their attention to realist explorations of social problems. But this is not to suggest that the comedy genre receded from domestic film culture. For a good example, Jarva worked with the rising comic Spede Pasanen on *X-paroni/X-Baron* in 1964 alongside Jaakko Pakkasvirta, with the three co-directing it. The often amusing but frequently nonsensical film about a count's visit to Finland would prove to be a key indicator of significant future directions in domestic film comedy. Not only did it provide both Jarva and Pakkasvirta an opportunity to explore national traditionalism through a comical angle, but it also brought Pasanen to cinema audiences.

Pasanen became the key force in Finnish comedy for the next thirty years or so, proving to be a literal one-man industry. Many of his earlier productions were directed by Jukka Virtanen or Ere Kokkonen and consisted of comical explorations of contemporary mores often in the context of genre spoofs. His most enduring claim to fame came with the solo debut of the character of Uuno Turhapuro in the eponymous film of 1973 (dir. Ere Kokkonen). The brainchild of actor Vesa-Matti Loiri and Pasanen, Uuno is a compendium of traditional stereotypes of the Finnish male as seen through the prism of excessive chauvinism. Despite all his negative characteristics, Uuno is incredibly successful in all his activities from sexual conquests to financial gambles, becoming the CEO of a major corporation and even the President. While Pasanen has produced a range of other comedies, it is still Turhapuro that remains his most endearing and beloved creation.

In addition to the disparaged, but frequently successful Pasanen productions, Finnish producers have had difficulty connecting with audiences throughout the 1980s and '90s. Aki and Mika Kaurismäki have produced many comedies, though these are often esoteric fare (*Leningrad Cowboys Go America* [A. Kaurismäki, 1989]) or farcical explorations of contemporary politics (*Cha cha cha* [M. Kaurismäki, 1989]). Also, while films such as *Ariel* (A. Kaurismäki, 1988) and *Zombie ja kummitusjuna/Zombie and the Ghost Train* (M. Kaurismäki, 1991) feature comic elements, any sense of mirth is constantly shadowed by deep sadness and melancholia. Thus, classifying these films as comedies would be limiting their range. Other dramas include comedy elements such as Markku Pölönen's *Kivenpyörittäjän kylä/ The Last Wedding* (1995), which wraps its comedy in the conventions of heritage drama.

It was not until the 2000s that a wide range of comedy products made connections with the domestic audiences. Some of these films use other genres such as Aleksi Mäkelä's *Pahat pojat/Bad Boys* (2003), with its allusions to the *häjy*-film, or *Vares: Private Eye* (2004) with its detective story framework. Films best described as lifestyle comedies have also been popular in their explorations of contemporary mores; for example, Ilkka Vanne's *Vieraalla maalla/Land of Love* (2003) depicts the problems of multicultural Finland while Johanna Vuoksenmaa's *Nousukausi/Upswing* (2003) critiques social class divisions. These films are important indicators of the state of the nation at the time of their production, and will provide important archival material for future analysis of twenty-first century Finland.

Indeed, within this very brief survey of dominant trends in Finnish comedy, the social relevance of the genre should be apparent. While these films have seldom been appreciated by critics at the time of their release, their popularity with audiences indicates their national cultural relevance. Furthermore, they are important archives of cultural knowledge and contemporary mores for audiences wishing to inspect the history or the contemporary state of the nation. Far from irreverent entertainment, they are to be considered as extraordinarily revealing social commentaries.

By Pietari Kääpä

Substitute Wife

Vaimoke

Production company:
Suomi Filmi Oy

Distributor:
Suomi Filmi Oy

Director:
Valentin Vaala

Producer:
Risto Orko

Screenwriters:
Valentin Vaala
Tauno Tattari, based on the
novel by Hilja Valtonen

Art director:
Armas Fredman

Cinematographer:
Theodor Luts

Composer:
Harry Bergström

Editor:
Valentin Vaala

Duration:
79 minutes

Cast:
Tauno Palo
Ansa Ikonen
Väinö Sola
Kirsti Suonio

Year:
1936

Synopsis

Kirsti Leivo (Ikonen) is the rebel of the family. Her five elder sisters have lived up to expectations, graduated and got eligible spouses. Kirsti quits school, wants to work and hangs out with her boyfriend Tanu (Kunto Karapää). Esko Latva (Palo) is the most eligible bachelor in the town. Friends tease him as he has courted all the eldest Leivo sisters but still hasn't married. Esko claims that he can marry the first woman he meets and a wager is made. The first woman is Kirsti. She doesn't take Esko's attempts seriously but enjoys both the kissing and a drive in his car. Soon Kirsti finds out about the wager and makes a plan with the sisters: she will get half of Esko's money in a divorce.

After the wedding, Esko takes control. He takes Kirsti for the honeymoon before the reception, and doesn't even allow her to take her clothes. Instead, he takes her to buy new ones as he hopes to tame her, but still refuses to dismiss the housekeeper, his ex-girlfriend. The couple initially lives separate lives, but their feelings grow, and Esko even admits his love for her. The housekeeper causes friction and eventually Esko moves out. Tanu tells him about Kirsti's true feelings, and at a New Year's party at the moment of midnight when the lights are turned off, men change places and Esko surprises his wife with a kiss.

Critique

Valentin Vaala and the leading couple Ansa Ikonen and Tauno Palo of *Substitute Wife* had started at Suomi-Filmi in 1935 with the successful *Kaikki rakastavat/Everybody Loves*. Both Palo and Vaala were experienced players in the film industry, but Ikonen was a newcomer – and an instant star. Together, Ikonen and Palo became the first couple of Finnish cinema. *Substitute Wife*, the follow-up to the introduction of the successful formula, was based on a text by Hilja Valtonen, the best-selling author of 'flapper' novels. Eight more Valtonen adaptations were to be made but none of them reached the fame of *Substitute Wife*. The time span of the novel is about one year, but the film was made in only a couple of winter months. All the exterior pictures are snowy scenes and there are even two chases in the midst of snow drifts: the first with a car when the couple escapes from the wedding, and the second with skis, train and car when Kirsti tries to run away during the honeymoon.

Vaala's films are fresh in style and lack theatricality. Even though some of the interior sets of *Substitute Wife* are a bit stuffy, and some of the supporting cast stiff, his cinematic style is even more obvious than usual. The film practically glows youthful liveliness as it illustrates what it was like to be young in the 1930s. This is especially evident in the character of Kirsti, who is both vivid and frisky. She is not an innocent girl as she admits that she loves to kiss and has been doing it ever since she was fourteen. She even curses twice by blurting out an abbreviation, 'HP!' that stands for something akin to 'Bugger off!' or 'Damn you!' It is not surprising that the role helped to establish Ikonen's status as the most adored film actress in Finland.

The most entertaining of the supporting characters are the elder sisters, all happily married but still longing for Esko. They are eager to criticize Kirsti when she turns down the first proposal, but when they find out about the wager, they draw up the scheme with the 'prenup' and divorce – although married according to mother's wishes, they understand the bliss of divorce! They call for revenge on Esko but, nevertheless, they look heartbroken at the wedding as their true love is married to their youngest sister.

Few of the golden age Finnish films have withstood the time as well as *Substitute Wife*. After his earlier success with *Everybody Loves*, Vaala had the opportunity to implement his vision and he succeeded triumphantly. Ikonen, the unconditional star of the film, stands out with her glimmering youth, beauty, vigour and rebellion. Palo deserves substantial credit as well as his character is perfect for testing the definition made by one of the elder sisters: 'In a modern marriage there are only two possible outcomes: you argue, until the divorce becomes inevitable, or you argue, until love atones for everything, and neither of the cases is life-threatening'.

Outi Hupaniittu

Beautiful Veera

Kaunis Veera eli ballaadi Saimaalta

Production company:
Suomen Filmiteollisuus

Distributor:
Suomen Filmiteollisuus

Director:
Ville Salminen

Producer:
T.J. Särkkä

Screenwriters:
Ville Salminen
Toivo Särkkä, based on the play by Tatu Pekkarinen

Art director:
Ville Salminen

Cinematographer:
Osmo Harkimo

Synopsis

The crew of tugboat Prinsessa Armada specialize in singing their way through the lakes of eastern Finland. On one occasion, their maid wins a beauty contest and decides to pursue a career in modelling. Thus, the crew set to find the ugliest girl they can, bumping into the mud-covered Veera (Nortia). She is on the run from her gypsy family who are forcing her to marry a rich travelling salesman. Veera gets hired as the new coffee girl and proceeds to charm the sailors. On a visit to St. Petersburg, the crew run into trouble with the Russian authorities. A Finnish lieutenant (Labbart) hitches a ride with them and an escaped prisoner from Siberia turns out to be Veera's long-lost father (Eino Kaipainen). On returning back to the Finnish lakes, the crew have to face the incompetent authorities and the gypsy (Veikko Uusimäki) suitor that still wants Veera back. Soon, corrupt authorities and thieving gypsies get their comeuppance as Veera regains her righteous place alongside the dashing and distinctly upstanding lieutenant.

Critique

Beautiful Veera is Ville Salminen's adaptation of Matti Jurva and Tatu Pekkarinen's popular song 'Kaunis Veera' and the subsequent play built around it. The song and the play were immensely popular with domestic audiences and was a massive hit with almost one million viewers on release. The film is a canonical example of national

Composer:

Harry Bergström

Editor:

Armas Vallasvuo

Duration:

79 minutes

Cast:

Assi Nortia
Rolf Labbart
Kalle Viherpuu
Elsa Turakainen

Year:

1950

cinema purely on the basis of its success, but there is also enough expressive cultural iconography to qualify its significance. The narrative of the film is flimsy at best and relies on circumstance and exaggeration for its impact. But this is not the point as the songs and the lively performances are what made (and still make) the film work with its audiences. The famed quartet Kipparikvartetti was established for the film and consisted of two tenors and two base singers. Their unique tone provides many of the musical scenarios' vibrancy that the choreography and narrative may not always match. Similar vibrancy is found in the visual setting as the film at times resembles a touristic advertisement for the Saimaa lakes, with frequent establishing shots of surrounding scenery and nature.

Contemporary reviewers emphasized its national romanticist appeal that is not only carried by the music and the scenery, but also in its narrative and themes. The geopolitical argumentation of the film simultaneously harkens to a timeless past and comments on the contemporary situation. The depiction of the tsarist armies and their inhumanity is created in caricatured terms as reflections of Stalin's Russia: for example, the Finnish lieutenant informs the crew that he is being hunted because he refused to beat his underlings. The father has been sent to the Siberian camps on flimsy charges and has now escaped this tyrannical victimization. Furthermore, the flippant upper-class heiress (Turakainen) that hitches a ride is clearly divorced from reality as she 'only' owns two gold mines and is thus considered poor in Russia. And finally, the authorities in Finland who aim to capture the lieutenant are either bizarrely creepy or brutally overbearing. The representation of tsarist Russia as inhumane can only be read as a contemporary comment on the post-WWII situation.

Beautiful Veera's problematic gender politics also reveal a lot about contemporary norms and expectations of appropriate gendered behaviour. Not only are women materialist and preoccupied with surfaces, they also pose problems for the established male order and need to submit to the rule of the dominant man. While Veera, of course, rebels against these confines, she is effectively domesticated by the soldier, and the Russian heiress becomes the wife of the patriarchal gypsy rebel as she finds such 'bestiality' appealing. Thus, patriarchal relations are naturalized or even made comically affable. This is still not the film's most problematic ideological aspect as its depiction of other ethnicities besides the 'whities' reveals a lot about contemporary norms. All of the gypsies are shown in the most caricatured and unfavourable of lights. When the gypsy rebel beats his wife in front of the whole camp, he justifies it as the way of the Roma. Meanwhile, Veera's 'parents' are aghast at people doing real manual labour. As they sell Veera off, they respond to her demand to explain why she is being sold off like a horse by saying that a horse is a lot more expensive. While many of these instances are so over the top as to be only taken comically, there is very little attempt to do anything with these stereotypes rather than to enforce homogeneity.

The narrative of the other has been a frequent topic throughout Finnish cinema and goes back to films such as *Kulkurin valssi/The*

Vagabond's Waltz (Särkkä, 1941) and its 'reassuring' revelation of the vagabond hero as a noble prince. *Beautiful Veera* performs the same role reversal as we find out that she was abducted by the gypsies and is in fact part of a family of anti-Russian activists. While this sort of criticism is clearly conducted from a retrospective perspective, the film is a reflection of the mores of the time and populist pandering to conventional fairy tale conventions. Meanwhile, the film is still revered for its nostalgic entertainment value and ability to evoke nostalgia for the national past. Many of the key themes of *Beautiful Veera* continued with Salminen's next music comedy Rion yö/*A Night in Rio* (1951), which once more starred Assi Nortia as a nightclub dancer. The film is a similarly infectious extravaganza with a bunch of Finnish sailors engaging in all manner of malarkey on the streets of Rio. It repeats most of *Beautiful Veera*'s ethnic and gendered assertions, while a disconcerting exoticism plagues the film, especially Salminen's performance as a dark-skinned white slaver, and we never see much of the realities of Brazil beyond this carnal carnivalesque fantasy. These musicals emphatically underline the ways in which studio-era cinema not only contributed to an archive of nationally significant iconography and cultural material, but reflected the ideological limitations of the times.

Pietari Kääpä

No Bodies in the Bedroom

Ei ruumiita makuuhuoneeseen

Production company:
Suomen Filmiteollisuus

Distributor:
Suomen Filmiteollisuus

Director:
Aarne Tarkas

Producer:
T.J. Särkkä

Screenwriter:
Aarne Tarkas

Art director:
Aarre Koivisto

Cinematographer:
Olavi Tuomi

Synopsis

Detectives Kaarna (Herala) and Luoto (Rinne) get embroiled with a gang of international money launderers as they journey to Malaga in Spain. The leader of the gang, Soto (Ture Junttu), hides Hitler's money printing plates in the detectives' luggage, which they then bring back to Finland. Soto's attempts to lure the detectives with dancing girls and threaten them with hoodlums fail one after another. The detectives fly to Las Palmas, where Soto's accomplice falls for Kaarna. Flying back home, they square up to Soto's gang, who prove no match for the witty detectives.

Critique

Aarne Tarkas' crime comedy is a lively if inconsequential film. The pairing of Helge Herala and Tommi Rinne works well and the inane banter between the characters keeps the largely arbitrary and circular narrative flowing. The film does occasionally achieve considerable comic momentum: for example, the detectives' humiliation of a pair of henchmen whom they force to clean their flat in their underwear is both absurd and hilarious. These sorts of silly interludes bring much to a rather formulaic narrative about detectives and the unruly dames that love them.

Director Tarkas was heavily influenced by genre Hollywood films, made evident by both the formulaic plot and the hardboiled

Composer:
Toivo Kärki

Editor:
Armas Vallasvuo

Duration:
104 minutes

Cast:
Anneli Sauli
Helge Herala
Tommi Rinne
Marjatta Kallio

Year:
1959

protagonists. He was never much of a sociocritical commentator, but the film showcases a 'new' Finland, a space of cosmopolitans in a modern international nation. *No Bodies in the Bedroom* is clearly conceived as a Finnish version of the international detective genre. The production was filmed in Spain and Mallorca, and there is little narrative motivation to keep returning to these locations beyond highlighting the international dimensions of the production. Curiously, the film often works as an advertisement for the Kar-Air airline company, for whom the detectives seem to work. Such product placement can be considered as part of the film's commercialism to which its internationalism attests. One of the criminals even exclaims: 'Finland – that is a nicely isolated land', upon deciding where to move their operations. The detectives are clearly modelled after figures such as Eddie Constantine and the film even contains commentary on how their lives are lacking in the exciting adventures seen in Constantine's films.

Appropriately then, the gender norms of *No Bodies in the Bedroom* are Neanderthal-like at best, especially as the main protagonists are portrayed as worldly Lotharios – international men of mystery indeed. There are occasional flashes of self-critical humour in the film's obsession with the detectives' childish and backwards ways and their endearing cohabitation of their flat. But mostly the film seems to love its characters almost as much as they love themselves. Thus, the film is revealing in both its reflection of dominant social norms and its unabashed sense of commercialism. While it can be considered an irreverent, populist effort, it is also an important reflection of the ways producers chose to internationalize domestic film culture.

Pietari Kääpä

Black and White

Mustaa Valkoisella

Production companies:
Jörn Donner Production
FJ-Filmi Oy

Distributor:
Finnkino

Director:
Jörn Donner

Producers:
Arno Carlstedt
Jörn Donner

Screenwriter:
Jörn Donner

Synopsis

Juha Holm (Donner) is an affluent advertising executive, living with his perfect family in one of the newly built suburbs of Helsinki. His life is full of modern conveniences, and his wife (Laaksonen) seems to relish her life in the suburbs. Yet, all is not as perfect under the surface. Holm is in the midst of an affair with his secretary Maria (Halkola), and they both seem to relish it as a noncommittal opportunity. Holm soon discovers that he needs something more stable in his life than this because his job is not fulfilling him. Yet, Maria does not want his commitment nor can he go back to his suburban transience.

Critique

Jörn Donner had authored a key article on the state of the Finnish film industry, *Finnish Film in Year Zero*, in 1959. In this work, he argued that film culture in Finland had reached its lowest point yet as it was only focused on rural melodramas and nonsensical com-

Cinematographer:
Esko Nevalainen

Composers:
Lasse Mårtenson
Georg Riedel

Editor:
Jörn Donner

Duration:
95 minutes

Cast:
Jörn Donner
Kristiina Halkola
Jukka Virtanen
Liisamaija Laaksonen

Year:
1968

edies. His criticism here is reminiscent of the rhetoric conducted by the *Cahiers du Cinéma* group in France. As with the French critics, the director produced his own version of what he thinks national cinema should be about. *Black and White* is Donner's contribution to the Finnish New Wave, which was spearheaded by figures such as Risto Jarva and Mikko Niskanen. Instead of the typical, rebellious young protagonists that we find in some of the key examples of the Wave, Donner focuses on the affluent thirty-something middle-classes. Through this, the film constructs an exemplary deconstruction of the contemporary moment of its production. Yet, *Black and White* is extremely ironic in its tone as it depicts the crumbling of the façade of the 'perfect' nuclear family. The postwar consumerist boom and the increasing middle-classicisation of society is ably captured in the opening moments. Holm and his family go about their daily routines; we hear a commentator's voice describe these routines in extreme depth while family members sprout peppy endorsements for commercial products and express their seeming contentment with their lives. The affairs Juha compulsively has with his secretary do not seem to impinge on this impression of moral security. But once he leaves home, this sense of harmony is revealed to be a construction not far from the consumerist advertisements Holm produces for a living.

Donner's films are highly interesting and often contradictory not only in their criticism of social conformity but also their attempts to strive for a certain feminist angle. *Black and White* reinforces the housewife stereotype on one hand, though this is inevitably cast in a critical light due to Donner's critical stance on suburban conformity. Similarly, the secretary's refusal to become yet another one of Juha's domesticated conquests indicates at least a primitive understanding of the basic principles of feminism. Donner has produced several films with a feminist angle, all which are simultaneously problematic and progressive in their gender politics. For example, the 1978 production *Miestä ei voi raiskata/Men Can't Be Raped* is a Finnish-Swedish version of the then popular cycle of US rape-revenge films. As with its American counterparts, the film bifurcates the role of the woman as either a victim or a cold killer with little room for complexity, though it does manage to be a lot less sleazy and exploitative in its approach to the topic.

Black and White combines its feminist politics with its formative New Wave-inspired rethinking of national cinema conventions in the final moments of the film. As Juha Holm pursues Maria out to the edges of the city to a zone of development where the city meets the countryside, the film plays with our expectations of national/gender politics. Initially, we are led to think the film will culminate in the expected romantic coupling as we follow the couple through forests, underscored by romantic folk-like music. Suddenly this scenario is interrupted as the music cuts out and is immediately replaced by the jarring sounds of traffic. We are again at the side of the road as Juha desperately tries to keep up with Maria. The film concludes in mid-shot, in motion, denoting the uncertain and ongoing process of social metamorphosis. This ambiguous conclusion connects interpersonal relations with wider social movements as the private concerns of individuals extend into public affairs.

Black and White was controversial for its times due to its frank sex scenes, though these were to be upstaged a few years later by Donner's own *Naisenkuvia/Portraits of Women* (1970). While Donner was clearly intending to shock the docile public into critical awareness, his attention-grabbing techniques are not merely sensationalist. There is a clear intention here to attack conventional morality, to effectively put the rhetoric of his Finnish cinema article into action. Moral concerns are tied to class politics, which may be surprising considering Donner's roots in Finland's Swedish-speaking elite. While Donner is dismissive of his leftist phase, we must consider all of these critical activities in an ironic and complex light as Donner also pokes fun at himself in *Black and White*. Starting out from a positive evaluation of the consumer boom and then deconstructing its hypocritical lifestyles, Donner's intellectual public image is similarly open to question. He has explored similar themes of public appearances and private lives in his many novels and the Swedish-language *Dirty Story* from 1984. Never settling for easy preconceptions, Donner remains the first Finn to win an Oscar for his role as producer of the Ingmar Bergman's *Fanny and Alexander* (1982). He also had a vital role in Nordic film culture as one of the founding members of the Finnish Film Foundation and the head of the Swedish Film Institute.

Donner's career in politics has overshadowed his film-related work, having served in both the Finnish and the European parliament. Yet, his achievements in cinema should not be underestimated as his return to directing, *Kuulustelu/The Interrogation* in 2009 demonstrates. The film again inspects national history from a critical perspective, this time focusing on undercover Soviet spies operating in Finland during the Second World War. Continuing the theme of unravelling conventional morality already seen in *Black and White*, the film is not as visually inventive as his early work. But this testifies to Donner's ability to adapt to the critical needs of cinematic expression at different historical periods. Out of all the experimental films he produced throughout the 1960s, *Black and White* is perhaps the most cohesive and indicative of the complexities that his idiosyncratic career would take.

Pietari Kääpä

References

Donner, Jörn (1959), 'Suomalainen Elokuvan Vuonna Nolla', *Studio*, Helsinki: SES, pp. 17–58.

Olympian Holiday

Loma

Production company:
Filminor

Distributor:
Suomi-Filmi

Director:
Risto Jarva

Producer:
Kullervo Kukkasjärvi

Screenwriters:
Jussi Kylätasku
Risto Jarva
Kullervo Kukkasjärvi

Art director:
Matti Marttila

Cinematographer:
Antti Peippo

Composer:
Markku Kopisto

Editors:
Risto Jarva
Matti Kuortti

Duration:
113 minutes

Cast:
Antti Litja
Tuula Nyman
Eija Pokkinen
Jukka Sipilä

Year:
1976

Synopsis

A poetic fan of winter sports and a precise bank officer, Aimo Niemi (Litja) mistakenly ends up in the wrong aeroplane on his trip to the 1976 Winter Olympics. Ironically, instead of snowy Innsbruck in Austria, Aimo finds himself alone with his skis and a woolly hat on a tour of the origins of the Olympic Games in Greece. At the airport of the island of Rhodes, Aimo receives the suitcase of 'Mrs A. Niemi', full of feminine properties, and he is made to share a hotel room with a female reporter. Aimo's roommate, Marjukka Notkola (Nyman), suffers from hunger for love due to a recent break up with her lover, a married man. Aimo, for his part, suffers from concrete hunger – due to a precise travel budget and a full-board plan in Innsbruck, he has no extra money with him. During the holiday, the Finnish tourists open up and start romantic relationships, but Aimo only daydreams and writes secret poems for a distant beauty queen who he does not dare to approach. Marjukka finds the poems and believes that she must be the object of Aimo's passion. At the end, also Aimo realizes that Marjukka indeed is a better companion than the mysterious, unattainable lady.

Critique

Olympian Holiday was the second film of Risto Jarva's trilogy (*Mies joka ei osannut sanoa ei*/*The Man Who Couldn't Say No* [1975]; *Olympian Holiday*; *Jäniksen vuosi*/*The Year of the Hare* [1977]) in which he turned away from strictly artistic and political film-making to producing more popular comedies that were mostly directed at large domestic audiences. This approach is crystallized in the collective scene in which a Finnish tourist group sings a traditional Finnish song in a Greek tavern, far away from home, yet together.

As in a proper comedy, the storyline of *Olympian Holiday* is based on unfortunate mishaps, unexpected encounters and changing identities that the trope of travelling enables. Working men become business managers, nurses turn into medical doctors, chief executives act as blue-collar workers, and loving husbands find wild Casanovas in themselves as they leave their home country behind. At the end, all false identities are revealed and everyone has learnt something when away from home. These identity performances resemble Judith Butler's famous idea of genders as performative, which is highlighted especially in drag: in the excessive gender imitation of drag, the general imitative character of genders is also revealed. Similarly, the excessive imitativeness of identities in the film shows how cultural identities are constructed through imitation and repetition of particular gestures, expressions and positions. The totally liberated changeability of the identities in the film, exclusively enabled by the travelling trope, also shows that, in real life, identities are not results of free choice, but always performed under culturally determined constraints and prohibitions. The imitated and repeated gestures, expressions and positions are not only particular, but also definitely designated and restricted.

Aimo's desperate and fatefully failed cross-dressing, performed for a meal in a Greek restaurant, ironically finalizes Butler's ideas about genders performed under carefully determined constraints and prohibitions which are painful, if not even fatal, to resist.

Olympian Holiday seems to share characteristics, such as cross-dressing, with screwball and even romantic comedies, without quite comfortably fitting into either of the categories. Although considered a comedy, there are no signs of slapstick or crazy, senseless college humour in *Olympian Holiday*; but it instead relies on quiet, warm and sympathetic humour, saturated with the idea of the fundamental and always-as-fateful irony of human life and human relationships. What is more, Jarva's 'gentle comedy' seems to contain a hint of 'compassionate tragedy'. His protagonists and characters either meet great losses or misfortunes, and even the minor losses, as well as minor misfortunes, have a great effect on their personal lives. This does not mean, however, that the characters of the trilogy would be tragic; quite the opposite. Jarva's attitude towards his characters is goodhearted and understanding, while most of them can also be seen as contrarians of the contemporary urban, hectic, individualized and opportunistic lifestyles that Jarva's films seem to criticize as a whole.

Sanna Karkulehto

Uuno Turhapuro in Spain

Uuno Epsanjassa

Production company:
Filmituotanto Spede Pasanen Oy

Distributor:
Eini Carlstedt

Director:
Ere Kokkonen

Producer:
Spede Pasanen

Screenwriter:
Ere Kokkonen

Art director:
Kristine Elo

Cinematographer:
Mara Kakko

Synopsis

One of the most successful entries in the long-running Uuno Turhapuro series, *Uuno Turhapuro in Spain* takes place in a coastal resort. Uuno (Loiri) has accepted a job as a tour guide and currently disposes his home-grown wisdom to hapless *señoritas*. Uuno's nemesis, his father-in-law Minister Tuura (Hämäläinen), is also at the resort as he needs to get a signature of approval from a minister for his business plans. The by-now well-established farcical scenario involving Uuno's haphazard success in thwarting Tuura's plans plays out on the beaches with little variation to the formula.

Critique

The Uuno Turhapuro (Numbskull Emptybrook) series consists of twenty theatrical films produced between 1973 and 2004. The brainchild of Finnish comic Vesa-Matti Loiri and director Spede Pasanen, they have been consistently successful, exemplified by the period between 1984 and 1992, when eight out of the ten most popular domestic films were Turhapuros. While the Turhapuro series consists essentially of low-budget farce productions – a formula that appears in most national cinemas – they are impressively ideological, if scattershot, in their satirizing of contemporary norms. Targets range from contemporary popular culture to the media industries, from private enterprise to capitalism in the welfare state. The approach taken in the Turhapuro series serves to

Composer:

Jaakko Salo

Editor:

Eva Jaakontalo

Duration:

107 minutes

Cast:

Vesa-Matti Loiri
Marjatta Raita
Tapio Hämäläinen
Marita Nordberg

Year:

1985

unmask accepted stereotypes and critique prevailing social norms. Uuno's invincible success with everything from presidential office to conquering members of the opposite sex confirms him as a male fantasy where the man can act as he pleases and not only get away with it, but be congratulated for it. As Uuno becomes a successful farmer in a matter of minutes or meteorically rises through the ranks of the army, the legitimacy of these institutions becomes questionable. Uuno's ambiguity as both a folk hero and a negative projection of the Finnish male allows him to become a stereotype in the Brechtian sense, where he serves to generalize meaning and demystify established power relations as a site of contradiction.

Of course, one could argue that the success of such easy mainstream parodies only works to suppress real criticism or supplant it to the margins. Thus, these 'harmless' ideological critiques may deflect more considered critically constructive arguments or even reinforce misogynistic attitudes. But they also function as the sort of ironically effective parody that keeps a culture alive and thriving. In any case, the real attraction with Turhapuro's Spanish adventure is not so much the narrative and certainly not the film production style. Rather, the key attraction is Loiri's performance, which once again excels in providing Uuno with a paradoxical sense of fantasy-induced reality. The particular instance of bravado in Uuno's Spanish adventure includes a matador show which admittedly halts the narrative flow for an irrelevant scene of performance spectacle. But as Uuno functions more akin to the cinema of attractions rather than conventional narrative cinema, this type of digression is entirely expected. Furthermore, as these films were produced independently without funding from the Finnish Film Foundation until 1988's *Double Uuno* (dir. Hannu Seikkula), they indicate important industrial developments within Finnish film culture. It is not surprising that the Turhapuro series are nowadays considered as key contributions to national film culture and politics. Comprising of over thirty years of cultural history, they span a considerable range of thematic concerns and exemplify transformations in the role of entertainment cinema in domestic film politics.

Pietari Kääpä

Just Great!

Hei kliffaa hei!

Production company:

Filmituotanto Spede Pasanen
Oy

Distributor:

Eini Carlstedt

Synopsis

Auvo (Loiri) is a conman of many talents, of which the most successful is his ability to talk absolute nonsense to anyone in such measures as to make them ultimately agree with his harebrained schemes. He finds a new target in Kultsi (Salminen), who is competing with his cousin for the inheritance of a large sum of money from their uncle. The deceased has set a condition that whoever first spends 20 million in the most productive ways receives the inheritance. Kultsi hires Auvo for the job and the two set out to win the prize.

Director:
Ere Kokkonen

Producer:
Pertti Pasanen

Screenwriter:
Ere Kokkonen

Art director:
Vesa Tapola

Cinematographer:
Mara Kakko

Composer:
Aarno Raninen

Editor:
Alf Ekström

Duration:
100 minutes

Cast:
Vesa-Matti Loiri
Simo Salminen
Hannele Lauri
Riitta Väisänen

Year:
1985

Critique

Just Great! is a good example of the type of comedy Spede Pasanen and Vesa-Matti Loiri produced amidst the more iconic Uuno Turhapuro series. Critics at the time dismissed the film as an irreverent and nonsensical production, much like they had done with most of Pasanen's work. While some of the film could be characterised in these terms – it is enthusiastically misogynistic and displays a real absence of logic – much of its content is very topical in its politicized commentary. This has often been the case with many of Pasanen's films as they take aim at most traditional and commonly-held values. *Just Great!* satirizes the increasing acceptance of capitalism as a key pillar of society, and the ways certain individuals can manipulate this acceptance for their own benefits. Vesa-Matti 'Vesku' Loiri makes an excellent villain (or antihero) in his portrayal of Auvo, a compulsive liar and confidence man. The character of Auvo is clearly a sort of ironic caricature of the yuppie businessman with his obsession on outlandish 'style' and money. Auvo sprouts nonsensical idiosyncratic slang constantly, adapting terms from English and Swedish liberally amidst his own perversions of contemporary slang. Auvo's linguistic molestations can be considered as a parody of the specialist terminology employed by neo-liberalist economists and policy-makers during Finland's entry into its then contemporary Reaganist adoration.

The film is not exactly cinematically ravishing as it was produced with television technology to keep the costs down. Yet, this lack of visual panache is not able to deter from its topical content. As is typical for Loiri, he performs a virtuoso sketch during the film which involves juggling in a restaurant. The film is thus a clear attempt to emulate the successful conventions of the Turhapuro series by adapting characters from the producers' television shows, the *Vesku Show* (1988–91) and the *Spede Show* (1968–87). Both shows were successful throughout the 1970s and '80s, and provided the comics a chance to cultivate crossover streams. While they produced a number of comedies aimed at popular audiences, none of them connected to the extent that Turhapuro did. A question often asked was why would one have to pay for something that could be seen for free on television? Turhapuro was thus kept as an elite brand, while 'Vesku' and Spede attempted to strike success with their other characters, as with the case of *Just Great!*. Spede's success in a range of media formats indicates his abilities with the business side of the industry. Effectively he was able to create a media brand to which all individual films and shows contributed. While critics and even audiences were quick to dismiss these films, their thematic contemporaneity and engagement with popular culture makes them an important, and as yet largely under-researched, archive of national culture. Tommi Aitio's insightful work on Spede acts as a key recognition of the cultural-historical validity of Pasanen's contributions to film culture in Finland. Meanwhile, further academic work on the individual films, especially those produced throughout the 1980s, is certainly to be recommended.

Pietari Kääpä

Land of Love

Vieraalla maalla

Production company:
Matila Röhr Productions (MRP)

Distributors:
Columbia TriStar Nordisk Film
Distributors
Nordisk Film International Sales

Director:
Ilkka Vanne

Producer:
Marko Röhr

Screenwriters:
Mika Ripatti
Seppo Vesiluoma

Art director:
Pentti Valkeasuo

Cinematographer:
Jani Kumpulainen

Editor:
Joona Louhivuori

Duration:
91 minutes

Cast:
Irina Björklund
Ville Haapasalo
Vesa Vierikko
Katja Kukkola

Year:
2003

Synopsis

Tuomas (Haapasalo) is a sociologist who is conducting research on the immigrant 'experience' in Finland. To get more insightful field data, he assumes the identity of his friend Omar and attempts to view the society from his perspective. Soon, he meets language teacher Hanne (Björklund) and starts to fall in love with her. The only problem is that Hanne only knows his immigrant alter ego and despises the real Tuomas due to a variety of misunderstandings. His problems get deeper as Omar's past catches up with him, especially his pregnant girlfriend from the Ostrobothnian plains.

Critique

Land of Love is one of the first Finnish films to explicitly tackle the issue of multiculturalism. While ethnic and other racial matters have occasionally featured in Finnish cinema, these have predominantly been marginal issues. Vanne's comedy is set in the increasingly multicultural contemporary Finland, where occasional conflicts exist between immigrants and the host population. The film has to be commended for its attempts at tackling this acute issue, but the ways it approaches multicultural coexistence leaves a lot to be desired. Much of the film relies on extensive stereotypes as the construction of two opposing dichotomies – restricted Finns and the amiable immigrants – limits any real introspection on cultural conflict and exchange. While the film has its heart in the right place in criticizing racism and prejudice, it portrays everything in black and white terms.

The film culminates with Tuomas joining the immigrant team Lainajussit ('Borrowed Jacks') for a game of Finnish baseball. Not only does this establish a superficial creation of equality, it also symbolizes the ways in which immigrants are expected to learn to play along with the rules of the dominant host society by adopting its customs. The problem here is that any sort of adaptation is actually premised on expecting the immigrants to forsake their own national customs and assume the normative frameworks of the dominant culture. This illustrates a weak version of multiculturalism in that it sees adaptation as a one-way system, where all the obligations rest with the immigrants. In comparison, the host population is only expected to tolerate them and provide them with the framework in which to live. This problematic multiculturalism is not helped by the film's depiction of the immigrants as somewhat naïve and childlike. For example, a lot of the humour is constructed on the basis of linguistic misunderstandings and stereotypes of immigrant behaviour. Any solution it poses to the problems of ethnic conflict seem on surface to be sound, but they are also indicative of its somewhat limiting and problematic perspective.

The perspective of a Finn adopting an immigrant identity is an intriguing approach in theory, but it also sidelines the immigrants to a secondary position. The poster for the film emphasizes a marked contrast between the two roles of the protagonist – the serious and studious character of Tuomas and the leering Omar with long hair and 'bling' paraphernalia. The tagline of the film reads that this is a comedy about Finns, indicating a somewhat liberal inclusion of the immigrants into the category of the Finns. But the marketing campaign simultaneously relies on a comical role-play on identity, which is still reliant on a dichotomous conceptions of Finns and their stereotyped Others. The suggestion that the film works more as a form of whitewashing feel-good cinema aimed at native Finns is also underlined by the conclusion, where Tuomas comes to realize that he is a better person as Omar than he is as himself. This is of course a very problematic proposition where real and tangible social problems are only used for the white man's self-realization. There are no real attempts to propose a solution to the problems and instead the immigrant community is depicted as an inherently Other cultural sphere. While one could argue that the film aims to strip away racist prejudices amongst the native Finns (its target audience), a topic of this sensitivity deserves more complex and insightful interrogation.

It is also somewhat surprising that Finnish cinema has not been able to produce a film on multiculturalism in a more critically balanced vein. Whereas the other Nordic film industries countries have provided key roles for immigrants both behind and in front of the camera, few such efforts exist in Finland. Increasingly, films such as Lenka Hellstedt's *Maata meren alla/Overseas and Under Your Skin* (2009) provide more complex depictions of the multicultural, as well as the overwhelming feeling that Finnish film producers insist on speaking for the immigrants. The latter is especially awkward and points to a systematic failure in Finnish film culture to provide opportunities for cinematic diversity. Recently, Tonislav Hristov's *Sinkkuelämän säännöt/The Rules of Single Life* (2011) can be considered part of this advanced mode of strong multicultural cinema as it chronicles the love lives of a couple of immigrants in Finland without making the film *about* the immigrant experience. But as the director himself suggests, this is still a real anomaly rather than a sign of structural transformation of domestic film culture. Finnish cinema thus remains somewhat underdeveloped in its engagement with the changing social realities.

Pietari Kääpä

References

Tirronen, Lumi (2011), 'Tonislav Hristov ja Sinkkuelämän Säännöt', http://www.film-o-holic.com/haastattelut/tonislav-hristov-sinkkuelaman-saannot/. Accessed 20 July 2011.

Upswing

Nousukausi

Production companies:
Kinotar Oy, Yleisradio (YLE)

Distributors:
FS Film Oy, Yleisradio (YLE)

Synopsis

Katri (Lymi) and Janne (Summanen) are a thirty-something couple, living a life of contentment in the upper echelons of information-age Finland. Janne is about to resign from the company which gave him his start in the business as he has just been offered a job at a rival computing firm. The couple wants to go on a vacation somewhere unusual, where none of their colleagues have gone before. They find an advertisement for a holiday in the Helsinki suburb of Jakomäki, a place of ill reputation. Janne and Katri move in, and place their

Director:

Johanna Vuoksenmaa

Producer:

Lasse Saarinen

Screenwriter:

Mika Ripatti

Art director:

Päivi Kettunen

Cinematographer:

Peter Flinckenberg

Composer:

Kerkko Koskinen

Editor:

Kimmo Kohtamäki

Duration:

98 minutes

Cast:

Petteri Summanen
Tiina Lymi
Katja Kukkola
Juha Veijonen

Year:

2003

belongings in the care of Heino (Antti Virmavirta), the unscrupulous travel agent. Initially enjoying their new back to basics life, they soon tire of living on the meagre unemployment allowance. Demanding to get their property back, they discover that Heino has conned them and sold their house to the next breed of internet entrepreneur. As Janne and Katri struggle to regain their old lives, the suburb and its peculiar inhabitants comes to offer them a new home.

Critique

A satirical tale of yuppie excess and the shallowness of the information-age Finland, *Upswing* is a reflection of the conflicts between the neo-liberalist utopia of the upper-classes and the realities of the welfare state. The film in many ways exemplifies the complications emerging from the globalization of the Finnish society. The roles and traditions of the nation are uprooted with few stable structures remaining to guide individuals through the social fluctuations. Media saturated complicity urges individuals to strive for the 'idyllic' lifestyles of the *nouveau riche*. According to the film, this fosters a new type of embourgeoisement that cuts off individuals from their communal roots. The young professionals operating in the IT and consultancy firms seemingly hold few obligations or any sense of loyalty to the firms that trained them, and cynicism and a sense of elitism prevail amongst this emerging upper-class.

The film constructs its critique of contemporary Finland and its lifestyles in two main ways. The first is a critique of consumerism, targeting the commodification of authenticity seen in parts of the mainstream media. As these IT professionals operate in an ephemeral industry predicated on transient interpersonal relationships and lack of tangible production, authenticity or any sense of rootedness is inherently scarce. The film establishes the run-down suburban neighbourhood as the locus of authentic life in a globalizing nation. Jakomäki in reality is an infamous neighbourhood, but the film erases most problems of class difference and ethnic inequality out of the picture. It constructs a typical 'localized' approach to depicting a globalizing society by emphasizing the sense of rootedness and authenticity one can find in these idyllic neighbourhoods. Thus, any sense of social or political engagement in the film is more to do with middle-class wish fulfilment than any sustained societal criticism. The erasures contribute to a sense of ideological whitewashing that promulgates class divisions rather than addresses them in any constructive fashion. This is especially the case with the film's coda, where all the protagonists gather at the reclaimed house of the newly reinstated couple. While integration between the different classes can take place, this is only possible if the hierarchical structures of the society remain in place.

Upswing's politics of localization are very short-sighted in their critical range and contribute to a wider 'leftist' turn in the commercial cinema of the early 2000s. Many popular comedies similarly focus on critical explorations of socially relevant contemporary issues: for example, *Saippuaprinssi/Soap* (Kuusi, 2006) satirizes the world of commercial television and the influence of reality TV on cinematic art. Simultaneously, it is a rather silly comedy relying on conventional plotting and slapstick humour for its content, producing a film that closely resembles the products it seeks to criticize. Other issues, such as the multicultural politics of *Vieraalla maalla/Land of Love* (Vanne, 2003) or the gender equality called for in Aku Louhimies' *Kuutamolla/Lovers & Leavers* (Louhimies, 2002), continue to exhibit a seemingly leftist perspective in their attempts to critique conservative, often patriarchal, mores of the society. Meanwhile, depicting race and the roles available for women only as social problems results in 'Othering' the non-white, non-male stratum of society just as the 'lower-classes' of *Upswing* are subordinated to our bourgeois protagonists. Thus, these products can, at least in theory, play for a wide range of domestic audience segments, providing all of them something with which to identify. The evocation of a unified national collective in commercial film production is a tactic deemed to be essential for the survival of national cinema, though the unfortunate ideological dictation of social mores by the hegemonic stratum of society is a more problematic aspect of this type of cinema. The ideological dimensions of *Upswing* are then distinctly conflicted, but it remains a testament of the cultural mores of its time as well as the tactics adopted by domestic producers to ensure their survival.

Pietari Kääpä

Producing Adults

Lapsia ja aikuisia – Kuinka niitä tehdään?

Production companies:
Blind Spot Pictures Oy
Sonet Film AB
Film i Väst

Distributors:
Celluloid Dreams
FS Film Oy
Peccadillo Pictures

Director:
Aleksi Salmenperä

Producers:
Petri Jokiranta
Tero Kaukomaa

Screenwriter:
Pekko Pesonen

Cinematographer:
Tuomo Hutri

Synopsis

Venla (Haapkylä), a psychotherapist at a fertility clinic, wants a baby with her long-term boyfriend, Antero (Toivonen), but he fears a child could derail his ambitions to win an Olympic gold medal for speed skating and so secretly feeds her contraceptives. When Venla discovers this, she is comforted by Satu (Mustakallio), a fertility doctor, and the two women develop feelings for each other. When Venla gives Antero an ultimatum, he agrees they should try for a baby but secretly has a vasectomy. Suspicious of his behaviour, Venla and Satu secretly test his sperm count and, finding it exceptionally low, Satu attempts to inseminate Venla using sperm from a donor physically similar to Antero. The plan is interrupted, but brings the women closer and they go to bed together. However, they are interrupted by Antero and Rönkkö (Eronen), Satu's casual boyfriend. Antero and Venla attempt to reconcile, while Satu discovers she is pregnant with Rönkkö's child.

Critique

Producing Adults takes the complex and improbable plotting of a romantic comedy, but applies it to characters who behave not like characters in a romantic comedy but like real people. Pekko Pesonen's script has them perpetrate all kinds of deceptions in attempts to conceal all kinds of absurd secrets, and fall into unlikely romantic entanglements while doing so, but it does not allow their actions to exist in the moral vacuum inhabited by so many film comedies. This exposes the absurdity and irrelevance of many films with similar plots but smaller ambitions.

Composer:

Timo Hietala

Editor:

Kimmo Taavila

Duration:

102 minutes

Cast:

Minna Haapkylä
Minttu Mustakallio
Kari-Pekka Toivonen
Tommi Eronen

Year:

2004

It also makes watching *Producing Adults* an unusual experience. Because of the tension brought about by witnessing events that appear to be guided by an overarching comic plot, but that concern characters who behave as idiosyncratically as any ordinary person and whose actions can therefore not be predicted, the film is always compelling. However, because the characters' deceptions are unmitigated by the witty one-liners or general lightness of mood that would accompany them in a standard comedy, the characters are often not attractive to the audience and the general viewer may, quite understandably, feel they are not ones about whom he or she can care.

A man who proposes marriage to his girlfriend knowing she is desperate to become pregnant, but who crushes contraceptive pills into the champagne she drinks to celebrate (and who later has a secret vasectomy) will always be unlikeable – but a woman who, upon discovering his deceit, at first attempts to trick him into impregnating her and, when this fails, violates the ethical standards of her profession by trying to illegally inseminate herself is scarcely more sympathetic.

Salmenperä, Pesonen and the cast of fine and nuanced actors with whom they work are to be applauded for creating such rich and often unpalatable characters. Doing so costs the film some of the basic entertainment value and no doubt some of the box-office takings that would have resulted from presenting the same story in a more light-hearted manner, but makes the film's central theme – that it is the process of producing children that truly produces adults – far more resonant than it would have been in a less substantial film.

Salmenperä and Pesonen are also to be applauded for the attention they give to their supporting characters. A film that is ultimately the story of two women beginning a lesbian affair will, of course, focus chiefly on its female characters, but the male characters here are also admirably well-developed. The feelings of frustration and inadequacy felt by Antero and Rönkkö when they are confronted with the realities of parenthood, and with the relationship between Venla and Satu, highlight the difficulties encountered by men caught between the demands of modern ideas of individualism and sexual equality and those of more traditional paternal roles. This creates a powerful secondary narrative, which adds depth to an already deep film, and is an example of the rigour and intelligence that is characteristic of *Producing Adults*.

Scott Jordan Harris

One Foot Under

Toinen jalka haudasta

Production companies:

Dionysos Filmi
Yleisradio (YLE)

Synopsis

Visa Vuorio (Zilliacus) is a gardener who discovers that he is suffering from a condition that will result in his imminent death. As Visa makes his final preparations and attempts to come to terms with his condition by attending a 'degriefing' group, he meets reporter Hanna (Vierikko) and swiftly falls in love. Hanna's coverage of him makes him into a national celebrity and he gets to conserve a piece of woodland as his dream garden. But soon Visa receives

Distributor:
Sandrew Metronome
Distribution

Director:
Johanna Vuoksenmaa

Producer:
Riina Hyytiä

Screenwriters:
Mika Ripatti
Seppo Vesiluoma

Art director:
Christer Andersson

Cinematograper:
Peter Flinckenberg

Composer:
Kerkko Koskinen

Editor:
Kimmo Kohtamäki

Duration:
100 minutes

Cast:
Tobias Zilliacus
Susanna Mikkonen
Helena Vierikko
Tuomas Rinta-Panttila

Year:
2009

the latest shock news – the hospital mixed up his test results and the prognosis is incorrect. As Visa now struggles with being a fake celebrity and using Hanna's pity to care for him, he faces a moral struggle where all options seem to be wrong. Yet, fate has another complication awaiting him as Visa's perception of everything that has taken place may not be entirely correct.

Critique

Johanna Vuoksenmaa's black comedy provides something as yet unique in Finnish cinema: a twist in the climax that calls us to question everything we have seen previously. The film combines elements from a range of film genres: it is at times a comedy and a tragedy, even venturing into action and more metaphysical thriller territory. The narrative works well as a character study, allowing us to feel the pain of the protagonist, but in its attempts to combine as much as possible into a relatively short running time, it occasionally loses its grip. This is especially the case with many of the comedic side characters that play no real role in the main narrative. Regardless, the film is not to be dismissed as an irreverent comedy.

One Foot Under is in many ways a thematic and stylistic follow up to Vuoksenmaa's previous work on *Upswing* with its focus on the shallowness of modern urban life. But whereas *Upswing* was more conservative in its politics and went for an easier resolution to its depiction of class conflict and the immorality of the capitalist welfare society, Vuoksenmaa's latest is considerably darker in its emphasis on the fragility of human life. As we find out that Visa's condition has not in fact been a hospital error, his self-perception and with it our understanding of the film's critical perspectives crumble. What started out as a fable about the superficiality and opportunism of the media industries turns into a more profound existentialist exploration of human self-perception.

This is a pleasingly inventive theme as it connects to an intriguing eco-philosophical narrative strand, which urges us to consider the relationship between humanity and the environment. While Visa's job as a gardener certainly betters our living environment, it can also be considered as a form of conserving the environment for human consumption. Visa's perception of himself as a saviour of the environment is confronted with his realization of his own mortality and, by extension, as an organic part of this environment. The twist in the narrative reveals to us the ways we construct fantasies to cover our inherent existence as part of the ecosystem, not as something superior to it. It is thus entirely appropriate that Visa dies in a church as religion is another theme that humanity uses to provide hope and achieve dominance over the environment. All trappings of modernity are ultimately pure simulacra, and Visa has to face his mortality and organicity. The film shows human life as a fragile and integral part of the ecosystem, from which it tries, but is ultimately unable, to separate with all its trappings of convenience.

Pietari Kääpä

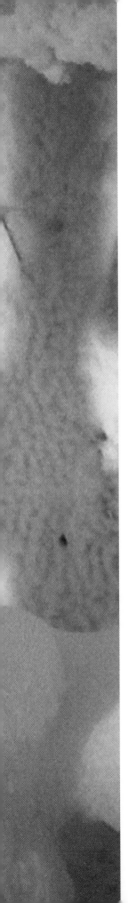

Although Scandinavian children's films have gained substantial international attention, children's cinema has been comparatively marginal within Finnish film culture, at least in terms of public support. The scarcity of films oriented at children is especially visible in the early years of the twentieth century as historian Kari Uusitalo estimated in 1978 that only slightly over 2 per cent, or altogether 15 films of all films made before 1978, could be categorized as children's films.

Finland's first feature-length children's film was *Tottisalmen perillinen/Tottisalmi's Heritor* (1940), based on a popular youth novel by Anni Swan, and directed by Orvo Saarikivi. It was followed by four child-oriented films by director Edvin Laine, including *Prinsessa Ruusunen/Sleeping Beauty* in 1949. Often during the golden age of Finnish cinema, the films could be characterized as films for the whole family or as adult films with characters that appealed to child viewers. Certain films aimed at young audiences were heavily pedagogical, such as Laine's 1947 film *Pikku-Matti maailmalla/ Little Matti*, which warned about the dangers of alcohol. Later, *Molskis sanoi Eemeli, molskis!/Plums, said Eemeli, Plums* (Salminen, 1960) also gained success with its comedic tones, as did *Pikku Ilona ja hänen karitsansa/Little Ilona and her Lamb* (Nortimo, 1957). In 1962, another Anni Swan novel about a rural girl in the big city was produced with the title *Pikku suorasuu/Little Iris Klewe*, featuring the contemporary child star Nora Haque in the title role. Of the frequently popular adult characters that appealed to children, the *Suomisen perhe/The Suominen Family* series (1941–45) and slapstick comedy characters Pekka and Pätkä (Woodhead and Shortie), are perhaps the best known from the 1950s.

From the 1960s onwards, short children's films were produced by television companies, especially the state-financed YLE. A particularly successful example is Heikki Partanen's humorously educational cut-out animation series *Käytöskukka/Good Behaviour* (1966–68). Partanen's students and colleagues from the University of Industrial Arts Helsinki (now Aalto University) were a generation of artists who intended to bring Finnish children's films to the forefront: Päivi Hartzell, Liisa Helminen, Riitta Nelimarkka, Marja Seiloja, Riikka Tuomari and Tarja Lapila were among the names producing wide-ranging forms of children's cinema. One of the successes, a cooperation between film director Matti Ijäs and satirical singer-songwriter M. A. Numminen was *Herra Huu Jestapa jepulis, penikat sipuliks/Mr Huu* (1973). Riitta Nelimarkka and Jaakko Seeck produced animation films on domestic historical and literary themes, including one of the two feature-length children's films produced during the 1970s, *Seitsemän veljestä/Seven Brothers* (1979), based on the nineteenth-century literary classic by Aleksis Kivi.

During the 1980s, the situation looked slightly brighter with five or six (depending on the categorization of children's cinema) feature-length films, most of which included fantasy elements. Päivi Hartzell and Liisa Helminen co-directed *Kuningas jolla ei ollut sydäntä/The King Without A Heart* (1982) and Heikki Partanen's *Pessi and Illusia* (1984) provided symbolic or allegorical readings of adult themes (war, power) set in a world where fantasy and dark realities coexist.

Left: *Joulutarina*, Snapper Films.

Perhaps the most prominent of these feature length productions was Päivi Hartzell's *Lumikuningatar/The Snow Queen* (1986), based on the Hans Christian Andersen fairy tale. This artistically ambitious film featured carefully built fantastical sets and wonderful orchestral soundtrack music by Jukka Linkola.

Discussion around children's cinema and audio-visual culture has gone through many stages. The 1970s saw the political generation raise children's culture to the forefront with domestic children's cultural production and media education in high demand against American mass culture. The Centre for Film and Television Pedagogy (ETTK) was a central organization, one goal of which was to introduce media and film education into the school curriculum. Another important development was the establishment of the Finnish Film Contact in 1970, under the auspices of which many children's films toured day-care centres, schools and municipal film clubs. Other programmes for the promotion of children's film culture were run by the regional film centres, especially the Oulu Film Centre, Pirkanmaa Film Centre in Tampere, as well as the Swedish-language minority Finlandssvensk Film Centrum. These public networks were complemented by the children's film theatre K-13 at the Finnish Film Foundation. Another trend was to support film-making by children and youngsters themselves. This initiative gained success with the establishment of municipal video workshops. The Centre for Film and Television Pedagogy (ETTK) cooperated with local film centres on 'Minun elokuvani' ('My Film'), a film- and video festival for young film-makers.

The second wave of discussion on cinema and children related to concerns around the influence of films, especially impact of violence on children. Gradually, a more radical approach was formed to answer the question of what children actually want to watch, as opposed to the earlier approach of rejecting popular culture as harmful for children. Film and media scholar Jukka Sihvonen analyzed children's cinema from 1920s onward, and his 1987 study came to the conclusion that children's films mirror more the world and values of adults than those of children themselves. Sihvonen's work led to a partial change in emphasis from educating children to discussing the reception and application of media by children, yet the discussion around cinematic violence raged on.

During the 1990s attention was directed into picturing the microcosmic world of preteenagers, such as the boys in Hannu Tuomainen's *Matokuningas/The Worm King* (1993) and the preteens in Kaija Juurikkala's films. Juurikkala, who draws from her experience as a school teacher prior to enrolling in film school, has underlined the necessity to work together with her young actors, and she lets them improvise a lot of the dialogue. Her film *Rosa Was Here* (2001) highlights her film-making philosophy by creating a fictional world where everyone over 13 has disappeared.

Olli Soinio's *Rölli – hirmuisia kertomuksia/Rölli – Amazing Tales* (1991) brought the beloved Rölli troll from TV children's programming to the silver screen. The character continued his adventures in 2001 with *Rölli ja Metsänhenki/Rölli and the Wood Sprite* in a more traditional fantasy/adventure mode. Rölli has also appeared in an animated film *Röllin sydän/Quest for a Heart*, directed by Pekka Lehtosaari in 2007. The Rölli films use the natural environment as a pedagogical environmentalist tool, which is an approach shared by Raimo O. Niemi's *Poika ja ilves/Tommy and the Wildcat* (1999), about the friendship between a boy and a lynx.

The turn of the century saw new directors enter the production of children's cinema. Klaus Härö's debut film, *Näkymätön Elina/Elina: As If I Wasn't There* (2002), was set in the Finnish-speaking minority community in 1950s Sweden, whereas the more established art house director Kaisa Rastimo made the charming girl film *Heinähattu ja Vilttitossu/Hayflower and Quiltshoe* (2002). The tropes of reality and fantasy also meet Liisa Helminen's delightful *Pelikaanimies/Pelicanman* (2004), which continues her focus on the lives of Finnish children as also seen in several of her documentaries about the topic. Recently, preteen oriented musical Ricky Rapper films directed by Mari Rantasila have been successes at the domestic

The Snow Queen, Neofilmi.

box office, as was the case with *Onni von Sopanen* (Vuoksenmaa, 2006), in which a boy goes through an identity crisis when he starts suspecting that he might be adopted. While children's film culture in Finland is diverse in scope and receives plenty of attention from cultural authorities, approximately only one domestic feature-length children's or youth film reaches the screens annually.

Eija Niskanen

References

Sihvonen, Jukka (1987), *Kuviteltuja Lapsia*, Helsinki: SES.
—— (1988), *Liekehtivät Nalleverhot*, Helsinki: LIKE.
—— (2001), 'Lastenelokuva 1980-luvulla'. *Suomen Kansallisfilmografia*, 9, pp. 336–39.
Uusitalo, Kari (1978), 'Suomalaisen Lastenelokuvan Historiasta', *Sinä-Minä-Me*, 1–2, pp. 11–14.

Christmas Story

Joulutarina

Production company:
Snapper Films Oy

Distributors:
Sandrew Metronome
Distribution (Finland)
Revolver Entertainment (UK)

Director:
Juha Wuolijoki

Producer:
Juha Wuolijoki

Screenwriter:
Marko Leino

Art director:
Olli-Pekka Rahikainen

Cinematographer:
Mika Orasmaa

Composer:
Leri Leskinen

Editor:
Harri Ylönen

Duration:
82 minutes

Cast:
Hannu-Pekka Björkman
Otto Gustavsson
Kari Väänänen
Mikko Leppilampi

Year:
2007

Synopsis

Niklas (Björkman) is orphaned as a child in rural northern Lapland and subsequently sent to stay with different families of his home village. Every year he devises a way to pay the families back for their kindness by leaving presents outside their front doors on Christmas Day. He is eventually sent to stay with his Uncle Iisakki (Väänänen), who at first treats Niklas as an unwelcome and unnecessary burden. Niklas proves to be a fine carpenter and soon Iisakki adopts him as his protégé. Niklas is thus given the chance to build his own workshop for his altruistic operations as Santa Claus.

Critique

Juha Wuolijoki's adaptation of the Santa Claus legend was a massive success on its release, becoming the domestic box office champion of 2007 and earning generally positive reviews. The film was also bought for distribution by Miramax and later released with John Turturro vocalizing the part of Niklas. This success is not surprising as the film is generally well-made, showcasing a dynamic narrative and a pleasing audio-visual style. It is thus an exemplary case of popular film-making oriented at the family audiences.

According to Wuolijoki, the film was intended as a response to the overt commercialization of the meaning of Christmas and its celebrations. It was thus conceived as a way to reorient the representation of Santa Claus as a figurehead for Coca Cola and the capitalist appropriation of the philanthropic spirit of Christmas. Yet, as many of its critics noted, the film is very carefully crafted to appeal to as many spectator groups as possible. The score by Leri Leskinen notches up the excitement with John Williams-inspired fanfares, and the cinematography captures the snowy landscapes in expansive terms. The narrative is not only content with repeating the tropes of Santa Claus films, but presents an origin-story. This is, of course, a currently popular technique for 'rebooting' established franchises, and it would not be out of place to consider *Christmas Story* in this vein. There are ultimately two ways in which we can approach the film: firstly, it is an attempt to undermine or ground the contemporary perversion of Christmas into a celebration of superficiality and spectacle; or, alternatively, it combines spectacle and familiar traditional content in an easily digestible commercial package. Thus, as some of its more cynical critics commented, it stands for all that is wrong with Christmas.

While the film achieved popular success, we should not only consider it as a cynical exercise in presenting commercialism in an anti-commercialist package. The sense of philanthropy emerges especially in the sacrifices and hardships Niklas has to endure, and the sense of moral goodness is further complemented by Hannu-Pekka Björkman's strong performance. The occasional light-hearted moments puncture what is a surprisingly gritty and downbeat narrative. Indeed, many parents complained about these qualities of *Christmas Story*, suggesting that it is too grim and realistic for a fantasy film. But certainly, such a weighty take enables a previously disparaged fantasy 'genre' to accumulate credibility and cater for wider audiences. Undoubtedly, these play a part in the film's critical and financial success, and its ability to reach international success with Miramax. The film's domestic marketing campaign was accompanied by a hit soundtrack album and heavy online promotion. Attempts were thus made to reach audiences through the channels and technology available to imported blockbuster cinema. Crucial in this success is the film's stylish poster, which depicts an iconic image of a child looking at his reflection as an old Santa Claus in the frozen ice of the lake.

As a reflection of its time of production, the film is largely successful in displaying the constant development of Finnish cinema into a more commercial populist industry. Crucial in this is its combination of an appealing visual and aural package, which assures viewers of a quality product capable of competing with the best of Hollywood while its thematic content offers nationally specific material. As a part of the ongoing development of Finnish children's film culture, the film is a significant leap forward in its populist appeal. As with the CGI-animated features *Röllin sydän/ Quest for a Heart* (Lehtosaari, 2007) and *Niko – Lentäjän poika/ The Flight Before Christmas* (Hegner and Juusonen, 2008), Finnish producers have demonstrated that they are capable of competing with their foreign counterparts.

Pietari Kääpä

The Flight Before Christmas

Niko – Lentäjän poika

Production companies:
Anima Vitae
Cinemaker Oy
A Film
Animaker
Magma Films
Ulysses
The Weinstein Company

Distributor:
Nordisk Film Theatrical
Distribution

Synopsis

Niko (Jantunen) is a part of a herd of reindeer living an isolated life in a secluded valley. Niko has been told his father is one of the famed Santa's reindeer who fly his sleigh on Christmas Eve. Determined to find his father, he sneaks out of the valley to practice flying and accidentally attracts a pack of wolves. Now the herd has to leave their home valley and, feeling dejected, Niko decides to journey to Santa's Fell in search of his father. Squirrel Julius (Björkman) accompanies him on the way, but the pair soon attracts the attention of the wolves. Upon reaching the fell, it turns out that the truth about the magnificent reindeer is a bit more unglamorous than the popular impression. As the wolf pack close in on the Fell, it is not only Niko in peril, but the whole reindeer way of life, and even Christmas itself.

Critique

As a large scale Finnish animation film, *Niko* represents an innovative project for the domestic film industry. *Niko* was a co-production between Finland, Denmark, Ireland and Germany, and the

Directors:
Kari Juusonen
Michael Hegner

Producers:
Petteri Pasanen
Hannu Tuomainen

Screenwriters:
Hannu Tuomainen
Marteinn Thorisson

Art director:
Mikko Pitkänen

Cinematographer:
Antti Ripatti

Composer:
Stephen McKeon

Editor:
Per Risanger

Duration:
75 minutes

Cast:
Olli Jantunen (voice)
Hannu-Pekka Björkman (voice)
Vuokko Hovatta (voice)
Vesa Vierikko (voice)

Year:
2008

production was divided equally amidst the four nations, though most of its thematic work originated in Finland. It was one of the most expensive Finnish-originated productions in the nation's history, and also one of the most successful at that. The film won the Jussi Award for Best Film in 2008, which is a considerable feat considering its animation form.

The film is a well-made and morally sound depiction of family dynamics, especially threats to the constitution of the nuclear family by social instability. Both directors emphasize the notion of the disappearing family structure as a central theme of the work. The theme of absent fathers is well-handled, though the film does succumb to a more simplistic and problematic conception of the 'inadequacies' of single motherhood. In this, it reflects some of the still dominant norms about the centrality of fatherhood in the dynamics of the contemporary family structure.

The film won a Jussi Award for Best Screenplay, which is surprising considering the derivative narrative of the film which, especially in its underdog qualities, seems to be modelled after *The Lion King* (Allers and Minkoff, 1994) and the *Ice Age* (Wedge and Saldhana, 2002; Saldhana, 2006; Saldhana and Thurmeier, 2009) series. While some of the Finnish critics considered this derivation as a considerable negative aspect of the film, others suggested that the film maintains a distinct Finnishness in its original dubbing. But these qualities are certainly lacking in the English version, where many of the characters communicate in something close to an Irish brogue. The film is not ashamed of its status as an international co-production, nor should it be. Thus, the use of Nordic imagery and cultural exoticism is an understandable tactic as it enables the film to gain a sense of distinction in the marketplace. Indeed, *Niko* is the most successful international release of a Finnish film to date having garnered over three million viewers globally. It has also broken records in its domestic market, and holds the lead in the number of domestic DVDs sold and also in its range of ancillary products.

Niko is an important aspect of the revamped Finnish film culture as its success at marketing and branding is something that has ensured the producers are embarking on the soon-to-start-production sequel. According to early comments, the producers are laying much more emphasis on its commercial aspects and similarities with the *Ice Age* brand with an eye on breaking out to the international markets. While there are obvious problems in such unabashed commercialism, this is also much to do with the realities of contemporary big-budget-small-nation film production. But producers ought to be simultaneously aware that part of *Niko*'s draw is its combination of exoticism with the conventions of mainstream entertainment. Emphasizing cultural specificity in favour of entertainment qualities can be counterproductive but, simultaneously, negating specificity in favour of commercialism is also highly problematic. This is directly related to concerns of how to specialize a film like *Niko* out of dozens of similar products vying for attention in an increasingly cluttered marketplace. This is something very difficult to achieve even with the backing of the Weinstein brothers, who have a patchy record in animation. The development of this budding franchise will thus be intriguing to follow as its concerns align with wider developments in Finnish film culture.

Pietari Kääpä

References

Vahäkylä, Liisa (2010), 'Animaatioalan strategia', http://www.finnanimation.fi/dokumentit/fa_raportti_01_2010_final_0312101221.pdf. Accessed 21 July 2011.

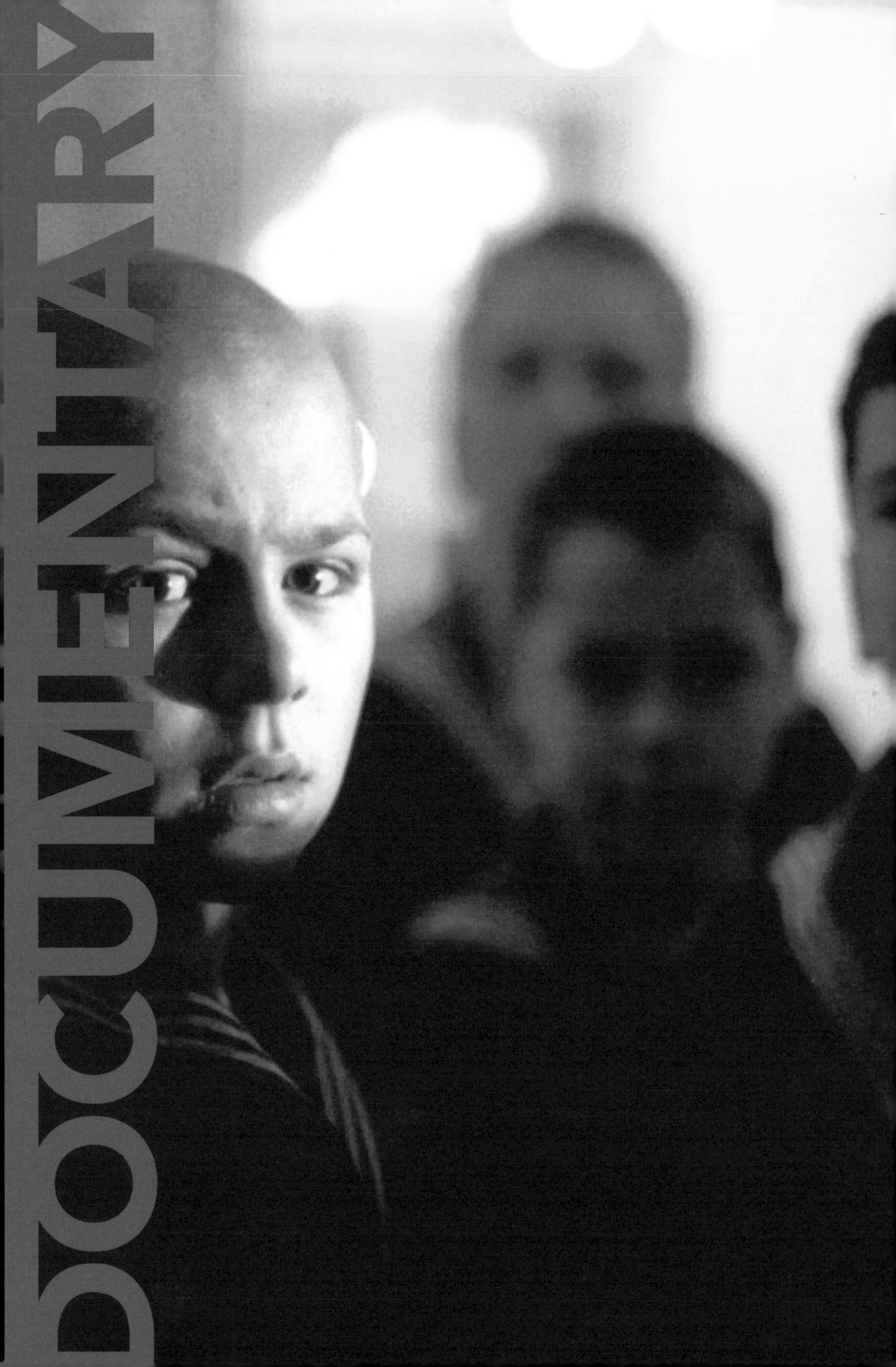
DOCUMENTARY

When it comes to awards recognition at foreign film festivals, Finnish documentaries have beaten Finnish fiction films around the world. Domestically, they have also started to draw audiences to theatres, though they are primarily still seen on television. The first documentaries produced in Finland focused on views of the boulevards of Helsinki in 1904. Soon the young nation began documenting its roots and national customs. During 1917–19, Sakari Pälsi was searching for his Fenno-Ugrian roots in the documentary series *Arktisia matkakuvia/Arctic Travel Scenes*. The Aho & Soldan production company, established by Heikki Aho and Björn Soldan, produced some 300 made-for-order documentaries during the 1930s on topics such as nature and increasing industrialization, as well as such well-known Finns as the composer Jean Sibelius. Their view of Finland was of a rising modernizing nation, whose achievements in wood, paper and steel industries, as well as in design and travel, were seen through a camera lens influenced both by Soviet cinema and Walter Ruttmann. The Winter War (1939–40) led the duo to depict a nation united in the war effort and resulted in the Finlandia documentary series, which continued for another 20 years.

One of the central cameramen of Aho & Soldan, Eino Mäkinen, started production company Kansatieteellinen Filmi Oy (National Ethnographic Film Co), through which he filmed labour methods and skills such as burning the brushwood and carving boats. During the Continuation War (1941–44), Mäkinen worked for the Finnish Army Headquarters as a war cameraman. After the war, he went to work for Erik Blomberg, and together they filmed, amongst others, the award winning documentary *Porojen parissa/With the Reindeers* in 1947. One reason for the flourishing documentary production was the tax cut system practiced in 1933–64. When a film theatre screened a domestic short film prior to the feature, the theatre owner received a 5 per cent tax reduction.

As elsewhere, a new generation of documentary film-makers was established amongst the political unrest and new social understanding of the 1960s and '70s. Jörn Donner, Aito Mäkinen and Risto Jarva were some of the '60s' generation of film-makers, moving between fiction and documentary productions. During the 1970s, the clear preference for leftist and Marxist politics continued with the second wave of political film-making, characterized best by Lasse Naukkarinen's film *Solidaarisuus/Solidarity* (1970), a direct call for class struggle. Jörn Donner's *Perkele! Kuvia Suomesta/Fuck Off!! – Images of Finland* (1971) paints a critical portrait of the nation, a trait also seen in Hannu and Erkki Peltomaa's *Rantojen miehet/The Shadow of a City* (1971), depicting those left behind in the society. Other documentarians of this generation are Kari Karmasalo and Claes Olsson. Timo and Tarja Lapila concentrated on the Finnish countryside, while Peter von Bagh (also a well-known film critic) made many compilation documentaries. Also Timo Linnasalo, Jarmo Jääskeläinen, Arvo Ahlroos and Elina Katainen started their careers during this time. The establishment of Tampere Film Festival in 1970 provided the producers a central arena for the screening of both Finnish and international documentary films. Another vehicle was the Finnish Film Contact, also established in 1970, which distributes documentaries, as well as shorts and children's films, then in 16mm, and later in video and DVD formats.

Later, the political movement's strict commitment to Soviet-style leftism was questioned in documentary films. In 1988, Kanerva Cederström and Riikka Tanner, both who had participated in the left-wing political movement, made *Lenin-setä asuu Venäjällä/Uncle Lenin Lives in Russia*, highlighting the post-revolutionary movement hangover in Finnish cultural circles. The topic was discussed in a more humorous way in Yrjö Tuunanen and Lasse Saarinen's *Jos Lada olisi auto/If Lada Were a Car* (1992), about the Soviet car brand's popularity in Finland. Jouko Aaltonen examined the topic through the history of the political singing movement in *Kenen joukoissa seisot/Revolution* (2006), contrasting footage from the 1960s and '70s with the singers' current life in post-industrial Finland, where rebellion seems to have been consumed by the economic rise of the country.

A shift to a more subjective style of documentary took place at the turn of 1980s and '90s. Influential here was Antti Peippo whose film *Sijainen/Proxy* (1989) contrasts the first seven years of his life against the historical events of the time. A clear attempt was made in separating documentary cinema from television documentaries and educational films. Belief in documentary as an objective depiction, or alternatively, as an open call for struggle, were replaced by a more internal inspection on the relationship between the film-maker, the topic and the film-making process. This period saw the rise of women documentarians, which became a strong feature of Finnish documentary history. Kiti Luostarinen's very subjective *Sanokaa mitä näitte/Tell Us What You Saw* (1993) garnered attention as a different kind of documentary from those produced before as the film-maker and her siblings' childhood memories are connected to and contrasted with the collective memory of the nation. In *Naisenkaari/Gracious Curves* (1997), Luostarinen studies the female body, including her own, from infanthood through adolescence and pregnancy to middle age. In a similar vein, Anu Kuivalainen's *Orpojen joulu/Orphans' Christmas* (1994) concerns the director's search for her father, whom she has never met before. Kristiina Schulgin's examination of her Russian émigré family *Miksi en puhu venäjää/I Don't Speak Russian, Why?* (1993) can also be considered an important contribution to the subjective documentary produced by female directors. Their male colleagues were slow to take up the subjective documentary form, emerging half a decade later than their female colleagues. During 2003–04, Visa Koiso-Kanttila, Markku Heikkinen and Jouni Hiltunen all made films about their relationships with their fathers.

The subjective phase was replaced by a return to socially-committed topics by the end of the 1990s. Susanna Helke and Virpi Suutari studied three jobless drifters from eastern Finland in *Joutilaat/The Idle Ones* (2001). John Webster, a Brit resettled in Finland, focused on a small-town police station in his film *Sen edestään löytää/What Comes Around* (2005). Experimentation with documentary's long-take camera aesthetics and concept of time can be seen in Kanerva Cederström's Siberian railroad documentary *Trans-Siberia, Muistiinpanoja leireiltä/Trans-Siberia – Notes from Camps* (1999). Other directors such as Mika Taanila merge documentary and experimental film in conceptual masterpieces such as *Optinen ääni/Optical Sound* (2005). Experimentation also characterizes Arto Halonen's *Pyhän kirjan varjo/Shadow of the Holy Book* (2007), about the political pressure state of Turkmenia, where he uses a Michael Moore-type of approach to representing political problems with a director as a catalyst within the documentary.

Somewhat outside of these trends exist film-makers like Pirjo Honkasalo, whose subjects range from Russian Greek Ortohodox religion in *Mysterion* (1991) and *Tanjuska ja 7 perkelettä/Tanjuska and the 7 Devils* (1993), to an Indian man's pilgrimage in *Atman* (1997), from the influence of the Chechen War on children in *Melancholian 3 huonetta/The 3 Rooms of Melancholia* (2004), to a Japanese man's struggle to be a Buddhist monk in *Seitti – Kilvoittelijan päiväkirja/Ito: A Diary of an Urban Priest* (2009). Markku Lehmuskallio has, since his debut in 1982, continued the ethnographic film tradition with highly artistic results in his documentaries on the Siberian Nenetsi nation (many made together with Nenets film-maker Anastasia Lapsui), as well as on Finnish Lapland and northern Canada.

Central to the production of documentaries has been the cooperation between the public broadcasting company YLE, Finnish Film Foundation and the Promotion Centre for Audio-visual Culture (AVEK); currently also foreign co-funding is a necessity for many documentaries, meaning cooperation with European television broadcasters Nordic Film and TV Fund (Oslo) and the European Union's MEDIA-program. Of importance in the public recognition of documentary films has been Iikka Vehkalahti, commissioning editor at YLE's TV2, in charge of a documentary series programme called *Dokumenttiprojekti* ('document project'). In raising a new generation of documentary film-makers, the University of Art and Design (Aalto University) study programme in documentary production has been instrumental, especially as it has been chaired until recently by Kanerva Cederström, herself a documentary director with a long career. Also important for launching new documentaries has been Docpoint, a film festival established in 2002 by documentary film-makers in Helsinki.

This millennium has seen a generation of film-makers taking interest in investigating their homeland. Mervi Junkkonen's graduation film *Hiljainen tila/About a Farm* (2005) covers one year of the director's parents' life, during which they resign from farming. Jukka Kärkkäinen's *Kansakunnan olohuone/The Living Room of the Nation* (2009) places cameras in ordinary Finn's living rooms and covers their everyday activities. Joonas Berghäll and Mika Hotakainen went to a sauna with Finnish men and took their camera with them in the surprisingly intimate confessional *Miesten vuoro/Steam of Life* (2010). Joonas Neuvonen's *Reindeerspotting – pako Joulumaasta/Reindeerspotting* (2010) became a media sensation with its open depiction of the life of a young drug addict, this time seen from an inside perspective, as Neuvonen had been part of the same drug-addicted youth group. Of note is the recent surge in documentaries dealing with Lapland and its aboriginal Sami culture as, for example, the films of Paul-Anders Simma focus on issues such as the forced Finnish language schooling of Sami-speaking children, and the turning of Lapland into a commercial tourist spot. These films continue to be both personal and political and indicate the substantial health of the documentary scene in Finland.

By Eija Niskanen

References

Aaltonen, Jouko (2005), 'Kolmas sukupolvi – kun dokumenttielokuva taiteeksi tuli', *Suomen Elokuvakontaktin 20-Vuotisjuhlakatalogi.*
Hirvenoja, Eero J. (2005), 'Elämäntyönä ja intohimona elokuva', *Kulttuurivihkot*, 2, pp. 23–24.
Kiiskinen, Heljä (2005), 'Uusi suomalainen kulttuurituote: dokumenttielokuva', *Kulttuurivihkot*, 2, pp. 18-24.
Sedergren, Jari (n.d.), 'Aho & Soldan', www.docpoint.info.

The 3 Rooms of Melancholia

Melankolian 3 huonetta

Production company:
Millenium Film Oy

Distributor:
Finnkino (DVD)

Director:
Pirjo Honkasalo

Producer:
Kritiina Pervilä

Screenwriter:
Pirjo Honkasalo

Cinematography:
Pirjo Honkasalo

Composer:
Sanna Salmenkallio

Editors:
Nils Pagh Andersen
Pirjo Honkasalo

Duration:
106 minutes

Cast:
Pirkko Saisio (narrator)

Year:
2004

Synopsis

Honkasalo's The 3 Rooms of Melancholia is divided into three parts, appropriately for its title. Room 1, 'Longing', is set in a military academy in Kronstadt, near St. Petersburg, and follows a group of young boys, orphans or from poor families, aged 9 to 14, in their day-to-day military training.

Room 2, 'Breathing', is filmed in Grozny, the capital of Chechnya, and follows the humanitarian volunteer Hadizhat Gatayeva as she visits a sick mother and her children in a bombed-out apartment house. Hadizhat takes the children out of Grozny, with the camera capturing the town in rubbles.

Room 3, 'Remembering', is filmed in the neighbouring Islamic republic of Ingushetia, where Hadizdat runs a private orphanage for Chechen children. The testimonies of children, including a boy who at the age of 11 was raped by a group of Russian soldiers, are heard. The episode ends with a religious ceremony of a goat being slaughtered.

Critique

The 3 Rooms of Melancholia may be one of the strongest films ever made about war. With handheld long takes of children's faces, be they Russian boys raised to be soldiers or the Chechen War orphans, the film captures the psychological damage of war on children on both sides of the war. Honkasalo's method of showing this is simple: there is very little explanation; minimal use of voice-over narration; simple sets; Sanna Salmenkallio's wistfully evocative score. The film gains its power through close-ups of children's faces. Memorable are the serious eyes of the child soldiers, the haunting black-and-white images of the ruined Grozny, and a long scene in which Hadizhat gently wakes up the orphanage children in the morning. Honkasalo was able to shoot in Grozny, in places where the international news reporters never dared to go. The film was originally supposed to be one part of an American film series about the Ten Commandments. When Honkasalo found out that the final cut right would, in that case, not belong to her, she started looking for funding elsewhere, and completed the film with her producer Kristiina Pervilä. As appearing in this film might have been dangerous, the director gave the people appearing in it the right to comment on the final edit.

The overwhelming feeling encompassing the film is one of sorrow. The film's thematic range widens its scope from the too little reported Chechen War to any of the conflicts recently ravaging Europe and the Middle East. What prevails and stays with the viewer are the young people with their serious eyes, whose affiliation to any of the sides of the conflict matter little to them.

Eija Niskanen

Vesku from Finland

Production company:
Marianna Films

Distributors:
FS-Filmi Oy
Yleisradio (YLE)

Director:
Mika Kaurismäki

Producer:
Mika Kaurismäki

Screenwriter:
Mika Kaurismäki

Cinematographers:
Tahvo Hirvonen
Jari Mutikainen

Editor:
Jukka Nykänen

Duration:
90 minutes

Cast:
Vesa-Matti Loiri

Year:
2010

Synopsis

Vesku from Finland is a documentary on the life of Vesa-Matti Loiri, one of the nation's most respected multi-talented artists. The documentary chronicles the career of Loiri from his early years as a child performer to a popular comedian, and to an award-winning musical performer and dramatic actor. Along the way we learn about his tribulations with fame, his turbulent love life and family relationships. We also get unique revealing insight into a man most Finns would profess to know – he is after all one of the most uniquely talented and well-known of Finnish popular culture icons.

Critique

Mika Kaurismäki's documentary is, on the surface, a rather conventional biographical work. We follow a largely chronological order as the film charts Loiri's life and both positives and negatives of fame. We also see many talking head interviews with former colleagues and friends who share insights and introspection into this much-loved figure. But slowly, out of all this, a more complex picture emerges, one of a complex individual, fragile in his beautiful humanity. This is not a simple whitewashing celebration of a talented man – it is that but also so much more. Loiri's regrets about his treatment of his family and neglect of his health come through in self-reflexive moments of contemplation, but this is not some attempt to set things straight by a man who has done wrong. Instead we see the very real individual who just desires the same things everyone else does: privacy and a little respect. This is the main theme of *Vesku from Finland* – the notion of fame and the pervasive impression that everyone thinks they know who you are once they have seen you perform.

Loiri certainly has done his share of performances: from the iconic early role in Mikko Niskanen's *Pojat/The Boys* (1962) to the most enduring popular creation in Finnish cinema history – Uuno Turhapuro (spanning close to thirty years). We also get insight into the jazz fusion music he performs, which is substantially different from the sketches he does in his role as a comedian. Furthermore, as Loiri has played a large role in the different tribulations Finnish cinema has undergone, so the documentary charts this very progress, making it a key inspection of Finnish film culture. What makes the documentary especially important is that it functions as an important part of national cultural history, but it also makes us see the reality behind our shared sense of culture. It raises pertinent questions about the role of national culture and individual lives – do we collectively own this culture?

It is in some ways a shame that the film is so enthusiastically national as this restricts its audiences. Kaurismäki's films are frequently about something more than national culture even if they take place inside the normative national sphere. *Vesku from Finland* follows suit by highlighting different aspects of culture with which domestic audiences are immediately familiar, but it also asks us to maintain a distance from it, seeing it for the creation it is. Through this, it reveals the costs of producing a national icon. And as much as Vesku should never be taken at face value as only a low-brow comedian, so the film makes it very clear that this is not only the story of an individual man and his experiences in the entertainment industry. While *Vesku from Finland* is a respectful depiction of a national icon, the film interrogates the wider problem of performers of culture becoming the property of the people. The purpose here is not to criticize celebrity, but to allow its personal consequences to seep through. And in the final moments of reflection with Loiri at his North Lapland cabin, glamour and any sense of fame dissipates. What we are left with is a real human being, but also one who has created something lasting and truly important.

Pietari Kääpä

Reindeer-spotting

Reindeerspotting – pako Joulumaasta

Production companies:
Bronson Club
Yleisradio (YLE)

Distributor:
Nordisk Film Theatrical
Distribution

Director:
Joonas Neuvonen

Producers:
Jesse Fryckman
Oskari Huttu

Screenwriters:
Joonas Neuvonen
Sadri Cetinkaya
Venla Varha

Cinematographer:
Joonas Neuvonen

Editor:
Sadri Cetinkaya

Duration:
85 minutes

Synopsis

Jani Raappana, a user of heroin substitute Subutex in the far northerly community of Rovaniemi, 'stars' in this shocking depiction of the (extra)ordinary lives of young Finnish drug addicts. Director Joonas Neuvonen chronicles the lives of his friends and the ways their lives revolve around, and are consumed by, drugs in the banal but ordinary northern community. Eventually Jani is able to break free of the confines of this periphery for a trip to Europe. But upon his return to Rovaniemi, he ends up in a long-lasting cycle of incarceration.

Critique

Reindeerspotting made a huge splash in Finland upon its release. A widely-known but little discussed problem of drug use amongst teenagers was suddenly unavoidable and in your face. What made the documentary more shocking was that the users were not 'bad people' but ordinary young teenagers. A sense of shock at the suddenly visible gaps in the structure of the welfare state generated discussion in the media as well as in parliament. The film had a major impact on Finnish society, but it is also an accomplished work as a cinematic documentary. Neuvonen was also a user, so his expertise and immediacy with the lifestyle provides *Reindeerspotting* with an extraordinary level of access to this subculture. The cinematic style follows a predominantly participant perspective though occasionally the film form takes on the blurry and hazy demeanour of the individuals. Its feelings of pity are mixed with many scenes of horror, including one particularly terrifying accident as the camera captures the fall of one of Jani's friends from a roof to the street.

The subtitle of the film is 'Escape from Santaland', which references both a touristic impression of Lapland as the home of the authentic Santa Claus and Finland as a welfare state. According

Cast:

Jani Raappana

Joonas Neuvonen

Year:

2010

to the film, it is precisely the dulling confines of the comfy welfare state that makes these youngsters act in this way. The film needs to be considered exemplary national cinema due to its attempts to discuss a problem that is inherently rooted to the national context. The welfare state and its self-projected image of comfortable existence constructs a harmonious façade, which hides a multitude of social problems out of sight. Many fictional films take issue with these problems, ranging from the works of Aku Louhimies to Aki Kaurismäki, as they recreate narratives of social angst and depression. While these films make important contributions to discussing social issues, the documentary form provides a more tangible, if not as popular, mode for tackling them. While fiction films can always be ignored for being fictional, this is much more difficult with the realist claims of the documentary.

Reindeerspotting was the source of much controversy on its release and was restricted by an 18 certificate. This is practically unheard of for domestic films, especially documentaries. While the production company of the film tried to repeal the rating, it was to no avail. Indeed, restricting the film from what is arguably its target group is questionable and effectively neuters most of the educational value it may have. This is especially ironic as its fictional antecedent, Danny Boyle's *Trainspotting* (1996), is only rated 15. Additionally, documentaries and news frequently broadcast material that can be considered as shocking as the material available in the film. But perhaps this testifies to the power of what we see on the screen as, for some, it may also represent questionable entertainment. The 'narrative' of the film is, accordingly, linear and even conventional in its dynamics of captivity and liberation. But, simultaneously, the sense of despair the film exudes in scenes of a friend digging through the garbage for used needles is anti-drug campaigning at its most effective.

As Jani takes off for Europe with stolen cash, we see his face brighten for this brief interlude as he transcends his stupor and actually engages with the world. It soon transpires that his main desire on the journey is to make it to France where Subutex is legally accessible. And as he holes up in a seedy motel with a bed full of the drug, his eyes light up in a moment of childlike ecstasy. There is no avoiding the sense that these are real people, individuals one could see on the street every day in both the centres and the peripheries of the nation. Thus, the suggestion that all these individuals need is an escape from their morose Santaland is even more harrowing. *Reindeerspotting*, then, works on two levels. On one hand, it achieves a sense of social relevance to which many similar features aspire but never achieve, instigating self-reflection on the lax availability of supposedly harmless drugs and societal short-comings. It is also a substantial challenge to other documentarians – and not only Finnish ones – in its access to the lives of these individuals and the substantial empathy it is able to build around a much maligned group of Finnish society.

Pietari Kääpä

CINEMA
AND THE
ENVIRONMENT

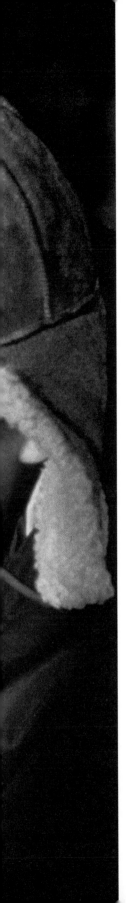

Since its conception, Finnish cinema has fostered a close relationship with the natural environment. Traditionally, such a relationship has been envisioned from a human-centric basis, where the natural environment functions as an integral element in the construction of the national imaginary – nature, as an uncontaminated, untouched pure concept, is utilized as a mirror for the 'national mentality'. This preoccupation is present throughout the history of Finnish cinema. Nature is said to both reflect and emphasize certain aspects of the national character (the stoic and stubborn but hardworking and perseverant Finnish male). Meanwhile, women stand for the purity of the nature, the wide skies and the pure lakes of nationalist romantic imagination. The intertwined relationship between landscape and the national character has taken multiple guises. While most national cinemas use landscape for nation-building purposes, Finnish cinema, especially during the so-called golden age, has had an especially productive relationship with landscape imagery to which the sheer number of films focusing on rural matters can attest. Rural life was depicted in the Niskavuori series and Nyrki Tapiovaara's *Juha* (1937). Nature/man parallels were another recurrent feature of the golden age in films such as Valentin Vaala's *Tukkipojan morsian/The Lumberjack's Bride* (1937) and Erik Blomberg's *Valkoinen peura/The White Reindeer* (1952). Cinematic studies of the national character, such as Erkki Karu's *Nummisuutarit/The Village Shoemakers* (1923) or Edvin Laine's *Tuntematon sotilas/The Unknown Soldier* (1955) draw on the landscape for their impact.

Depictions of the environment are wide-ranging and span genre, history, industrial mode of production and status in culture: for example, the 1960s saw the emergence of New Wave film-making (films produced to challenge and rework established conventions). While many of these films are distinctly urban, the natural environment plays a central role even here. Key films of the era, such as Risto Jarva's *Yhden miehen sota/One Man's War* (1973), feature protagonists who inhabit the liminal schism between the countryside and the city. The natural environment lingers in the background of all these narratives as a signifier of something lost. Nature also takes the place of a collective point of reference, an idyllic signifier of a communal national memory. It plays this role in more contemporary depictions like the films of Markku Pölönen such as *Kivenpyörittäjän kylä/The Last Wedding* (1995). Here, nature occupies the role of a largely imagined signifier of authenticity that provides an antidote to the preoccupations and false simulacra of the city. When the environment is appropriated for nation-building purposes, nature essentially functions as the property of the nation-people, as something that belongs to the human part of the ecosystem. It thus occupies two distinct roles, either as a suturing device to undo problems inherent in any conceptualization of the national collective, or as the locus for debating these schisms.

Contemporary studies in ecological cinema interrogate the relationship between humanity and the environment. Here, the very idea of nature reflecting human characteristics is questioned as it provides a way for appropriating the environment for human-specific considerations instead of conceiving of this relationship in more

Left: Tommy and the Wildcat, Suomi-Filmi/ Wildcat Prod.

reciprocal and balanced ways. In ecophilosophy, humanity is conceived to be a part of the ecosystem and not its master, but cinematic examples of such interrogative perspectives are rare. Risto Jarva's *Jäniksen vuosi/The Year of The Hare* (1977) is a key text in attempting to reach this more philosophical plane of existence. It captures the sense of claustrophobia of an increasingly urbanizing society in its narrative of an advertising executive who gives up his life in the city for a nomadic existence in a cabin in the wilderness. Through this, it provides one of the most affecting arguments against man's superiority over the environment. The metaphoric simplicity of the executive turning into the rabbit in the climax of the film to escape his jail cell and the pervasive confines of 'civilization' impart a clear and powerful message.

Similar modes of rethinking this relationship emerge in some of Aki Kaurismäki's films: for example, *Mies vailla menneisyyttä/The Man Without a Past* (2002) uses nature in distinctly fresh ways that do not always bind themselves with these superficial and simple distinctions of the human appropriation of the environment for self-realization. In this important film, the protagonist is displaced outside of contemporary society by an attack that results in him losing his memory and thus his identity. He has to move to the outskirts of the city to a village of the homeless to build a new life. He takes up residence in an abandoned shipping container located next to the harbour of the city. While containers are used as one of the predominant instruments with which capitalist ideology sustains itself (and depletes the environment), Kaurismäki's film demonstrates how individuals displaced outside of the naturally-depleting system can reappropriate these instruments for alternative and perhaps more beneficial purposes of community building. Thus, the rusting and useless piece of scrap metal becomes something which can find an alternative purpose in the ecosystem. The recycling of the container is an example of the ways in which environmentally conscious texts operate. While the film is not explicitly environmentalist, it shows how individuals can rethink the norms of human/environment interaction in positive ways.

The use of nature as a material element in the construction of the national narrative is a technique which is by no means restricted to the Finnish context. Indeed, we can find similar ideas in most national cinemas. Other examples of environmentally aware films are Mika Kaurismäki's *Amazon* (1990), a multinational production set in Brazil, though it also qualifies as a distinctly Finnish film due to its production history and financing. In *Amazon*, we are made privy to a clear environmentalist argument about the need to preserve the Amazonian rainforest. But, simultaneously, it maintains many of these problematic binaries, such as humanity's exploitative relationship with nature. It only notes the problems and does not propose any clear ways to counter the destruction, at least in terms of unravelling the dominant paradigms. Finnish cinema thus exhibits two predominant paradigms in environmental awareness. For one, many of them attempt to use the environment to vindicate ideological aims or mirror the human psyche. Secondly, some of them seek to criticize or rethink the appropriation of nature for human consumption and profitability.

Lately, documentaries such as John Webster's *Katastrofin aineksia/Recipes for Disaster* (2008) have contributed to the burgeoning ecological documentary genre. Webster's film provides an intriguingly localized exploration of global environmental issues as we are made privy to the travails of his Finnish-British family undergoing an experiment to live without plastic for a year. The film is inspirational in its arguments for maintaining sustainable consumption levels, even though all of this is seen through the complacency of middle-class lifestyles. Indeed, its environmentalist rhetoric is problematic as it mainly focuses on the threats 'green awareness' brings to the equilibrium of the 'ordinary' nuclear family. Furthermore, the depiction of John's escalating obsession can be seen as typecasting of environmental activism in an idealistic and over-the-top light – it seems as if environmentalism leads to a malfunctioning psychological state. The consumerist ideology of the film (the holiday in Italy by train instead of the plane is presented as one of the family's biggest achievements) is another instance of its myopia. While, certainly, the film wants to convince ordinary Finns to think about how reducing waste in their everyday lives can be beneficial, the rhetoric of the film also works as a justification of a middle-class-based consumer society rather than a thoroughly dynamic or inspirational rethinking. While extreme rhetoric about the need to go green is also easily dismissible, ignoring the fundamental underlying societal problems that normalize environmentally harmful consumption levels is not productive either. This Finnish contribution to an increasingly relevant genre is important, if conceptually muddled, environmentalist work.

Meanwhile, many films take the topic of humanity's relationship with nature as a key question: for example, the Rölli films (dir. Olli Soinio, 1991/dir. Olli Saarela, 2001) and Raimo O. Niemi's *Poika ja ilves/Tommy and the Wildcat* (1998) aim to increase environmental awareness in children, their target audiences. Others, such as Kai Lehtinen's *Umur* (2002) and Tapio Suominen's *Mosku – lajinsa viimeinen/Mosku – Last of His Kind* (2003), focus on protagonists who work in border control, where part of their job is to prevent illegal poaching of indigenous animal species. The protagonists of both films are effectively eco-warriors in their protection of the unspoiled environment from the destructive influence of the humans. And while such activity is to be commended, this is still a largely conservationist approach to the human/environment relationship. Thus, humankind is envisioned as the protector (and thereby the master) of the environment. While conservationism has many advantages beyond simplistic dominance of nature, it still maintains boundaries between humanity and the natural environment, and thus reinforces their separation. Environmental themes are thus frequent topics in Finnish cinema, but for a form of cultural expression so reliant on connections between humanity and the environment, it remains surprisingly conservative in its ecologicalism. Ecophilosophical approaches are also still somewhat immature in their argumentative reach, but film producers like Suominen and Niemi demonstrate increasing viability in Finnish cinematic environmentalism.

By Pietari Kääpä

The Lumberjack's Bride

Tukkipojan morsian

Production company:
Suomi-Filmi Oy

Distributor:
Suomi-Filmi Oy

Director:
Erkki Karu

Producer:
Erkki Karu

Screenwriter:
Erkki Karu

Art director:
Karl Fager

Cinematographer:
Eino Kari

Composer:
Tapio Ilomäki

Editor:
Erkki Karu

Duration:
91 minutes

Cast:
Urho Somersalmi
Helena Koskinen
Hemmo Kallio
Aku Käyhkö

Year:
1931

Synopsis

Erkki (Somersalmi) is a poor logger, part of a group of men whose work involves coordinating the drive of felled trees to their factories via the rivers of Finland. On respite from one such trip, Erkki falls in love with Leena, the affluent daughter (Koskinen) of a respected villager (Kallio). But conflict soon festers as Eetu (Käyhkö), the spoilt son of the richest villager, has also set his eyes on Leena. Erkki and Eetu duke it out over Leena, and the fighting soon expands beyond them as both loggers and the villagers start antagonizing one another. The film culminates in a daring stand-off at the rapids of the river.

Critique

The Lumberjack's Bride holds the distinction of being the first sound film produced with an entirely Finnish crew (though it does make occasional use of intertitles). The film was produced right on the brink of the era generally seen as the 'golden age' of Finnish cinema, when the large majority of Finnish films were produced by a studio system dominated by the two major production companies, Suomi-Filmi Oy and Suomen Filmiteollisuus (the latter to be established in 1933). During this era, a high level of production corresponded with a sizeable domestic audience, thus enabling the studios to enjoy a somewhat autonomous existence free of direct intervention from the government. While cinema was derided for its entertainment-based values by those in positions of cultural authority, the films produced during the period cannot be ignored on such narrow-minded grounds.

The Lumberjack's Bride can be considered a vital player in providing the foundations for many of these developments in the national film culture as it consciously used national content as an antidote against imported cinema. To meet these demands, the film provides an early contribution to a persevering genre in Finnish cinema – the logger film. The narrative of the film is a very typical class-based plot built on romantic interludes and spectacular action. It contains a number of intriguing thematic elements which it uses to comment on the conflict between wilderness and civilization. This is not only to do with the more 'cultured' occupants of the village or the untamed wild loggers (at least in the view of the villagers); it is also about the changing frontiers of Finnish society and thus it's transforming sense of self, occupying much of a similar role as the Western genre does in American culture. Canonical tales by writers such as Aleksis Kivi have focused on this dichotomy, and Karu's film can be productively understood as a cinematic extension of the theme.

Adding a new twist on these dynamics, the film does not portray the loggers as only the wild element. Instead, it is the villagers who are depicted in an aggressive light, especially in their attempts to push this 'external' element back to the wild. This is part of the film's ideological work as it emphasizes a Protestant work ethic where the idle life of the villagers is seen in less favourable terms to the hard physical work of the loggers. The scenery, with its emphasis on picturesque vistas, complements the film's preoccupation with nation-building. Most of the action takes place during the Midsummer festival (Juhannus) and involves such potent signifiers of nationhood as the lake scenery, folk dances, the open fire (*kokko*) and excessive alcohol consumption. According to its producer, Karu, '*The Lumberjack's Bride* is a cinematic Our Land, which can be understood by everyone and which is meant to be seen by everyone'.

In providing this important contribution to the archive of national knowledge, *The Lumberjack's Bride* fulfils the premise of the title of its production company ('Suomi-Filmi' translates to 'Finland Film'). It proved to be one of their biggest successes and was thus able to keep the struggling studio – the leading company of the industry – afloat during the difficult depression era. As part of the industry rhetoric of building a wider audience for Finnish cinema, *The Lumberjack's Bride* succeeded in catering for diverse audience demographics and providing a considerable challenge to imported films. Simultaneously, its marketable exoticism was used to distribute the film abroad and it received releases in Germany as well as other markets. In these important moments in the consolidation of Finnish national cinema, Karu's production was an integral element in fostering the development of the Finnish film industry and film culture as a whole.

Pietari Kääpä

The Earth Is a Sinful Song

Maa on syntinen laulu

Production company:
RM-Tuotanto

Distributor:
Suomi-Filmi

Director:
Rauni Mollberg

Producer:
Rauni Mollberg

Screenwriters:
Rauni Mollberg
Panu Rajala
Pirjo Honkasalo, based on the novel by Timo K. Mukka

Synopsis

The story of young Martta's (Viitamäki) ill-fated affairs, set in the Finnish Lapland, tells of the struggles and difficulties of village life. Following the death of a drifter at a public dance, we learn that Martta's family acts as the local undertaker, a duty that she shares with her whole family. As the men go out to the timber harvest, a neighbour and her son, Hannes (Jouko Hiltunen), come to Martta's home begging for some spare money, suggesting that Hannes is Martta's father's (Aimo Saukko) illegitimate son. Later that day, Martta ventures off with a family friend with whom she is having a budding relationship. Martta makes it clear she won't have sex with him, but he rapes her regardless. Martta is dishevelled, but is quickly lured away by the annual slaughter of reindeer. There she falls in love with Oula (Aikio), a Sami, who Martta's father claims, 'has a child in every village'. After Hannes' mother dies, her children move in with Martta's family, leading to a brief liaison between Martta and Hannes. Their brief encounter reveals to the family that Martta is pregnant, and she tells her family the child is Oula's. Dejected, Martta runs away to Oula, who tries to convince her to elope with him before Martta's father arrives and chases Oula. The chase ends

Art directors:

Ensio Suominen

Seppo Heinonen

Cinematographers:

Kari Sohlberg

Hannu Peltomaa

Composer:

Hannu Sinnemäki

Editor:

Marjatta Leporinne.

Duration:

95 minutes

Cast:

Maritta Viitamäki

Pauli Jauhojärvi

Niiles-Jouni Aikio

Milja Hiltunen

Year:

1973

in tragedy when Oula breaks through the ice and drowns. The climax of the film sees Martta giving birth in the summer, indicating the child wasn't Oula's, but from her earlier rape.

Critique

The Earth Is a Sinful Song is based on a moderately successful novel by Timo Mukka, published when the author was just 19. Using amateur actors, it captures the village's harsh life realistically, if melodramatically. The film won the Jussi for Best Cinematography as well as Best Director, before going to sell over 700,000 tickets. The film was acclaimed abroad, culminating in its nomination for the Golden Bear in Berlin. As Lawrence van Gelden of the New York Times understates, the rare arrival of a good Finnish film in America is 'an occasion of more than ordinary note'.

An early and startling scene of a cow in a troubled labour concludes with the farmer deciding to butcher the unborn calf and remove it piece by piece to save the otherwise doomed animal. The scene strikes the brutal and stoic tone which saturates the film. The simple pleasures of the villagers are never exempt from death and violence. Sex, drink, and celebration are undifferentiated from the pain, suffering and death that form the yin and yang of village life. The film captures life in ambiguous and non-moralizing terms,

The Earth Is a Sinful Song, Rm-Tuotanto.

filming a hell-bent fire-and-brimstone sermon with the same lusty passion as the villager's drunken celebrations. The difficult life of the villagers makes them use every outlet available for escapism, even if a preacher's sermon is the only entertainment. The ferocity which the people consume life is obvious and frank, and death and pain is totally inescapable. A community dance can't escape the murder of a drifter, Martta's initiation to love includes rape, death and possible incest, while drinking is the favoured pastime and the inevitable end to anyone who survives long enough to die by it.

The film's natural beauty aligns the two disparate worlds that the villagers inhabit. The slaughtering of a calf and the ugly sex is filmed as beautifully as the more romantic images of a herd of reindeer crossing the snow-crested landscape and a fishing boat lackadaisically resting beside a misty lake. The forbidding arctic land the villagers inhabit becomes a metaphor for the pained life of Martta and the villagers as the film-makers, in their unbiased and natural approach, suggest that the pain and suffering of the villagers' barbarous life is as natural and beautiful as the emphatic landscape that surrounds them. The romanticism of Mukka's source novel isn't pushed aside, but is instead manifested through the film's intentional beauty when filming the painful as well as the majestic. Mukka suggested through poeticism the intricate relationship shared by pain and beauty, a relationship encapsulated in the beauty with which the film-makers capture the villagers' pain. While the melodramatic nature of the film's plot tends to exploit the Sami as primitive or exotic figures to watch and judge accordingly, the film's common denominator is the eternal subject of how we cope with pain amidst the beauty of life, and the more cerebral subject of nature's own brutality within its innate beauty.

John Saari

The Year of the Hare

Jäniksen vuosi

Production company:
Filminor Oy

Distributor:
Suomi-Filmi

Director:
Risto Jarva

Producer:
Kullervo Kukkasjärvi

Synopsis

Disillusioned advertising executive Kaarlo Vatanen (Litja) forsakes his stressed and claustrophobic city life for the existential freedom of the wilderness of Lapland. With only a wounded hare for company, Vatanen adapts surprisingly well to the naturalistic lifestyle, subtly implying that this is the natural environment of the Finn. A group of American tourists interrupt Vatanen's solitary bliss as he is involuntarily hired as a sort of cultural mannequin for the tourists. Soon, he feels the need to elope further and finally transforms into the rabbit to achieve total immersion.

Critique

The Year of the Hare works as both a critical commentary on the state of the nation and as a traditionalist examination of national culture and its values. The film is very much a product of its time, as the immense restructuring of Finnish society in the 1960s

Screenwriters:
Risto Jarva
Kullervo Kukkasjärvi
Arto Paasilinna (based on his novel)

Cinematographers:
Antti Peippo
Erkki Peltomaa
Juha-Veli Äkräs

Composer:
Markku Kopisto

Editors:
Risto Jarva
Matti Kuortti
Tuula Mehtonen

Duration:
129 minutes

Cast:
Antti Litja
Kauko Helovirta
Markku Huhtamo
Paavo Hukkinen

Year:
1977

and the 1970s – what became known as the Great Migration – resulted in the fracturing of traditional national mentality. The film connects with the national traditions by focusing on grandiose, ravishing shots of uncorrupted nature, while it chronicles Vatanen's metamorphosis from a city executive into an idealized national character evoked in premodern narratives. The impression of tradition is further underlined by Markku Kopisto's folk-styled music, which evokes aural images of 'authentic' rural Finland. Despite the homogeneous impression created by these elements, *The Year of the Hare* underlines the dual nature of Finnish identity as conceptualized through the nature/city paradigm. Vatanen's transgression of the rural/urban border, his incapacity to return to urban life, the subsequent incarceration and the fantastical (fantasized?) escape back into nature underline the notion that these opposites have been permanently divided, and the urbanized can only dream of the perfect, 'authentic', rural existence.

In focusing on this fundamental division caused by the onslaught of the urban mindset, the film is able to create an ecophilosophical conception of humanity's place in the environment. Vatanen escapes urbanity by going back to nature to rediscover his 'authentic' self and slowly becomes physically and psychologically immersed into the surrounding environment around him. Instead of understanding humanity as separate or superior to nature, the natural environment dictates the main directions human self-conceptualization and self-realization takes. But this harmony is only temporary as Vatanen is made into a touristic icon with the arrival of a group of American tourists, and his attempts to transcend 'civilisation' is enslaved to commercial considerations of national culture. To overcome this enslavement, the film uses irony to question the ways humanity appropriates the environment for its own purposes. While Vatanen comes up with a range of oft-putting techniques to repel the tourists, it is precisely these attempts at rudeness and rudimentary barbarism that makes the Americans appreciate him more – by transcending the nation, he becomes its Other and a commercial symbol for reinforcing social conventionality. Through this combination, the film is able to criticize the ways in which nation-building and the appropriation of the environment for the rhetoric of nationalist communality are social constructs. Thus, arguments for any sense of organic national communality are revealed to be only fabrications. Through this, the film can be considered as a culmination of Jarva's wide-ranging exploration of the construction and meaning of national identity which began with *Yö vai päivä*/*Night or Day* (with Jaakko Pakkasvirta, 1962). Unfortunately, this would prove to be his final film as he died in a car accident on his way from the premiere of the film.

Pietari Kääpä

The Last Wedding

Kivenpyörittäjän kylä

Production company:
Dada Filmi Oy

Distributor:
Buena Vista Home
Entertainment (DVD)

Director:
Markku Pölönen

Producer:
Kari Sara

Screenwriters:
Markku Pölönen, based on the
novel by Heikki Turunen

Art director:
Minna Santakari

Cinematographer:
Kari Sohlberg

Composer:
Vesa Mäkinen

Editor:
Jukka Nykänen

Duration:
91 minutes

Cast:
Martti Suosalo
Henrika Andersson
Tarja Kortelainen
Jarmo Mäkinen

Year:
1995

Synopsis

Pekka (Suosalo), a Finn currently living in Sweden in an unhappy marriage and an unsuccessful career, comes to visit his home village in north-eastern Finland. Not much has changed in the village – people maintain their traditional ways of life and roles though socio-economic change looms inevitable in the background.
The school building is under threat from an opportunistic estate developer and the village has to come together to find its inner strength. Meanwhile, Pekka's estranged wife, Meeri (Andersson), is drawn into the developer's arms as she finds modernization a more appealing idea than the persistent traditionalism of the village. Tensions build and are eventually unleashed during the wedding ceremonies. As Pekka succumbs to outpouring his disappointment with his immigrant adventures, Mervi reassesses what is important in her life. The film ends on an ambiguous note as it captures Pekka and Meeri in stasis, their marriage to be rebuilt as much as traditional Finland needs to be restructured to account for the changes.

Critique

Markku Pölönen's The Last Wedding is national cinema at its most deliberate. There is no ambiguity here as to its intentions: to reinterpret the national past with excessive reliance on symbolism and nostalgic conventions. While the narrative is set during the Great Migration of the early 1970s, the film needs to be interpreted in the framework of the mid-1990s Finland, slowly emerging out of the Depression of the early parts of the decade, and entering a new era with its upcoming EU-accession.

The film provides a multi-character meditation on the coalescence of the past and the present, where the contemporary urban perspective, exemplified by Pekka's cynical wife Meeri, is juxtaposed with rurality, heritage and tradition as manifested in the colourful and vibrant portrait of the village folk. The village is represented as a 'national village', as a strictly defined community of shared belonging with its own peculiarities, customs and traditions, which Pekka longs for whilst in Sweden. An interesting display of conflicting views on belonging occurs when Meeri's frustration with the stubborn, 'primal' mindset of the village folk explodes in an extended rant on the 'qualities' of rural life. Meeri's sarcastic perspective brings a dissenting voice to the national village, unable to understand the customs of the village or to participate fully in its ways of life. When taken in context with the somewhat negative portrait of Meeri's character and the idyllic portrait of rural life, her comments take on another layer of meaning as they reveal the film's critical stance towards the narrow-minded, self-obsessed city dweller.

The film addresses the national audience symbolically through Pekka's homecoming, with the film providing a portal to the traditionally recreated village and to a facsimile of an authentic national past. The homecoming implies that both Pekka's identity, and by extension that of the Finnish audiences, is still deeply entrenched in the traditions of the village. Such a notion is, of course, problematic as the film both invites the contemporary audience to participate in national nostalgia, whilst symbolically excluding them from narrative participation. While *The Last Wedding* aspires to an authentic 'pure' Finnishness, uncorrupted by the destabilising effect of urbanization, idealization proves to be only an approximation, a metaphoric portrait of what contemporary Finnishness ought to be and what it is ultimately lacking. This doubled connotation reveals the limited scope of the national village, where the proposed homogeneity of *The Last Wedding* is revealed to be internally fragmented and contested by the rural/urban and nature/modernity schisms that dominate contemporary Finnish national discourse: the idyllic national village is inadequate in scope and cannot sustain the heterogeneous forms of contemporary national existence.

But, interestingly, the film is not some type of uncritical, unquestioning *Heimat* film; instead it chooses to construct an open, multifaceted impression of the national past. It is this complexity that arguably allows Pölönen's films to reveal the problematic nature of national representations, which are highly dependent on subjective cultural memory. Audiences are expected to have access to this shared memory and to interpret the subjectivity of Pölönen's vision through it. Where does this leave audience members with different frames of reference, such as ethnic minorities and the urbanized? As emphasized by the narrative of *The Last Wedding*, the excluded Others remain outsiders, despite their nominal participation in the activities of the national village. The notion of a national cultural memory is revealed as a constant topic of negotiation as it becomes evident that the elements that constitute such a memory are interpreted differently and mean different things at different times. Thus, while Pölönen's films may seem like homogeneous representations of the Finnish past, they also function to reveal its impossibility

Pietari Kääpä

Umur

Production company:
FantasiaFilmi Oy

Distributor:
Finnkino

Director:
Kai Lehtinen

Producer:
Asko Apajalahti

Synopsis

Umur takes place in the northern borderlands of Finland, a space also closely associated with the Samiland and its indigenous forms of culture. It focuses on Poika (Rantanen), a lonely guard who lives in harmony with the environment. He becomes obsessed with a mysterious woman named Umur (Turunen) and eventually consummates his relationship with her. Yet Umur keeps disappearing every so often, prompting Poika to unravel her mysterious existence in the city. It turns out that she is mortally ill, and her visits have been a final desperate attempt to connect with something tangible

Critique

Kai Lehtinen's *Umur* is perhaps the most advanced example of ecological cinema from Finland. Lehtinen is a passionate environ-

Screenwriters:
Kai Lehtinen, based on the
novel by Petter Sairanen

Cinematographers:
Timo Heinänen
Jouko Seppälä

Composers:
Carl-Johan Häggman
Pekka Karjalainen
Wimme Saari

Editor:
Kauko Lindfors

Duration:
102 minutes

Cast:
Heikki Rantanen
Minna Turunen
Rea Mauranen
Juhani Niemelä

Year:
2002

mentalist and both stars in (*Mosku – lajinsa viimeinen/Mosku: Last of his Kind* [2003]; *Havukka-ahon ajattelija/Backwood Philosopher* [2009]) and directs such cinema. While *Umur* uses many similar methods for envisioning the relationship between the environment and humanity as conservationist films like *Mosku*, its suggestive range is much richer. The film sets its targets from early on as we are introduced to Poika through a sweeping helicopter shot of the northern tundra and a voice-over discussing the main themes of the film: the relationships between humanity and the natural environment. The voice-over, initially in Sami, situates the film's approach in the sphere of ecophilosophy: 'A human like the migrating bird finds their way back home. This is inevitable'. From early on, the film understands humanity in organic, instinctive ways as a holistic part of the natural world. The voice-over establishes this perspective further by discussing the situatedness of the human soul in the natural world: 'To where does your soul long to? To what does your soul attach itself? [Poika] does not yet know that paradise is an inner state. It is in you if you know where to look'. While *Umur* seeks to discuss the very essence of humanity, this depiction does not seek to emphasize difference or separation. Instead, Poika and Umur are repeatedly shown immersed in the natural environment as they strip down and frolic in the riverbed or in the snow, merging their corporeal bodies with the environment. This holistic perspective is maintained in all aspects of this film, even extending to the longing Poika feels for Umur as he relates his loneliness and his emotional state to the environment:

> One stands here alone, amongst his peers. Like the trees. And there is nothing else in the world but the trees and the rivers and the absolute longing. One goes to the windy plains and thinks that that is where one belongs. The whole of the sky arches over me.

Instead of the post-Great Migration society of Jarva's *Jäniksen vuosi/The Year of the Hare* (1977), *Umur* is set in the information society of Finland in the 2000s. On several occasions the film contrasts its holistic concerns with the functions of the national state. Early on in the film, we see a somewhat comical depiction of the border guards, whose outmoded language skills and persistence with superstitious ideas prevent them from doing their job properly as a pair of foreign poachers are reprimanded and let off. The nation does not care for the environment, nor does it protect Poika from his hardships with Umur. Urbanity and the 'organized society' are depicted in wholly negative terms as something that hinders the natural alignment of Poika and Umur, something that can only result in corruptive disease and death. In contrast, when Umur eventually perishes, the final images of the film focus once more on the natural environment where she and Poika can transcend mortality and conjoin together. As the film culminates on an ambiguous note, a sense of optimism suggests the potential of reincarnation, of organic recycling, where Poika and Umur can join the natural order and the endless cycle of reproduction. Meanwhile, one could also criticize the film for its tinge of patriarchal thinking (Umur is depicted as 'wild' and untamed), which seeks to other her as something impossible to integrate into the structures of conventional society. And while this is initially a problem for Poika, he comes to realize that Umur's bizarre behaviour is to do with her acceptance of mortality (a part of the natural cycle). Poika's realization that no part of the modernized organized society can help her makes him question his part in the machinery of the nation-state. This sort of rejection of all aspects of conventional society can of course be considered idealistic and even counterproductive for contemporary society. But simultaneously, it works as a powerful subversive contribution to Finnish cinema's obsession with nature.

Pietari Kääpä

Backwood Philosopher

Havukka-ahon ajattelija

Production companies:
Matila Röhr Productions (MRP)
Yleisradio (YLE)

Distributor:
Nordisk Film

Director:
Kari Väänänen

Producers:
Marko Röhr
Mikko Tenhunen

Screenwriters:
Kari Väänänen, based on the novel by Veikko Huovinen

Art director:
Markku Pätilä

Cinematographer:
Timo Salminen

Composer:
Pessi Levanto

Editor:
Benjamin Mercer

Duration:
113 minutes

Synopsis

Konsta Pylkkänen (Lehtinen) is a bit of an 'odd hawk' around his part of the woods. Fancying himself as a philosopher, Pylkkänen has an alternative perspective on most aspects of life and is not afraid to put forth his view. One day, he is asked to look after two doctoral candidates (Korpela and Björkman) studying the environment around the lake region. Pylkkänen figures he can start to exchange some of his perspectives with these learned scholars. As the two philosophical perspectives meet, both sides discover something about independent thinking and mutual understanding. Indeed, rurality and city-based learning are not incompatible, but contribute to one another in mutually productive ways. And as Pylkkänen accidentally discovers a new species of bird, he becomes a celebrity worldwide, resulting in readjustment of the dubious attitudes of his villagers.

Critique

Backwood Philosopher is an adaptation of Veikko Huovinen's seminal 1952 novel, and provides a great showcase for Kai Lehtinen's gruff performance. The novel is one of the rare breed of texts that gets labelled 'the whole nation's literature', alongside such classics as Väinö Linna's *Tuntematon sotilas/ The Unknown Soldier* and a few others. To tackle this through cinema is certainly a considerable undertaking. Kari Väänänen, an esteemed actor in his own right, took the challenge as his directorial follow-up to the comic male exploration *Klassikko/ The Classic* (2001). While *Backwood Philosopher* shares thematic similarities with Väänänen's debut, it is a definite expansion on its visual qualities. Timo Salminen's grandiose vistas contribute to a truly cinematic film, with many astonishing shots of stunning landscapes. Furthermore, Pessi Levanto's expansive orchestral score provides additional life to the visuals.

Much of the film is national romanticist in its evocation of traditional norms of Finnish masculinity, but the depiction of hard-drinking and gruff men of nature is almost ironic in its excessive qualities. When Konsta sees himself travel through the universe to comprehend its structure, we get some insight into this lovable yet

Cast:
Kai Lehtinen
Tommi Korpela
Hannu-Pekka Björkman
Vesa Vierikko

Year:
2009

self-satisfied mind. As he then decides to build walls around it to contain his comprehension of it, we get the type of common sense idiot savant behaviour that has sustained the *rillumarei* genre, for example, for decades. The key to conveying this type of humour to contemporary audiences lies in Lehtinen's performance. Instead of overplaying Pylkkänen's 'hickness', the performance provides a distinctly humoristic streak to the film's exploration of Finnish characteristics. This is well complemented by Väänänen's assured direction, drawing on both natural spectacle and interpersonal humour to a great extent. While the film does thus rely on appropriating the environment for visual spectacle, it also approaches all areas of its narrative from a distinctly ironic perspective. It would be overstating the case to say that we can see a similarly complex ecological perspective emerge here as in *Umur* (2002) as it is far too romanticist against the former's bleakness. Yet, *Backwood Philosopher* is still part of the more environmentally-aware domestic cinema, which does not treat nature only as a mirror to the national character, but contributes new perspectives on cinematic environmentalism. As part of the ongoing dialogue on the role of nature in Finnish cinema, *Backwood Philosopher* is not particularly progressive. Yet, it also indicates the key role nature continues to play even in the information age Finnish society.

Out of the many relatively big budget domestic productions of 2008–09, *Backwood Philosopher* is something of an anomaly as it is predominantly funded by Finnish production companies. Most domestic productions nowadays include a substantial role for international coproduction, yet only the pan-Scandinavian Nordisk has pitched in to handle the distribution of *Backwood Philosopher*. Its take on cultural specificity illuminates potential reasons for this because the film's humour, for one, is largely based on vernacular idioms and knowledge about Finnish cultural history. Through this, the film is able to establish a solid way of communicating with domestic spectators. As Väänänen suggests, *Backwood Philosopher* touches on something indelibly Finnish in its emphasis on being different from the dominant norms. According to him, Finns are never going to be ordinary Europeans as their different mentality will set them apart from the rest of Europe. It is thus not surprising that Konsta's life philosophy has been so readily embraced by audiences and cultural historians. The film is part of heritage cinema that has prospered through the existence of the Finnish film industry. And while there is still a lot of life left in this genre as the substantial critical and financial success of the film demonstrates (over 220,000 spectators domestically), drawing in the increasingly important international audience is considerably more difficult. Heritage products such as these have their key roles in domestic film culture, but increasingly their unexportable potential will come under scrutiny.

Pietari Kääpä

References

Kahila, Janne (2009), 'Kari Väänänen ja Havukka-ahon ajattelija', http://www.film-o-holic.com/haastattelut/kari-vaananen-havukka-ahon-ajattelija/.

In policy and cultural discourse on contemporary Finnish cinema, two concepts dominate the discussion: internationalization and the more ambiguous notion of globalization. On a comparative level with other small national cinemas, Finnish cinema is a rather isolated and insular entity. Most of the producers and industry personnel are indigenously Finnish, and the majority of the films receive few chances of international distribution and acclaim. Yet, an increasing drive for internationalism has characterized the policy decisions of the Finnish Film Foundation and the activities of domestic producers, including the establishment of organizations like FAVEX and Filmland, devoted to the promotion and distribution of Finnish cinema abroad. As these developments escalate, the discourse of national cinema is constantly shifting as international co-productions and thematic explorations of the global dimensions of Finnish culture become not only more frequent, but also essential ingredients of the overall plan.

Yet, Finnish film has been international from its inception. For example, the Suomi-Filmi production *Anna-Liisa* (Puro and Snellman, 1922) was distributed in Europe and the US and received positive reviews in both markets. Several films throughout the years have received success in festival (*Valkoinen peura/The White Reindeer* [Blomberg, 1952]) or commercial (*Tuntematon sotilas/The Unknown Soldier* [Laine, 1955]) distribution and the films of Aki Kaurismäki and Aku Louhimies have recently received commercial distribution abroad. On a thematic level, crossing borders and transcultural interaction have been present in cinema from its early years in films such as *Korkein voitto/The Highest Victory* (Von Haartman, 1929) and *Jääkärin morsian/Soldier's Bride* (Orko, 1938). These are both examples of war-related film production and thus exhibit a clear propagandistic function in their depictions of Finland's international connectivity. In addition to bolstering the internal unity of the nation by focusing on external threats, films such as *Ei ruumiita makuuhuoneeseen/No Bodies in the Bedroom* (Tarkas, 1959) or *Rion yö/ A Night in Rio* (Salminen, 1951), or even more contemporary examples like *Loma/Olympian Holiday* (Jarva, 1976) and *Uuno Epsanjassa/Uuno Turhapuro in Spain* (Kokkonen, 1985), use exoticism and scenarios involving Finns abroad to reflect on Finnish identity.

More complex evocations of Finnish identity in a global world emerge, for example, in the films of the Kaurismäki brothers. Their films are clearly about a world where cosmopolitanism is a very real option to consider, especially as it seems that Finland rejects the protagonists of the films and/or is already a space integrated in global cultural flows. Here, we see movement across borders and willingness to establish a new life in cultural space outside of Finnish confines. Aki Kaurismäki's films explore the dynamics of outsiderness and permanent movement in a global world in films such as the Leningrad Cowboys trilogy (1989–94). Whereas the Cowboys films are best read as metaphoric suggestions about Finland's geopolitical circumstances, other films take a more literal approach to depicting diasporic movements. Mika Kaurismäki's films such as *Helsinki-Naples All Night Long* (1987) and *Zombie ja Kummitusjuna/Zombie and the Ghost Train* (1991) feature cosmopolitan protagonists adapting to life outside of Finland.

Many narratives of Finns in Sweden, especially during and after the Great Migration, are frequent. Klaus Härö's *Äideistä parhain/Mother of Mine* (2005) and Nanna Huolman's *Aavan meren tällä puolen/Kid*

Svensk (2007) explore the experiences of children moving across these borders. In Härö's film, we follow the experiences of children sent to Sweden during WWII for safeguarding against the onslaught of the Soviet Union. Huolman's film examines the post-Migration lives of Ester (Milka Ahlroth) and her daughter Kirsi (Miia Saarinen), two Finns in Gothenberg. Kirsi is willing to adapt to their life in Sweden, whereas Ester works as a cleaner and refuses to learn Swedish. A vacation to rural Finland provides a chance to return to her idealized homeland. The film also takes this nostalgic route as it recreates an impression of Finland through the diasporic imagination, a fantastical place of authenticity and beauty. Ester's diaspora is not as severe as those experienced by individuals escaping political and religious persecution, and thus the politics of the film play out this fantastical scenario in largely glamorized terms. Yet, there is a sense that a return to Finland would imply giving up and also separating Kirsi from her life in Sweden. Thus, both of them inhabit a space in between the two lands as the film attempts to negotiate the complexities of diasporic liminality.

Similar themes are explored in Lauri Törhönen's *Ameriikan raitti/Paradise America* (1990), though these are addressed from an entirely different angle from Huolman's film. The film is a critical examination of the ideological mores of the 'casino economics'-era Finland, where capitalist excesses and yuppie culture were increasingly valorized. Erkki Hakala (Kari Sorvali) flees to the tax haven of Florida to escape the law and his unscrupulous business partners. The initial experience of Florida is of a capitalist paradise full of expensive cars and the *nouveau riche*. But Finns are often criticized for being too backwards or uncivilized for the outside world, and Törhönen's film makes full use of these stereotypes. Indeed, it is not long before Erkki's business goes sour and real gangsters come after the Finns. Being a stranger in a (not-so) strange land is presented here as little more than an inconvenient holiday, and continues the problematic exoticism of previous 'Finn-abroad' films, also seen more recently in Aleksi Mäkelä's *Lomalla/The South* (2000).

In addition to fictional travels and the circulation of films abroad, the careers of several directors demonstrate further international integration. Renny Harlin, for example, has maintained a complicated relationship with Finland while carving out a career as a director of Hollywood blockbusters. As discussed in another article (Kääpä 2011), the incidental uses of Finnish iconography and his frequent comments in the press negotiate his national identity in complex ways, simultaneously marginalizing Finland as a northern periphery whilst attempting to intertwine it with global cultural currents. Other Finnish directors have taken advantage of the opportunities available in international co-production with Aki and Mika Kaurismäki leading the way in both thematic content and the extent of their production/financing networks. Klaus Härö is another director who has explored the notion of pan-Nordic connectivity both on a thematic and industrial level, producing films with both Finnish and Swedish material and financial backing (Kääpä 2011). Antti Jokinen is the latest helmer attempting to break into the Hollywood market with the Hilary Swank film *The Resident* (2011), with Renny Harlin, unsurprisingly, the executive producer. While this functional thriller demonstrates Jokinen's skills at producing professional and even effective genre cinema, it has only received an international release on DVD and a very limited domestic theatrical outing. Jokinen is nevertheless in pre-production on an epic animation film taking its inspiration from the canonical text *Kalevala*. While the final quality of the product is still to be determined, Jokinen's approach to success is clearly modelled on the Harlin experience in Hollywood. While producers and companies strive for international connectivity, it is somewhat ironic that the most recent international successes have been Jalmari Helander's *Rare Exports* (2010) and Dome Karukoski's *Napapiirin Sankarit/Lapland Odyssey* (2010), both films with emphatically exoticized Finnish content.

Pietari Kääpä

References

Kääpä, Pietari (2011), 'Born American: Renny Harlin and the American Dream', *Film International*, 2.

Jade Warrior

Jadesoturi

Production companies:
Blind Spot Pictures Oy
Ming Productions
Fu Works
Film Tower
Troika Entertainment

Distributor:
Sandrew Metronome
Distribution
Grindstone Entertainment
Group

Director:
Antti-Jussi Annila

Producers:
Margus Õunapuu
Petri Jokiranta
Tero Kaukomaa

Screenwriters:
Antti-Jussi Annila
Petri Jokiranta
Iiro Küttner

Art director:
Jukka Uusitalo

Cinematographer:
Henri Blomberg

Composers:
Samuli Kosminen
Kimmo Pohjonen

Editor:
Iikka Hesse

Duration:
110 minutes

Cast:
Markku Peltola
Tommi Eronen
Zhang Jingchu
Krista Kosonen

Year:
2006

Synopsis

Antique dealer Berg (Peltola) requests blacksmith Kai (Eronen) to reform a mythical ancient machine named Sampo, which provokes flashback to his former life as a martial arts master called Sintai in ancient China. While prophecy designated that Sintai the warrior was to eradicate a rampant demon threatening the world and be rewarded with immortality, he fell for Pinyu (Zhang) (an earlier incarnation of Kai's girlfriend). Distracted from his mission, Sintai only held the demon captive in the Sampo and committed suicide after discovering that she was already engaged to his best friend. The storyline of the past unfolds through Kai's flashbacks, which are provoked by Berg, who is now possessed by the unleashed demon. Kai again confronts his doomed fate as he reconstructs the Sampo in the contemporary Finland and plans his final battle with his nemesis.

Critique

Jade Warrior is the very first cross-cultural Finnish martial arts film, directed by kung fu enthusiast Antti-Jussi Annila and partly co-produced with mainland Chinese funding and crew. With its prologue suggesting a mysterious relationship between the Finnish national epic *Kalevala* and ancient China, the film wittily legitimizes its co-production roots and its appropriation of Chinese cultural elements. Genuine efforts have been made to recreate an authentic martial arts flavour in the well-known world of transnational Wuxia genre – Tommi Eronen's use of Mandarin dialogue is complemented by his stylish martial arts costume; his Shaolin monk troop is a typical (or stereotypical) component of the Wuxia genre; and the use of the widely-recognized signifiers of Chinese culture – jade and even chopsticks – are clearly highlighted in the narrative.

But such adherence to stereotypical ideas in cultural specificity seems too deliberate and calculated, lacking in cultural substance by default. Martial arts, and kung fu scenes in particular, are cursory emulations from popular genre films such as *The Matrix* (Wachowski and Wachowski, 1999) and *Hero* (Zhang, 2002). Furthermore, the image of China is relegated to ancient times, while Finnish elements are foregrounded throughout the whole narrative. Cultural symbols, such as the Sampo, the Kantele (a Finnish traditional instrument) and the folk-like musical score pervade the film, attesting to its heavy reliance on *Kalevala* and traditional Finnish national culture. While we can understand such Fennocentrism as self-exoticization pandering to cross-border audiences, this results in an unbalanced dynamic with the Chinese elements (Kääpä 2010).

The ideological preoccupation of *Jade Warrior* revolves around Sintai, who fights evil in a self-sacrificing manner. On one hand, this seems closely connected to conventional Chinese hierarchical politics of collectivism and social responsibility rather than any essential notion of Finnishness. Yet alternative interpretations are plausible as the film highlights the glory and holiness of such obedience less and, instead, emphasizes the consequence of the conflict between social responsibility and the protagonist's individual desire. Indeed, the melancholic emotional world of Sintai forges a central narrative line of the film – in both his lives, Kai/Sintai is doomed to an inability of enjoying a personal life, suffering from his fate to pursue a love he has never had while fighting for honour he may never gain. Such pathos and a suggestive downbeat acceptance of the more depressive aspects of obedience lie at the thematic centre of the film. Shying away from overcooked melodrama and tear-jerking techniques, the attraction of the pathos lies in the ways it is rendered throughout the film by seemingly plain and deadpan emotional expressions and interactions between its characters. Such ethereal and profound sorrow has resulted in some viewers equating the minimalism of the film's emotional scope with the renowned cinematic world of Aki Kaurismäki. The film thus exhibits an inclination to art cinema that preserves a sense of cinematic Finnishness, resisting 'self-Hollywoodization' with which some other internationally-ambitious films from Europe have engaged.

The combination of *Jade Warrior*'s commercial and art cinema tendencies refuses categorization in any absolute terms. Rather, it is more productive and necessary to interrogate the ways the specific local cinematic context (Finnish, mainland China) manifests in its distribution and reception. For example, *Jade Warrior*'s art film qualities are magnified by its connections with the Chinese market, where cinematic commercialism may have very different implications than it does in the Hollywood and even European markets. Upon its release in mainland China, critics suggested that the exhibition of *Jade Warrior* in China significantly diversifies the range of available programming as mainland screens are largely dominated by domestic commercial entertainment and Hollywood blockbusters. *Jade Warrior*'s comparatively 'European' art film credentials allow it to distinguish itself in this market, but it also highlights a more problematic conceptualization of all European films as art cinema. However, in this case the local contributions of the Chinese crew and production team were met in largely welcoming terms.

If *Jade Warrior* is more of a transient 'guest' to Chinese cinema, its function in Finnish cinema is of more significance. Of the film's contested artistic qualities, a frequently discussed, if not completely undisputed, idea is that it clearly contributes to a more vibrant Finnish film culture, mobilizing it from a largely excluded periphery to global popular spectacle. Hence, it also manifests the feasibility of expanding the frontiers of Finnish cinema into more concretely international directions, albeit as an eccentric text that moves away from staple Finnish cinematic conventions. But perhaps the eccentricity is precisely its value in the wider scope of Finnish cinema; as arguably a strategic effort on part of the Finnish producers to align with the emerging economic super power, *Jade Warrior* dynamically increases the possibilities of Finnish cinema in a (relatively) more popular and culturally inclusive form. Such eccentricity is to be considered less as a random adventure but more as an exploratory attempt to respond to the constant challenges of increasing globalization.

Guan Wenbo

References

Kääpä, Pietari (2010), 'Imaginaries of a Global Finland: Patterns of Globalization in Finnish Cinema of the 21st century', *Journal of Scandinavian-Canadian Studies*, 19: 2.

Kamome Diner

Kamome Shokudo

Production companies:
Nippon Television Network (NTV)
Video Audio Project (VAP)
Gentosha
Shasha
Paradise Café
Media Suits

Distributor:
Sandrew Metronome Distribution

Director:
Naoko Ogigami

Producers:
Mayumi Amano
Hanako Kasumizawa
Kumi Kobata
Enma Maekawa

Screenwriters:
Naoko Ogigami, based on the novel by Yôke Mure

Cinematographer:
Tuomo Virtanen

Composer:
Tetsuo Kondô

Editor:
Shinnichi Fushima

Synopsis

Kamome Diner (or Ruokala Lokki in Finnish), a small Japanese-style restaurant, opens on a street corner in Helsinki. The restaurant's menu consists of rice balls called onigiri, soul foods which carry the Japanese spirit according to its owner Sachie (Kobayashi), a 38-year-old Japanese woman. Sachie hopes the diner will become a place where neighbours can easily drop by, enjoy the tasty food and have a relaxed time. Although the only customer is a Japanese enthusiast Tommi (Jarkko Niemi), a Finnish boy, Sachie's sincere optimism and work ethic makes her believe that everything will go well for her. 'If we keep working steadily, we will get customers. If not, then I'll just have to close up shop. But it will work out,' she states.

Soon, Sachie meets Midori (Katagiri), a Japanese lady who has just arrived in Finland without any definite plans. She comes to help Sachie's diner and soon joins to work at her diner with Masako (Motai), another Japanese woman, whose baggage has been lost by an airplane company. The café gradually gains more customers, as the Japanese women make more friends with the local people.

Critique

Kamome Diner is the first Japanese film set in the Finnish capital Helsinki. The film's premiere in Japan took place in one theatre as it was a small-scale film with no PR or marketing budget. But it soon captured the hearts of audiences, especially those of the female audience, and slowly gained a massive following, becoming a box office hit. It was a true word-of-mouth success, ultimately reaching the top five at the Japanese box office in 2006.

The popularity of the film is closely connected with the 'Finland boom' in Japan as Finnish design, fashion and architecture have become an obsession for many Japanese women. Thus, various brands of Finnish origin, such as Iittala and Marimekko, are frequently present in the Japanese media. Simultaneously, media coverage of the good results of the Finnish OECD program for

Duration:

102 minutes

Cast:

Satomi Kobayashi
Hairi Katagiri
Masako Motai
Markku Peltonen

Year:

2006

International Student Assessment bolstered Finland's popularity as a nation with high educational standards. Resulting from this boom, Finnish design, lifestyle and education expanded the Japanese conceptualization of Finland, previously limited to Moomin, Nokia and high-quality social security. *Kamome Diner* had a vital role to play in the increasing interest in this seemingly distant Nordic nation.

In addition to its Fennophilic dimensions, *Kamome Diner* contribution to Japanese cultural politics extends to gender considerations. The main audience group for the film in Japan consisted of middle-aged women; not surprising seen as its focus on three middle-aged women, who have an open mind to different cultures and enough ability to adapt and change their lives, were widely considered attractive by the Japanese female audiences. The film's non-judgmental attitude was also seen as a positive quality because the protagonists' past lives are not mentioned to any large extent, and they have no particularly strong reasons to come to Finland. Instead, this is truly a utopian chance to start over, creating a new world in a new place. Previous to the film's release, a '*Make-inu*', meaning an independent woman of more than thirty years of age with no husband and kids, was seen as a derogatory term. The main characters challenge these preconceptions as the film's representation of different social mores functions as a form of empowerment.

However, the popularity of *Kamome Diner* resulted in a small-scale backlash. One of the Finnish actors of the film, Markku Peltola, the star of Aki Kaurismäki's *Mies vailla menneisyyttä/ The Man Without a Past* (2002), and its minimalist narrative and aesthetic style were often criticized for too closely resembling Kaurismäki's films. Some Kaurismäki fans interpreted *Kamome Diner* based on these similarities, but insisted that its representation of Finland is too idealistic and more a fairy tale than any attempt to chronicle the realities of the nation. Why did the Kaurismäki fans reject *Kamome Diner*, even though they have some similarities, especially their minimalist narrative and aesthetic style? One of the reasons seems to be related to the representation of Kaurismäki in Japanese media. In interviews in Japanese magazines, Kaurismäki's speech, originally in English, would be translated into the tone of Japanese hardboiled style. The articles described how Kaurismäki would be smoking during the interview, and sometimes even the smell of alcohol could be detected. Through this, Kaurismäki was represented as a hardboiled person who fought against social injustice. However, whereas Kaurismäki's protagonists expressed their marginality by rebelling against injustice, *Kamome Diner*'s protagonists did not exhibit any sense of social commitment beyond ambiguous ideas on female collectivity and multiculturalism. For some reviewers, the lack of explicit (male-centric?) social commitment was a distinct fault. Thus, *Kamome Diner* triggered irritation from some of the critics who favoured similar ideas in Kaurismäki's films and only saw Ogigami's film as an inferior, ideologically-lacking copy.

Another important contribution of *Kamome Diner* to Japanese film history is as part of a genre of films which focus on food as their main topics. Films such as Yasujiro Ozu's *Ochazuke no Aji/ Flavour of Green Tea Over Rice* (1952) and Juzo Itami's *Tampopo* (1985) use the symbolic motive of food to reflect on wider social conventions. *Kamome Diner* also places food in the centre of the story as it is no longer a tool of sustenance but a means to enjoy life. The onigiri rice balls and cinnamon rolls (*korvapuusti*) function as symbolic facilitators of connectivity between the Japanese and the Finns. At first, the Finns are unable to accept Japanese food at Sachie's diner, but gradually they start to understand the Japanese affection to their food by comparing it to the Finnish attachment towards cinnamon rolls. The foods provide the grounding for both Japanese and Finnish people to understand each other and, finally, Sachie's diner is full of Finnish customers. Ogigami follows the logic of simple cultural communication throughout the film and constructs the cinematic world by avoiding exaggerated, theoretical or argumentative gestures. Although her concepts are profound, she explains them in simple words with humour. This may be one of the biggest reasons why this film has been accepted by a large audience. The following lines of dialogue illustrate the idea of strong female protagonists perfectly:

> Masako: 'I envy you. Doing exactly what you want'.
> Sachie: 'No, I just don't do what I don't like'.

Does such willing abandonment of social conventionality make the film a fantastical dream or a politicized statement for female empowerment?

Rie Fuse

The Visitor

Muukalainen

Production company:
Helsinki Filmi Oy

Distributor:
Sandrew Metronome
Distribution

Director:
Jukka-Pekka Valkeapää

Producers:
Aleksi Bardy
Alain de la Mata

Synopsis

Life is hard if stable in a downtrodden rural household besieged by endless forests. The son (Bobrov) and the mother (Ikäheimo) of the family toil away on the premises mostly in silence while their father (Tommila) is incarcerated. He sends a note telling them that they are to look after a stranger (Liska) visiting the farm. The stranger, wounded by a bullet to the stomach, is nursed back to health and soon he moves from the stables to the mother's bed. Meanwhile, the son frequents an old well from where he takes tobacco and a mysterious product to his father. War planes are often seen circling above the farm and the police soon come looking for the stranger. He manages to evade them but knows it is time to leave. It seems the woman is now pregnant, but still more alive than she was before the stranger came. As the stranger leaves, he makes for the old well but falls to his demise. The woman who had briefly blossomed to life at the farm withers away and the son escapes into a fantasy world.

Screenwriters:
Jukka-Pekka Valkeapää
Jan Forsström

Cinematographer:
Tuomo Hutri

Composer:
Helena Tulve

Editor:
Mervi Junkkonen

Duration:
100 minutes

Cast:
Vitali Bobrov
Jorma Tommila
Pavel Liska
Emilia Ikäheimo

Year:
2008

Critique

The Visitor is an atmospheric, 'rural gothic' exploration of complex family dynamics. A co-production between production companies from four nations – Finland, Estonia, Germany and the UK – it was also the final dissertation project of its director Jukka-Pekka Valkeapää for the Cannes Film Festival Cinéfondation's 'Résidence du Festival'. This programme provides twelve young directors the chance to perfect their ideas and network with colleagues, and judging from the outcome, Valkeapää made the most of the experience. He intended to make a film about the world of children and the often frightening subjective perspective through which children view adult reality. According to him, the film blurs these ideas into a singular world, where the barriers between imagination and fantasy merge into one. He attracted the attention of the well-known Wild Bunch production company, and the final product displays the logos of over ten different production entities of which only the SES and Helsinki-Filmi are Finnish.

The Visitor's aesthetic and thematic world is clearly inspired by the work of Andrei Tarkovski and David Gordon Green. The emphasis on reflective surfaces and the virtuoso use of the natural environment complement the film's oppressive atmosphere, as does the expansive soundscapes created by the first-time designer Micke Nyström. The film also exhibits clear adherence to the moral austerity of Robert Bresson and the visual grandeur of the natural environment found in Terrence Malick's films. The score, with its atonal stutterings and disturbing strains, further creates a pervasive sense of unease.

Critics have commented that the film is largely divorced from time and space. This certainly seems to be the case as it is set in an almost Stalkerian dystopian landscape, which is complemented by the film's shooting locations in Estonia. Situating the 'southern gothic' stylings of Green or the reflective metaphorism of Tarkovski onto a downtrodden unnamed farm allows the film to achieve unique openness that enables it to work as a mood piece and a political commentary. There are nevertheless plenty of indicators of a wartime Finland as the costumes and lack of technology signify WWII. The prison where the father is held is governed by men in Gestapo-like outfits and planes often circle above the farm, and at one point cause the death of the farm's horse. These are some of its signs of a general historical context of a world at war, while they also suggest the acrimonious relations between Finland and the USSR. Meanwhile, other elements, such as the relationship between the father and the visitor, seem to suggest the Civil War of 1918. The ambiguity of the world allows us to read a range of meanings to the text, and as with the best of these kinds of deliberately ambiguous texts, we can link it to wider existential perspectives on humanity and war.

The Visitor's domestic reception was a source of controversy as it flopped at the domestic box office and critics were largely nonplussed, expressing dismay at its abstract and unclear narrative structure. In contrast, the film won the main prize at the largest

Nordic festival at Gothenburg, where it was commended for its ability to create an original and affecting cinematic experience. A few of the critics commented that the film is not clearly a part of national cinema due to its ambiguity and thematic range. This led many respected authorities, such as the former head of the Finnish Film Foundation Olli Soinio and commentator Kalle Kinnunen, to ponder the role of the professional critic. While no-one was arguing that *The Visitor* should be considered only as some sort of restrictively Finnish cinema, it was the role of the critics in debating and promoting national cinema that came under the spotlight. Should they participate in promoting esoteric and difficult, yet artistically rich and satisfying films? Or should they reflect the opinions of the multiplexes, maintaining populist standards that dominate the domestic box office?

Furthermore, is it ultimately productive to insist on the nationality of a film like *The Visitor*? After all, it has been produced abroad with production funding from multiple national sources and does not explicitly deal with national themes. Yet, most of its production crew and its genesis come from Finnish sources and most of its actors (and language of course) come from the domestic industry. Perhaps the controversy that emerged in the wake of its release demonstrates the ways in which it fundamentally challenged audience/critical preconceptions of national cinema. Could it be that it is precisely such non-adherence to traditionalist or 'authentically national' tropes which enables it to dynamically extend the scope of the national film industry? This is not some simplistic copying of international art trends but involves an ongoing dialogue with both national and global developments in film culture. Simultaneously, it may be difficult to locate such films easily within the confines of the domestic film culture.

While such ambiguity may restrict a film's commercial success, the producers of *The Visitor* have made a film to expand the framework of national cinema. There is certainly a lot to celebrate in the film from the expressive and visually stunning cinematography to its aural sonorities. The acting is also strong with excellent work from Vitali Bobrov as the boy and a typically threatening performance from Tommi Eronen. *The Visitor* is thus national cinema at its very finest and at its most ambiguous.

Pietari Kääpä

References

Kinnunen, Kalle (2009), 'Muukalainen ja Kriitikon Vastuu', http://suomenkuvalehti.fi/blogit/kuvien-takaa/muukalainen-ja-kriitikon-vastuu. Accessed 21 July 2011.

Overseas and Under Your Skin

Maata meren alla

Production companies:
Silva Mysterium Oy
Yleisradio (YLE)
Flying Moon Filmproduktion

Distributor:
Sandrew Metronome
Distribution

Director:
Lenka Hellstedt

Producers:
Mika Ritalahti
Niko Ritalahti

Screenwriters:
Lenka Hellstedt, based on the
novel by Riikka Ala-Harja

Art director:
Saara Joro

Cinematographer:
Mark Stubbs

Composer:
Anna-Mari Kähärä

Editor:
Kimmo Taavila

Duration:
85 minutes

Cast:
Amira Khalifa
Marja Packalén
Leena Uotila
Matti Ristinen

Year:
2009

Synopsis

Ida (Khalifa) is a young adult who is on the lookout for her place
in the world. She has been adopted from Africa when she was a
small child and has grown up with Finnish customs and language.
Yet, she still faces different levels of prejudice from the society. She
gets the chance to go to Germany for the summer and stay at her
aunt's. Here, she has her real experiences of growing up as she has
to survive on her own and act outside of her comfort zone. Her
experiences of insider-outsiderness in both contexts make her reassess her core values and her identity.

Critique

Lenka Hellstedt's adaptation of the novel by Riitta Ala-Harja is perhaps the most mature and complex depiction of Finnish multiculturalism to date. The condition of diaspora (of inhabiting a space
outside of one's homeland) is interrogated from multiple angles in
Overseas and Under Your Skin. Firstly, Ida has grown up with the
customs of Finnish culture most of her life and she is perfectly fluent
in Finnish. Yet, she is still perceived to be different due to her skin
colour, facing all sorts of explicit and implicit prejudice on a daily
basis. As she goes to Germany, she experiences a double sense of
liminality as she is characterized both by stereotypes of Finnishness
and her 'ethnic' Otherness in Germany. The film includes a number
of Finnish stereotypes in relation to Ida, from her obsession with
herrings to her shyness. Thus, her diasporic sense of self exists on
a complex level of difference. She is not part of Germany nor is her
'real' homeland accepting her for who see is; neither is a return to
Africa a possibility as this has little to do with her identity, a typical
problem facing many second-generation immigrants.

Overseas and Under Your Skin makes a powerful case for not
only interrogating the dominant prejudices of society, but also
inspecting one's own perspectives and how these may also be
shaped by prejudice. The film addresses the implicit racism of sections of the Finnish society by highlighting the ways Ida's biological
features shape her employment opportunities. But it is also mature
enough not to make too much of a mention of this later in the narrative. This sort of strong multiculturalism makes race a non-issue,
at least once she is outside of Finland, where her sense of Finnish
identity becomes the concern. Initially, she acts in a very touristic
manner, taking everything at face value and not understanding
the customs that shape the society. She experiences a pervasive
sense of nostalgia for Finland, making it clear that Finland is her
homeland and her diasporic existence is one to do with living in
Germany. Yet, she is also able to build a life for herself in Germany
and be accepted for who she is. The film thus adds a powerful
sense of cosmopolitanism to its palette of cultural themes. Firstly,
it challenges the exclusivist categorization of the Finn with Ida's
identity. Secondly, it shows how such a Finnish identity is able to
adopt and even thrive in mainland Europe.

Overseas and Under Your Skin is thus relatively optimistic of Finnish cosmopolitanism and integration to Europe. Missing from it largely are the more problematic and troubling depictions of the hardships facing ethnic minorities and immigrants to Fortress Europe seen in a range of other national cinemas from Denmark to Germany. While this is a problem for any sense of complex critical qualities of the film, it can also be considered a positive example of interrogating ethnic differences in a global society. *Overseas and Under Your Skin* may be idealistic, but it is also a positive role model for achieving a sense of ethnic harmony. The production methodology of the film complements the need to open one's personal borders as it is a co-production between German and Finnish production companies. Thus, the depiction of both nations is very colourful, almost as if the film was a piece of advertising for them. While it is still reliant on exotic depictions of both its national contexts and a certain level of idealism, it is also reassuring that film producers from Finland are able to produce mature explorations of ethnic difference.

Pietari Kääpä

Iron Sky, Blind Spot Pictures Oy.

THE FUTURES OF FINNISH CINEMA

This volume has discussed a range of thematic and industrial developments throughout Finnish cinema history. While this discussion reveals both problems of ideology and lack of infrastructural support, we can also observe constant attempts by producers to remain socially relevant and try out new formative and thematic innovations. Policy decisions and the work of governmental and other cultural authorities play key roles in such endeavours, but it is the film-makers and, perhaps most importantly, the audiences who are instigating these transformations. Taking these perspectives into account, a complex picture of reciprocal cultural experimentation and stagnation, limitation and innovation emerges. This concluding section explores some of the ongoing developments in Finnish film culture, especially in the field of new media production and distribution, including the ways crowdsourcing and user-generated content challenges established structures.

Convergent models of collaboration between the new media and film industries are expanding dynamically in Finland. One of the earlier contributions to this is the independent production *Kohtalon kirja/The Book of Fate* (2003), produced and directed by Tero Molin and Tommi Lepola, two graduates from the Tampere University of Applied Sciences. The film is comprised of five segments that complement an overarching fantasy narrative about a book that can manipulate time and space. The makers of the film used it as a showcase for their professional technical capabilities and their abilities to produce commercial cinema in the fantasy genre. The film has been criticized for being a shameless copy of mainstream American films with its emulations of different genres in a low budget setting. Regardless, it won Best Film at the New York International Independent Film and Video Festival and has been released on two different DVD editions. The film's production was also supported by veteran actors such as Vesa Vierikko and Åke Lindman, and the heavy metal band Nightwish contributed a song to the film's soundtrack. The film was thus not a total grassroots production, nor was it a breakout success. But it can be considered an important attempt at genre productions of the type that film-makers such as Antti-Jussi Annila would produce years later.

A more intriguing development in Finnish cinematic new media is the increasing prominence of Timo Vuorensola and Samuli Torssonen's production company Energia. The initiative began in 1992 when Torssonen produced an animated spoof of *Star Trek* using rudimentary animation. Over the next years, *Star Wreck* grew into a multipart narrative, often spoofing conventions from Finnish culture and, of course, science fiction. Torssonen and Vuorensola cultivated the 'franchise' to a feature length production with *Star Wreck: In the Pirkkining* (2005). This epic tale tells us of Captain Pirk's (Torssonen) plan to conquer the Earth with the help of the Russian Federation. After several large space battles, Pirk and his crew end up in an alternative reality where they must do battle with a race of aliens. While the productions of Energia may not be up to the technological standards of Hollywood CGI spectacles, they are nevertheless important contributions to the ongoing development of the Finnish film industry. The use of online communities to both accumulate crew and capital is just one aspect of the innovative nature of this enterprise. The invaluable contribution of online word of mouth has expanded the fanbase of *Star Wreck* well beyond its roots. According to some estimates, *Star Wreck: In the Pirkinning* is the most watched Finnish film of all time with over 4 million individual downloads. As it has been distributed under a creative commons licence, it has not had to meddle with copyright or other potentially problematic ideas that would disallow its distribution and reception.

Energia has demonstrated that immediate financial benefits or critical acclaim need not be the only (or even the main) benefits of film production. The company's operations are significant because of the reputation the company has accumulated through its grassroots networking and independent spirit. This has begun to pay off as they are currently in the midst of production on their follow up *Iron Sky* (Vuorensola, 2012). Using fan donations and crowdsourcing as the building blocks in funding, *Iron Sky* has turned out to be the most expensive Finnish film ever made. Produced with a budget of over 7 million, the film is about Nazis who have been hiding on the moon since WWII, and who are now in the process of returning to Earth with flying saucers to reclaim it for their Führer. This rather outlandish narrative is clearly modelled after the type of cult sci-fi with which directors such as Peter Jackson and Sam Raimi made their fame. The 'fanboy' audiences have been the targets of the production from the beginning. Here, word of mouth has been used to show the viability of the project and accumulate interest from established production companies such as Blind Spot Pictures. The release of the first teaser in 2008 spread wide on the Internet and accumulated substantial interest. The focus is on the impressive visual effects, as it displays the moon base from where the Nazis launch their attack. It culminates in a shot of an iron eagle punctuating the punch line of the teaser: 'In 1945, the Nazis went to the moon. This year they come back'. Signing the Slovakian metal band Laibach to compose the score for the film has been another part of its targeting of specific yet wide audiences.

Iron Sky has met with commercial success and largely positive critical reaction, and it has already generated more interest among online fans than most, if not all, Finnish films have before. While any celebration of the film's impact on the course of Finnish cinema is, of course, premature, *Iron Sky* is clearly at the forefront of technological innovation. As media convergence in both production and distribution technologies increases, it is important for producers from this small nation to embrace these at this nascent stage. The conscious deployment of genre tropes in a denationalized setting has enabled the production to thrive, though it is still unclear as to what type of benefit Finnish film culture will gain from this. Whereas Peter Jackson's *Lord of the Rings* (2001–03) films transformed the cinematic landscape of New Zealand, *Iron Sky* is more about pan-European connectivity. While most areas of the production concern denationalization, the conscious use of genre ideas with more outlandish cult appeal can provide a marketable way to expand the parameters of small national cinemas.

Energia certainly establishes a formidable example for Finnish producers, but it remains to be seen whether its approaches will yield similar results with other production entities. For this, we may consider the example of Blind Spot Pictures on their production of the Finnish-Chinese kung fu epic *Jade Warrior* in 2006. While the film was certainly successful and the production largely unproblematic, it has not generated sustainable connections with other film industries. If more transnational productions emerge with China or other nations, they will certainly have to be innovative in their theme and include culturally-specific material from the partner context. Furthermore, Finnish producers need to consider what they can offer in return for capital investment and production collaboration. If this is only a form of exotic cultural capital, the need to foster mutual interests may result in hybridized productions which come close to the disparaged 'euro-pudding' syndrome (negating cultural specificity). It seems that fostering links only on an incidental basis will only lead to incidental productions. Generating substantial long-term investment is more difficult and requires stable production infrastructures for the film industry. The Finnish Film Foundation is certainly encouraging such collaboration and co-production especially in the field of animation, but there is still ways to go before this increasing level of vitality can be considered infrastructurally sustainable. This section and the volume concludes with a quotation from Dome Karukoski, one of the most successful directors of contemporary cinema:

> I'm very excited to be part of Finnish cinema today. There is a New Wave, a generational shift. A lot of directors, scriptwriters are in their 30s and are reinvigorating film. I believe many great films will come out of Finland over the next five years. Last year, we had great success with over 30 festival awards for my previous film *Kielletty hedelmä/Forbidden Fruit* (2009) and for Klaus Härö's *Postia Pappi Jaakobille/Letters to Father Jacob* (2009). This year should again be very good. (in Pham 2010)

While 2010 was indeed very good for the diversity of Finnish cinema, some of the more intriguing developments of the film industry remain in a nascent stage.

Pietari Kääpä

References

Pham, Annika (2010), 'A film about underdog male shame in Finland', *Cinemauropa*, http://cineuropa.org/interview.aspx?documentID=153073.

RECOMME READING

Ahonen, Kimmo, Rosenqvist, Janne, Rosenqvist, Juha and Valotie, Päivi (eds)
(2003), *Taju Kankaalle: Uusin Suomalainen Elokuva*, Helsinki: Suomen Elokuva
Arkisto.

Bacon, Henry, Lehtisalo, Anneli and Nyyssönen, Pasi (eds) (2007), *Suomalaisuus
Valkokankaalla*, Helsinki: LIKE.

Connah, Roger (1991), *A Couple of Finns and Some Donald Ducks*, Helsinki:
VAPK-publishing.

Cowie, Peter (1990), *Finnish Cinema*, Helsinki: VAPK-publishing.

Hietala, Veijo, Honka-Hallila, Ari, Kangasniemi, Hanna, Lahti, Martti, Laine,
Kimmo and Sihvonen, Jukka (1993), 'The Finn-between: Uuno Turhapuro,
Finland's Greatest Star', in Richard Dyer and Ginette Vincendeau (eds), *Popular
European Cinema*, London: Routledge, pp. 125–40.

Honka-Hallila, Aki, Laine, Kimmo and Pantti, Mervi (1995), *Markan Tähden: Yli
Sata Vuotta Suomalaista Elokuvahistoriaa*, Turku: Turun Yliopisto.

Koivunen, Anu (2003), *Performative Histories, Foundational Fictions: Gender and
Sexuality in Niskavuori Films*, Helsinki: SKS.

Laine, Kimmo (1998), *Pääosassa Suomen Kansa: Suomi-Filmi ja Suomen
Filmiteollisuus Kansallisen Elokuvan Rakentajina, 1933–1939*, Helsinki:
Suomalaisen Kirjallisuuden Seura.

Kyösola, Satu (2001), 'Des Ombres et Des Nuages: Dynamiques Mélancoliques
dans L'oeuvre d'Aki Kaurismäki', Ph.D. thesis, Paris: Sorbonne Nouvelle.

Kääpä, Pietari (ed.) (2007), 'Aki Kaurismäki and the Politics of Contradiction',
Wider Screen, 2.

—— (2010), *The National and Beyond: the Globalization of Finnish Cinema in
the Films of Aki and Mika Kaurismäki*, Oxford: Peter Lang.

—— (2011), *The Cinema of Mika Kaurismäki: Transvergent Cinescapes,
Emergent Identities*, Bristol: Intellect.

—— and Gustafsson, Tommy (eds) (2011), 'Adapting National Identity', *Film
International*, 2.

Nestingen Andrew (2003), 'Nostalgias and Their Publics: The Finnish Film Boom,
1998–2001', *Scandinavian Studies*, 75: 4, pp. 538–66.

—— (ed.) (2004), *In Search of Aki Kaurismäki: Aesthetics and Contexts*,
Beaverton, ON: Aspasia Books.

—— (2008), 'Crime and Fantasy in Scandinavia: Fiction, Film and Social Change',
Seattle: University of Washington Press.

—— and Elkington, Trevor (eds) (2005), *Transnational Cinema in a Global North:
Nordic Cinema in Transition*, Detroit: Wayne State University Press.

Närhi, Harri (2004), *Pölönen*, Helsinki: Maahenki Oy.

Pantti, Mervi (2000), *Kansallinen Elokuva Pelastettava. Elokuvapoliittinen Keskustelu Kotimaisen Elokuvan Tukemisesta Itsenäisyyden Ajalla*, Helsinki: Suomalaisen Kirjallisuuden Seura.

Sihvonen, Juha et al. (eds) (1991), *UT: Tutkimusretkiä Uunolandiaan*, Helsinki: Punamusta.

Soila, Tytti et al. (eds) (1998), *Nordic National Cinemas*, London: Routledge.

—— (ed.) (2005), *The Cinema of Scandinavia*, London: Wallflower Press.

Thomson, C. Claire (ed.) (2006), *Northern Constellations: New Readings in Nordic Cinema*, Norwich: Norvik Press.

Toiviainen, Sakari (1975), *Uusi Suomalainen Elokuva*, Helsinki: Suomalaisen Kirjallisuuden Seura.

—— (2002), *Levottomat Sukupolvet: Uusin Suomalainen Elokuva*, Helsinki: Suomalaisen Kirjallisuuden Seura.

Tucker, John (ed.) (2010), 'Nordic Cinema', *Scandinavian-Canadian Studies*, vol. 19: 2.

Von Bagh, Peter (2000), *Drifting Clouds: A Guide to Finnish Cinema*, Helsinki: Otava.

—— (2006), *Aki Kaurismäki*, Helsinki: WSOY.

FINNISH CINEMA ONLINE

AVEK
www.kopiosto.fi/avek
Audiovisuaalisen kulttuurin edistämiskeskus (The Promotion Centre for Audio-visual Culture) is a key organization in supporting all aspects of Finnish film culture, from production to distribution.

Elonet
www.elonet.fi
The website is a database run by the National Audio-visual Archive and the Finnish Board of Film Classification. It contains information on all aspects of film production, especially on production personnel and film companies.

Episodi
www.episodi.fi
Episodi is a monthly populist magazine on film culture in all its forms. A solid (if basic) source for film news and interviews with Finnish film personnel.

FAVEX
www.favex.fi
Finnish Film and Audio-visual Export is an organization devoted to the promotion, marketing and sales of Finnish films, and they especially aim to distribute Finnish films internationally.

Filmland.fi
www.filmland.fi
Filmland is a networking tool for both Finnish and international producers. It provides a search engine for contacts in different production areas and also functions as a way to market Finnish cinematic know-how internationally.

Film-o-holic
www.film-o-holic.com
Film-o-holic is an online journal devoted to all aspects of cinema. It is an invaluable source for interviews with producers as well as insightful reviews of both

domestic and foreign films. The website also hosts the Wider Screen section, which is an academic resource devoted to debating film culture. Wider Screen publishes 2–4 issues per year and covers a wide range of topics, including contemporary and historical research on Finnish cinema.

Filmihullu
www.filmihullu.fi
Filmihullu is the oldest film magazine in Finland. It specializes in intellectual but often non-academic discussion of cinema, and the organization's topics range from Finnish film history to specialist theme issues on film festivals.

Finnanimation
www.finnanimation.fi
Finnanimation is a producers' association devoted to promoting and advancing all aspects of Finland-related animation. It also provides access to research on different aspects of the animation industries.

The Finnish Film Foundation
www.ses.fi
The Finnish Film Foundation is the prime source for production related matters in Finnish film culture. They act as an independent subsidiary of the Ministry of Education, and are tasked with supporting and promoting film production, distribution and exhibition. They promote the distribution of Finnish cinema abroad as well as maintaining co-production links with the cinemas of other nations. SES also commissions research work on Finnish film culture.

Journal of Scandinavian Cinema
http://www.intellectbooks.co.uk/journals/view-Journal,id=192/
An Intellect journal devoted to academic studies of Scandinavian film culture. Published twice a year, this is a peer-reviewed collection with a wide reach.

Lähikuva
www.lahikuva.org
Lähikuva is the leading peer reviewed academic film journal in Finland. It is published four times a year and the edited collections comprise a range of topics on media culture, from Finnish film history to cognitive media philosophy.

The National Audio-visual Archive
www.kava.fi
The National Audio-visual Archive is an invaluable source for all aspects of Finnish cinema and media culture. The organization hosts the national film library with invaluable collections of archival material, including films. Part of the organization's operations is the restoration of individual films and also the running of the cinema Orion. The cinema hosts film clubs and specialist events and regularly screens less commercial films. KAVA also publishes the National Filmography, which is the leading source for information on Finnish film culture.

Varsinais Suomen Elokuvakeskus
www.vselokuvakeskus.net
Varsinais Suomen Elokuvakeskus is devoted to archiving and promoting film culture. Their activities comprise a large public library and film club activities.

TEST YOUR KNOWLEDGE

Questions

1. Who famously remarked that Finnish cinema has reached its nadir, its year zero, in an article published in 1959?
2. How many Uuno Turhapuro films star Vesa-Matti Loiri?
3. Name the three well-known director cameos in Mika Kaurismäki's *Helsinki-Naples: All Night Long* (1987)?
4. Name the only two domestic titles released in 1974, dubbed the 'worst year of Finnish cinema'?
5. Who directed the James Bond parody film *Agentti 000 ja kuoleman kurvit/Agent 000 and the Curves of Death* (1983)?
6. What was the name of the Sibelius composition used to underscore the climax of Risto Orko's *Soldier's Bride* (1938)?
7. What was the original title of Åke Lindman's *Jengi/The Gang* (1963)?
8. Who was the first female Finnish commercial feature film director?
9. Name the song performed by Leo Jokela in *Komisario Palmun erehdys/Inspector Palmu's Error* (1960)?
10. Who was the first and only Finn to win an Academy Award?
11. Name the Finnish films to receive domestic distribution in China?
12. In his plans to establish dominance over the Finnish film industry, what type of architectural monument was at least tentatively commissioned by the director/producer Erkki Karu?
13. What was the title of Mika Waltari's epic novel adapted by the Hollywood studio?
14. When did the production company Suomen Filmiteollisuus officially go bankrupt?
15. What was the first Spede Pasanen production to receive funding from the Finnish Film Foundation?
16. What is the name of the real life model Auvo chases in *Kadunlakaisijat/Street Sweepers* (1991)?
17. When was the Finnish Film Foundation established?
18. Which well known Canadian actor stars alongside Mikko Nousiainen in *Going to Kansas City* (1998)?
19. Who is the famous actress spouse of Hannu Leminen?
20. In which film did Carl Von Hartmann act as military adviser?
21. Which Hella Wuolijoki story does the film *Eteenpäin – elämään* adapt?
22. Tuomas Kantelinen composed the score for which Renny Harlin film?

23. How many spectators did the original *Tuntematon sotilas/The Unknown Soldier* (1955) attract (approximate)?
24. Name the two films Antti Tuuri adaptations produced by Pekka Parikka?
25. How often has Kenneth Colley appeared in Aki Kaurismäki's films?
26. Name the two actors who have played the character Vares on the big screen?
27. Which actress stars in a short cameo alongside George Clooney in *The American* (Corbijn, 2010)?
28. Which well-known film historian directed the documentary *Helsinki, Forever* (2008)?
29. Name the three directors who collaborated on X-paroni/X-Baron (1964)?
30. Which Finnish actor appears in Renny Harlin's *Born American* (1986) as a prisoner named Kapsky?
31. How many of the Niskavuori films did Valentin Vaala direct?
32. Which documentary film received the K-18 rating in 2009?
33. Which Finnish actor appeared in a leading role in the Russian-produced *The Cuckoo* (2002)?
34. What film is the directorial debut of actor Kari Väänänen?
35. Which Nordic distribution company is the parent entity of Solar Films?

Answers

1. Jörn Donner
2. 19
3. Samuel Fuller, Wim Wenders and Jim Jarmusch
4. *Karvat, Pi pi pil…pilleri*
5. Visa Mäkinen
6. 'Jääkärin marssi' ('The March of the Yaghers')
7. 'Ota minut nuorena' ('Take me when young')
8. Glory Leppänen (*Onnenpotku* [1936])
9. 'Silmät tummat kuin syksyinen yö'
10. Jörn Donner
11. *Jadesoturi/Jade Warrior* (2006) and *Joulutarina/Christmas Story* (2007)
12. A skyscraper
13. *Sinuhe*
14. 1963
15. 1988
16. Kata Kärkkäinen
17. 1969
18. Michael Ironside
19. Kara
20. *Wings* (1927)
21. *Justiina*
22. *Mindhunters* (2004)
23. 2,800,000
24. *Pohjanmaa/Plainlands* (1988) and *Talvisota/The Winter War* (1989)
25. Twice (*I Hired a Contract Killer* [1990] and *La Vie de Bohème* [1992])
26. Juha Veijonen and Antti Reini
27. Irina Björklund
28. Peter von Bagh
29. Risto Jarva, Spede Pasanen and Jaakko Pakkasvirta
30. Vesa Vierikko
31. Three
32. *Reindeerspotting* (2010)
33. Ville Haapasalo
34. *Klassikko/The Classic* (2001)
35. Nordisk Film

NOTES ON CONTRIBUTORS

The Editor

Pietari Kääpä is a postdoctoral researcher and an Academy of Finland research fellow in the School of Film and Television Studies at University of Helsinki. His research focuses on transnational cinema in a range of cultural contexts and theoretical frameworks. In addition to multiple articles, he has published two monographs on the globalization of Finnish cinema. He has also published articles on Chinese cinema, transnational Nordic film culture, ecocinema, and audience studies. He is currently working on several projects focusing on eco-cinema, including editing a special issue ('Ecocinemas of transnational China') of the journal *Interactions* and the Intellect collection *Transnational ecocinemas: film culture in an era of ecological transformation*. He is contributing articles for both collections, the first on Chinese ecoaudiences, and second on ecophilo-sophical transformations in global film culture.

Contri

Emőke Csoma has graduated with an MA degree from the Babe -Bolyai University of Cluj-Napoca, Romania, Faculty of Political, Administrative and Communication Sciences, majoring in sociocultural communication. Besides preparing for further studies in Scandinavia, she works as an editor for an online Hungarian film magazine (*Filmtett*). In addition to numerous reviews she has also published a range of essays about Nordic film history.

Rie Fuse has an MA in cultural studies from Japan and she is now a postgradu-ate student at the University of Tampere, Finland. She is preparing her disserta-tion on "Using Otherness to Construct National Identity: Japaneseness in Film reviews of Aki Kaurismäki's Works," supported by a fellowship of the Finnish Government. Her research interests are communication theory, film studies and contemporary Japanese culture. Fuse is also a writer and a translator. She has written essays on diverse topics including film reviews and traveling culture.

Scott Jordan Harris is editor of *The Spectator*'s arts blog, the international film magazine *The Big Picture* and several volumes of Intellect's *World Film Locations* books series. His film criticism has been published in several books and by numerous magazines, websites and academic journals, including world lead-ers like *The Spectator* and *Fangoria*. Roger Ebert lists @ScottFilmCritic among his top 50 'movie people' to follow on Twitter, alongside David Lynch and Sir Michael Caine, and featured Scott in his article 'The Golden Age of Movie

Critics' as one of the writers he believes is doing most to contribute to that golden age. Scott's work has been quoted by, among others, *The Washington Post*, *The New York Daily News*, The British Film Institute and The Fred Rogers Company and in 2010 his blog, *A Petrified Fountain*, was named by *Running in Heels* as one of the world's twelve 'best movie blogs'.

Outi Hupaniittu is a doctoral student at the University of Turku. She is writing her doctoral thesis on Finnish film business in 1900s–1920s and her article, 'Industrial Spotlight' is based upon the preliminary result of the study. In addition to her studies on film business she has published numerous articles on Finnish film stars and international stars adored by Finnish audience from the 1910 to the 1950s.

Sanna Karkulehto is Professor of Literature at the University of Jyväskylä, Docent of Literature and Cultural Studies at the University of Oulu and Docent of Women's Studies (Multidisciplinary Research of Gender and Media Culture) at the University of Lapland.

Kimmo Laine is a lecturer of film studies at the University of Oulu and a docent of media history at the University of Turku. He has published two books (in Finnish) and a number of articles (in Finnish and in English) on film and genre history, as well as co-edited books on film directors Valentin Vaala and Hannu Leminen. He is the editor of Lähikuva-magazine and a member of the editorial board of the Journal of Scandinavian Cinema.

Eija Niskanen received an MA from UCLA Critical Studies in Film and Television, and is writing a Ph.D. dissertation on Japanese anime industry and style for University of Wisconsin-Madison, Department of Communication Arts. Eija has been a programmer for Helsinki International Film Festival since 1989. Eija's interests are East Asian and South East Asian cinema and world animation in general, as well as documentary film.

Pasi Nyyssönen has written his licentiate theses on Hugo Münsterberg's film theory and published articles about psychological aspects of early film theory. He has held a position of lecturer of Film and Television Studies in the University of Oulu, Finland, and lectures currently at the University of Helsinki. He has edited, together with Henry Bacon and Anneli Lehtisalo, *Suomaisuus valkokan-kaalla* (2007) and written Finnish reviews to *1001 Movies You Must See Before You Die* (Finnish edition, WSOY 2008). Currently, he works as programmer in the National Audio-visual Archive, Finland.

John Saari is an award-winning experimental film-maker. He recently received his BA in History and Film Studies from Hofstra University. His film thesis was on Jean Pierre Melville and Aki Kaurismaki's use of narrative form, a subject he hopes to continue studying. Currently he is working on a number of film projects but is on hiatus hiking the Appalachian Trail.

Jaakko Seppälä is Ph.D. student at University of Helsinki. His major research interests lie in the field of silent cinema, with a particular focus on Finnish film culture. He is the author of several articles and essays published in miscellany work. At the present he is finishing his dissertation on the reception of Hollywood films in Finland in the 1920s.

Guan Wenbo is a PhD student at Lingnan University, Hong Kong. Her research is focused on audience studies and transnational cinema.

FILMOGRAPHY

Akseli and Elina	116
Anna-Liisa (1922)	78
A Time of Roses/Ruusujen Aika (1969)	181
Backwood Philosopher/Havukka-ahon ajattelija (2009)	248
Beautiful Veera/Kaunis Veera eli ballaadi Saimaalta (1950)	204
Black and White/Mustaa Valkoisella (1968)	207
Black Ice/Musta Jää (2007)	191
Blue Week/Sininen viikko (1954)	132
Born American/Jäätävä Polte (1986)	182
Christmas Story/Joulutarina (2007)	224
Cross of Love/Rakkauden risti (1946)	109
Dark Floors (2008)	193
Dog Nail Clipper/Koirankynnen leikkaaja (2004)	120
Eight Deadly Shots/Kahdeksan surmanluotia (1972)	136
Eyes in the Dark/Silmät Hämärässä (1952)	177
Falling Angels/Putoavia Enkeleitä (2008)	123
Filth/Sauna (2008)	196
Forbidden Fruit/Kielletty Hedelmä (2009)	165
Friends, Comrades/Ystävät, toverit (1990)	96
Frozen Land/Paha maa (2005)	160
Here, Beneath the North Star/Täällä, Pohjantähden alla (1968)	115
Here, Beneath the North Star/Täällä Pohjantähden alla (2009)	117
Here, Beneath the North Star II/Täällä Pohjantähden alla II (2010)	118
Home for Christmas/Jouluksi kotiin (1975)	139
If You Love/Jos Rakastat (2010)	197
Insiders (1989)	149
Inspector Palmu's Error/Komisario Palmun erehdys (1960)	178
Jade Warrior/Jadesoturi (2006)	253
Judge Martta/Tuomari Martta (1943)	131
Juha (1937)	105
Just Great!/Hei kliffaa hei! (1985)	212
Kamome Diner/Kamome Shokudo (2006)	255
Land of Love/Vieraalla maalla (2003)	214
Letters to Father Jacob/Postia pappi Jaakobille (2009)	167
Man's Job/Miehen työ (2007)	162
No Bodies in the Bedroom/Ei ruumiita makuuhuoneeseen (1959)	206

North Express/Pikajuna Pohjoiseen (1947) 174
Olympian Holiday/Loma (1976) 210
One Foot Under/Toinen jalka haudasta (2009) 218
One Man's War/Yhden miehen sota (1973) 137
Overseas and Under Your Skin/Maata meren alla (2009) 260
People in the Summer Night/Ihmiset suviyössä (1948) 111
Plainlands/Pohjanmaa (1998) 119
Producing Adults/Lapsia ja aikuisia – Kuinka niitä tehdään? (2004) 217
Rare Exports 9
Reindeer-spotting/Reindeerspotting – pako Joulumaasta (2010) 234
Restless/Levottomat (2000) 155
Right on Man!/Täältä Tullaan Elämä (1980) 141
Run Sister Run!/Sisko tahtoisin jäädä (2010) 168
Shadows in Paradise/Varjoja Paratiisissa (1986) 146
Skin, Skin/Käpy selän alla (1966) 135
Soldier's Bride/Jääkärin Morsian (1938) 89
Star Wreck: In the Pirkinning (2005) 189
Substitute Wife/Vaimoke (1936) 203
The 3 Rooms of Melancholia/Melankolian 3 huonetta (2004) 232
The Bothnians/Pohjalaisia (1925) 80
The Boys/Pojat (1962) 93
The Butterfly from Ural/Uralin perhonen (2008) 98
The Collector/Neitoperho (1997) 152
The Earth Is a Sinful Song/Maa on syntinen laulu (1973) 241
The Final Arrangement/Tilinteko (1987) 185
The Flight Before Christmas/Niko – Lentäjän poika (2008) 225
The Geography of Fear/Pelon Maantiede (2000) 153
The Highest Victory/Korkein voitto (1929) 82
The Last Wedding/Kivenpyörittäjän kylä (1995) 245
The Lumberjack's Bride/Tukkipojan morsian (1931) 240
The Man Without a Past/Mies Vailla Menneisyyttä (2002) 157
The Moonlight Sonata/Kuutamosonaatti (1988) 186
The Niskavuori Saga 112
The Song of the Scarlet Flower/Laulu tulipunaisesta kukasta (1938) 106
The Unknown Soldier/Tuntematon Sotilas (1955) 91
The Unknown Soldier/Tuntematon Sotilas (1985) 92
The Vagabond's Waltz/Kulkurin valssi (1941) 108
The Village Shoemakers/Nummisuutarit (1923) 79
The Visitor/Muukalainen (2008) 257
The Well/Kaivo (1992) 150
The White Reindeer/Valkoinen Peura (1952) 175
The Winter War/Talvisota (1989) 94
The Worthless/Arvottomat (1982) 143
The Year of the Hare/Jäniksen vuosi (1977) 243
The Year of the Wolf/Suden vuosi (2007) 122
Thomas (2008) 163
Umur (2002) 246
Upswing/Nousukausi (2003) 215
Uuno Turhapuro in Spain/Uuno Epsanjassa (1985) 211
Vares: Private Eye/Vares – Yksityisetsivä (2004) 190
Vesku from Finland (2010) 233